The Risk Management Universe

The Risk Management Universe

A guided tour

Edited by
David Hillson

BSi
Business Information

First published in the UK in 2006
Second edition 2007 by BSI
389 Chiswick High Road
London W4 4AL

Typeset in Sabon by
Florence Production Ltd, Stoodleigh, Devon
Index compiled by Indexing Specialists (UK) Ltd
Printed in Great Britain by
MPG Books, Bodmin, Cornwall

British Library Cataloguing in Publication Data
A catalogue record for this book is available from the British Library

ISBN 978–0–580–50346–7 2nd edition

(ISBN 0–580–43777–9 1st edition)

Contents

Figures

Tables

Notes on the Contributors

Richard Anderson is a Director of Corporate Risk Group (http://www.co-risk.com) which he founded in conjunction with Professor Robert Baldwin of the London School of Economics in 2001. Corporate Risk Group advises organizations on how to develop their risk management programmes so that they are focused on generating performance gains rather than simply being compliance exercises. Richard worked with Professor Baldwin to develop a suite of diagnostic tools to help in this process and to assist companies in becoming Risk Intelligent Organizations. Richard has a particular interest in developing understanding around Balanced Risk and Risk Maturity. Richard advises organizations that include some of the world's largest companies headquartered in the UK and public sector equivalents.

Richard is a Chartered Accountant and a graduate of the London School of Economics. He regularly speaks at conferences and contributes articles to journals.

Dr Keith Blacker BSc FCA MBA FIIA DBA is a Director of Risk DNA Limited (http://www.riskdna.co.uk), a specialist risk management consultancy business. His expertise in risk management and business analysis has developed over many years both as an operational manager and as an adviser to businesses. Most of his 30-year career has been spent in the financial services industry both in the UK and abroad and he has been actively involved in implementing risk management frameworks in a number of organizations. Keith has a doctorate in Operational Risk Management from Henley Management College and has published a number of papers on the subject.

Keith is also a Director of the Henley Centre for Value Improvement, a research centre at Henley Management College, and Protection & Investment Ltd, a firm of Independent Financial Advisers regulated by the UK Financial Services Authority, where he has responsibility for all corporate governance matters.

Dr David Bobker MA DPhil ACA is founder and Director of Real Assurance Risk Management (http://www.realassurance.com) which specializes in risk management, regulatory compliance, corporate governance and internal audit, delivering both consulting and training. He holds a First Class BA, MSc and DPhil in Mathematics all from Oxford University and is a Chartered Accountant.

David has spent a long and varied career in the financial services industry where he worked as an external auditor and an internal auditor (having been Head of Group Audit both for Alliance & Leicester plc and Norwich Union plc). He has authored a number of articles on internal audit and spoken widely at conferences in the UK and abroad. His interests also include corporate governance, having taken a keen interest in the original Turnbull consultation, and compliance, having been a group compliance officer and a supervisor at the Building Societies Commission (now part of the FSA) with responsibility for capital adequacy rules.

As well as supplying outsourced internal audit services, his recent consulting work has included quantified risk analysis and systems for clients. Always taking a keen interest in IT, he has now developed specialist Monte Carlo modelling software for the assessment and management of operational risk, as well as carrying out credit and market risk assignments. The other active area of work is training where over a three-year period he has delivered specialist courses on quantified risk methods to over 200 senior internal auditors and operational risk managers.

Dr Tyson R. Browning is Assistant Professor of Enterprise Operations at the M J Neeley School of Business at Texas Christian University in Fort Worth, Texas, USA. He teaches Operations Management (MBA Core) and Project Management (MBA elective) and conducts research on enterprise operations, process modelling, product development, project management, engineering management and systems engineering. He previously worked for Lockheed Martin Aeronautics Company, where he was the technical lead and chief integrator of the enterprise process architecture and author of company policies and processes driving the transition to a process-based company. Before joining Lockheed Martin, he worked with the Lean Aerospace Initiative at the Massachusetts Institute of Technology, conducting on-site research at Boeing, Texas Instruments, General Electric, Daimler Chrysler and several other companies. Browning has also worked for Honeywell Space Systems and Los Alamos National Laboratory. He received a Bachelor's degree from Abilene Christian University and two Master's degrees and a PhD (in Technology Management and Policy) from MIT. He has authored over 20 papers on engineering management, risk management, the design structure matrix, organization design, process modelling and value measurement – publishing in *IEEE Transactions in Engineering Management*, *Systems Engineering*, *Project Management Journal*, *Technology Management Handbook* and others. He is a member of the International Council on Systems Engineering (INCOSE) and the Institute for Operations Research and the Management Sciences (INFORMS), and he also serves on the Editorial Board for *Systems Engineering*.

Anthony Cherry is a Partner in the national law firm, Beachcroft Wansbroughs. After graduating in Law from Manchester University in 1976 and serving Articles in the City he worked for three years in the legal department of ICI. Since 1983 he has been with his present firm and its predecessors. He is responsible for developing and delivering services, including Risk Counsel, which bring legal skills and experience to bear on business risk and opportunity in new and flexible ways. He also chairs the firm's Risk Management Directorate and contributes to its policy on Corporate Social Responsibility. He lives in Clevedon, North Somerset with his wife and three children.

Jon Finch retired in 2002 after 31 years in risk management, most recently as ICL/Fujitsu Services Group Business Risk Manager where he carried corporate responsibility for business risk management policy and processes. Based in corporate Internal Audit he worked to achieve protection against business risk. Jon Finch is well regarded within the UK risk management community as a specialist in business risk and practical business problem resolution. He was employed in commerce from 1961, in the UK Electricity and Gas Industries before ICL, initially as an accountant and later in IT system design and development. After joining ICL in 1971 he performed a significant number of internal and customer related troubleshooting assignments on behalf of the Board of ICL, of STC, and on secondment to major clients. Over the years Jon has succeeded in resolving crises in over 40 mainly litigious situations on behalf of ICL in 18 countries including Hong Kong, South Africa, New Zealand, Malaya, France, Germany, Hungary and Portugal.

Jon is semi-retired, writing and speaking on business risk management topics. He has the reputation of being an entertaining speaker in his field. He is married to an actress, has three children and lives in the Fens near Cambridge.

Richard Flynn BSc (Hons) MSc RGN FRSA is a serving Police Officer and is currently seconded to a national police unit providing protective security advice to the business community. He is the author of national guidances 'Expecting the unexpected' and 'Secure in the knowledge', both written to aid the business community in the development of security and business continuity plans. He has a wealth of experience working with the business community and his research interests include how organizations perceive and manage risk, and how crime prevention strategies can assist in the prevention of terrorism.

Dr David Hillson PMP FIRM FAPM MCMI is an international risk management consultant, and Director of Risk Doctor & Partners (http://www.risk-doctor.com). He is a frequent conference speaker and author on risk. David is recognized internationally as a leading thinker and practitioner in the risk field, and has made several innovative contributions to improving risk management. He is well known for promoting the inclusion of proactive opportunity management within the risk process, and has recently been working on applying emotional literacy to understand and manage individual and corporate risk attitudes.

David is active in the Project Management Institute (PMI) and was a founder member of its Risk Management Specific Interest Group. He received the 2002 *PMI Distinguished Contribution Award* for his work in developing risk management. He is an elected Fellow of both the Institute of Risk Management (IRM) and the Association for Project Management (APM), as well as being a member of the Chartered Management Institute.

Terry Kendrick is Director of the Centre for Marketing and Risk at the University of East Anglia (UEA). He has been a strategic marketing planning consultant for the past 18 years and has undertaken marketing planning projects in 17 countries for over 50 large organizations. He is particularly interested in the risks to effective marketing planning and has written both academic papers and managerial briefings on this topic. Terry is a member of the Chartered Institute of Marketing and contributes sessions to the MBA programme at UEA.

Robert J Politowski ACIB Dip Mgt Stud. MCMI LCIPD is a Director of IMS Risk Solutions. Rob has accomplished managerial and advisory skills at senior level with particular interest in Operations, Risk Management, Customer Service and Human Resources. Rob has over 20 years' experience in the retail financial sector in the UK. During this time he worked in various departments of a major UK Clearing Bank. He has substantial experience in the management and delivery of operations support through centralized operating centres including back office processing, customer service delivery and call centre operations. Additionally, he has significant experience in the management of operational risk issues within a wide range of banking operations encompassing credit risk, compliance and a range of special investigations having been an Auditor in the Group Audit function.

Professor Simon Pollard was appointed to the Chair in Waste and Environmental Risk Management at Cranfield University in September 2002. He obtained his PhD in Environmental Engineering from Imperial College in 1990. Simon has formerly held appointments at the Universities of Alberta and Edinburgh, with consultants Aspinwall & Company, with the Scottish Environment Protection Agency, and as the Environment Agency's Head of Risk Analysis. Simon's research and teaching interests are in sustainable technology systems, the management of wastes, contaminated land and environmental risk. He is the author of over 100 publications, Associate Editor of *Science of the Total Environment* and Director of Cranfield University's Integrated Waste Management Centre, coordinating activity on waste and resource management across the University. Simon has held professional appointments on the Government's Interdepartmental Liaison Group on Risk Assessment (ILGRA), the Executive Committee of the engineering institutions' Hazards Forum and has recently been elected to the Scientific and Technical Committee of the Chartered Institution of Wastes Management.

John Sharp FBCI (Hon) FCMI MCIM is recognized worldwide for the contributions he has made to Business Continuity Management. In 2004 he was made an Honorary Fellow of the Business Continuity Institute and received a special award for his outstanding contribution to the industry. Currently John is Policy and Development Director with Continuity Forum, an educational and development body. From 1997 until 2004 he was the Chief Executive Officer of the Business Continuity Institute where he was responsible for delivering services to members throughout the world and working with all facets of industry, commerce and government to enhance the understanding and commitment to business continuity as a key management discipline.

John Sharp was chair of the committee that produced BSI's *Guide to Business Continuity Management* (PAS 56), and was also a member of the team producing BCM guidance for the UK Civil Contingencies Act. He works closely with government, regulators, police, security organizations and is a member of the London Resilience Business Team. John is a regular conference speaker and author on Business Continuity Management and has provided input to newspaper articles, radio, television and educational films.

David A Smith BSc MSc Chartered Chemist is Managing Director of IMS Risk Solutions with many years' experience of Health and Safety and Environmental Management Systems. He chairs a variety of important BSI Committees and represents the UK on ISO and CEN Committees on management systems standards and has substantial international experience in training, consultancy and auditing for a wide variety of clients in industry, government and the academic sector throughout the world. He has authored and edited a variety of books on management systems, most recently including a series of nine books on Integrated Management Systems published by British Standards Institution (BSI). He is co-author of the BSI publication *Managing Risk for Corporate Governance* – PD 6668:2000. Further publications include *Managing the Environment the 14001 Way* (1999, 2nd edn. 2005) – published by British Standards Institution – which is an award winning publication and provides comprehensive guidance on appropriate methodologies for effective environmental risk management systems. *Managing Safety the Systems Way* (1998) is a comprehensive guide to the implementation of Occupational Health and Safety Management systems to meet ILO and UK standards including the internationally recognized specification OHSAS 18001:1999 and BS 8800:2004.

Stephen Ward is Professor of Risk Management at the School of Management, University of Southampton, UK. He holds a BSc in Mathematics and Physics (Nottingham), an MSc in Management Science (Imperial College, London), and a PhD in developing effective models in the practice of operational research (Southampton). He is a member of the PMI and a Fellow of the UK Institute of Risk Management. He is Director of the School's MSc program in Risk Management.

Professor Ward's teaching interests cover a wide range of management topics including: decision analysis, managerial decision processes, insurance, operational and project risk management, and strategic management. For more than 20 years his research and consulting activities have been concerned with project risk management systems and the effective management of uncertainty. His latest book, *Risk Management – Organization and Context* (2004), discusses organization-wide approaches to integrated risk management, building on emergent issues in project risk management.

Peter Young has over 25 years experience as an environmental consultant specializing in research, policy and practical implementation of risk management programmes associated with waste, soil and water contamination. He has a First Class Honours degree in Environmental Chemistry from Edinburgh University, is a Chartered Chemist and an active member of the Chartered Institutes of Water and Environmental Management and Waste Management. He is currently Strategy Director of Enviros Consulting formed some years ago by the amalgamation of several UK consultancies, including Aspinwall and Co. where he was formerly Managing Director. He has published over 80 scientific and technical papers, contributed to statuary environmental guidance published by UK, Singapore and Hong Kong governments, and is a long-term member of the UK BSI Soil Quality Committee EH/4 and ASTM Committee D34 on Waste.

Arif Zaman BA (Hons) MBA FRSA is Visiting Fellow in the John Madejski Centre for Reputation and the Centre for Board Effectiveness. He is the author of *Reputational Risk* (Financial Times Executive Briefing, 2004) developed from research at Henley Management College. He recently returned to British Airways, where he leads several commercial projects, after a two-year sabbatical as an Associate Fellow at Chatham House, where he authored *Corporate Responsibility in Japan* (2003), and managing projects for policy-makers and corporates in Asia as an Advisor to the Commonwealth Business Council (CBC) and the Asian Productivity Organisation. In 2005 he was a member of Mitsubishi Corporation's Stakeholder Panel and in 2004 served on the drafting committee of the European Conference on CSR, at the invitation of the Dutch Presidency of the EU. He remains an advisor to the CBC. Previously he was Global Market and Industry Analyst at BA from 1993 to 2002 where he received a 'Recognising our People' award for his contribution to the Code of Conduct and BA's first Social Report and Sustainability Policy, and the leading award from the air cargo industry for his research on logistics and global supply chains. Prior to this, he was at Valin Pollen, a leading financial PR consultancy, and HSBC. He is on the Board of the Strategic Planning Society and the Editorial Board of the US-based *Journal of Business Strategy* and was a contributor to *Strategic Thinking in Tactical Times* (Palgrave, 2004). He is a Director and trustee of the Strategic Planning Society and the Red Shift Theatre Company. He is also an Associate of the Foreign Policy Centre, a Fellow of the Royal Asiatic Society and a Fellow of the Royal Society of Arts.

Foreword

'Everybody's Business': an introduction to the risk management universe

Steve Fowler, CEO, Institute of Risk Management (IRM)

Just what exactly is risk management? Until quite recently, the response to this apparently simple question would depend on who you asked: ask a safety expert and you'd get one interpretation; ask a banker and you'd get a completely different one. If you didn't know otherwise, you'd assume these two interpretations came from different worlds. Increasingly, however, organizations are beginning to appreciate that these different worlds make up parts of the same universe – the risk management universe.

This book brings together insights into this universe from a range of leading commentators. Indeed, rarely has such a breadth of risk authors contributed to the same work. Whilst each paints a picture of risk management from their own viewpoint, a number of significant common themes come through time and again, the foremost amongst these being:

- uncertainty;
- opportunity;
- communication;
- complexity;
- leadership;
- skills.

Risk is not a finite science. Whilst mathematics can help us calculate probabilities, as David Hillson remarks in Chapter 1, we cannot know, understand, calculate or control everything. Risk is everywhere and derives directly from unpredictability. Risk management provides us with a framework for dealing with and reacting to such uncertainty. This is particularly important given the pace of change in life today. Ours is a world where product life cycles are typically measured in months not years and technological innovation makes whole industries, not just individual companies, obsolete almost overnight. In the space of less than 30 years, the main format used by the recorded music industry has moved from LP to cassette to CD to MP3 download: what will the next 30 years bring? To survive and thrive, organizations must keep one eye and an open and fertile imagination on the future through so-called 'horizon scanning', and at the same time learn from past experiences. Risk management provides an invaluable framework within which horizon scanning can be integrated into 'business as normal' activities. It's a way of consciously thinking about change rather than just reacting to it, a theme raised by David Smith and Rob Politowski in Chapter 3. John Sharp echoes this in Chapter 5 with his comment that, with today's faster speed of business, there is little time for gradual recovery when disaster strikes.

For businesses, taking risk is intrinsically linked to profit and value creation. 'Who dares wins' as the old adage goes. Richard Anderson gets this message over loud and clear in Chapter 2 and it is echoed again throughout the book. Proactive risk and opportunity management can be used by senior managers to drive performance: in such a context, compliance and governance are a by-product of risk management and not just primary drivers in their own respect. I particularly like Anderson's idea of the 'risk intelligent organization'. Such an organization optimizes future opportunity and current risk through the spread of good risk management practice.

Risk management also provides us with a common language for dealing with uncertainty, enabling professionals from different functions to better communicate with each other. At its most fundamental level, organizational and project failure is often driven by individuals speaking their own professional languages but failing to truly communicate: sales failing to communicate with production, and finance with IT for instance. Whilst each author writing in this book inevitably speaks from their own perspective, it is heartening to see an increasingly common 'risk language' also in use. This is echoed in the emergence of standards, mentioned throughout the text, and an area in which my own organization, the Institute of Risk Management (IRM), is very active.

Risk management involves everyone and everything throughout an organization. Keith Blacker stresses this in Chapter 8 but again it is a common theme raised throughout the book. Whilst it is often relatively straightforward to identify and deal with pure risk in simple processes and systems, most of these do not stand alone and almost all require human interaction at some point. Reliance therefore on engineering solutions alone to minimize adverse risk will almost always fail: not only must the human element be considered, but the interactions between different systems in different functions are often so complex that in practice they can only be partly managed. In practice, the failure of such interactions is directly responsible for many well publicized risk failures. This in turn links back to my earlier point on the 'ghetto-ization' of professional languages and the opportunity this presents for the risk practitioner to step in to facilitate understanding between functions. This is an area where risk managers can add real value – through understanding, explaining and simplifying complexity, and consequently dealing with the sense of being overwhelmed that many directors feel.

A further sign of the growing maturity of risk as a field of study is the inclusion of many 'softer' non-engineering focused areas in this book, such as reputation, marketing and legal risk. Increasingly these regularly score highly in surveys of CEO risk attitudes, perhaps because failures in these areas are inexorably and directly linked to value destruction.

Effective approaches to risk management require strong and visible leadership. As a number of authors point out, without proactive leadership, risk management becomes a backroom function more concerned with technicalities, reporting and risk logs than with business development and performance. Risk management requires skills, not just in its technical execution but in creating the framework within which it can be exercised. Risk education organizations such as IRM have recognized the need for a broad range of education solutions. Consequently, programmes are now available to equip everyone from technical risk specialists up to CEOs with the risk skills they need.

In the future, risk specialists increasingly will need to become much more multi-skilled: able to understand and work with risk from the full range of perspectives discussed in this book. My own view is that only through such multi-skilling will risk management properly be recognized as a true vocation alongside accountancy, law, engineering and the like. Risk, however, is also becoming a core part of general management education for all executives, whether in industry, commerce, public sector or charity.

Managing risk is something that everyone does. As Peter Bernstein (1996) comments in *Against the Gods: The Remarkable Story of Risk*, certainty is hugely seductive, and the history of mankind is the history of our attempts to transform uncertainty into risk. Acting effectively within a context where we understand risk will help differentiate tomorrow's winning organizations from those that will be less successful. In contrast, aiming for the elimination of all risk is like the quest for Eldorado: largely illusory and ultimately unfulfilling. The person that risks nothing, does nothing, has nothing, is nothing and will be nothing. To quote Baz Luhrmann's 1992 film 'Strictly Ballroom', 'A life lived in fear is a life half lived'. Through understanding and applying the range of insights, tools, skills and knowledge provided by this book, the reader will be better equipped for their exploration of the risk management universe.

Reference

Bernstein, P L (1996) *Against the Gods – The Remarkable Story of Risk*. New York: John Wiley & Sons.

Editor's Note: The UK Government announced in November 2005 its intention to withdraw the requirement for full implementation of the proposed Operating and Financial Review (OFR). This announcement was made after the text for this book had been finalized. Consequently references to the OFR appear in Chapters 2, 3, 5, 6, 7, 11 and 13. We apologize for this small inaccuracy, which is the inevitable consequence of describing current conditions in a fast-changing environment.

DH

1

Surveying the Risk Management Universe – Where Are We Now?

David Hillson

Risk in history

The earliest records of human history and prehistory include stories of risk and its management. Historical documents, sacred writings, myths and legends – all tell tales of the human struggle against nature, the gods or the odds. Accounts of mankind's earliest origins describe the urge to break boundaries, go beyond current confines, explore the unknown. Narratives describe risk-taking individuals ranging from Abraham, revered by three of the world's great religions for his faith in leaving home and setting out to find a new country, through mythological heroes like Jason or Odysseus who undertook epic journeys, to modern entrepreneurs and innovators who change the lives of millions through ground-breaking discoveries and inventions. The broader sweep of human development has included risky phases as hunter-gatherers and agrarians, leading to the establishment of great civilizations like Egypt or the Mayans, to the present day.

Seen from a certain perspective, risk is everywhere. The world we inhabit is unpredictable, strange, incomprehensible, surprising, mysterious, awesome, different, other. This is true from the macro level of galaxies to the exotic nano-realm of subatomic particles, and everywhere in between. Irrefutable evidence forces people to accept the truth that we neither know nor understand everything, and we cannot control everything. Consequently, the word 'risk' has become a common and widely used part of today's vocabulary, relating to personal circumstances (health, pensions, insurance, investments, etc.), society (terrorism, economic performance, food safety, etc.) and business (corporate governance, strategy, business continuity, etc.).

And it seems that mankind has an insatiable desire to confront risk and attempt to manage it proactively. Many of the institutions of humanity could be viewed as frameworks constructed to address uncertainty, including politics, religion, philosophy, technology, laws, ethics and morality. Each of these tries to impose structure on the world as it is experienced, limiting variation where that is possible, and explaining residual uncertainty where control is not feasible. Sense-making appears to be an innate human faculty, seeking patterns in apparent randomness, applying a variety of templates or heuristics until a workable resolution is reached which allows an acceptable degree of comfort in the face of uncertainty.

As a result, not only is risk everywhere, but so is risk management. Just as the presence of risk is recognized and accepted as inevitable and unavoidable in every field of human endeavour, so there is a matching drive to address risk as far as possible. This has led to a proliferation of areas where the phrase 'risk management' is used to describe efforts to identify, understand and respond to risk, particularly in various aspects of business. Indeed it is possible to speak of a multidimensional 'risk management universe', with the word 'universe' derived from the Latin words *unus* (one) and *versum* (turn), describing a concept that combines all into one whole. Perhaps it is not too far-fetched to describe risk management as offering an integrative framework for understanding many parts of the human experience, if not all.

Risk in business

In the world of business, risk management has a special place, being recognized as a management discipline in its own right, with a broad supporting infrastructure. Elements of this support include:

- *Academic base:* Many universities and educational establishments offer basic and advanced teaching in risk management, at degree, masters and doctoral levels, and both theoretical and applied research programmes are also available.
- *Professional bodies*: Many professional societies exist specifically to promote and support the discipline of risk management. Some of the most prominent are listed in Table 1.1.

Table 1.1 Risk management professional bodies

Professional body	*Web address*
ALARM – The National Forum for Risk Management In the Public Sector	www.ALARM-UK.org
Association for Project Management Risk Management Specific Interest Group (APM Risk SIG)	www.APM.org.uk/RiskManagement/RiskProfile.asp
Association of Insurance and Risk Managers (AIRMIC)	www.AIRMIC.com
Business Continuity Institute (BCI)	www.theBCI.org
Engineering & Construction Risk Institute (ECRI)	http://ECRIonline.org
European Institute for Risk Management (EIRM)	www.EIRM.com
Federation of European Risk Management Associations (FERMA)	www.FERMA-asso.org
Global Association of Risk Professionals (GARP)	www.GARP.com
Institute of Risk Management (IRM)	www.theIRM.org
International Council on Systems Engineering Risk Management Working Group (INCOSE RMWG)	www.INCOSE.org/practice/techactivities/wg/risk
Professional Risk Managers' International Association (PRMIA)	http://PRMIA.org
Project Management Institute (PMI) Risk Management Specific Interest Group (PMI Risk SIG)	www.RiskSIG.com
Public Agency Risk Managers' Association (PARMA)	www.PARMA.com
Public Risk Management Association (PRIMA)	www.PRIMAcentral.org
Public Risk Management Organisation (PRIMO)	www.PRIMOeurope.org
Public Utilities Risk Management Association (PURMA)	www.PURMA.org
Risk & Insurance Management Society (RIMS)	www.RIMS.org
Risk Management Association (RMA)	www.RMAhq.org
Risk Management Institution of Australasia (RMIA)	www.RMIA.org.au
Society for Risk Analysis (SRA)	www.SRA.org

Table 1.2 Risk management standards and guidelines

Reference/title	*Standards body/publisher*	*Date*
AS/NZS 4360:2004, *Risk Management*	Standards Australia, Homebush NSW 2140, Australia, and Standards New Zealand, Wellington 6001, New Zealand.	2004
BS 25999-1:2006, *Business Continuity Management – Part 1: Code of Practice*	British Standards Institution, London, UK.	2006
BS 6079-3:2000, *Project Management – Part 3: Guide to the Management of Business-related Project Risk*	British Standards Institution, London, UK.	2000
BS 8444-3:1996 *Risk Management – Part 3: Guide to Risk Analysis of Technological Systems* (previously issued as IEC 300-3-9:1995)	British Standards Institution, London, UK.	1996
CAN/CSA-Q850-97 R2002, *Risk Management: Guideline for Decision-Makers*	Canadian Standards Association, Ontario, Canada.	2002
CP142, *Operational Risk Systems and Controls*	Financial Services Authority, London, UK.	2002
ISO/IEC FDIS 16085-2006, *Information Technology – Systems and Software Engineering – Lifecycle Processes – Risk Management* (previously issued as IEEE 1540-2001, *Standard for Software Life Cycle Processes – Risk Management*)	International Organization for Standardization, International Electrotechnical Commission, Geneva, Switzerland.	2006
ISO 14001:2004, *Environmental Management Systems – Requirements with Guidance for Use*	International Organization for Standardization, Geneva, Switzerland.	2004
ISO 14004:2004, *Environmental management systems – General Guidelines on Principles, Systems and Support Techniques*	International Organization for Standardization, Geneva, Switzerland.	2004
ISO/IEC 17799:2000, *Code of practice for Information Security Management*	International Organization for Standardization/International Electrotechnical Commission, Geneva, Switzerland.	2000
IEC 62198:2001, *Project Risk Management – Application Guidelines*	International Electrotechnical Commission, Geneva, Switzerland.	2001
JIS Q 2001:2001 (E), *Guidelines for Development and Implementation of Risk Management System*	Japanese Standards Association, Tokyo, Japan.	2001
NS 5814:1991, *Krav til risikoanalyser*	Norges Standardiseringsforbund (NSF).	1991

Table 1.2 Risk management standards and guidelines (*continued*)

Reference/title	*Standards body/publisher*	*Date*
PD 6668:2000, *Managing Risk for Corporate Governance*	British Standards Institution, London, UK.	2000
PD ISO/IEC Guide 73:2002, *Risk Management – Vocabulary – Guidelines for Use in Standards*	British Standards Institution, London, UK.	2002
A Guide to the Project Management Body of Knowledge (PMBoK®), Third Edition, Chapter 11 "Project Risk Management"	Project Management Institute, Philadelphia, US.	2004
A Risk Management Standard	Institute of Risk Management (IRM), Association of Insurance and Risk Managers (AIRMIC), and National Forum for Risk Management in the Public Sector (ALARM), London, UK	2002
Continuous Risk Management Guidebook	Software Engineering Institute (SEI), Carnegie Mellon University, USA	1996
Enterprise Risk Management – Integrated Framework	The Committee of Sponsoring Organizations of the Treadway Commission, USA	2004
Guidelines for Environmental Risk Assessment and Management	DETR, Environment Agency and IEH/The Stationery Office, London, UK.	2000
Management of Risk – A Strategic Overview (The Orange Book)	HM Treasury, London, UK	2001
Management of Risk – Guidance for Practitioners	UK Office of Government Commerce (OGC)/The Stationery Office, London, UK.	2002
New Basel Capital Accord – Consultative Document	Basel Committee on Banking Supervision, Switzerland	2001
Project Risk Analysis & Management (PRAM) Guide, (second edition)	Association for Project Management/APM Publishing, High Wycombe, Bucks UK.	2004
Risk Analysis and Management for Projects (RAMP, (second edition))	Institution of Civil Engineers, Faculty of Actuaries and Institute of Actuaries Thomas Telford, London, UK.	2005
Risk Management Guide for DoD Acquisition, 5th edn., Version 2	US Department of Defense/ Defense Acquisition University, Defense Systems Management College. Published by DSMC Press, Fort Belvoir, VA, USA.	2003
The Combined Code on Corporate Governance	Financial Reporting Council, UK.	2003

- *Qualifications*: A range of examinations and qualifications are available for the risk professional, offered by academic institutions and professional bodies, though there is no clear consensus on a single certification which is recognized across all industries or countries.
- *Literature*: In addition to the wide range of national and international risk management standards and guidelines (see Table 1.2), there are a number of refereed journals covering the topic, as well as a huge variety of books on various aspects of risk.
- *Tools*: Software vendors offer a wide variety of tools to support all aspects of the risk process, as well as specialized tools for particular applications. There is also a growing market in enterprise risk management solutions, offering an integrated approach to managing risk across the organization. The current generation of risk tools have powerful functionality, good user interfaces and increasing integration capability.
- *Consultancies*: Solution providers also offer risk management support, allowing clients to benefit from their expertise and experience, and sharing best practice thinking and practical implementation.

Part of the recognition of risk management as an important management discipline has been the development of standards and guidelines which aim to capture and describe 'best practice'. These are increasing in number, with some aiming to address risk management in its broadest sense while others have more limited scope. Some of the most widely used are listed in Table 1.2. The problem with having such a wide variety of 'standards' is the lack of 'standardization'! The standard originally described a flag carried onto the battlefield to provide a rallying-point for the troops in the midst of the conflict. Having more than one standard in such circumstances would be a recipe for disaster. Yet in the professional arena it seems perfectly acceptable to have many standards in the same field, dividing the troops who rally to one or another, and leading to confusion and lack of focus.

Purpose and structure of this book

There seems little doubt that risk management has been part of human activity for a very long time, and it is today a vital component of business. As a result, anyone asking the simple question 'What is risk management?' will not find a simple answer. Hence this book.

Even the most cursory exploration reveals a huge variety of differing perspectives, all claiming to represent the best way to address risk management. In fact risk management is not a single subject at all; it is a family of related topics. Application of risk processes has reached ever further across the boundaries of business. Risk management is not only practised formally in most industries, in many countries, and in both government and the private sector, but it also plays an important role at all levels in organizations. Types of risk management found in business today include:

- strategic risk management;
- corporate governance;
- financial risk management;
- business continuity and disaster recovery;
- reputational risk management;
- risk-assessed marketing;
- operational risk management;
- project risk management;
- environmental risk assessment;
- legal and contract risk management;
- technical risk management;
- fraud risk management;
- counter-terrorism risk management.

Even this long list is not exhaustive, as new and specialized applications are found in different areas of business. There are many common elements shared by these different types of risk management, but each has its own distinctive language, methodology, tools and techniques. They vary in scope from the broadest application to very specific areas of risk. They are at different levels of maturity, with some types of risk management being quite recent developments while others measure their history in decades. But each is important in its own way, representing part of the response of business to the uncertain environment within which it operates.

This book brings together leading experts from various risk management fields to share key insights into what makes their part of the risk management universe unique. While it would not be possible to include every aspect of risk management in all its diverse forms without making this a very large volume indeed, the main application areas found in most businesses are covered here. Each contributor describes current best practice in his area of expertise, as well as outlining areas for future development. Following this unique guided tour of the main dimensions of the risk management universe, the book concludes with a final integrative discussion which attempts to draw the threads together, identifying underlying themes which unify all types of risk management, and setting the scene for new developments to maximize the effectiveness of risk management in all its diverse areas of application.

As a result, this book has something for everyone: business leaders who need to know where their risks are coming from and how they can be addressed; risk professionals seeking a broader and deeper understanding of their subject; lay people interested in developments of a key theme of our time; and teachers and students of business and management. All aspects of life have always been and still are risky, and this guided tour of the risk management universe provides essential insights into how to manage risk in business wherever it arises.

References and recommended reading

AS/NZS 4360:2004, *Risk management.* Homebush, Australia: Standards Australia; Wellington, New Zealand: Standards New Zealand.

Association for Project Management (2004) *Project Risk Analysis & Management (PRAM) Guide* (second edition), High Wycombe, Bucks, UK: APM Publishing.

Basel (2001) *New Basel Capital Accord – Consultative Document.* Basel: Basel Committee on Banking Supervision.

Bernstein, P L (1996) *Against the Gods – the remarkable story of risk.* New York: J Wiley & Sons.

BS 25999-1:2006, *Business Continuity Management – Part 1: Code of Practice.* London: British Standards Institution.

BS 6079-3:2000, *Project Management – Part 3: Guide to the management of business-related project risk.* London: British Standards Institution.

BS 8444-3:1996, *Risk Management – Guide to risk analysis of technological systems.* London: British Standards Institution.

CAN/CSA-Q850-97 R2002, *Risk management: Guideline for decision-makers.* Ontario, Canada: Canadian Standards Association.

COSO (2004) *Enterprise Risk Management – Integrated Framework.* Washington DC: The Committee of Sponsoring Organisations of the Treadway Commission.

DETR, Environment Agency and IEH (2000) *Guidelines for Environmental Risk Assessment and Management.* London: The Stationery Office.

Dorofee, A J *et al.* (1996) *Continuous Risk Management Guidebook.* Pittsburgh, PA: SEI Carnegie Mellon University.

Financial Reporting Council (2003) *The Combined Code on Corporate Governance.* London: Financial Reporting Council.

Financial Services Authority (2002) *CP142 Operational Risk Systems and Controls.* London: Financial Services Authority.

Hillson, D A (2002) What is risk? Towards a common definition. *InfoRM (Institute of Risk Management)*, April, pages 11–12.

HM Government Cabinet Office Strategy Unit (2002) *Risk: Improving government's capability to handle risk and uncertainty*. Report ref 254205/1102/D16. London: HM Government Cabinet Office Strategy Unit.

HM Treasury (2001) *Management of Risk – A Strategic Overview (The Orange Book)*. London: The Stationery Office.

IEC 62198:2001, *Project risk management – Application guidelines*. Geneva: International Electrotechnical Commission.

IEEE 1540-2001, *Standard for Software Life Cycle Processes – Risk Management*. New York: The Institute of Electrical and Electronic Engineers.

Institute of Risk Management (IRM), Association of Insurance and Risk Managers (AIRMIC), and National Forum for Risk Management in the Public Sector (ALARM) (2002) *A risk management standard*. London: IRM/ALARM/AIRMIC.

Institution of Civil Engineers, Faculty of Actuaries and Institute of Actuaries (2005) *Risk Analysis & Management for Projects (RAMP)* (second edition). London: Thomas Telford.

ISO 14001:2004, *Environmental management systems. Requirements with guidance for use*. Geneva: International Organisation for Standardisation.

ISO 14004:2004, *Environmental management systems. General guidelines on principles, systems and support techniques*. Geneva: International Organization for Standardization.

ISO/IEC FDIS 16085:2006, *Information technology – Systems and software engineering – Life cycle processes – Risk management*. Geneva: International Organisation for Standardisation/International Electrotechnical Commission.

ISO/IEC 17799:2000, *Code of practice for information security management*. Geneva: International Organisation for Standardisation/International Electrotechnical Commission.

JIS Q2001:2001(E), *Guidelines for development and implementation of risk management system*. Tokyo: Japanese Standards Association.

NS5814:1991, *Krav til risikoanalyser*, Oslo: Norges Standardiseringsforbund (NSF).

PAS 56:2003, *Guide to Business Continuity Management*. London: British Standards Institution.

PD 6668:2000, *Managing risk for corporate governance*. London: British Standards Institution.

PD ISO/IEC Guide 73:2002, *Risk management – Vocabulary – Guidelines for use in standards*. London: British Standards Institute.

Project Management Institute (2004) *A Guide to the Project Management Body of Knowledge (PMBoK®)* (Third Edition). Philadelphia, PA: Project Management Institute.

Raz, T & Hillson, D A (2005) A comparative review of risk management standards. *Risk Management: An International Journal*, 7:4 53–66.

UK Office of Government Commerce (OGC) (2002) *Management of Risk – Guidance for Practitioners*. London: The Stationery Office.

US Department of Defense (2003) *Risk Management Guide for DoD Acquisition* (Fifth edition, Version 2). Fort Belvoir, VA: Defense Systems Management College.

2

Strategic Risk Management

Richard Anderson

Why risk management?

No one can turn a profit unless they are taking risk. Equally, everyone intuitively knows that turning risk to positive organizational advantage is not easy. That is what makes risk a strategic issue. The risk management issues discussed here are equally applicable to smaller companies, not-for-profit organizations and public sector bodies as they are to large multinational groups.

Risk management is the optic through which senior managers are now able to drive better performance. Improved performance is being driven by more effective processes, closer collaboration with partners and better motivated people in a finely tuned organization. This is a contrary view to one held by many people who regard risk as negative and risk management as bureaucracy. Viewing risk as a strategic issue and risk management as a strategic tool can turn negative, energy-sapping, compliance-driven risk management programmes into performance-enhancing, energy-releasing, positive programmes.

Corporate governance is a theme of the time, whether it is Higgs and the Combined Code (Financial Reporting Council, 2003; Higgs, 2003), the Financial Services Authority's (FSA's) new principles for listed companies, the new Operating and Financial Review (OFR), the Sarbanes-Oxley Act of 2002 or activist shareholders. Risk management is at least a part of the response demanded by all of these corporate governance initiatives. This has fostered a negative perspective of risk management in many organizations. In sharp contrast the aim of strategic risk management should be to help managers to remove the downside bias of many risk programmes and to liberate energy around a positive risk management approach that enhances an organization's ability to achieve its legitimate objectives. Regulatory compliance should be a by-product of good risk management; it should not drive the risk management agenda, a phenomenon that is only too apparent in many industrial sectors today.

In the UK risk management is now on the board agenda for all quoted companies, all charities, all public sector bodies and increasingly it is on the agenda of private companies as well. Three factors have put it there, but only one will keep it on the list. The first of these three factors is *corporate failures*: coverage of Enron, WorldCom and Andersen in the US has been relentless: in Europe, Maxwell, BCCI, Barings, Marconi, Equitable Life and many others are equally well documented. On both sides of the Atlantic, corporate disasters have led to strident demands for increasing levels of the second factor: *corporate governance*, an important part of which encompasses risk management. The third factor that has put risk management on the agenda is *regulation*: since privatization first established itself as a phenomenon in the UK, regulation has become a dominant theme with an increasing number of regulatory bodies, each of which promulgates a risk management approach, both to their regulation strategies and also in guidance to companies that are subject to their remit. But the onslaught of regulation does not rest with UK regulators: the EU and increasingly the SEC (Securities and Exchange Commission) in the United States all have stakes in the regulatory agenda. Directors face a heightened risk of falling foul of an increasingly complex regulatory agenda.

These drivers have all had far-reaching impacts on the way in which businesses are run in the UK as well as in many other economies of the world. However, given the short memory spans of many management teams evidenced by the surprisingly short average tenure of a CEO in a quoted company, and the intense difficulty of maintaining focus on the plethora of regulations that all businesses now face on a daily basis, there is only the fourth driver that will keep risk management on the board agenda over the long term, and that is *performance*. Risk management should produce four outcomes: to help organizations to perform better, to achieve their objectives with fewer slip-ups, to build greater shareholder value and to hit performance targets more easily. If this is achieved, then risk management will have earned its permanent place on the board's agenda.

These four issues (corporate failures, corporate governance, regulation and performance) are not the only drivers of risk management for organizations: many are concerned about insurance premiums, especially in the light of hard insurance markets with low capacity that were seen in the aftermath of 9/11. Banks and other financial service organizations spend considerable time and money measuring credit, market and liquidity risk. Increasingly large numbers of organizations are concerned about project risk. Important as they are, these have not historically been the issues that have driven risk management on to the board agenda nor are they the factors that will sustain its position there. It is accordingly necessary to understand in the first instance how these drivers led to the current position.

Driver 1: corporate disasters

Over the last few decades of the 20th century and the beginning of the 21st there have been waves of corporate disasters. In the UK, Polly Peck, Maxwell, BCCI and Barings started the ball rolling. They were subsequently followed by Equitable Life, Marconi, AIB, MyTravel and others. In the US, the early wave was in the financial sector with failing Savings and Loans corporations and more recently Enron, Andersen and WorldCom. But that is not the end: many others have followed on both sides of the Atlantic where management has failed to keep the pressures for performance at bay in their organizations. And this is not limited to the Anglo-Saxon world: Royal Ahold (The Netherlands), Vivendi (France) and Parmalat (Italy) have all blazed trails in their own countries and left their imprint across the world.

There are three reasons why these failures are important from a risk management perspective: first, the influence that they have on the behaviour of other companies, second, the influence they have on other stakeholders, and third, because valuable lessons stand to be learnt from the specifics of the failures.

In some circumstances these global and domestic failures can make a significant impact on the behaviour of other organizations. There have been two main responses: 'It couldn't happen here' was the response to Enron from Government, senior professionals and regulators. The reason 'it' could not happen 'here' (in the UK), it was maintained, was that regulation in the UK and more particularly corporate governance regulation and accounting rules are maintained on a series of principles rather than a series of rules as in the US. The contrary evidence is provided by Marconi, MyTravel and Mayflower, each of which took place after the Cadbury, Rutteman, Hampel and Turnbull reports (Cadbury *et al.*, 1992; Committee on Corporate Governance, 1998; Internal Control Working Party, 1994; Turnbull *et al.*, 1999). Attempts to differentiate Enron from Marconi are unhelpful: they both resulted from greed and arrogance. They both had serious accounting failures, either in the application of principles or in the systems that were needed to run them. They both had major strategic flaws. In other words they both had serious corporate governance and risk management failures. And they both resulted in massive financial losses to shareholders, pensioners, employees, suppliers and their sectors as a whole.

The second major thread of response is to try to ensure that 'it' does not happen over here. This is the response of organizations that look to the outside world for lessons that can be applied to their own organizations. Some commentators argue that the evolution of risk management is a continuum that starts with problems in management's own organization, continues with problems in neighbouring organizations and ends up with the pursuit of value. In other words, in the first instance, internal controls are put in place to deal with problems that arise in a manager's own organization. For example, a company that finds it regularly suffers from bank frauds committed by its own staff has a problem that has to be addressed by management. A possible response might be to implement a process of regular bank reconciliations, divide responsibilities for authorizing payments and signing cheques between different members of staff and insist on more rigid account mandates with their bankers. The internal controls are therefore a response to a risk, which has evidenced itself in losses. These control responses are implemented with a view to dealing with the risk of bank fraud that has occurred internally.

The next stage of evolution is dealing with problems that have occurred in neighbouring organizations (neighbouring in terms of size or industry as much as neighbouring in terms of geographical location). For example, a management team sees that other organizations are facing severe bad debts on credit sales. They have not yet suffered any themselves, but, given that they have weak procedures and are in the same industry, they can see that they might. Their response might be to institute proper credit checks, to introduce account limits and to place 'stop' instructions where credit limits are breached, until the position is brought under control. In other words internal controls are developed to ensure that problems that first occurred externally in neighbouring organizations do not impact the business.

It would be difficult to describe risk management of this nature as being strategic, but the responses, in particular to Enron and WorldCom, do mean that the subject of internal controls has begun to appear as a discussion item in the boardroom for the first time in very many years. And there again, these issues of control are significant: the very survival of an organization may well depend on them.

Driver 2: corporate governance

Where organizations are not putting control onto the agenda for themselves, those that look after the codes of corporate governance are trying to do so for them. However, there are at least two different approaches: that adopted in the UK and that adopted in the US. It is not the purpose of this chapter to address corporate governance in detail, but there are important aspects that are relevant to risk management as a boardroom agenda item. This is because corporate governance is founded on three pillars: organizational structure, board activities and compliance. Of these, in the UK, the most developed pillar is organizational structure, a bias that was significantly reinforced both by the Higgs report into the effectiveness of non-executive directors, and the Smith report (Smith *et al.*, 2003) which looked at audit committees. The second of the three pillars of corporate governance is the activities of the board which in turn consists of three main strands: reporting, risk management and assurance. It is the last two of these that are relevant to the position of risk management at the board table. The third pillar, compliance, is largely underdeveloped in the UK, in that compliance is a matter of 'comply or explain' with sanctions being imposed only by institutional stakeholders and lobby groups. It is therefore rare for compliance with the Combined Code to be a major hurdle or cause for concern driving substantial organizational activity. Indeed, after the introduction of each of the major reports on corporate governance, there has been considerable activity focused on simply meeting the requirements of the report rather than addressing the underlying issues. This is a position which is at variance with current experience in the US, where the Sarbanes-Oxley Act envisages penalties for errant directors of up to 25 years in prison. Not surprisingly, Sarbanes-Oxley compliance has driven the compliance industry to a feeding frenzy, based on a fear of non-compliance.

In the UK, the presence of risk management in the Combined Code originated with the Cadbury report which included a paragraph that required directors to review the effectiveness of their internal controls. The thinking behind this was to be found in the COSO report (COSO, 1994). COSO was important because it defined internal control, for the first time, in terms of corporate culture and risk as much as the actual activities of checking and exercising control. Essentially the key concepts that it introduced to the debate were that without a proper control environment (internal culture) any control activities were just being built on foundations of sand. Secondly, internal controls were there to respond to risks, and therefore it would be sensible to undertake a form of risk identification and assessment process before launching into risk management. Thirdly, the authors of COSO asserted that internal controls needed to be built in to the organization rather than being bolted on as afterthoughts. There were two further important themes coming out of the COSO report. The first was that control had three major objectives: the continuity of operations, timely and effective reporting and compliance with local laws and regulations: these were to have the effect of broadening out a debate from finance departments into something that had wide ramifications for the entirety of the organization. And this led to the second important theme: control was not just for finance, it was for everyone, whether at head office or a subsidiary on the other side of the world.

The Cadbury report was followed by a succession of subsequent reports on corporate governance and reports providing guidance to directors. However, it is worth noting that the Turnbull report was designed to encourage all organizations to develop their risk and internal control review processes up to the standards that were viewed as 'better' if not 'best' practice at the time. It also specifically sought to avoid prescription, on the basis that the approach needed to be tailored to each organization's own particular circumstances. This lack of prescription has been perceived in some quarters as an opportunity for organizations to do just as they wish. However, the Turnbull report does say that 'the system of internal control should be embedded in the operations of the company and form part of its culture; should be capable of responding quickly to changes as risks evolve and from changes in the environment; and should tell management where failings have happened, together with details of corrective action'.

The legacy of Turnbull is that it firmly placed risk management on the agenda of all organizations that are required to comply with the Combined Code.

Driver 3: regulation

Regulation is an inevitable consequence of a society that demands accountability from its politicians and businesses. Politicians create a regulatory framework and delegate responsibility to regulatory bodies, which in turn create the rules which businesses have to follow. Modern regulatory approaches dictate a risk-based approach to regulation, both by the regulator and in turn by the regulatee: this determines the rules that the company should follow and those which it can afford to be more relaxed about. Regulators frequently demand risk assessments from the regulatees. In some circumstances, failure to comply with regulation can result in severe adverse outcomes including financial penalties, reputational damage, suspension of licences to operate and even jail for directors and senior managers. Consequently, regulatory risk management, or compliance, can be a major driver for the creation of a risk management approach within a corporate environment.

With regard to regulatory risk, research shows that the fear of damage to corporate reputation is cited by nine out of ten senior managers as one of their four top drivers of risk management activity. Perversely perhaps, the same research showed that, amongst the same population of managers, six out of ten regard the lack of clear leadership at board level as being one of the key inhibitors of further risk management activity. This is perverse because increasing numbers of regulatory laws impose personal liabilities on directors and officers. These laws include the Competition Act 1998, the Data Protection Act 1998, the Proceeds of Crime Act 2002, to name a few. There are no less than 257 offences under the Companies Act 1985 with sanctions of up to seven years' imprisonment and/or unlimited fines.

With this in mind, the plethora of regulation continues to grow: research for the Federation of Small Businesses shows that since 2000 legislators have passed over 40 new statutes that provide for entry and seizure. Strategically, organizations must take on board the chilling effect of regulatory risk on entrepreneurial risk-taking by both executive and non-executive directors. Behaviour that would have been acceptable yesterday has become unacceptable overnight. Moreover, many regulators see it as being their job to ensure that a cultural sea change favouring more responsibility is truly embedded within companies. Their armoury includes licensing (both at a personal and a corporate level) through to sanctions that include imprisonment and unlimited fines. There is little doubt that companies that fail to appreciate the implications of the new punitive regime of regulation are liable to lose their competitive position while their more nimble competitors will race ahead through more effective management of what has become a punitive regulatory environment.

Driver 4: performance and the operating environment

The fourth driver, the driver that keeps risk management on the board table, is performance. Risk management is inextricably linked with performance because of three major changes in the operating environment in which all organizations exist and which have presented major challenges to managers. Those three are the speed of change, the consequent lack of history and the development of much more permeable boundaries between organizations.

It is difficult to argue with the notion that the pace of change continues to accelerate. Product life cycles are reducing, innovation is ever faster and more far-reaching, and obsolescence arrives even quicker than was previously imaginable. Combine this with changing global power: one global superpower, non-statal ideologies and the changing dimensions of Europe, and they all add up to an unpredictable and shifting environment that can make long-term planning obsolete. The commercial exploitation of the internet, the unlocking of the human genome, genetically modified organisms, biotechnology and nanotechnology all represent fundamental paradigm shifts for producers and consumers. Some people see opportunity in these changes: better lifestyles, longer life, opportunities to be exploited. Others see little more than gloom and despondency: exploitation of the balance of nature which will result in devastation, famine and uncontrolled harm let loose on an unsuspecting world. Some people see a need to exercise the precautionary principle; others simply duck and say there is nothing that anyone can do once the genie (the idea) is out of the bottle.

What is clear is that nobody has any real, hard-edged, agreed-upon data that says what will happen. There are no controlled experiments. Therefore people are liberated to argue from their own prejudices, ignorance and personal interests. This represents a quantum leap in the scope of risk management, away from bank reconciliations and on to global change. But it is this speed of change that is forcing organizations to reappraise their thinking about the nature of risk and how it impacts on themselves and their organizations. This is the first major change organizations are seeing in the environment in which they exist.

The second major change in the organizational environment is the lack of corporate history. The comparatively short period of tenure for CEOs in major corporations noted earlier is echoed by staff turnover rates. Companies are facing low levels of morale amongst staff and low levels of trust. This is the reciprocal, the payback for the downsizing, cost-cutting business process re-engineering exercises of the 1990s. It reflects the trend to outsourcing, off-shoring and reshaping organizations. It also reflects the collapse of major corporations and the loss of hard earned pension provision that was supposed to see staff through retirement. As a consequence of the constant churning of staff, corporate memory is regularly wiped clean. Frequently the experienced members of staff who knew how to respond to a given issue have left the organization.

The third change in the environment is the nature of economic activity between organizations. Rigid organizational boundaries have all but disappeared as a feature of the organization of economic activity. Large businesses, government departments, universities, health care trusts, all of them depend on the existence of other organizations in order to achieve their objectives. Boundaries that used to be defined by legal corporations are now permeable, allowing risk to transfer across and between legal entities at the flash of an internet connection. It is no longer good enough for organizations to rely on representations from its suppliers to the effect that its second and third tier suppliers are not using 'sweatshops' or child labour in the production of consumer goods. This now has to be verified and to be provable beyond any doubt.

This issue of permeable boundaries manifests itself in two distinct situations: first, where a long supply chain originating in third world countries leaves organizations open to accusations of exploitation, or of failing to care for the environment, and second, where an industry is fragmented into many small players, each of whom is dependent on other members of the industry. Accusations of child labour in Nike's supply chain some years ago were an example of the former, and resulted in considerable amounts of work to remove the accusation hanging over them.

An example of an industry-wide dependency is the rail industry in the UK. Following privatization, tracks, rolling stock, train operators, maintenance and supervision were all fragmented. Problems in maintaining tracks in one location may result in severe operating difficulties for the train operators in geographically diverse locations, whose track may be maintained by other contractors. Permeable boundaries mean that operational and reputational risks slip between organizational boundaries.

The consequences of these three changes in the operating environment are profound. It is no longer possible to manage risk within the boundaries of an organization. Nor is it sufficient any longer to rest on what was good enough in the past. Rapidly changing environments demand flexible and dynamic strategies. Employees, both of the organization itself and those of its key partners, need to understand the nature of the strategy, how it affects them and how they can support it. The implications of rapid changes in strategy and fluctuating organizational boundaries are that everyone must have a much more instinctive feel for risk and their part in managing it.

A definition of risk

For strategic risk management, the generally accepted definition of risk is: *an event which may occur in the future and which if it happens might impact on the ability of the organization to achieve its objectives.*

This definition is useful, because it incorporates a number of issues in a single comparatively straightforward sentence. It implies a need to understand the nature of the event, an issue with which many organizations find it surprisingly difficult to get to grips. This is largely because managers frequently mistake their position in the system, whether or not they are talking about the circumstances or the event, and whether they appreciate the difference between the event, the actions required to manage it and the consequences of the event. In order to define a risk accurately, it is important to bring clarity to these issues.

The definition also implies a need to understand the timing: when might the risk impact? Soon? Or in a year's time? Or 50 years? Equally, the likelihood needs to be clear: is the risk almost a certainty, or no more than a small cloud on the horizon?

Finally the definition addresses the impact on the organization's objectives. This requires a departure from much of the historical perspective of risk as a purely negative subject. Current best practice envisages three attributes of a risk. Risk certainly has a negative attribute: there is a range of possible outcomes that can be worse than expected. However, it also has a range of outcomes that might be better than expected. This is often known as the upside of risk, and the argument runs that unless organizations manage with a view to capturing the upside, they are unlikely to do so by simply leaving matters to fortune. The third attribute of risk is the distribution: how much worse than expected does the range extend, and how much better than expected? This three-part set of attributes is derived from a heroic assumption that risks typically follow a normal distribution curve. This is by no means necessarily the case: many risks do not have a normal distribution curve. However, by thinking in these terms, managers are looking for alternative outcomes which might otherwise be missed. All of this presents a formidable set of data for an organization to collect around a large range of issues. In practice there is usually simply insufficient information and the analysis often boils down to a single point estimation of high, medium or low, possibly with an indication of whether the impact is getting better, worse or staying the same.

Impact is also a multifaceted word in this context in that it is possible to identify many different 'impacts'. Most commonly organizations use a hybrid financial definition, but this can be broken down to the impact on profit, or cashflow or the balance sheet. In some cases it is possible to calculate the impact on shareholder value. Increasingly organizations are finding that financial measures are inadequate and they resort to using indicators such as reputation, staff morale or visibility to the regulator.

A definition of risk management

At its simplest, risk management is sometimes seen as a process of identification, assessment and management of risks such that the expected value (impact times likelihood) of a gross (uncontrolled) risk is reduced to an acceptable net (controlled) risk. However, this is a very prosaic approach to the management of risk. As a strategic issue, risk management encompasses:

- the management of the portfolio of risks – the nature and type of risk that the organization is uniquely skilled at addressing;
- the way in which the organization wishes to engage with risk; and
- the manner in which the organization exercises control over risk.

These areas of strategic risk management are addressed in the rest of this chapter.

Types of risk

One of the big problems faced by risk managers is the very breadth of the definition of risk set out above. Examples range at one end of the scale from bank frauds to the threat of global warming at the other. Most risk practitioners attempt to deal with this by creating classifications to organize their risk data. There are broadly three main traditional approaches: organizational approaches, objective approaches and model-based approaches.

All of these approaches have attractions in that the risk 'buckets' are all recognizable to managers throughout the organization, and it is comparatively easy to draw up a departmental or business unit risk register using such approaches. It is also easy to compare Unit A with Unit B: which one has a more complete listing, which one is more successful and so on. It is also easier to provide a rudimentary 'consolidation' or 'aggregation' of risk data across a whole group to ensure that a high level view can be prepared. However, while some of these approaches have the benefit of being familiar and are recognized by many regulators, they have the disadvantage of not saying anything particularly valuable about the risks from a strategic perspective.

A new approach to categorizing risk

Professor John Adams puts forward a new grouping of risk under three categories (Adams, 1995): directly discernible, visible through science and virtual. Each is explained more fully in the following paragraphs.

1. Directly discernible risks are those risks in respect of which it is almost unimaginable to conceive of living without running into them and dealing with them in day-to-day life. For example, an individual gets up in the morning, dresses, has breakfast and steps out of the front door but does not get knocked down by the bus as it passes. In fact, the chances of this individual being knocked down by the bus are almost incalculably small, because the individual is culturally attuned to managing that risk as part of daily life.

   These directly discernible risks are evident in organizations as well. It is difficult to imagine, in a well-run and organized business, the consequences of the risks arising from leaving bank accounts unreconciled. In fact, any manager in a well-established business is unlikely to be able to estimate the possible costs of undetected bank fraud arising from a failure to carry out bank reconciliations. The manager, and the organization, are both culturally attuned to organizations with completed bank reconciliations. In effect then, directly discernible risks are those events that are rendered almost unimaginable because the required avoiding actions are taken as a matter of course.

Given that directly discernible risks are almost always dealt with by day-to-day control activities, should they be on the board agenda? It might be argued that the almost 600 US listed companies that as at January 2005 had filed reports of inadequacies in their accounting systems under the Sarbanes-Oxley law are probably largely reflecting their managements' and auditors' concerns about controls that respond to directly discernible risks. This US preoccupation with what is described in the legislation as Financial Reporting Controls stems directly from one of the perceived causes of failure in Enron and WorldCom, respectively.

2. The second type of risk might be described as being visible through science. For example, if a returning traveller is diagnosed as suffering from cholera, the doctor can see the bacterium through a microscope, and based on lots of experience and well defined treatment regimes it can be treated very simply and effectively such that the patient can be completely cured.

   The relevance of this example is that there are large numbers of risks where the gross risk (death by cholera) can be reduced to a perfectly acceptable net risk (the patient can be completely cured) through the use of a widely agreed-upon set of procedures (treatment regimes). By substituting any number of business issues into the brackets, it is possible to see the business relevance. For example:

Gross risk:	Adverse exchange rates adversely impact earnings from US subsidiary.
Net risk:	The impact of adverse currency movements can be largely eliminated.
Procedure:	Appropriate hedging of exchange rate positions.

   In this foreign exchange example, the procedure can theoretically be applied by anyone in the organization, although in practice it is usually left to a corporate treasurer who has the overall picture to manage the group-wide exposure and who has the expertise to ensure that it is done in an appropriate manner. This therefore leads to a set of rules for defining a business equivalent to risks that are visible through science: they require expertise if they are to be managed properly; there are agreed approaches that would be described widely as best practice and they probably need an enterprise-wide perspective.

   Other examples of risks that are visible through science might include items such as taxation and information security. Equally they might include certain manufacturing processes or the provision of some services, for example, expert legal advice. None of these things is necessarily understood throughout an organization, but each of them has a body of knowledge that is broadly agreed upon by a group of appropriately qualified practitioners.

3. The third type of risk is much more ephemeral: nobody can be absolutely sure about the extent of the risk, how it might impact or what should be done about it. These risks can be described as virtual risks, in the sense that they cannot be tied down to a fact-based interpretation or treatment. This sort of risk is typified by the debate over bovine spongiform encephalopathy (BSE) and its linkage with new variant Creutzfeld–Jacob brain disease (vCJD). The debate resulted in predictions of numbers dying from vCJD ranging up to 10 million individuals. Predictions are now down to the region of 7,000 individuals by 2080. This is still a serious issue; however, it is simply not of the same dimensions as was originally predicted. The absence of an agreed-upon body of knowledge allowed individuals to predict, comment and prophesy on the basis of their own ignorance, preconceptions and prejudices.

   This type of risk translates directly into the day-to-day world in which most organizations operate. These virtual risks include ones mentioned earlier: the commercial exploitation of the internet, the unlocking of the human genome, genetically modified organisms, biotechnology and nanotechnology. But virtual risks also include more mundane issues such as mergers and acquisitions. The literature suggests that the failure rate for acquisitions is something in the region of 50 to 80 per cent. And yet, while acquisitions are acknowledged to be a major source of value destruction, some companies do them extremely successfully. The implication of this is that many acquiring companies are entering into an area of virtual risk where managers are able to argue from their ignorance, preconceptions and prejudices. However, those that are successful at the acquisition process have taken a virtual risk and moved it into the realms of risk visible through science: they know what it takes to effect a successful acquisition.

This all has important ramifications. Is there a pure definition that categorizes risks as being directly discernible, visible through science or virtual? The implications are that these are not fixed: one company's virtual risk (acquiring another company) is another company's expertise: thereby making the risks visible through science. Equally, what is pure science to one company, for example, sophisticated treasury operations, may be directly discernible to a banking boutique or hedge fund which operates with these risks on a daily basis.

This is the core of risk as a strategic issue: understanding the nature of the risks that a company faces and which ones management are uniquely able to address is one of the essential ingredients to a successful strategy. The other side of the coin is that setting out to deliberately change the nature of the portfolio of risks faced by an organization is inevitably a high risk strategy. When in the 1980s Reed International embarked on the demerger and disposal of many formerly core businesses, it was embarking on a substantial change of its risk profile. It moved from a series of manufacturing businesses with risk profiles that were well managed into new areas which gave rise to substantial virtual risk. However, management were supremely successful. In the late 1990s GEC embarked on a series of equally transformational transactions to create Marconi. In contrast to Reed International they failed to manage the transformation into new areas of what was still to them virtual risk. The problems are threefold: to recognize what an organization is already good at (what is the nature of the risk that they already manage successfully), to understand the nature of the risk that the organization is taking on and third to ensure that the organization has the capability to manage the newly acquired risk as effectively as it manages the tried and tested former risk profile.

Reason for engagement with risk

Of equal importance to understanding the nature of risk and how that impacts strategy is the need to understand why organizations engage with risk. Clearly, the reasons for avoiding bank frauds and entering into a major corporate acquisition are different. Each has a place in strategic risk management: there are four reasons for entering into engagement with a given risk, and these four reasons fall naturally into two pairs of tensions.

The first reason for engaging with a risk, the reason that most commercial organizations exist, is the need to make profit. To make profit and to continue doing so, an organization must continue to take more managed risk. If it stops taking more managed risk, then it will watch margins on its existing businesses erode, markets decline and profits evaporate. The profit motive does not have to be the sole driver in this equation. The same drive for more managed risk is equally true of charities, public sector organizations and indeed governments. Organizations that fail to take more managed risk will inevitably fall into disuse and eventually fail. It is worth emphasizing the word 'managed' in the phrase 'more managed risk'. There may be a strategy about simply taking risk, but this does not, on balance, seem to be a sensible strategy for a sustainable organization, whether commercial or not-for-profit.

The second major reason for engaging with a risk is to avoid pitfalls. This is the home territory of risk management: how to stop bank frauds; how to stop Enron or Marconi from recurring. It is also the home territory of the regulator: the Health and Safety Executive strap line is 'reducing risks – protecting people'. Not an inherently bad strap line, especially for anyone with an awareness of social history and the exploitation of the Victorian workforce, but not one that is likely to encourage people to make more money or to take more risk, one of the fundamentals of a successful and dynamic economy. And yet, organizations must avoid pitfalls, or else they will face value destruction and ultimately failure.

Clearly there is a tension between these first two reasons for engaging with risk. They both go to the heart of value: creation on one side and destruction on the other. But it is the difference that is important: the avoidance of destruction is no more a creative activity than the creation of new value is a defensive activity. This is why they require different skill sets that are bound to be in tension.

The third major reason for engaging with risk is that organizations must have a performance culture. It does not matter whether the organization is a commercial operation, a university or a hospital. There has to be something in the lifeblood of the organization that persuades its people to do extraordinary things for it as well as for themselves. In a commercial organization this might be about bonuses for meeting sales targets; in a charity it might be about helping the homeless; in a university it might be about teaching or research. But what all these things imply is the taking of risk with a view to improving both personal and organizational performance.

The fourth major reason for engaging with risks is to ensure that the organization remains within the boundaries of acceptable corporate ethics and behaviours. This is about a proper engagement with stakeholders: staff, customers, suppliers, the public at large, employees of third world suppliers and the environment. In fact, it is about the way in which an organization interacts with any grouping that has a legitimate interest in the way in which the organization is run. Any organization that believes that it can ignore the legitimate interests of stakeholders is fooling itself: at the very least it has to have a dialogue. Failure to engage with stakeholders is likely to result in anything from disenchantment through to outright hostility which will reduce the ability to drive the business forward, will take up valuable management time and adversely impact the effectiveness of the organization.

There is a potential for tension between these last two reasons for engaging with risk. If the organization is to drive its people, through a performance culture, what is going to stop those same people from ignoring, or harming, the interests of less powerful stakeholders? The salesman who bends the rules, the finance director who flatters the results, the supervisor who pushes their team – somewhere there is a dividing line between ambition, good accounting, getting the job done and breaking the law, hiding black holes and putting people in danger.

The bottom line is that all organizations need to demonstrate each of these attributes in considering risks: no managed risk equals no profits; no avoidance of pitfalls equals impending disaster; no performance culture equals zero employee buy-in; no corporate ethics equals disaffected stakeholders. So should the organization push the boundaries on each of these fronts as far as it can? The answer is a categorical 'no'. If it does it is at just as much danger: it will get to the stage where it is taking so much more managed risk that the organization can no longer cope. It will suffer from initiative fatigue, its people will be unable to exercise control over all of the balls that are up in the air and they will become stressed. This is true also of the other three reasons for engagement with risk: if a company spends all of its time avoiding pitfalls, it is always operating with an eye on problems and regulators rather than an eye on the future, innovation and development. Such organizations become stuck in a quicksand of negativity that is overwhelming. Organizations that push the boundaries too far on the performance culture will find that individuals are pushed beyond their abilities, suffer burnout and probably begin to bend the rules to persuade themselves and their managers that they are coping. On the other hand, those that have overly stifling relationships with their stakeholders begin a permanent dance on eggshells which results in a stiffening of resistance to change as they stop making decisions in favour of consultation and deference to other people's concerns.

So by mapping each of the individual reasons for engagement with risk against long-term performance, it is possible to show the relationship whereby improvements in performance in the organization are derived from increases in the attention paid to any of the four reasons for engagement with risk. However, the marginal benefits begin to tail off and then become negative. Figure 2.1 shows the relationship with long-term performance on the *y* axis and any of the four attributes shown on the *x* axis. There are broadly three key zones: in zone one the organization is insufficiently interested in the reason for engagement with risk. In zone two they are interested and the marginal benefits from additional attention are either significantly positive or at least have not yet become negative. Zone three is where the marginal benefits have become negative and are potentially damaging the organization. Zones one and three can be described as 'dead zones' and zone two as the 'performance zone'.

All four of these relationships can be shown on the same diagram. Figure 2.2 shows the four axes going in each case from very little to lots as the circumference is approached. The inner circle shows a dead zone: the organization has no ambitions, is buffeted by the winds that blow it every which way, its people could not care about performance and furthermore it does not much care about its stakeholders either. Such organizations have little future. The outer ring shows where organizations are obsessed by the reasons for engagement with risk. This is where individuals and business can no longer cope.

To test the usefulness of this model imagine a company with the following attributes: it is a leader in its field. Its field is new and they are making great strides in dominating the market-place. As it approaches restrictions on its ability to grow, it encourages acquisitions, opening up new markets, using new financial instruments and so on. Its people are remunerated well for extraordinary performance. Stock options, cash bonuses, all the rewards of success in a company where people are always successful are plentiful. It has a team of people who analyse new business opportunities to death: due diligence, enterprise risk, credit, market and derivative risk are measured, recorded and analysed. And yet, with a puff of adverse wind, the organization collapses in record time. This is an organization that has no ability to avoid pitfalls: it has never known reverses in its fortunes; it has no resilience strategies and simply does not know how to stop problems from arising. Equally, item number two on the board agenda is the waiver of the ethics statement so that 'interesting' transactions which do not accord with the ethics statement can be entered into. Item three on the agenda is the transaction in question and item four is the reinstatement of the ethics statement. What we see in this case is a risk management profile as depicted in Figure 2.3. With a degree of

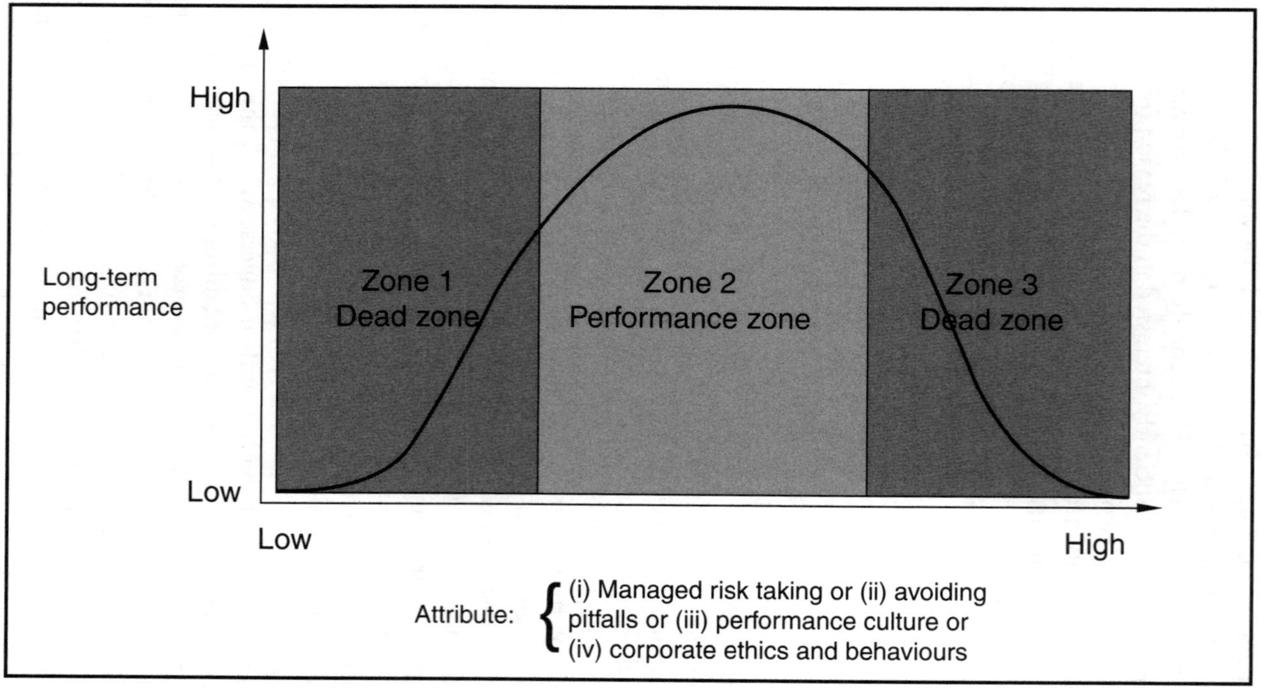

Figure 2.1 Relationship of attribute to long-term performance

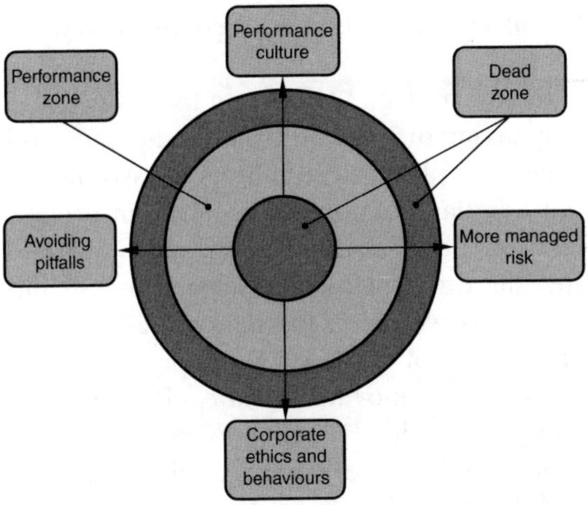

Figure 2.2 Balanced risk: mapping all four attributes

imagination this might describe the situation at Enron: change the circumstances somewhat and it describes Barings Singapore.

It is therefore interesting to note the reaction of US legislators: the Sarbanes-Oxley Act deals with directly discernible financial reporting controls, the structure and remit of audit committees and the relationship between audit firms and their clients. What it fails to do is to take into account the four dimensions that are set out above, although some might reasonably argue that it does to some extent push a risk profile

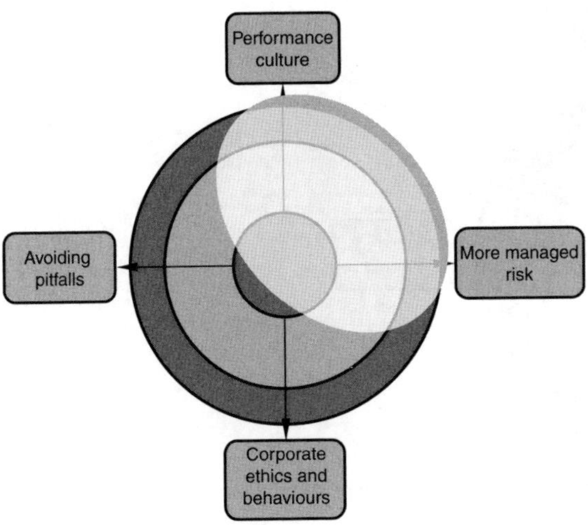

Figure 2.3 Enron risk culture

to the left and down by dint of the sheer volume of compliance work that is required.

It is interesting to speculate how to depict UK plc on this model. It is probably fair to summarize by saying that the British are generally good at avoiding a lot of pitfalls: there are plenty of regulators to assist in this regard, and this is anyway the heartland of risk management: insurance, IT security and the practice of auditing. British organizations are also generally good at corporate ethics and behaviours: being honest and doing the right thing by others sits well with the national conscience. However, British organizations are a lot less good at taking more managed risk: look at the poor history of innovation and exploitation, the low levels of cooperation between industry and university research. All of these suggest an approach to taking more managed risk that could be substantially better. In addition the British press are often accused of knocking directors who take risks that go wrong; this is compounded by analysts in the City who look for growth, but are extremely cautious about high risk strategies. There is also a culture of negativity to performance. The acreage of newsprint given over to 'fat cats' and excessive pay indicate a hard-wired attitude to performance that is almost impossible to change. All of this suggests that the typical risk profile for UK plc looks more like Figure 2.4 than the Enron picture above.

Is there an optimal position on the grid? This is an area that would benefit from long-term research. However, it is reasonable to speculate that the optimal position would be more like Figure 2.5: in the centre of the profile.

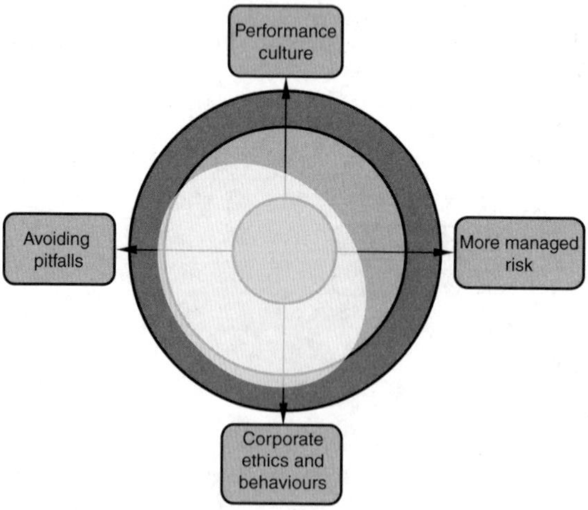

Figure 2.4 UK plc risk culture?

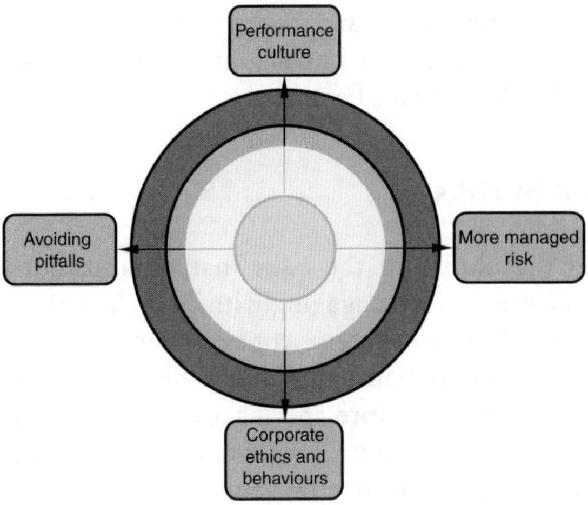

Figure 2.5 Target risk culture?

However, in a sense the group-wide position is almost irrelevant. Reverting to Barings, it was the attitude to risk from one person in one subsidiary that destroyed the bank. Therefore, more important than the group-wide profile are the profiles of all business units, territories or operational groupings. Where an organization pursues a particular profile for the group as a whole, visibility of significant differences in the balance of these reasons for engagement in risk in specific units should raise alarm bells in the boardroom or within the audit committee.

While this approach has obvious benefits in terms of looking at a business from the top down, it also lends itself as a framework in devising a strategy for responding to new risks. Having identified whether the risk is directly discernible, visible through science or virtual, management can ask why they are engaging with a particular risk. It may be, for instance, that a competitor is facing class actions from employees in the US. How should management respond to the risk when it has not yet manifested itself within its own organization? The initial take would probably be to review what needs to be done to avoid falling into that particular pitfall: legal reviews, reviews of procedures, modifying the HR processes and so on. But it might soon seem obvious that this is more than simply a legal pitfall: how does the treatment of individuals resonate with the company's corporate ethics and behaviours? Might it be that, by treating people in a way that is consistent with respecting their beliefs, morale and consequent performance is improved? If there is now no longer a threat of these class actions, and our people both recognize and respect the ethics and performance culture, is there not scope for pushing at risk boundaries that increase the amount of risk that can be taken?

Approaching the control of risks

This chapter has explored the nature of the risks that organizations face; it has also looked at the reasons for engaging with risks. The third key element of the equation is how to exercise control over risks.

As noted earlier the COSO report had a significant impact on the development of corporate governance. More specifically it represented the first definitive definition of internal control. COSO defined internal control as consisting of five main components: the control environment, risk assessment, control activities, information and communication and monitoring activities. This is often shown as a pyramid, as set out in Figure 2.6.

At the base of the pyramid is the control environment. This defines the way in which the company behaves. It includes its moral and ethical approaches, the values by which it operates and its attitudes to control. Without a firm foundation from the control environment, there is little prospect of establishing an effective system of internal control.

The second component is risk assessment. COSO was the first authoritative statement to link risk with internal control. For the first time, control was not just about pieces of paper moving around the organization, it was about things that might go wrong in achieving an

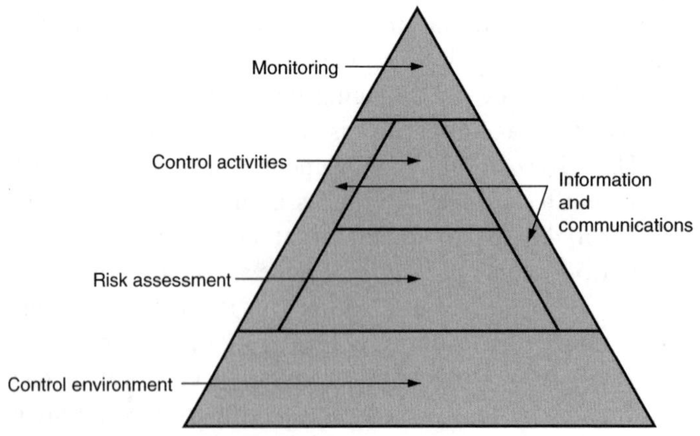

Figure 2.6 COSO: elements of control

organization's objectives. COSO established the requirement to assess risks prior to engaging in control activities – the third component. Control activities take place right round the organization. They are the things that happen to make sure that objectives are achieved and include all of those traditional tools of control including segregation of duties, reviews and analyses.

The fourth component that binds the whole process of control together is information and communication: information that rises to the top about the control environment, about the risks and the control activities and communication from the top that influences the direction of the organization. This in turn facilitates the fifth component, being the monitoring activities: this is the role of senior management and the board and, given the nature of linking risk to objectives, it provides evidence to ensure that the organization is on target to achieve its objectives.

Figure 2.7 shows the three-dimensional nature of control. There are three objectives, shown on the top of the cube, which represent the objectives of control: to ensure the continuing operations of the company; to ensure accurate and timely financial reporting; and to ensure compliance with local laws and regulations. But more than that, control is something that happens throughout the organization. This aspect is represented on the third face of the cube.

Recently, work by Professor Robert Baldwin of the London School of Economics has formed the basis of a new approach that can be used to review control responses. This model explores the relationships between five key headings across which the organization must manage. They include strategy, people, detail, tasks and drivers, as set out in Figure 2.8.

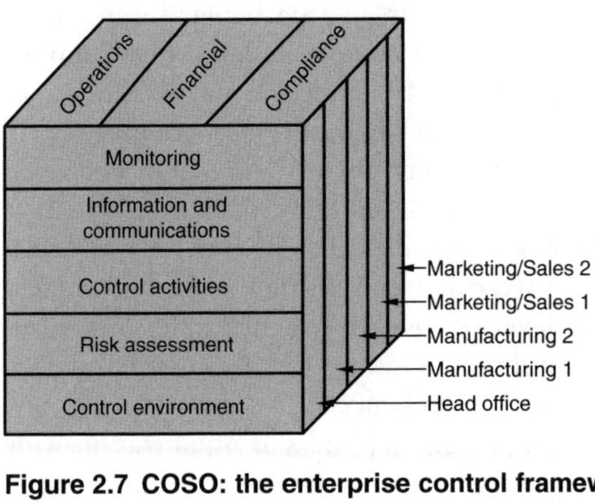

Figure 2.7 COSO: the enterprise control framework

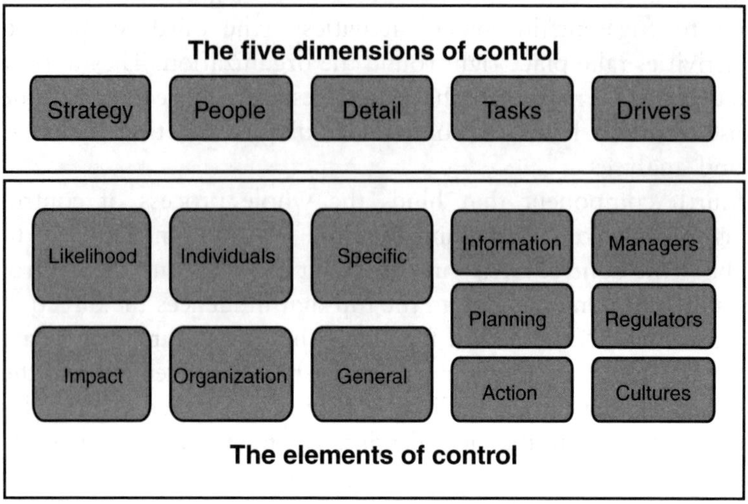

Figure 2.8 A new approach to controlling risk

What this model does initially is to emphasize the difficult decisions that have to be taken when deciding on the tactics of exercising control: there are many different ways in which control might be influenced by taking varying approaches to control. It is therefore important to get to grips with each of the five dimensions of control and each of the elements that are addressed within the dimensions.

By 'strategy' the model is referring to the balance between reducing the likelihood of a risk crystallizing or alternatively limiting the impact when it does. In some instances an organization may decide that it does not want to face the risk of loss arising from a particular future event, or wishes to reduce the likelihood to an acceptable level. For example, a financial services company may wish to reduce the likelihood of employees or directors being banned for regulatory non-compliance. In order to reduce the likelihood, they may go through significant regulatory hoops, establish procedures and undertake training. In other instances, perhaps where the risk is considered to be relatively unlikely, organizations may choose to invest in a contingency plan that reduces the impact to an acceptable level of loss. In practice many organizations will look for a blended approach: reduce the likelihood and then think about the remaining need for resilience.

Under the heading of 'people' the model looks at organization-wide responses to hazards and the behaviours of individuals. In the wake of perceived audit failures in the 1980s and 1990s, all of the major audit firms instituted organization-wide responses to the acceptance of new audit clients, the review of audit work and the avoidance of claims. In effect they were driving the management of this risk down to a directly discernible risk. On the other hand, as discussed earlier, many risks, for example, treasury or taxation risks, might only need the attention of specific individuals.

The third heading of 'detail' refers to the difference between managing specific problems that require specific focus and a general set of issues. For example, in one organization, perhaps where debts are settled in sterling using normal banking procedures, it might be sufficient to be aware of and manage generic risks arising from the possibility of bad debts. For another organization it might be that a particular class of overseas customer that settles its debts in foreign currencies which are not stable will require particular attention.

'Tasks', the fourth heading, refers to the key activities that an organization undertakes in managing a risk: does the organization collect information about the risk? Does it set policies or procedures to ensure that the risk is managed? And finally, does it ensure that appropriate action is taken to manage the risk? For example, where a company is exposed to a risk of foreign exchange losses, it would make sense to firstly gather data about the impact of the risk, where and when it might impact and how often it might be a problem before deciding what the policy or procedure should be for dealing with the risk. It might then make sense for someone to be tasked with ensuring that the policy is followed and reporting compliance to an appropriate member of the management team. It is not uncommon for organizations to have the balance wrong at any level of this part of the model.

The last of the five headings of the model is 'drivers'. This looks at the key motivators that make risk management work in an organization. We have already looked at the impact of regulation as a driver of risk management generally. Clearly, regulators can be a big determinant of risk management activity: for example, the Financial Services Authority clearly sets the pace in some of its regulatees for risk management activity. The fear of regulatory activity can act as a considerable spur. On the other hand, it may be an area that is close to the heart of management itself, in which case they will drive risk management activity because they see the benefit. The third driver that the model looks at is the culture of risk management. In some organizations the culture of risk management is embedded to the extent that regulators or management can take a secondary place in driving risk management activity.

It is not the absolute levels of any of the components of the model that matter. What is important is how all of the elements bind together to form a comprehensive and cohesive approach to managing risk. The importance is that the approach taken sets the propensity of the organization to exercise control. A higher propensity to exercise control within the organization will result in a lower likelihood of adverse net risks impacting the ability to achieve the organization's objectives. This therefore forms an important part of determining the appetite for controlling risk. As a consequence, all organizations need to be able to identify the approach taken to exercising control, both over risk at large and specific key risks or categories of risk, not only at a high level, but across operating units and between different functions. It is in the gaps between organizational units, where different approaches are adopted, that control is lost and organizations are most vulnerable to hazards.

Risk appetite

Many commentators have looked at the concept of risk appetite, often with a view to defining a single appetite or a single number. By contrast, a strategic review of risk appetite needs to address the three strands of thinking set out above. Economists might argue that organizations are largely fiction made fact by legal trickery. An organization cannot feel the rewards of risk or the costs of failure. Those rewards and costs are felt by the individuals who are the constituent parts of the organization. Psychologists might argue that an individual's behaviour, his or her own personal risk appetite, will be conditioned by the system within which they are operating: how they respond to a risk situation for their small children when at home will be very different from how they respond for their work colleagues in the organizational environment. Therefore it is possible to influence the nature of the collected risk appetite of the individuals who make up the organization by determining the nature of the environment within which their system works. A third view is offered by the anthropologist who would be looking for the norms of behaviour or rules of engagement for the group as a whole or for groups of people within the organization.

These contrary views of the ability of an organization to have a risk appetite lead to the suggestion that a corporate risk appetite depends on three key factors: the nature of the risk that is under consideration, the reason for engagement with the risk and the propensity of the organization to exercise control. This mix of contributing factors can be different between different parts of an organization, in different geographies or at different levels of the hierarchy. Because of the legal trick of imagination that creates an organization there is no such thing as corporate DNA or the corporate genome that determines how an organization responds to risk: it is therefore a matter of aggregating and influencing the behaviours of individuals such that they become attuned to risk as a group that expects certain norms of behaviour when facing threats or presented with opportunities. By creating a truly risk aware organization managers are creating the nervous system, complete with sensory organs and rudimentary brain capability, to deal with risk in the same way as is demonstrated by all living creatures which have benefited from millennia of accumulated experience of dealing with risk.

The risk intelligent organization

An organization that is able to manage risk in this way is truly a risk intelligent organization. There are indicators that suggest whether or not an organization is risk intelligent:

- It has risk management woven into the organization.
- It is able to differentiate responses according to the type of risk.
- It is aware of the basis on which it engages with risks.
- It understands how to optimize the response to a given risk.
- It expects line managers to seek their own assurance.
- It builds risk management into the development of managers.
- All activities have a risk management perspective.
- It balances its attention to opportunities and risks.
- It deals with outsourced and inter-organizational risks.
- It is constantly conscious of its risk management performance.

Such organizations will generally be conscious of the risks that they encounter. They will keep risk data up to date and will have a board and senior management team that pay attention to risk. The best will be confident about their abilities to make the most of opportunities, deal with new risk developments efficiently, coordinate their various risk management tools and cultures, spread best risk management practices throughout the organization, embed risk awareness into day-to-day business decision-making, prioritize their risk control activities effectively and take risks free from fear.

A risk intelligent organization deals with risk systemically throughout the organization, deals with risks arising from delivering services in association with partners, is nimble in responding to new issues, is able to take more, better managed risks, gets hit by fewer surprises, lives by its established principles and expects excellent performance from its staff.

Risk intelligent organizations typically have CEO buy-in and visible commitment to risk management, link their risk management to strategic planning, have regular dialogues based around the risk agenda, aim for simplicity and action rather than complicated theory and bureaucracy, have woven risk management into all major business activities and are constantly conscious of their risk management performance.

By developing into risk intelligent organizations, organizations can explicitly decide to manage risk to create and sustain long-term durability. Becoming a risk intelligent organization implies a high degree of commitment from the senior management team.

The extended enterprise

Successfully transforming an organization into a truly risk intelligent organization is not the end of the story. It is equally important to understand the risk management skills of partners, suppliers and other critical members of the value chain. They too must live up to the same high standards if the exercise is to be worthwhile. As discussed at the beginning of this chapter, economic activity is increasingly being carried out by organizations with permeable boundaries: Company A's objective, Company A's risk, but Company B's controls. Where traditional boundaries become permeable through alliances, joint ventures or outsourcing, the relationship between objective, risk and response is broken with a third party taking on responsibility for a part of the chain. The relationships become much more difficult to control once the internal linkages are broken.

It is often too easily assumed that outsourcing exports risk. Outsourcing can frequently produce risk importing through risk dependency. Where the linkages are broken and Company A is responsible for the objective, but Company B manages the likelihood and timing of achieving those objectives (because it manages the risks or the risk responses), this gives rise to the dependency risk conundrum: who is managing what? For whom? And why? And how?

Exactly the same issues arise whether the organization is involved in alliances, joint ventures or outsourcing: the complicating factor is the number of parties to the relationship. The more there are, the harder it becomes to exercise control; therefore such relationships in extended enterprises demand risk management attention. Traditional responses, many of which remain valid, even in today's world of virtual and real joint ventures and alliances, include good definition of the scope of the joint venture, respective responsibilities, appropriate management, good legal documentation and appropriate insurance cover.

All of these responses have their shortcomings. The exercise of management control is more difficult by orders of magnitude. Legal documentation should only be relied upon as a last resort – where the objectives of a joint venture and its operation have broken down. Insurance is a 'sticking plaster' approach to risk management in that it deals with the symptoms of problems, but not the root causes.

Consequently there are new approaches that need to be exercised in order to ensure that the extended enterprise can work. Essentially, the answer is to create a risk intelligent partnership, which implies the creative collaboration of two or more risk intelligent organizations.

What steps next?

For too long now risk has been confined to the back rooms of organizations, a function kept for compliance purposes rather than as a means of supporting business performance. Risk management is tarred by an image of negativity and bureaucracy. At the extremes, it is as unimportant as listing the top 10 risks of an organization. This is not using the emerging discipline to its full potential; indeed far from it. Risk management is about radically changing the perception and management of risk throughout an organization. It is about developing the organizational equivalent of a nervous system: impulses that seek gain, but avoid pain; sensory organs that can detect risk; nerves that conduct information; a brain that can analyse and interpret data; and organs that can implement the decisions, with immediate feedback. The developments that are moving risk management in this direction are what will drive risk as a strategic issue and risk management as a strategic tool.

With this in mind, this chapter has set out a number of challenges for any organizations that make risk a strategic issue and risk management a strategic tool. Whilst there are some traditional viewpoints, many of the areas covered by this chapter are new concepts or new applications in the arena of strategic risk management. Challenges for all organizations are to:

- understand the nature of the risks the organization faces;
- determine the reasons for engagement with risk;
- review organizational approaches to control;
- pull these three into line and develop a risk intelligent organization;
- ensure that the extended enterprise operates to the levels of risk management that you expect.

Once management have done this, then it will be ready to move the art and science of risk management to the next level.

References and recommended reading

Adams, J (1995) *Risk*. London: UCL Press.

Adams, J (2002) *Do We Have Enough Injidents?* London: The British Journal of General Practice.

Anderson, R (2003) The three pillars of corporate governance. *International Corporate Governance*, no. 115 (May).

Anderson, R (2004) Risk Intelligent Partnerships – Are Alliances, Joint Ventures and Outsourcing a Means of Risk Mitigation – or Risk Nightmare? *Strategic Risk* (December). London: Newsquest Financial Media.

Baldwin, R (2001) *Harnessing the Power of Risk Management – The Dimensional Control Diagnostic*. Available at: http://www.co-risk.com/_private/_articles/DimensionalControl.pdf

Baldwin, R and Anderson, R (2002) *Rethinking Regulatory Risk*. DLA Piper Rudnick Gray Cary. Available at: http://www.co-risk.com/_private/_articles/RethinkingRegulatoryRisk.pdf

Baldwin, R and Anderson, R (2005) *Inspector at the Door 2005: The Real Costs of Regulation*. Federation of Small Businesses.

Baldwin, R and Cave, M (1999) *Understanding Regulation*. Oxford: Oxford University Press, ch. 11.

Cadbury, A *et al.* (1992) *Report of the Committee on the Financial Aspects of Corporate Governance*. London: Gee and Co Ltd. See also: http://www.ecgi.org/codes/all_codes.htm

Committee on Corporate Governance (1998) *Committee on Corporate Governance: Final Report*. London: Gee and Co Ltd. Available at: http://www.ecgi.org/codes/documents/hampel.pdf

The Committee of Sponsoring Organizations of the Treadway Commission (COSO) (1994) *Internal Control – Integrated Framework*. New York: American Institute of Certified Public Accountants. Available at: http://www.coso.org/Publications/executive_summary_integrated_framework.htm

Financial Reporting Council (2003) *The Combined Code on Corporate Governance*. Available at: http://www.asb.org.uk/documents/pagemanager/frc/combinedcodefinal.pdf

FSA Handbook. LR 7.2 The Listing Principles. Available at: http://fsahandbook.info/FSA/handbook.jsp?doc=/handbook/LR/7/2

Great Britain (1985) Companies Act 1985. London: The Stationery Office.

Great Britain (1998a) Competition Act 1998. London: The Stationery Office.

Great Britain (1998b) Data Protection Act 1998. London: The Stationery Office.

Great Britain (2002) Proceeds of Crime Act 2002. London: The Stationery Office.

Higgs, D (2003) *Review of the Role and Effectiveness of Non-Executive Directors*. London: Department of Trade and Industry. Available at: http://www.dti.gov.uk/cld/non_exec_review

Internal Control Working Party (1994) *Internal Control and Financial Reporting – Guidance for Directors of Listed Companies Registered in the UK*. London: ICAEW Technical Department.

Power, M (2004) *The Risk Management of Everything. Rethinking the Politics of Uncertainty*. Demos. Available at: http://www.demos.co.uk/catalogue/riskmanagementofeverythingcatalogue/

Smith, R *et al.* (2003) *Audit Committees – Combined Code Guidance*. London: Financial Reporting Council. Available at: http://www.icaew.co.uk

Turnbull, N *et al.* (1999) *Internal Control – Guidance for Directors on the Combined Code*. London: Institute of Chartered Accountants in England and Wales. Available at: http://www.icaew.co.uk/internalcontrol

United States of America (2002) Sarbanes-Oxley Act of 2002. Available at: http://www.sec.gov/about/laws/soa2002.pdf. See also: http://www.sec.gov/spotlight/sarbanes-oxley.htm

3

Corporate Governance

David Smith and Rob Politowski

This chapter outlines the background for governance and provides a framework for managing the issues raised in the chapters that follow. Governance applies to governmental bodies, charitable bodies, corporate entities and private companies.

The beginnings

Corporate governance is the way in which organizations are directed and controlled. More specifically, 'corporate governance involves a set of relationships between a company's management, its board, its shareholders and other stakeholders. Corporate governance also provides the structure through which the objectives of the company are set, and the means of attaining those objectives and monitoring performance are determined' (OECD, 2004a).

The need for rules and guidelines on corporate governance arises from the separation of ownership and control that is one of the principal features of our industrial society. No such problems arise in the case of a one-man business who is free to decide what he wants to do and does not have to worry about the effects on other shareholders.

The need for guidelines on corporate governance has come to the fore in recent years principally following a number of well-publicized scandals and failures of large organizations where management actions resulted in significant losses to shareholders. It was perhaps the economic crisis in Asia in the late 1990s which brought the need for rules on governance to the fore. At the Asia-Pacific Economic Cooperation (APEC) finance ministers' meeting in 1998 it was noted that 'wherever there had been a corporate disaster, bad corporate governance had invariably been a key factor'.

This was by no means the first time that major corporate failures had led to the realization that new rules were needed to govern the way in which corporations were controlled and monitored. The problems were inherent from the invention of the limited liability company and the divorce that was then created between those who owned the company and those who managed it. As long as the owners received what they considered to be a fair dividend for the risks that they had taken, they were content to leave the management in the hands of others. In general small shareholders were, even if they were not satisfied, in practice powerless to exert any effective influence on the management as they could not muster sufficient support from other shareholders. This was true even if the corporate failure was clearly due not merely to negligence or misjudgement on the part of the managers but to their deliberate malfeasance. The classic case of Equity Funding Corporation of America in the 1960s resulted in a revision of the function and duties of the auditors of a public corporation, but there was no call for a new definition of the rules of corporate governance. Similarly in the UK the De Lorean Motor Car Company in the 1970s obtained £83 million in loans and guarantees from successive governments on the promise of providing much-needed employment in Northern Ireland before failing less than four years later. Again it was the auditors, Arthur Andersen, who were blamed for inadequate auditing and millions of pounds were recovered, but this did not lead to any fundamental revision of the way that companies are controlled.

It was, however, at that time that matters started to move on the corporate governance front. In 1992 the *Report of the Committee on the Financial Aspects of Corporate Governance*, the Cadbury report (so named after the chairman of the committee), was published in London (Cadbury *et al.*, 1992) and similar studies were starting in other parts of the world. The Cadbury committee emphasized that 'It is for the shareholders to call the directors to book if they appear to be failing in their stewardship . . . and they should use this power'.

The London Stock Exchange issued a 'combined code' to which all companies listed on the Exchange would be expected to conform, and in 1999 the Institute of Chartered Accountants of England and Wales issued *Guidance for Directors on the Combined Code,* the Turnbull report (Turnbull *et al.*, 1999), which has since become one of the principal authorities on the subject. This recognized three key components for successful management for corporate governance, as shown in Figure 3.1.

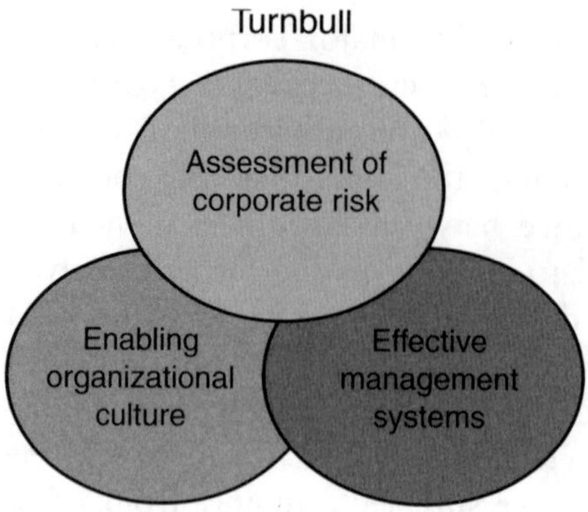

(after Turnbull *et al.*, 1999)

Figure 3.1 Components of successful corporate governance

At the same time the California Public Employees Retirement System (CalPERS) came into the field with the publication in 1997 of *Global Principles*, 'the first articulation of specific minimum governance principles for worldwide' (CalPERS, 1997). As the guardian of massive pension funds the organization was concerned that these should be safeguarded, and hence committed themselves to pursuing good corporate governance in the companies in which the funds were invested. The CalPERS concern was with the financial results, and hence the share values of their investments, and six 'global principles' were enunciated which they felt would be universally applicable and would not impinge upon the legal, economic or cultural traditions of any country. These were:

1. director accountability to shareholders;
2. transparent markets;
3. equitable treatment for all shareholders;
4. easy and efficient proxy voting methods;
5. codes of best practice defining the director–shareholder relationship;
6. long-term corporate vision which at its core emphasizes sustained shareholder value.

To widen the impact of these principles a new body was formed, the International Corporate Governance Network (ICGN), of which CalPERS was a founding member and which included a number of similar organizations whose total assets amounted to over six trillion US dollars, a massive influence on the adoption of global principles of corporate governance, which soon became recognized internationally.

In 1999 representatives of the 29 governments which make up the Organisation for Economic Co-operation and Development (OECD) endorsed the OECD Principles of Corporate Governance, which had been negotiated in consultation with major interested bodies in the market, including ICGN. These principles were recognized and welcomed by the G7 leaders at their meeting in June 1999 and have since been recognized by international bodies such as the UN, the IMF and the World Bank. These original principles were revised after consultation with countries outside the OECD and a new version was published in 2004 (OECD, 2004a).

These principles have accordingly received virtually universal acceptance throughout capitalist countries, although it would be idle to believe that they are strictly followed in all countries which have nominally agreed to them. They cannot, however, be regarded as adequate safeguards on the activities and responsibilities of corporate bodies.

Legislation

Codes of practice and statements of principles are fine as long as people can be expected to abide by them. Too often lip service is paid to them, and often companies will start out with the best of intentions, but when circumstances arise that make this difficult or inconvenient they may be ignored, some excuse being found why they should not be followed in that particular instance. To reassure the public in general and the investing public in particular something stronger is needed, and the demand is for legislation. Only in that way will the public be satisfied that the government is doing something to curb the excesses that have been evident.

The most comprehensive piece of legislation to be passed in the Western world following the Enron debacle was the Sarbanes-Oxley Act passed in the US in 2002. It was seen that there was an urgent need to restore the faith of shareholders, both individual and corporate, in the way that business works and to protect the investor from the malfeasance of management. The objective was to make investors feel more secure and more comfortable. This was to be achieved by requirements of the structure of company boards, with great reliance placed on non-executive directors to oversee the activities of the executives, and the publication of much more detailed information about the activities of the organization.

It is probably fair to say that at the time of writing the Act has not yet been in operation for long enough to judge whether it will prove effective in its aims. It certainly has created a lot more work for the companies and their auditors and so far has had only a marginal effect on investor belief in reduced fraud, less risk and greater confidence. Such is the power of the US economy, however, that the requirements of the Act are likely to become a world standard and adopted by most industrial economies in due course almost irrespective of their success in achieving the objectives.

The success of Sarbanes-Oxley in the US and Turnbull in the UK will largely depend on the extent to which corporations set out merely to conform, as a minimum; or whether they will adopt and embrace the principles and use them as a basis for their strategy development. In the latter instance they could achieve much but such organizations are those that have least need of such regulation. Whether they can curb the self-interested activities of a dominant chief executive will need to be seen. This will largely depend on the extent that the company's auditors find it possible to live up to the standards now imposed upon them.

The concern of CalPERS and other similar bodies was, quite rightly, to safeguard the investments that they had made on behalf of their members. Virtually all the legislation and rules are concerned with the ways in which corporate bodies must be structured and conduct their affairs to ensure that the rights of their owners, i.e. shareholders, are protected. The maintenance of share values becomes the only criterion, but this is only part of the requirement.

Wider concerns

Shareholders are not the only people who are affected by the activities of a company. The OECD principles do, it is true, make mention of stakeholders as well as well as shareholders, but this aspect is not developed. The need for risk management does not figure apart from the final influence on the share values.

There are many people who are affected by the activities and performance of a company other than shareholders. Employees, suppliers, neighbours may all be affected long before the share price starts to suffer as a consequence. It is only by identifying risks and managing them throughout the organization that the situation can be controlled. Whilst all failures will in due course have financial impacts which will finally affect share values, failure or collapse can be avoided only if the risks are managed at a much earlier stage. By the time the share price is affected it is usually too late.

In the UK the main corporate risks are generally considered to be:

- reputation;
- people; and
- regulatory compliance.

All these subjects receive more detailed attention elsewhere in this book. They are considered here only briefly to demonstrate that the extent of corporate governance requirements is much wider than is commonly assumed.

Reputation

Environmental disasters such as that associated with the Union Carbide plant at Bhopal and the Exxon Valdez oil pollution in Alaska have long-term effects on the reputation of the organization directly concerned. In both these instances there were massive financial costs involved in the short term: the clean-up operation in Alaska and the compensation for all those affected in India. Much longer term than these, and probably greater, were the effects on the reputation of the companies involved.

Both these corporations have survived, but frequently the loss of reputation can be fatal. Following the Enron scandal leading to the largest corporate bankruptcy in American history, their accountants, Andersen, one of the largest accountancy firms in the world, were so irreparably damaged that they have virtually disappeared.

These are spectacular and well-known examples, but almost every day companies are failing because in some way their reputation has suffered for some reason – usually a product failure involving a recall, or a failure of service. A reputation that has been built up over years can be destroyed almost overnight, and even if the company survives rebuilding its reputation will be a long haul. The name Perrier used to be synonymous with mineral waters but following an unfortunate incident in quality control the name suffered to such an extent that it has never truly recovered. The only safeguard is to be alive to the risks. For this to be achieved there has to be an awareness of the importance and principles of risk management embedded in the culture of the business – and this is, unfortunately, rare.

Reputation loss does not only affect the organizations directly involved. In the recent scandals it is the auditors who have largely been pilloried and punished even though they were not the principal wrongdoers. Even more remotely, there is the taint of 'guilt by association' which can severely damage a business even if they themselves were not involved in any wrongdoing. An example is that of Citigroup, the world's biggest bank. Although it has been found guilty of a number of infringements, it is perhaps that the bank has been named in connection with Enron, WorldCom or almost any of the major scandals that has resulted in its current poor reputation, although this is probably a function of its scale of operation rather than any shortcoming in its behaviour. This the bank recognizes as its major corporate problem at the present time, leading to the announcement in February 2005 by the chief executive, Charles Prince, of a five-point plan to overcome these problems.

People

The second cause of concern is people. Every organization finally depends upon the people who work for it, and they represent the greatest risk to its profitability and survival.

This people risk has many dimensions, but in general it falls into a number of areas, for example:

- skills and skill retention;
- honesty; and
- morale.

The question of skills covers both quantity, quality and retention of the workforce. Companies that have relied in the past on large numbers of unskilled or semi-skilled labour may suddenly find their futures threatened by social factors – populations move away; there is an increasing unwillingness to do certain types of work which are regarded as dirty or strenuous or dangerous or unpleasant; or there are competitive demands on the labour supply. A large engineering company employing large numbers of semi-skilled labour was threatened by the fact that a new large hospital was being built nearby which would employ several thousand tradesmen of the type that the company needed for its production. Certain skills can rapidly become unavailable – some kinds of tool-setters, for example – as the basic technology became obsolescent and apprentices were no longer being trained. The young people concerned saw their future in new technology even though more traditional methods would still be in use for a long time to come. The recent growth in call centres offered alternative employment to large numbers of young women (mostly) who had previously been relied upon to fill clerical positions; and so on. Unless the risk is recognized and managed it can be fatal to the future of the company.

In the same category is the case where a company is dependent on the skills or experience of one or two individuals. This tends to arise in small companies, often where they have started as owner–manager businesses which have grown with success but have failed to plan for succession, not only for the chief executive but frequently senior colleagues who were old associates of the owner and have been with the business since its inception. This can result in a situation where all the principal managers approach retirement at the same time, presenting the company with an impossible problem of replacing them all at once. Management buy-outs not infrequently lead to this situation as the original members of the buy-out team reach retirement at about the same time. In such circumstances liquidation may be the only practicable course, to the detriment of external shareholders as well as all the other stakeholders.

An allied difficulty can arise when a company has built its business on the name or reputation of a particular person – perhaps the designer of a range of clothes or of a household appliance. If that name suddenly became unavailable, due perhaps to a disagreement or death, the company might not survive unless it had recognized the risk and made plans to meet it as part of its risk management programme.

Employee risks are by no means restricted to senior management. A small specialist company had an experienced, well-trained and contented group of employees and had never considered that it had to worry in this respect. Unfortunately (from the company's point of view) they had formed a syndicate to bet on the National Lottery, and one day they achieved a major win, such that they all wanted to retire immediately. It is not suggested that this possibility should have been foreseen by the management, and it is not easy to see what they might have done about it – except perhaps insure – but the example does serve to show that improbable risks do sometimes materialize.

Customers are people, and this is the class that can pose the biggest threat. The pace of technical development today can mean that a product that the public has been happily buying for years suddenly becomes outdated and people no longer wish to buy the article or pay the price. You may have the best factory in the world for making galvanized iron buckets, but that is no good if people can buy plastic ones which are just as serviceable, preferable in many respects and only a fraction of the price. It is unlikely to be financially attractive to equip to make plastic ones instead. Given an effective risk management system the company would have recognized its vulnerability. Achieving and maintaining customer satisfaction must be a principal concern of any organization, and the risks involved in failing in this area are among the greatest that a company has to face. The subject is a large one and outside the scope of this summary, but its importance is such that it needs some consideration. An organization is judged by its customers not only on the basis of the product that it offers but also in the way that it offers it. Many a company with an excellent product range has faced extinction because its customers will not put up with the inadequate service that they have received. It has to be recognized too that the quality of sales and service is important not only to commercial concerns. Whether the business is a school, a hospital or a government department, all have to offer a service which is, finally, acceptable to the customer (whoever they may be – not necessarily the person paying for the service) if the organization is to succeed.

One of the biggest people problems is that of honesty. The clerk who steals a few pounds from the petty cash is not likely to cause the collapse of the company, but dishonesty on a larger scale can be more serious. Information security is a major concern in these days of industrial espionage. All companies have information that they would rather others did not know, whether it relates to preferential terms offered to some customers, or perhaps the prices at which they buy supplies. Occasionally the details of the product itself are secret – either how it is made or what it consists of. There may be competitors to whom this information would be of value and who would be happy to pay handsomely for it. Disaffected employees are frequently a source of leaked information, and the risk is one which needs to be recognized and managed. Sometimes the means of stealing information are very sophisticated, and the whole subject of information security has become specialist and technical.

Occasionally the misdoings of one individual can cause the collapse of a whole business. The case of Barings, the greatly respected London Merchant Bank, is perhaps the best-known case. The alarming feature here was not so much that Nick Leeson did what he did in 1995, but that the management of the bank had never even recognized the risk that this could happen. There were no effective controls in place for the simple reason that no one thought that they might be necessary. They recognized the opportunities that arose from futures trading but ignored the threats that are associated with the activity.

There is also the issue of morale. If some of the organizational risks are not being well managed there is the risk of poor performance through disillusionment or disregard for some tasks that are fundamental to maintain good governance. The failures at BNFL over exports of processed radioactive waste have been attributed to such a malaise.

Regulatory compliance

The need to meet regulatory compliance is self-evident. Failure can lead to adverse publicity and loss of reputation. The size of fines can be dramatic but the reputational losses and sometimes the civil claims that arise are more costly. Compliance issues can arise across a huge number of areas as diverse as share dealings, financial transactions, health, safety and environmental breaches. A recent example that created a significant impact across a range of businesses, large and small, and upon the general public as a whole was the food colouring agent scare.

Scope of governance in organizations

So what is the scope of governance? This cannot be precisely specified to cover all organizations. Figure 3.2 gives an indication of what corporate governance risk control measures may need to cover within a business. The structure of the company, scope of activities and the stakeholders that have greatest influence on its operation will determine the exact scope for corporate governance activities. Those areas identified in subsequent chapters will give guidance on the threats and possible solutions. However, the scope of governance is much wider than those subjects covered and there is also the balance between threat and opportunity to be considered.

A BSI publication, PD 6668:2000, gives an approach to managing risk for corporate governance. The aim of this publication was to highlight the information given by Turnbull and others and give some structure to how governance could be managed. It was recognized that many organizations have multiple systems and that a coordinated approach for managing risks would be beneficial to ensure management of operational risk. PD 6668 gave a framework for managing risks.

Figure 3.2 Corporate governance organigram

There are various terms and terminology used for managing risks and this can cause confusion. The following definitions are taken from *Managing Risk for Corporate Governance* (PD 6668:2000), which covers the subject in much greater depth than is possible here:

- *management system* – part of the overall management system that includes organizational structure, planning activities, responsibilities, practices, procedures, processes and resources for developing, implementing, achieving, reviewing and maintaining the policy;
- *threat* – source or situation with potential to harm the organization's assets;
- *risk* – chance of something happening that will have an impact upon objectives, measured in terms of likelihood and consequences;
- *tolerable risk* – risk reduced to a level that can be tolerated by the organization;
- *audit* – systematic examination to determine whether activities and related results conform to planned arrangements, and whether these arrangements are implemented effectively and are suitable for achieving the organization's policy and objectives.

The relationship between threats and opportunities

It is fundamental when considering risks in relation to corporate governance to consider both the risks and opportunities. Figure 3.3 (taken from BS 6079-3:2000) demonstrates the need to balance the importance of an opportunity against the threat from the risk.

It is worth highlighting that risk management can have positive dimensions. It is natural that the risks that we are chiefly concerned with in our daily lives are the negative ones, the things that could go

(from BS 6079-3:2000)

Figure 3.3 Relationship between threat and opportunity

wrong. In some contexts – as in health and safety – risks are described as 'hazards', quite understandably.

In the context of managing a company, however, risks can be positive as well as negative. New opportunities may unexpectedly arise which could transform the business just as radically as would a complete disaster. New products, new markets, new materials, new methods: all these could make a significant impact. Just as the whole organization should always be on the lookout for things that could go wrong, so they should be looking out for things which might take a turn for the better. Such risks need to be managed just as much as negative ones. In recent years, for example, new markets have opened in various parts of the world. Would the business be able to meet the new demand? Could production manage it? Could the finance be made available? How would the business manage exchange rate fluctuations? Should arrangements be put in place now? And so on. The essential point is failure to spot an opportunity and to prepare for it is just as much a failure of good corporate governance as is a failure to prepare for hazards.

This balancing of opportunity and threat is something that we do almost subconsciously in our everyday lives in many different contexts, whether we are making an investment decision or placing a bet on a horse. The process can be simple when we are the only affected party. If we pick the wrong horse we have lost our money but that is our loss and nobody else's. In corporate and public matters the position is very different and a wrong decision may affect the livelihoods of thousands of people. The decisions still have to be taken but the process needs to be formalized so that it can be seen that all aspects have been identified and examined and impacts – the effects of the decision – fully considered. This is true at all levels in an organization. We expect the foreman of a production shop to make considered judgments on the plant and staffing levels that he or she needs to meet the production programme that he or she has been given. We do not expect them to concern themselves with the wider strategic problems facing the company, but unless he or she does the job properly and gets the production out the company will suffer just as surely as if a major decision went wrong. Identifying risks and managing them must be part of the culture of the organization at all levels if the company is to avoid unpleasant surprises. Just as the foreman cannot be expected to worry about strategic problems, neither should senior management have to worry about whether the foreman has got staffing levels right. The risk management system needs to be cascaded so that all risks are considered at an appropriate level in the organization, as is illustrated in Table 3.1.

Table 3.1 Cascade of risk management system

Operational level	*Responsibility*		
	Top management	*Middle management*	*Operational*
Strategic	✓		
Strategic/management	✓	✓	
Strategic/management/operational	✓	✓	✓
Management		✓	
Management/operational		✓	✓
Operational			✓

None of this will do any good if the risks are not identified in the first place. The legislation and regulations, whether they be Turnbull, Sarbanes-Oxley or OECD are aimed at preventing malfeasance by the management of the organization at the expense of stakeholders. It is to this end that reliance is placed on non-executive directors and auditors to see that the rules are followed. But it is not their function to second-guess the management on the decisions that they have to take, although they should assure themselves that an adequate system of risk management is in place. As shown previously, the worrying feature of the Barings case was not that Nick Leeson did what he did, but that such a possibility had not been foreseen by those charged with managing the company. Some disasters result from factors that clearly should have been foreseeable. If a captain in charge of an oil tanker is incompetent or drunk, it is highly likely that an accident will occur which may have major repercussions. Many disasters, however, arise from a set of circumstances which, even if the possibility had been foreseen, would have been considered so unlikely to arise that the risk would be considered negligible. The Piper Alpha oil platform disaster in the North Sea arose from a combination of failures, principally to adhere to procedures. The Bhopal catastrophe arose through a sequence of circumstances, principally equipment failures that led to the deaths and disablement of thousands. That such a coincidence of failures could arise had never been considered as a risk.

Only if all members of the management team can get into the practice of thinking continuously of what might conceivably go wrong (or right; risks can be positive as well as negative) can risk management be truly effective and the likelihood of nasty surprises be avoided.

Business is all about taking risks. The business that never takes a risk will never survive, let alone make a profit; the important thing is to recognize the risks, to assess their likelihood and their impact and then to decide on what needs to be done.

The organization needs to determine a process for identifying threats and for managing them in a similar way to the process it should have established for managing other risks, such as that required by law for occupational health and safety. The process used might follow the lines given in Figure 3.4.

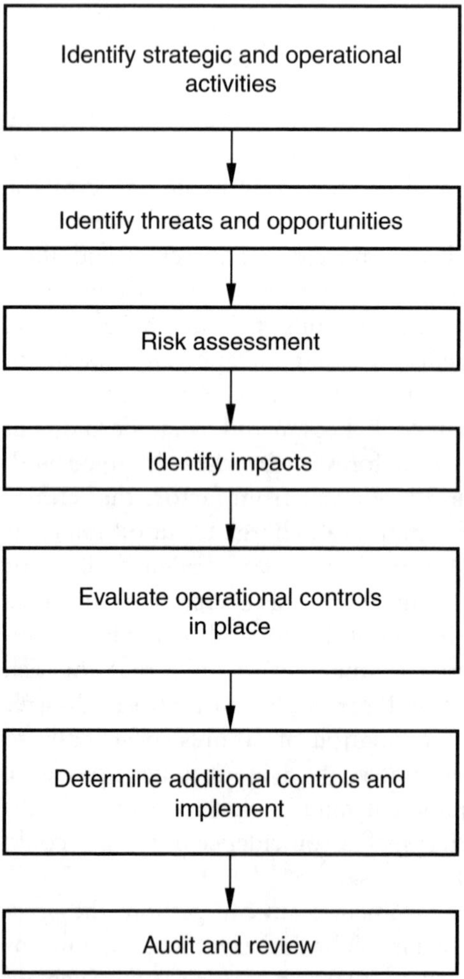

Figure 3.4 Process for managing threats and opportunities

The two essential elements, likelihood and impact, must always be considered together, along with the control measures that are in place. These must be not merely written in a handbook but embodied in the way that the organization works and thinks. If risk management is understood and adopted by everyone in the organization, then the worst will be avoided and the company will not find a Chernobyl or a Bhopal on its hands. Even if the activity of the company is not such that it could kill thousands, there are many people in all categories of stakeholders who will be affected by its performance, and everyone concerned has a duty to do the best for them that can be achieved within the activity of the organization.

The risks that an organization has to consider can be categorized in a number of different ways. A common classification is to consider risks in the four categories of:

1. strategic;
2. financial;
3. operational; and
4. unforeseen hazards.

This classification has the merit of pointing to those members of the management board who might reasonably be considered as the focus for risk identification in each area. Financial risks, for example, would include such factors as interest rates and credit risks, which concern almost everybody. To some companies exchange rates will be important. These may be considered as external factors, over which the company has little or no control. Internally, matters of cash flow will be equally critical and it will be up to the finance director to ensure that this is monitored.

Strategic risks would include subjects such as changes in the structure of the industry, or customer and demand changes. Again the distinction can be made between whether the drivers for the risks are external (competition, for example) or internal (perhaps research and development). These risks may be largely concerned with marketing or, in some organizations, the design functions, but clearly they will need the attention of the full management board.

Similarly the operational risks may be considered as externally driven (regulatory) or internally, such as supply. Hazards too may be similarly categorized, but all will need to be considered at all levels.

Whatever the risk, the significance may be assessed by the use of some system which considers the likelihood and the impact – that is

Consequence ↓ / Likelihood →	Unlikely		Very likely
Insignificant	1	2	3
	2	4	6
Significant	3	6	9

Figure 3.5 Risk matrix

to say, the effect if the event did arise – to assess the overall risk and to determine whether, at the lowest level, it is tolerable and can be lived with, or whether it is something that needs the urgent attention of the board. Any one of a number of methods can be used for making this assessment, but the matrix in Figure 3.5 is frequently used.

UK legislation

At the beginning of this chapter it was pointed out that the problems of corporate governance are intrinsic in the concept of the limited liability company and the separation of ownership and control. Right from the early days – one remembers the South Sea Bubble – it was recognized that some form of regulation was needed. In the UK this was principally achieved through the Companies Acts which laid down rules about the conduct of such companies. Progressively over the years these regulations have become more stringent as share ownership has become wider, the scale of operation of companies has become greater and the impact on society of failure has become greater.

In the UK the latest amendment to the Companies Act has just been published in draft in the form of the Operating and Financial Review (OFR) regulations (Department of Trade and Industry, 2005). These will require that all UK quoted companies as well as the larger unquoted companies will have to produce an Operating and Financial Review. This will be a separate report that will have to be laid before the company in a general meeting. It will not be part of the directors' report and accounts but will be a separate report. It will not have to be put to the shareholders for approval, although it is likely that this will become general practice.

The report is to be addressed to the shareholders and the contents have to include a number of items which are concerned with the future health of the company. For example, as well as reporting on the past year, the OFR has also to describe the main trends and factors which are likely to affect the group's development, performance and position in the future. There are safeguards which mean that the directors do not have to disclose future developments where such disclosure would be prejudicial to the interests of the company.

The report must also include a description of the organization's business, objectives and strategies, the available resources and, most significantly in the present context, the principal risks and uncertainties. This can be expected to include consideration of the risks attaching to the supply of materials and skills, dependence on major suppliers or customers, access to markets, and so on. Other subjects to be covered might include environmental issues, regulatory issues and product liability.

Another category to be reported is that of the organization's employees, and environmental, social and community issues.

There are numerous other financial aspects on which a report is required, and the fundamental focus of the OFR is again that of effects on share values. After all, it is a report to shareholders and this will be their prime concern. What is significant, however, is the recognition that risks at all levels and all fields have to be considered, and that it is not merely financial measures that need to be taken into account. Any failure in risk management will finally show itself in financial terms and ultimately in share value but, as stated earlier, by the time the share price is affected it is probably too late to take remedial action. The new regulations do (or will) emphasize to organizations that corporate governance is not just about watching the stock market values of the organization; it is about having an effective system of risk management at every level and in every corner of the business.

Achieving risk awareness

Considering the risks involved in all one's working activities is not something that comes naturally to any of us. In our daily lives we expect today to be much like yesterday and we are surprised if things turn out differently. Just occasionally, if we are about to embark on a long journey, perhaps, we will think about risk and even take out special insurance to cover it, but statistically we have probably incurred a much greater risk in crossing the road or in our daily drive to work than in a flight to Australia. Indeed, if we stopped to consider the risks attached to everything that we did we would probably never get out of bed. That is a perfectly natural and acceptable attitude to take in respect of our daily activities, but in the work that we do we have to learn to think differently. Here the actions that we take and the decisions that we make affect not only ourselves but also the organization that we work for, and by extension all the others who depend on that business or are affected by what it does.

Businesses have the same natural tendency to assume that today will be much like yesterday and that tomorrow will be the same, but everyone in a company (or any other kind of organization) has to develop the attitude of wondering what could go wrong (or right – risks can be positive as well as negative, an aspect developed later) which would make things different and affect the performance of the business. This has not been helped by the way in which businesses have traditionally been organized by functions. Typically there was (and still is in many cases) an overall general manager who is the only person with responsibilities right across the business. Then there is a manager who looks after sales, another who is in charge of production, others responsible for buying, for personnel, for accounts, for despatch and so on. Each tended to be focused on their own function and was concerned with others only to the extent that their activities impinged on their own. The sales manager would not be interested in the concerns of the production manager unless they affected the supply of goods that he or she could sell, and so on. Boundaries were not only set, in many cases they were stoutly defended such that the only communication between them was at the top, general management, level.

This functional specialization extended beyond the core activities into subsidiary fields such as quality, occupational health and safety or environmental management. This led not only to inefficiencies due to higher bureaucratic costs but failures at the margins through the inability to take an overall view. No one could perceive risks that might affect the organization unless they arose within their particular area of responsibility.

In recent years there have been two trends which are tending to improve this situation. The first is that the rigid vertical, functional organization is tending to be replaced by horizontal cross-functional general management units at a variety of levels. No longer is the person at the top the only one who can form a comprehensive view, even of a small part of the total activity, but there may now be a number of smaller units, each with its own general manager keeping a close watch on all the functions affecting a part of the total operation.

The second trend is that towards integrated management systems. The traditional vertical structure made it difficult for people to see that the business had to be viewed as a single system if it was to work effectively. The managerial divisions led to a similar attitude towards management systems. The accountant would have a system for recording the financial transactions of the business, and this may well have been formally defined. The sales manager would have a system for obtaining and handling orders from customers but this would more than likely be informal and not likely to be written down. Similarly, in the areas of production, purchasing, personnel, despatch, and so on there would be systems operating which for the most part were never formally designed and in all probability never written down. The production manager would regard the systems for production planning, scheduling, purchasing, etc., as being purely his or her concern and nothing to do with anybody else. In reality, however, all these are part of the overall management system of the business, and should be seen as such. Every system and subsystem will have some impact on other systems, and risks arising in one area may well give rise to risks in another. If the sales manager fails to obtain the orders, there will be an immediate impact on production schedules and longer-term impacts on every other aspect of the company's operations, finally reflecting in the share price. Production difficulties may have been responsible in the first place for the sales manager being unable to meet the sales targets. In another scenario the sales manager may have been much more successful than expected in obtaining orders. Here again the impacts will extend throughout the organization. Has production the resources needed to produce at higher levels? Is the plant up to it? Can the extra labour be obtained? Can suppliers respond to increased schedules? Can the additional working capital needed be made available and remunerated – a frequent source of trouble to rapidly expanding businesses?

It has to be recognized, therefore, that there is a single overall management system that the company follows. It may not be recognized as such – indeed it is probably not – and the inability to recognize the interactions of different parts of the organization is a frequent cause of failure.

A step forward in encouraging businesses to take an overall view was made in the international quality standard ISO 9001:2000 which required all processes to be identified. Admittedly there was no specific requirement that they should be mapped, and the standard applies only to production activities, but it has served to introduce many organizations to the value of process mapping. This demonstrates in an easily comprehensible way the relationship of one activity to another and can be valuably extended to the other functions of the business apart from production. This can be of value in several ways. (One of the unexpected but not inconsiderable benefits is that it enables any employee to see and understand, perhaps for the first time, their own place in the organization and the contribution that their activity makes to the whole.) The principal value of the process approach, however, is that it enables just about everybody to play their part in the risk management of the company. All levels of management, and ideally operatives too, should be instructed in the basic principles of identifying risks and considering how they should be managed. The basic question is 'What could go wrong?' A business may be highly dependent on the output from a particular piece of plant and the operator will probably be aware of danger signals before anyone else is. Or there may be great reliance on the skills of a particular person to an extent that is recognized only by their immediate superior. Every manager should be required to consider the activities for which he or she is responsible and the resources on which he or she is dependent in order to achieve their output. He or she should get into the habit of considering what might go wrong, how likely it is to happen and what safeguards could or should sensibly be put in place in case it does. Should you have a spare fax machine or computer? Is it time to train a backup for a critically important member of staff? These may be considered trivial matters but it should be remembered that many major disasters arise from a combination of small events, none of which appeared particularly significant when considered alone. It was only the coincidence of a number of such events that gave rise to Piper Alpha and Bhopal.

This need to be aware of risks and the need to manage them must become part of everyone's everyday thinking just as much as is concern for safety or for quality or cost or the environment. A necessary pre-condition to achieving this state is that concerns about a risk must be treated seriously even if the risk is negligible and hence tolerable in the eyes of management. If a junior manager or operative is ridiculed for raising an improbable risk he or she will be reluctant to voice a concern again, even if this time it is something serious. Just as in the best organizations concerns about occupational safety are always welcomed and treated seriously, so should expressions of concern about risk. They should be recorded, considered and the decision recorded. These decisions should be reviewed from time to time to make sure they are still valid, as the passage of time may turn a negligible risk into a serious one. Risk management must not be regarded as a specialist business, still less the province of the accountant or of top management. The accountant may well be involved in assessing the financial effects of a possible failure, or the costs of taking precautionary measures, but the decision will rest with management, not with him or her. In the same way, risk management cannot be left to the top levels of management. It may well ultimately fall to them to decide whether a significant risk is tolerable or whether remedial action needs to be taken, and quite possibly in drawing up contingency plans in the event of the risk becoming realized; but the first warning signals, the first indication that a risk exists, will come from below in the management chain. The principal duty of top management in this respect is to make sure that there is a system in place for identifying risks and managing them in every part of the business.

Integrating management systems

The separation of systems is not conducive to effective risk management. Whilst everyone is concentrating on his or her own area of responsibility they are less conscious of the ways in which a minor risk in one area could translate into a significant risk in another. One has often seen how a 'solution' to a problem in one department has a knock-on effect in another to which the originating department was quite oblivious. If, as suggested above, the mapping of processes is carried on throughout the business until every part is covered, then a team attitude will be fostered in the organization and decisions will not be taken without reference to any possible effects in other areas.

This leads back to the point that a business runs not through a melange of discrete systems but with an overall system of which the individual systems are subsets. In a typical business these subsystems will cascade into various layers of subsidiary systems. They will all be different depending on the subject they are dealing with (sales, quality, design, finance, etc.); some will be formally defined (occupational health and safety, perhaps quality), others will probably be less formal or not even written down at all. Even if they are not installed as formal systems, they must each have some common characteristics if they are to function efficiently as management systems. They will, for example, each need to be checked, or audited, occasionally to make sure that the rules are being followed; they will need to be reviewed by top management from time to time to make sure that they are still doing the job they were intended to do. There will be documentation and records associated with each one (almost certainly) and this documentation needs to be controlled to make sure that it is up to date. If all these facets are organized in a uniform way there are many benefits to be obtained. There can be one set of audits in place of many, duplication of document systems can be avoided, the management review can be comprehensive and so on. A full account of the merits of integrated management systems would be out of place here, but such a system can be of great value in ensuring that the risk management system is alive and active throughout the organization. The issue of developing a management framework was covered in Figure 3.2 and is an integral part of PD 6668:2000.

The most effective way of achieving the integration of management systems is by adoption of the integrated framework. This resulted from a government-funded study published by BSI into the most effective way of achieving integration (HB 10138:1997). It recognizes the elements common to all management system standards (and by extension into those areas where there are as yet no published standards) so that these can be handled as an overall integrated system, avoiding duplication in common areas (e.g. policy, audit, review, documentation) whilst allowing for the incorporation of those items specific to particular fields. BSI has published a series of guides in the IMS series (Hinch, 2003; IMS Risk Solutions, 2003, 2004; Kelly, 2004; Murray, 2003; Nowacki, 2003; Smith, 2001, 2002, 2003) covering the general method and the application to specific areas such as quality (as per ISO 9001:2000), environment (as per ISO 14001:2004) and health and safety (OHSAS 18001:1999). This has been extended to information security (ISO/IEC 17799:2005) and food safety (ISO 22000:2005).

The model shown in Figure 3.6 is just one option for implementing an integrated framework as recommended by PD 6668:2000.

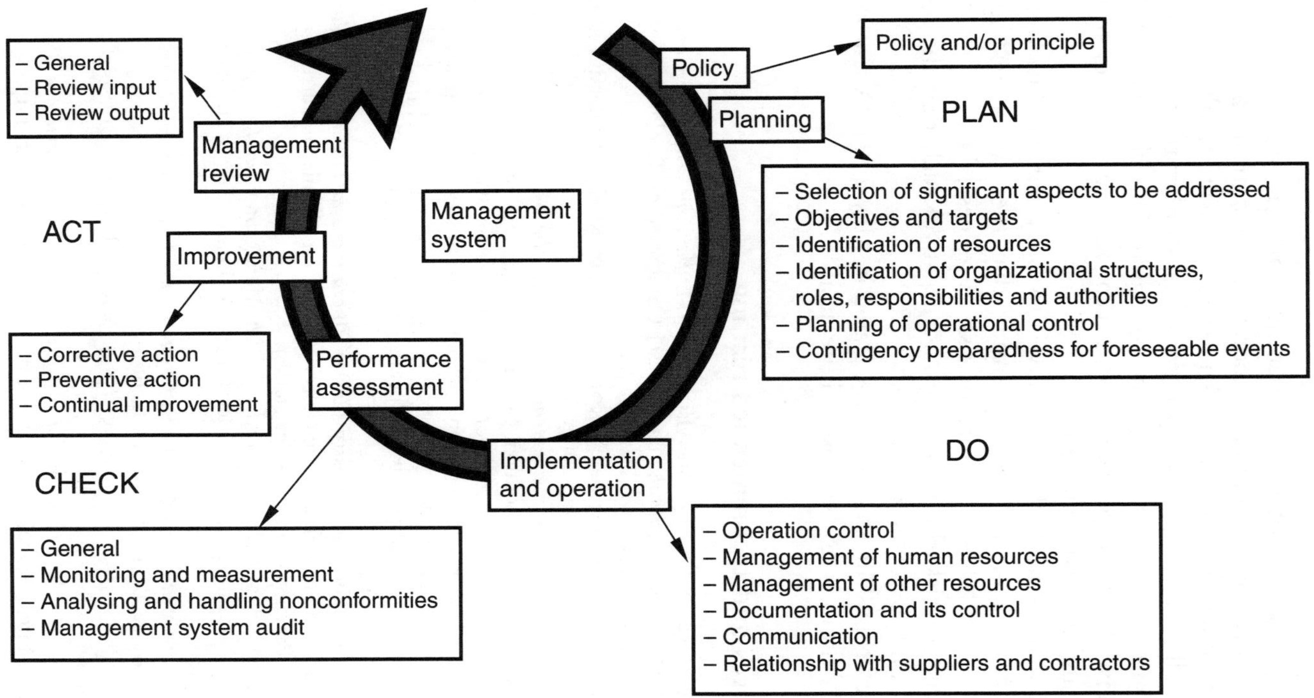

Figure 3.6 IMS model

Summary

Good corporate governance is about much more than appointing non-executive directors, requiring elaborate reports from auditors and sticking to books of rules. The organization needs to think widely and consider all its strategic and operational risks rather than just concentrating on those that are compliance oriented. This chapter and those that follow should help organizations recognize the risks they need to manage and how to manage them.

If the management of a company is to carry out its obligations to its stakeholders in full, it must ensure that there is imbued in the business at all levels a culture of risk awareness, identification and assessment (of risks both positive and negative) such that the law is followed and surprises are avoided.

As the Prime Minister of the UK stated in May 2005: 'A risk-averse business culture is no business culture at all'.

References and recommended reading

Basel Committee on Banking Supervision (1999) *Enhancing Corporate Governance for Banking Organisations*. Basel: Basel Committee on Banking Supervision. See: http://www.bis/org/bcbs/

Blair, A (2005) 'Risk and the State' speech delivered by Rt Hon A Blair at University College, London 26 May 2005.

BS 6079-3:2000, *Project Management – Guide to the Management of Business Related Project Risk*. London: British Standards Institution.

Cadbury, A *et al.* (1992) *Report of the Committee on the Financial Aspects of Corporate Governance*. London: Gee and Co Ltd. See also: http://www.ecgi.org/codes/all_codes.htm

CalPERS (1997) See: http://www.calpers-governance.org/principles/international/global/page03.asp

Department of Trade and Industry (2005) *Operating and Financial Review*. See http://www.dti.gov.uk/cld/financialreview.htm for details of current passage through Parliament into full legislation.

Federal Reserve Board (2004) *Trends in Risk Management and Corporate Governance*. Washington, DC: Federal Reserve Board. See: http://www.federalreserve.gov

HB 10138:1997, *Study on Management System Standards: A Report Prepared for BSI*. London: British Standards Institution.

Hinch, H (2003) *IMS: Managing Food Safety*. London: British Standards Institution.

ICGN (1999) *ICGN Statement on Global Corporate Governance Principles*. London: International Corporate Governance Network. See: http://www.icgn.org/documents/globalcorpgov.htm

IMS Risk Solutions (2003) *IMS: Risk Management for Good Governance*. London: British Standards Institution.

IMS Risk Solutions (2004) *IMS: Continual Improvement Through Auditing.* London: British Standards Institution.

Institute of Risk Management (IRM), Association of Insurance and Risk Managers (AIRMIC) and National Forum for Risk Management in the Public Sector (ALARM) (2002) *A Risk Management Standard.* London: IRM/AIRMIC/ ALARM.

ISO 9001:2000, *Quality Management Systems – Requirements.* Geneva: International Organization for Standardization.

ISO 14001:2004, *Environmental Management Systems – Requirements with Guidance for Use.* Geneva: International Organization for Standardization.

ISO 22000:2005, *Food Safety Management Systems – Requirements for Any Organization in the Food Chain.* Geneva: International Organization for Standardization.

ISO/IEC 17799:2005, *Information Technology – Security Techniques – Code of Practice for Information Security Management.* Geneva: International Organization for Standardization/International Electrotechnical Commission.

Kelly, J M (2004) *IMS: The Excellence Model.* London: British Standards Institution.

MORI (2003) *Focus on the Future of Corporate Governance.* London: MORI.

Murray, R P (2003) *IMS: Information Security.* London: British Standards Institution.

Nowacki, G (2003) *IMS: Customer Satisfaction.* London: British Standards Institution.

OECD (2004a) *The OECD Principles of Corporate Governance.* Paris: OECD. See: http://www.oecd.org

OECD (2004b) *Guidelines on Corporate Governance in State Owned Enterprises – Draft Text.* Paris: OECD. See: http://www.oecd.org

OECD (2004c) *Comments from Public Consultation on the Draft for Guidelines on Corporate Governance in State Owned Enterprises.* Paris: OECD. See: http://www.oecd.org

OHSAS 18001:1999, *Occupational Health and Safety Management Systems Specifications.* London: British Standards Institution.

PD 6668:2000, *Managing Risk for Corporate Governance.* London: British Standards Institution.

Smith, D (2001) *IMS: The Framework.* London: British Standards Institution.

Smith, D (2002) *IMS: Implementing and Operating.* London: British Standards Institution.

Smith, D (2003) *IMS: Creating a Manual.* London: British Standards Institution.

Turnbull, N *et al.* (1999) *Internal Control – Guidance for Directors on the Combined Code.* London: Institute of Chartered Accountants in England and Wales. Available at: http://www.icaew.co.uk/internalcontrol

United States of America (2002) Sarbanes-Oxley Act of 2002. Available at: http://www.sec.gov/about/laws/soa2002.pdf. See also: http://www.sec.gov/spotlight/sarbanes-oxley.htm

Weil Gotshal and Manges LLP in consultation with the European Association of Securities Dealers (EASD) and the European Corporate Governance Network (ECGN) on behalf of the European Commission, Internal Market Directorate General (2002) *Comparative Study of Corporate Governance Codes Relevant to the European Union and its Member States – Final report and Annexes I–III.* See: http://www.odce.ie/_fileupload/services/EU%20Comparison.pdf

4

Financial Risk Management

David Bobker

This chapter takes an unashamedly quantitative approach to risk management which is the best way to make sound, rational business decisions. Especially in the area of financial risk management, directors and managers who do not use figures relating to the levels of risk being run are in danger of making errors. It is the equivalent of driving a car with your eyes shut.

This chapter aims to elucidate *what* needs to be done to manage financial risks rather than to describe *how* to do it. It is a brief summary of the main principles and, hopefully, a spur to action where it is needed, rather than giving detailed quantitative methods.

At the end of the day, risk management is about trying to anticipate the future, which can never be known with certainty. There is never a guarantee that all of the actions taken will prevent future problems or disaster. Therefore, the question always to be asked is not 'Can risk be eliminated?' but rather 'Have I done everything the reasonable and rational person would be expected to do in the light of current knowledge?' Better to take a calculated risk and fail than to be surprised by a bolt out of the blue.

Principles of financial risk management

What is financial risk?

It is easiest to start with some questions: What is risk anyway? Why should you try to differentiate types of risk? What is different about financial risk?

There is no universally accepted definition of risk. Most people agree, however, that it has associated with it the connotations of potential adverse events and uncertainty. In financial risk management, risk is treated solely as a *downside* concept. Some people do consider there is an upside to risk, but for this author, this is a contradiction in terms – for example, one normally would not consider it a *risk* to win the Lottery. There may be confusion with decision-making and risk tolerance which has to do with balancing the possible upside of a decision with the potential for loss. This is covered later in the chapter; however, in my terminology, the upside is not the risk, only the downside.

This chapter covers *financial risk* and it is pertinent to ask, why identify it separately? In some ways the classification of a risk is not important, only how *big* it is. Indeed much energy and effort is probably wasted arguing over the correct classification of risks when what really matters is whether or not the risk is a potential killer to the business.

On the other hand, the measurement of the risk, and the tools and techniques to manage it, depend very much on the nature of the beast. What distinguishes many financial risks from others, such as operational risk, is the availability of data and the possibility to do more robust statistical analysis to draw quantified conclusions. On the other hand, as will be shown, the statistical analysis can lead to a sense of false security because at the end of the day the *future is not predictable.*

Having said all of that, the following definitions will be used.

- *Risk* is exposure to future adverse events whose timing and impact are uncertain.
- *Financial risk* is that risk arising from financial assets and liabilities. It is particularly associated with the *volatility* of financial markets.

Types of financial risk

There are at least four types of financial risk:

1. *Market risk* which arises from movements in financial markets. The markets considered would include the equity markets, interest rate markets (for loans, deposits, bills, bonds and notes) and the foreign exchange and commodity markets.
2. *Liquidity risk* – the inability to meet liabilities as they become due.
3. *Credit risk* arising from counterparty default.
4. *Investment risk* – the potential for investments in new products, systems or other business ventures to fail.

Due to space limitations credit risk and investment risk are not covered in this chapter, and the reader is referred to Ong (1999) for credit portfolio modelling and to Vose (2000) for an introduction to Monte Carlo and its application to investment appraisal.

The challenge of financial risk management

The key challenge is for non-specialists, especially board members and senior managers, to have sufficient understanding of the main risks to enable them to make sound decisions affecting their organizations' future. This challenge is the same for all technical areas underpinning business.

There are manifold examples of where things go wrong. Two of the most spectacular examples are those of Barings Bank in the UK (Board of Banking Supervision, 1995) and Long Term Capital Management in the US (Lowenstein, 2000). They each illustrate different aspects of how catastrophic failure can occur. Many other examples illustrate fraud on the part of management which really is the subject of operational risk and corporate governance, dealt with elsewhere in this book.

Whilst, of course, there is no space here to do justice to a detailed examination of the lessons (fuller references are given at the end of this chapter), there are some basic points that can be made.

In the Barings case, one of the contributory factors was a seeming unwillingness by top management to question in sufficient detail the level of risk being run in the face of what appeared to be a large incoming profit stream. It is clear that the majority of the board did not understand the workings of the Far Eastern derivatives markets but took it on trust that such profits from arbitrage were possible. 'Blinded by greed' is probably too strong an expression of what was going on here, but such psychological factors, including an unwillingness for members of boards to break ranks or 'rock the boat', undoubtedly play a significant role. This general effect may be termed 'risk blindness', which may be a common disease.

Why should this be? It is to be hoped that further research will be done in this area by psychologists and other researchers, but one reason may be simply that the skill set necessary to climb the corporate ladder (and, for that matter, the political ladder) does not necessarily include technical risk assessment skills near the top of the list. Whilst the ability to make judgements about risk is undoubtedly important, speed, decisiveness and the ability to perceive the motives of others usually count for more in the leadership role than robust technical analysis.

On the other side of the divide, the challenge for the professionals is somehow to make the nature of financial risks sufficiently comprehensible to, and open to, sensible questioning and challenge by the board. Often this is not easy as some of the concepts are complex and difficult to express accurately in non-mathematical language.

Quantifying potential movements in financial assets and liabilities

If financial risk is associated with the future uncertainty of the value of financial assets and liabilities, what is required is some methodology to estimate how large this uncertainty may be, and calculating the effect of this on the organization.

Referring to the chart of BP's share price (Figure 4.1), the US dollar vs. sterling exchange rate (Figure 4.2) and three-month US Treasury Bill rates (Figure 4.3), the similarity of the charts is striking. Each manifests rapid, jagged volatility movements superimposed on a general trend curve which moves up and down with much slower periodicity.

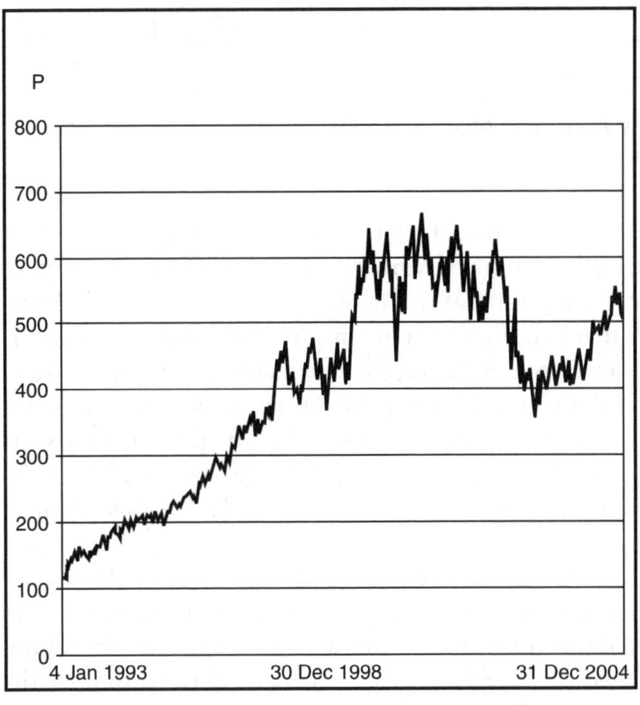

(from BP website)

Figure 4.1 BP Ordinary share price 4 Jan 1993 – 31 Dec 2004

(from Federal Reserve Bank of New York, 2005)

Figure 4.2 US$/GB£ Rate Oct 1993 – Apr 2005

The challenge is to be able to calculate with some reliability the best estimate of where such a financial variable might go in the future with the associated probability estimates. Financial models have been developed to deal with this situation. The main pitfall in such estimation is also apparent. For example, if the recent chart shows a steepish downward trend, is this the start of a long downward movement or is it a temporary 'blip' in a general upward trend. The art of financial risk is to get a systematic way of dealing with all the future possibilities to allow a rational basis for decision-making today. To do this requires financial modelling.

The basis of most of these models is the mathematics of 'Brownian motion'. Output from such a model is demonstrated in Figure 4.4 and it can be seen that the four charts, known as *sample paths*, follow similar sorts of jagged path as the FTSE chart. Each of the sample paths is based on the same calibration. However, their values at specified times differ greatly and this is precisely an expression of the future uncertainty, or risk.

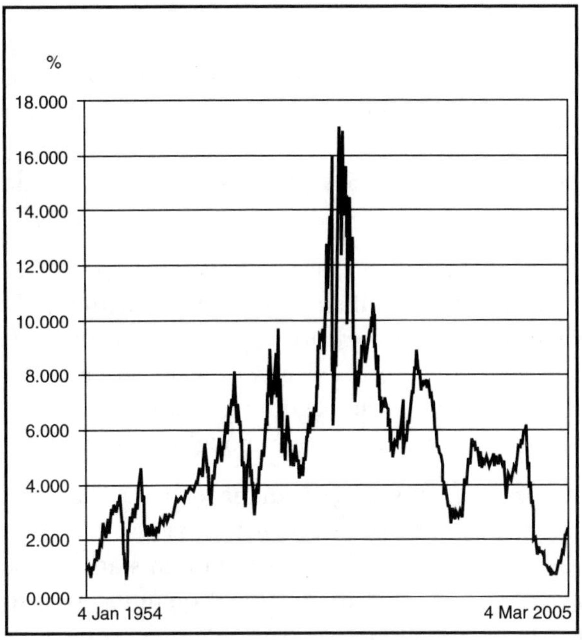

Figure 4.3 Three-month US Treasury Bill rate 1954–2005

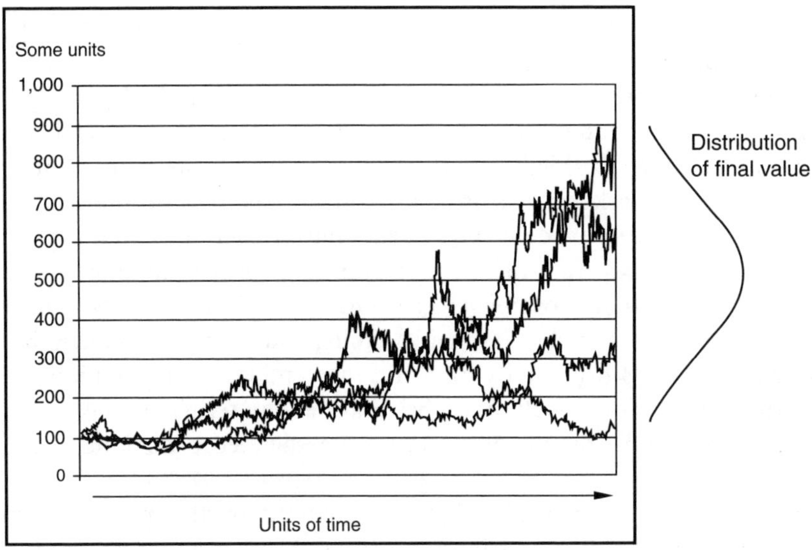

Figure 4.4 Four simulated Brownian sample paths

Why quantify risk?

It is suggested that there are two main reasons why risk should be quantified (as far as possible), as follows.

1. To understand it properly. The famous physicist Lord Kelvin said (1891–1894):

   > I often say that when you can measure what you are speaking about, and express it in numbers, you know something about it; but when you cannot measure it, when you cannot express it in numbers, your knowledge is of a meagre and unsatisfactory kind; it may be the beginning of knowledge, but you have scarcely advanced in your thoughts.

2. To evaluate the business benefits of risk management. The difficulty in making risk management decisions is that very often costs may be accurately estimated but the benefits are often stated to be intangible and hazy. What is required is rational quantification to allow more rational decision-making.

Quantitative risk analysis and probability distributions

How to quantify risk is more complex. In the introductory considerations of risk one often encounters the notion of the *probability* and *impact* of an event as being the basis of risk assessment. On this concept are built risk matrices, risk maps and all the multicoloured paraphernalia of modern 'enterprise risk management'. The problem with the Red/Amber/Green or High/Moderate/Low analysis, especially in relation to financial risks, is that it is just too simplistic to do the job. To illustrate, consider where you might put something like foreign exchange or interest rate risk in the probability/impact matrix.

The point is that movements in exchange or interest rates can be anything, within certain reasonable limits, and each movement has its own associated probability of occurrence and consequential impact. In other words, events need to be analysed in terms of the whole *distribution* of possible impacts and their associated probabilities, not just one.

Risk, especially financial risk, now needs to be thought about in terms of the probability distribution of possible consequences. Even if such distributions are at best based on estimates and guesses, the presence of this theoretical framework is the basis of best practice analysis.

The loss curve and VAR

Although detailed calculations can get a little complex, many of the basic concepts are straightforward enough. Assume it were possible to calculate the probability distribution of all impacts on the organization arising from currency exchange rate movements. The probability distribution curve might look something like Figure 4.5. This is the famous 'bell–shaped' normal distribution curve and has been generally assumed to be that governing market risk.

For other risks such as credit risk and operational risk, the corresponding curve is asymmetric, reflecting that credit and operational impacts can only be negative on the organization. Markets, by contrast, can move up as well as down.

Credit and operational risks are generally assumed to have curves of the general shape of Figure 4.6. This is anything but a normal distribution curve. First, the shape is skewed, that is, it is asymmetric, having

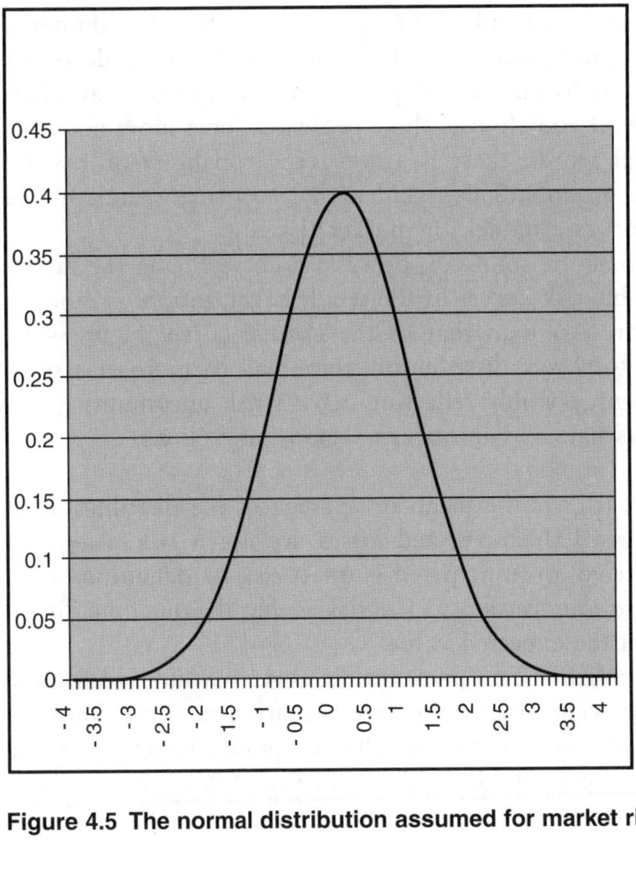

Figure 4.5 The normal distribution assumed for market risk

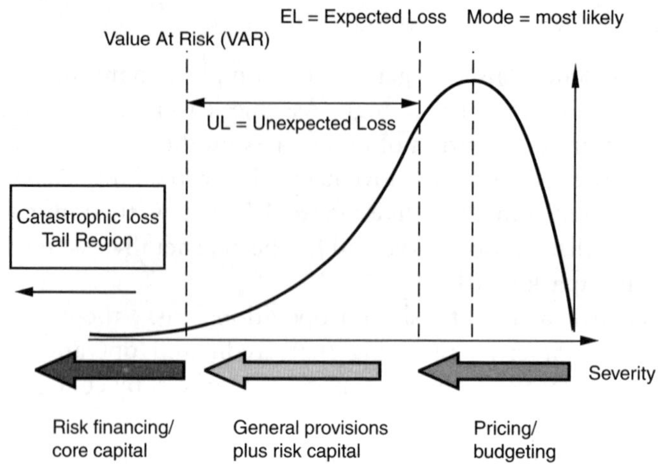

Figure 4.6 One-sided loss curve – credit risk/operational risk

a bulge near the upper end and tailing off to the left. Second, compared to a normal distribution, it has a *fat tail* which means that it decreases comparatively slowly to the left. Simply put, this means that, at whatever probability level you choose, there is always some more potential bad news! In other words, there is a non-zero probability of loss, no matter how large the loss. This, incidentally, is a major fault of the normal distribution as a model for market risk also.

It is assumed that the total corporate loss curve (being the aggregate of all applicable risk curves of the whole organization) is more of the shape of Figure 4.6 than that of the normal curve (Figure 4.5). Although for the total risk distribution, there will be more of a positive 'upside' element, possibly reflecting market risk uncertainty.

Figure 4.6 splits naturally into three regions, as follows.

1. Expected Loss (EL) is the mean or average of the distribution. It should be stressed that expected losses are not a risk. Anything which is 'expected' or anticipated is not a risk by definition, since risk is exposure to uncertainty. The risk is that the outcome differs adversely from the expected value.
2. Value at Risk (VAR) is the point on the curve beyond which there is a specified percentage probability of occurrence. For example, if there is a 1 per cent probability that corporate losses (over the next year) could exceed £50 million, then the VAR is £50 million *at the 1 per cent level.*

3. Unexpected Loss (UL) is the distance from EL to VAR and represents the potential normal level of volatility of profits.
4. The *tail region* which covers all losses beyond the unexpected loss level. Losses in this region are considered catastrophic for the business.

Managing the loss curve

Whilst it is important to manage financial risk in an integrated and coherent way, certain specific considerations apply to each of the three regions. It is important that management is clear on which area it is focusing; a common mistake is to direct actions suitable for one region to another.

Expected loss

As noted above, expected loss is not a component of risk. Rather, it needs to be considered as a cost to the business and treated accordingly as part of profit management. Examples include expected losses by banks on credit card business and 'shrinkage' in the retail industry.

In these cases management addresses the expected loss by a combination of pricing and cost control decisions. For example, banks, recognizing a certain level of loss on credit cards due to fraud and default, as well as taking anti-fraud and credit assessment measures, also build in part of the pricing to cover it. This is why the Annual Percentage Rate (APR) on your credit card is probably around three to four times the Bank of England's current base rate. Similarly, expected shrinkage loss in the retail sector will be covered partly by anti-theft measures and partly by pricing.

Unexpected loss

In this region of the loss curve management is addressing the risk to profit performance or *earnings volatility.* Surprises in results are fatal to share price management and volatility in earnings naturally leads to the requirement of a higher risk premium by investors which means either higher dividend payout or lower share price. As will be explained later, various financial management tools are applied all with the aim of reducing the UL to an acceptable level. These tools include the use of financial hedging instruments (forward and futures contracts, swaps, options, caps, collars, floors and so on) and *natural hedging* strategies which involve rearranging the business to reduce the financial risks. The main point is that this profitability management is done on the basis of ignoring the possibility of catastrophe. If, for example, assessments are done at the 1 per cent level for Value or Capital at Risk, this discounts the possibility of anything worse happening, which, if no other action is taken, could prove to be a grave mistake.

Catastrophe

An essential element of effective risk management requires the board to define the catastrophe level, beyond which the business would fail or be very severely damaged. An acceptable level of probability of catastrophe then needs to be stated as an expression of risk tolerance or appetite.

The possibility of catastrophe needs to be transparently acknowledged and addressed by management action within a coherently defined risk policy. As noted above, if risk management activity concentrates solely on the unexpected loss or earnings volatility, the business may be exposed to total failure due to the crystallization of events which are considered only very remote possibilities.

Consider as a parallel the occurrence of a tsunami. It is clear that what are needed are: an early warning system, a contingency plan and insurance. This assumes you live near the sea: the other option is to eliminate the risk entirely by moving out of the danger zone to higher ground. Similarly in financial risk management the first requirement is to assess whether or not the catastrophic danger exists and then determine a strategy to deal with it. The point is that to do this effectively you *must* consider adverse movements in the financial variables (interest and currency rates, etc.) well beyond what is usual and discount nothing for being too remote a possibility.

In summary, the train of reasoning which needs to be followed is:

1. What set of circumstances (scenarios) would result in catastrophe?
2. How likely do we believe them to be?
3. Are we content with that level of likelihood or do we need to do something about it?

Value At Risk and time horizon

Value At Risk (VAR) is defined to be the point on a loss curve beyond which there is a specified probability. For example, in the case of foreign exchange (FX) exposure limits based on a target VAR of £2 million at 99 per cent confidence may be chosen. This means the necessity to arrange things so that there is only a 1 per cent possibility of an adverse movement exceeding £2 million.

The aspect so far left out, however, is the time period over which the movements are measured. For example, in the banking industry, for regulatory reasons a time period of 10 days is used; the thinking being that this would be a reasonable period during which to 'trade out' of a position which has gone bad.

If the price of the financial asset follows the sort of Brownian motion path as exhibited in Figure 4.4, the significance of the time period becomes clear. The four lines represent four 'sample paths' based on the same uncertainty parameters. The value at risk represents the 99th percentile of the distribution of possible final positions of the path at a certain time. It may be seen how the paths tend to diverge from each other and the degree of divergence, or uncertainty, increases with time. In fact, much of the substance of advanced texts on risk quantification centres on what the resultant distributions will be at different times for different models.

Scenario analysis – the future may be more uncertain than you think

As already observed, financial risk analysis benefits from the availability of vast amounts of relevant data which allows the application of statistical analysis. Market movements are logged almost every moment so, for the most liquid markets, the availability of data is not a problem. However, at root, all of these methods make the heroic assumption that the past is a good predictor of the future. In addition to this, many models weight recent data more heavily than older data, which in terms of economic cycles may not be entirely logical. (It may be mentioned in passing a similar illogicality exists in some operational risk models where current losses are supposed to imply high risk. This ignores the fact that, after big loss events, systems and personnel are changed and controls tightened, so precisely the reverse may be true.)

This is recognized by international banking regulators where, of course, financial risk is most acute. The rules state that, where financial institutions use internal risk models (for financial and operational risks), there is an additional requirement to carry out testing under stressed scenarios. No detailed guidance is provided on exactly what is required, but the intention is clear – without additional input, the past is not a sufficiently reliable guide to the future. Banking regulators additionally require supplementary 'buffers' of capital over and above that predicted by the models, just in case the models prove to be over-optimistic.

Because the level of capital required to support a financial position needs to cover quite rare unexpected circumstances, this can *only* be carried out effectively using scenario analysis. VAR covers unexpected loss, but generally this is just not sufficiently unexpected for capital requirements purposes.

This aspect of financial risk management brings it into a close relationship with the strategic planning of the organization. In order to assess longer-term, strategic risks, the discipline of scenario analysis is often adopted by larger organizations.

Scenarios are expressions of different foreseeable futures which allow planners, and risk managers, to consider what actions taken now will best prepare the organization to take advantage of future opportunities and avoid being destroyed by catastrophe. They are not the same as plans, but help put the planning debates on a more rigorous, and better thought through, footing. The main financial risks are closely associated with the major economic variables (growth, interest rates, world economic and financial relationships and imbalances, etc.) and so financial risk assessment needs to consider these factors.

The portfolio view, correlation and hedging

A further complexity which needs to be added to the mix is that *risks do not add together linearly.* It has already been noted that it is not possible to represent risk as a single number but only by means of the whole loss distribution curve. The problem then arises: when two or more risks exist how then to *add* two probability curves?

Even though this can be done by the computer, more information regarding the possible *correlation* between the risks is still required. Correlation is a measure of the extent to which the levels of impact of the risks tend to be of the same order or not. Careful consideration of correlation can lead to the seemingly strange conclusion that in some circumstances *the aggregate risk of two risks may be less than the level of either of the individual risks.* This will occur when the risks are anti-correlated and, in the extreme case, the total risk may be eliminated altogether – this is the principle of hedging.

Generally, financial risk exposures arising from business operations are hedged using financial instruments. These may be liquid contracts, traded on exchanges (e.g. many futures and options) or they may be over the counter (OTC) trades, such as interest rate swaps, or foreign exchange forwards, which are not traded in the financial markets. However, care is needed as the following example demonstrates.

Suppose that a company manufactures a product using a commodity and its main market for the finished product is denominated in the same currency as that used to pay for the raw material. In this case, a *natural hedge* is in place because the foreign currency income may be used as finance for the foreign currency outgoings. It may also be observed therefore that the natural hedge may obviate the need for financial hedging transactions. Indeed, putting a financial hedge in place in addition would actually make matters worse because the company would be fully exposed to movements in the value of its future income stream.

Thus financial risks need to be considered together, in the round. It is generally dangerous to try to identify a particular financial risk and attempt to manage it in isolation.

Accounting rules and disclosure

A brief example may illustrate some of the issues. Suppose an organization were to invest £10 million in a long-dated UK government bond (a gilt-edged stock), whose purchase price were £125 per £100 nominal.

Because the price of a long-dated bond varies inversely with interest rates, if interest rates rise, the price of the bond will fall. Suppose rates do rise and the price of the bond falls to £100. What is the implication from a risk perspective?

In one sense there is none. If the organization holds the bond until maturity, it receives the coupon payments regularly twice a year and, although the current management will probably be long gone, the organization can look forward with certainty to receiving its £100 redemption payment in 20–30 years' time. Because it is a UK government bond (gilt-edged) the possibility of default (credit risk) is not considered. So where is the risk?

On the other hand, if the organization is required under accounting standards to value the bond at current market value, it is exposed, year on year, to considerable interest rate risk in terms of its *reported results.* Whilst the underlying cash flows change not one jot, to the outside world looking at the accounts, there may be considerable volatility in reported results arising from the exposure. This would be avoided (in the absence of hedging measures) only if the organization were able to account for the bond on the basis of amortized cost, which in this case would amount to spreading the purchase 'premium' of £25 over the life of the bond.

Thus, even where hedging transactions are put in place, much depends on the accounting treatment as well as the economic effects. In other words, for a hedge to be fully effective it needs to reduce reported profit volatility as well as cash flow volatility.

Risk appetite

Up to this point various aspects of building a picture of the financial risks have been examined. What needs to be done to complete the picture is to input this information to build an overall view of the probability distribution of total profit.

Suppose it were possible to build a model to calculate the probability distribution of the coming year's profit results. This model would be based on the usual operational plan and budget, except each of the key input assumptions would be replaced by assumed probability distributions expressing the level of uncertainty in the assumption. Thus instead of assuming the mid-point US$/GB£ exchange rate for the coming year were 2.0, you might assume it could be expressed as a normal distribution with mean 2, allowing the possibility of 1.5 to 2.5 with all the intervening values.

If this were done (and some larger companies are doing this regularly in practice), you might end up with a probability distribution for planned profit which looked like Figure 4.7, which is the output from a Monte Carlo simulator. Note the similarity of this to Figure 4.6 which is the abstract version.

It may be seen that this forecast is telling us that there is an expected level of profit of around £5 million (imagine these figures scaled to the size of your own organization e.g. £500,000 to £5 billion, etc.). There is a 5 per cent probability that profit will exceed £11.8 million, but a 1 per cent probability that there will be a loss exceeding £25 million. It would be possible using the information produced by the simulator to compute the probability of all intervening values also.

The question to be asked by the board is, 'Is this profile acceptable?'

In answering this question, the board would need to consider the three regions in the curve, namely:

1. the expected level of profit;
2. profit volatility, i.e. uncertainty around the expected level; and
3. the probability of catastrophic loss.

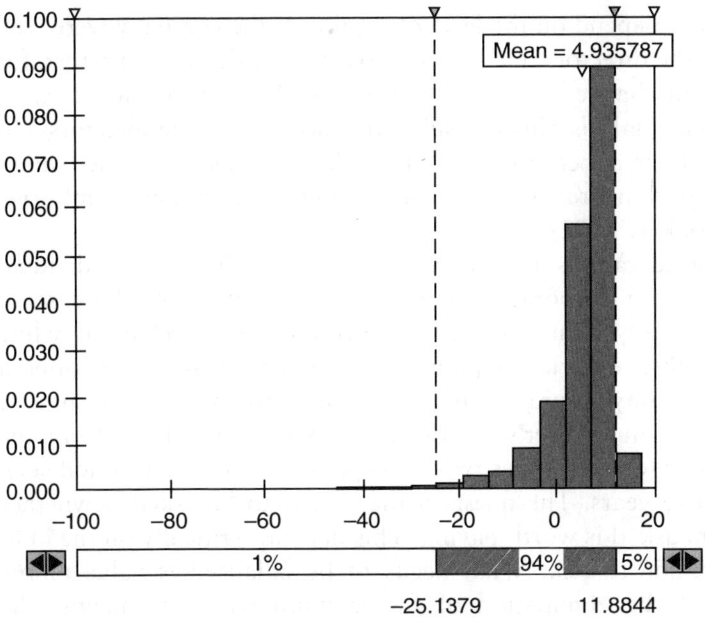

Figure 4.7 Simulated total corporate profit

All three need to be considered as part of a rational approach to managing the organization's risk profile.

In terms of considering the expected level of profit, this is really the same process, by another name, as approving the annual operational plan. The interesting part comes in looking at the other issues of profit volatility and catastrophe.

In the example, there is a 5 per cent chance of a profit in excess of £11.8 million and there is also a 5 per cent chance of a loss exceeding £9.2 million. This range might be termed the basic uncertainty because 5 per cent is quite a low probability.

This basic uncertainty is what is looked at by equity investors when it translates into annual results. Thus the company that runs with this sort of planned range of uncertainty is likely to have it translated, over the course of years, into volatility of earnings with a consequential impact on the attitude of investors.

On the other hand, major loan creditors, such as banks or corporate bond holders, are only interested in the probability of default, which is likely to be at the far left of the distribution curve, in the catastrophic region.

The question then is whether or not (in this example) the directors can live with a 1 per cent probability of a loss in excess of £25 million.

This may well depend on the level of capital. If the company were well capitalized, the directors may be prepared to run this risk in return for the 5 per cent chance of delivering over double the profit forecast.

In the final analysis, this is a subjective decision of the directors and depends on their appetite for risk. Indeed, decisions about the overall profit distribution are precisely what defines the organization's risk appetite (Bobker, 2002).

These considerations may be put more specifically into an individual (as opposed to a corporate) context. For example, take the case of extended warranty insurance. Each time you make a purchase of 'white goods' or other electrical equipment, you are likely to be offered extended warranty insurance. In return for a premium, the insurance extends the manufacturer's warranty for parts and labour from the usual one year (or sometimes two year) period, to a longer period such as four or five years. The question that needs to be asked is whether the premium asked is worth paying. This depends critically on the individual's attitude to risk. What needs to be balanced is value *to the individual* of the elimination of future unknown costs against the certain cost of the premium today.

Risk appetite and risk policy

It is essential that the key elements of risk management are clearly documented in risk policies adopted by the board and the following two statements of policy are suggested as providing the required framework. Furthermore, such statements will drive the organization down the more analytic route as there will need to be the appropriate measurement and monitoring infrastructure in place in order to test compliance with the policy.

The suggested statements would be along the lines of:

- profit volatility: the board aims to ensure that there is 90 per cent confidence that annual reported profit will be within ±£5 million of the forecast;
- catastrophe: the board will take such action as is necessary to ensure that there is no greater than a 0.1 per cent likelihood that the group will fail in the next year.

These are clearly defined statements of appetite. Currently most statements about risk published in annual reports are to a large extent 'woolly'. With the exception of banks, which often publish their VAR targets, many expressions of appetite are practically content-free.

Following on from the catastrophe statement, the organization may then proceed to review its level of capital against the corporate loss curve to determine its adequacy. From there, capital may be allocated around the business in line with the level of risk of each business unit. This latter process would form part of a risk adjusted performance measurement (RAPM) system.

Internal controls and operational risk

It should be mentioned in passing that implementing risk measurement and monitoring systems into an organization may increase operational risk exposure. This is the case, for example, in banks where sophisticated market and credit risk functions operate. Errors in the calculations ('model risk') or errors in reporting or in any other part of the measurement/monitoring processes may lead to high operational risk exposure. However, the risks are operational, not direct financial risks.

Eleven principles of financial risk management

Much of what has been said so far may be summarized in the following 11 basic principles of financial risk management.

1. As far as possible, risks should be quantified. This includes an acceptance that all forecasts (such as strategic plans, budgets and project plans) contain uncertainty which needs to be quantified.
2. Risk cannot be quantified as a single number. There is a range of possible consequences and financial impacts of an event, each with its associated probability of occurrence. The whole probability distribution represents the risk.
3. Expected losses are not a risk; 'probability' multiplied by 'impact' does not represent risk.
4. The aggregate of a multiplicity of risks needs to take account of correlations between risks; the effect of a risk cannot be evaluated in isolation from the other risks to which the organization is exposed; this is *portfolio thinking*.
5. Care is needed when entering into hedging transactions to ensure natural hedges are not imbalanced, thereby increasing risk.
6. Clarity is needed on which part of the risk curve is being managed: EL, UL or the tail.
7. The accounting treatment of hedging transactions is critical to their overall effectiveness.

LL recommendations!

8. Risk appetite should be formally stated in terms of the acceptable level, and probability of unexpected loss, and the definition and acceptable probability of catastrophic loss.
9. Risk analysis based solely on historic data is insufficient to assess catastrophic risk. This can only be estimated by considering adverse scenarios well beyond the limit of what is usual, and possibly beyond anything which has occurred up to the present time, using detailed analytic methods to assess the probabilities. This implies that capital requirements can only be assessed on the basis of scenarios.
10. The set of all potentially catastrophic events needs to be established and an assessment made of their combined likelihood against the organization's policy on risk tolerance.
11. Boards of directors are ultimately responsible for risk and need to ensure there is full collective understanding at a deep level of all the significant risk exposures of the organization. That can only be based on a thorough identification and quantified assessment programme overseen by a 'risk literate' board.

Having described the basic characteristics of financial risk management, it is now possible to describe in more detail some specific areas of concern, namely foreign exchange risk, interest rate risk and liquidity risk.

Foreign exchange risk

Foreign exchange (FX) risk arises from movements in exchange rates. Of course, if the business is based solely in one country, with assets and liabilities, and purchases and sales, all denominated in the same currency, there is no currency risk, but there may still be 'economic exchange risk' as discussed later.

The relationship between forward rates and interest differentials

There is an intimate relationship between forward exchange rates and the prevailing rates of interest on each of the two currency assets or liabilities. This is based upon a general *arbitrage* argument, applicable to all financial instruments, relating future prices to current ones via *the cost of carry*. This demonstrates that the forward rate does not really represent the current view of where exchange rates will be in the future, but essentially the difference in interest rates between the two currencies.

To understand this, suppose a company wished to buy 10 million US dollars (US$) in exchange for sterling (GB£) in three months' time in payment for a delivery of goods or services which has just been ordered. Rather than entering into a forward FX deal, it could borrow a sum of sterling today, sell it spot for dollars which it put on deposit for three months. Assume it purchased exactly a sum of dollars which, together with the deposit interest in three months' time, amounted to exactly US$ 10 million.

At the end of three months, the US$ 10 million would be available, but the company would need to repay its sterling loan, which then becomes precisely the forward cost for the dollars. If this equivalent forward rate differed at all from the quoted rate, arbitrageurs would soon bring it back into equilibrium.

In fact, for odd or lengthy periods, companies do carry out precisely that series of equivalent transactions.

Protecting the upside – options

Although the majority of transactions comprise spot deals, forwards and swaps, it may be observed that, whilst they may protect against downside movements, they lock-in a result and therefore the opportunity to profit from an upside movement is lost.

An option is a contract giving the holder the right, but not the obligation, to enter into a contract at some future date. Rather than entering into a forward contract, say to purchase Euros six months in the future, a company could, on payment of a premium, purchase an option to buy currency at that date at a specified price (called the *strike price*).

The point is that, if the spot price on the day is more favourable, the option need not be exercised so that the company may take full advantage of the situation. Of course all this comes at a price, namely the option premium whose cost is certain. It is a sort of insurance (although that word is not favoured due to its regulatory implications).

Transaction risk, translation risk and economic risk

The transactions discussed above were for the purposes of hedging a specific transaction and address the *transaction risk* arising from potential movements in exchange rates between a contractual order being placed and the cash being received in settlement.

However, over the longer term, if the exchange rate were to continue to move in a certain direction, the exporter would be unable to protect itself by these measures because the next contract would be made at the new rate. This is an example of *economic risk* which arises from the fact of doing business with another economic area. In this example, costs may be borne in the home country (in its currency) whilst income is received in the currency of the country being exported to. This is a basic economic imbalance as it stands and short-term hedging is not able to eliminate the risk.

For companies trading goods and services across currencies, the FX risk is not straightforward. Compared to banks whose assets and liabilities are all monetary, for a trader, there is the added complication that prices (and hence revenue) are determined by economic factors of competition, general economic circumstances and so on. Thus for a trader, when exchange rates move adversely, depending on the state of the internal market, it may be possible to pass on all or part of the impact onto customers. This situation exists for airline operators and holiday firms. When the price of jet fuel (driven by the oil price) rises, some or all of the increase has traditionally been passed on to customers. Thus most of the risk is eliminated.

A different situation might arise in the case of a UK manufacturer of goods who is competing with importers of foreign-made goods of the same type. It may be that the UK manufacturer has all costs and income arising in sterling in which case there is apparently no FX risk. On the other hand, if the importing currency devalues against sterling, the competitors would be able to lower their sterling prices at no (sterling) cost to themselves, whilst the UK manufacturer would suffer a hit to the profit and loss account if it tried to compete.

These economic risks are not at all straightforward to analyse. Nevertheless, in order to manage its risks, a company needs to examine the position not only of its own cost and revenue structure but also that of its competitors and the market for its goods generally.

The final aspect of currency risk arises when it comes to reporting profits. Exactly what is reported will depend crucially on the precise accounting treatment. When companies have overseas subsidiaries, the rates used to translate their assets and liabilities into the home currency and the way profits and losses are treated will substantially affect the risks to reported profits. This is known as *translation risk* and arises as a result of the precise accounting treatment of assets and liabilities. Imagine, for example, investment in an overseas subsidiary whose net assets at the start and end of the year are US$ 100 million. If the US dollar has depreciated during the year, on consolidation there will be a translation loss, even though in economic terms nothing has changed.

Should a firm hedge currency exposures?

The above considerations have been directed towards measuring FX exposure and carrying out hedging to reduce the risk. However, there is a general debate about whether or not firms *should* hedge their FX risks.

To get a flavour of this debate consider a UK exporter to the US. If the US dollar depreciates against sterling, the exporter's income is correspondingly diminished. However, economists might say that this merely indicates that the price of the export needs to rise in dollar terms. Depending on the extent that the exporter is competing against local producers, the competitive effect of that would need to be assessed.

Secondly, investment theorists might argue (and this could apply to risk management in general) that it is for the investor to consider his or her own diversification and not for the company to take those decisions. If a significant proportion of the company's income comes from exporting to the US, investors would expect this to imply volatility around the US dollar rate and would diversify their own portfolios accordingly. If the company's income volatility is less than expected due to their hedging strategies, in theory this might upset the investors' portfolios.

Interest rate risk

Interest rate risk is exposure to adverse movements in interest rates. Interest rate risk has an added complexity compared to other market risks in that there is not a single interest rate, but the whole *yield curve*. Some often overlooked elements of interest rate risk relate to possible changes in the *shape* of the yield curve as well as the absolute level of rates.

Whenever an organization pays or receives interest it may be exposed to interest rate risk. For example, investing in long-term bonds which pay a fixed rate exposes the holder to mark-to-market losses when interest rates rise.

For issuers of bonds, hitherto, liabilities have not been marked-to-market in the way that bonds held as assets have. So there was a basic accounting asymmetry between bonds as assets and bonds as liabilities. This, of course, is changed by new accounting rules. In economic terms, the mirror image considerations apply to bonds as liabilities as to bonds as assets. When rates rise, the value of the liability falls since the company would be able to repurchase the bonds in the market at a lower value.

The interest rate applicable to a financial instrument depends critically on the *maturity* of the instrument, that is, the time from now to the date of repayment of the interest-bearing asset or liability. For bonds issued by corporates, another aspect of the actual rate of interest relates to the *credit spread* which is determined by the credit worthiness of the borrower. In this section credit spread is ignored although it is essential to consider in practice.

The yield curve and spot rates

Short rates are normally quoted (in the UK) for overnight, 7 day, 1 month, 3 months, 6 months and 1 year. Longer-term rates are determined from quoted bond yields in bands, one to five years being short, 5 to 15 being medium and over 15 years being long.

As with all financial instruments, interest products are analysed in terms of the future cash flows and valued as the net present value of those cash flows.

Looking at bond rates quoted in newspapers, one normally sees the 'Gross Redemption Yield' or 'GRY' quoted. This is a figure applicable to bonds carrying regular coupon payments during the life of the bond. The GRY is just the internal rate of return which results in the quoted price of the bond if all the coupon payments and final payment on maturity are discounted at that rate. Of course, this is an unrealistic assumption and bonds are actually priced on the basis of discounting each cash flow at the specific rate applicable for the maturity at the date of the payment. It is for this reason that GRYs on bonds with different coupons may be different.

Because GRY introduces this complication, it is usual to examine interest rate positions in terms of *spot interest rates*. A spot rate is what the equivalent rate would be on a zero coupon bond of that maturity. For example, spot rates of three and six months are clear because Treasury Bills exist in those maturities and a Treasury Bill is an instrument without a coupon, sold at a discount to the nominal value.

To calculate longer-term spot rates, one can use a 'bootstrap' method to move up the maturities. If you know the six month spot rate, you can take a coupon bond of maturity one year, discount the six month coupon at the spot rate, subtract that from the price so that what remains is the final interest payment plus the nominal discounted at the one year spot rate. And so on.

More advanced pricing systems then need to find a way to work out the rate applicable to all the maturities between the various points found in that way and various *interpolation* schemes are used for that purpose.

Interest rate exposure

Once the spot rate curve has been calculated, to assess actual exposure the next thing to be done is a maturity analysis of all interest-bearing assets and liabilities normally in terms of *maturity buckets*. That is, future time is split into discrete ranges, for example, now to one week, one week to one month, one month to three months and so on. Each range is called a maturity bucket and the total assets and total liabilities with each maturity are aggregated. Where assets and liabilities are matched in a bucket, there is a low interest rate risk in that particular maturity bucket. The risk is low but not necessarily zero because, unless the cash inflows and outflows are matched exactly, there may be small effects *within* the bucket itself.

It is, of course, essential to include all hedging transactions within the analysis. Indeed, this analysis will be a test of the effectiveness of actual, or proposed hedges.

The value of the portfolio may be calculated by discounting all the net flows by the applicable spot interest rates. In theory, one would then want to calculate the probability distribution of the portfolio value implied by the probability distribution of possible future values of the spot rate curve. The portfolio probability distribution represents the interest rate risk.

This is much more complex than the case of a single variable (such as the FX rate): future movements of the whole *curve*, not just one value, must be considered. An unsophisticated approach might simply consider a discrete set of spot rates to be correlated variables and feed this information into a standard spreadsheet-based Monte Carlo package to compute the portfolio distribution.

In addition, following the method described above, initially one would also seek to establish the set of future spot curves which would result in a catastrophic fall in the value of the portfolio. This will highlight any exposure to changes in the *shape* of the curve as well as the absolute value of interest rates.

To do this, one needs to flex the spreadsheet maturity model with various extreme interest rate scenarios, testing just how extreme they need to be to cause catastrophe (or at least a severe downside). An assessment of the acceptability of the likelihood of such scenarios would then need to be made.

The sophisticated approach requires the use of specialist (probably expensive) software designed specifically to do the job. This would carry out the much more complex calculations based upon the full Brownian motion models and is the type of system used by financial institutions and traders.

However, much can be gained in the corporate (non banking) setting, even by the comparatively crude spreadsheet analysis recommended above. And, however brilliant the inventors of expensive models, there is no guarantee that their predictions of future behaviour will prove accurate.

Duration

Because of the computing power needed to analyse the exposure in the way just described, certain simplified methods have been developed based on the notion of *duration*. This is defined for a portfolio of bonds to be the sum of the values of the time to each cash flow (interest or final payment) multiplied by the NPV of the value of the payment divided by the overall price of the portfolio.

For a portfolio of bonds, the total duration gives a very broad brush picture of the interest rate characteristics. For example, it was observed that zero duration portfolios are immune to interest rate movements, provided the movements are very small and result in parallel shifts of the yield curve (i.e. no change in shape). This gave rise to the dangerous idea that short duration portfolios carry little interest rate risk because (as is usual in such matters) the caveats and assumptions are often overlooked.

Attempts are made to correct this with further sophistication in the theory but all of this, at root, is attempting the impossible by approximating whole curves with just one or two numbers which, as previously pointed out, cannot be done. The main issue is that so-called interest rate *immunization* is only guaranteed when there is an exact matching of cash inflows and outflows. Zero duration can exist for oddly constructed portfolios with unmatched cash flows leaving residual interest rate exposure.

Ultimately, there is no substitute for a full analysis of all the cash flows, maturities and applicable rates. With modern computers and software this is now feasible. On the other hand, the language of duration can be helpful for that broad picture of a portfolio and its simplicity of calculation is an advantage provided the potential pitfalls are kept in mind.

Hedging instruments – swaps, caps, collars, floors and futures

A range of hedging products is available of which the interest rate swap has the largest and most liquid market. In the most common swap, the company pays (or receives) a fixed rate of interest on a notional principal sum and receives (or pays) in return a floating rate, for example, based upon London Interbank Offered Rate – LIBOR. This would be most useful to a corporate which wished to borrow at a fixed rate of interest but had no access to the bond markets. It could instead borrow at a floating rate and swap into fixed. Similarly, if the corporate had a sum on deposit at a floating rate but wished to receive fixed, it could do so by entering into a swap in the other direction. The cost of the transaction is included in the actual rates of interest in the contract.

The interest rate swap thus permits organizations to match better their interest rate cash flows. Where swaps are clearly used to hedge specific transactions, and the accounting rules are satisfied, the hedged transactions may be disclosed with their modified characteristics.

Whereas the swap fixes the terms of the fixed and floating legs of the contract, caps, collars and floors allow movement of rates within limits. For example, caps entitle the buyer to interest payments when rates rise above an agreed level. Floors similarly apply when rates fall below a specified level, and collars when rates move outside a specified band of rates.

All of these contracts are off balance sheet. The underlying principal amount is entirely 'notional' and no principal is exchanged.

Other interest rate products include interest rate and bond futures and options on those contracts. Futures and options on futures are usually contracts which may be traded on an exchange.

Using the principles already stated, in order to assess the overall interest rate risk, it is essential to understand how future cash flows, including all underlying instruments, plus all derivative and hedging products, would change under different interest rate scenarios. This is the essence of managing the risk. The problems experienced by organizations using derivatives may usually be traced to a lack of understanding of exactly how they would behave (i.e. potential valuation as asset or liability) under different scenarios.

Liquidity risk

Liquidity risk is the risk that an organization fails to meet its financial obligations as they fall due, or in other words, it cannot pay its bills.

It is distinguished from solvency which is defined as assets exceeding liabilities and relates most directly to the timing of cash flows. The measurement and management of liquidity risk centres naturally, therefore, around cash flows.

Failure of liquidity may potentially be a catastrophic risk for an organization. In cases (now the norm) where bank or bond lenders have imposed covenants in loan agreements, failure to meet gearing and interest cover requirements may trigger action long before there is failure to meet actual interest payments. For a publicly quoted company, the attendant publicity may mean the end of the organization in its current form. In any case, under UK Company Law (Insolvency Act 1986), failure to pay a creditor on due date is grounds for the commencement of winding-up proceedings.

The main point is that, unless cash/liquidity and funding is adequately managed, a strong balance sheet in itself may not protect against disaster or at least major embarrassment.

For cash-rich organizations, there is the opposite problem, i.e. excess liquidity may be costing too much. In normal circumstances the yield curve is upward sloping meaning lower returns on shorter, more liquid funds.

Assessment of liquidity risk

In some ways liquidity risk is more straightforward to assess since it is more or less a yes/no type event; there are unlikely to be degrees of liquidity failure. Either the company fails to meet a required payment on time and is in deep trouble, or it does not. Whilst there may be intermediate levels of consequences, it is suggested that, because this is a relatively new area of quantification, that organizations start with the assessment of liquidity catastrophe in terms of its probability of occurrence over the next year.

This leads to the following definition: liquidity risk is the probability that, at some time during the next 12 months, breach of loan covenant or failure to meet a payment on time will result in major action against the company by its creditors.

Following on from this it is a simple matter to define the basis of *liquidity policy* which should have at its core a statement of the acceptable probability of catastrophic liquidity failure.

As with other financial risks, the major benefit of such a policy statement would be to drive the implementation of infrastructure to monitor the stated probability which in turn would be bound to lead to improved liquidity management.

In a similar way compared to other financial risks, to assess the threat of catastrophe, it is first necessary to clarify the full set of scenarios giving rise to it and assess the probability of occurrence of each. This requires detailed cash flow forecasting as its basis together with an assessment of all contingent liabilities and their probability of crystallization. For a bank where interest receipts and payments are a major element of cash flow, the liquidity analysis may be closely related to the interest rate risk maturity analysis. However, for banks, the driver of a liquidity catastrophe would be the scenario of sudden, unanticipated withdrawal of funds by depositors.

Liquidity management – assets and liabilities

As well as maintaining liquid funds (normally in the form of bank deposits and readily marketable securities), unless the organization is cash-rich with high levels of regular cash income (e.g. retailers), access to funds in case of need will need to be arranged. This can take many forms depending on the size of the organization and its access to the funding markets.

The most basic form of funding would be the bank overdraft. Larger organizations may be able to arrange committed facilities (at a cost of course) and commercial paper programmes. As with all risk management, what is required is a soundly based estimate of the change in probability of crystallization of the worst-case scenarios to be balanced against the cost of achieving them.

For example, suppose the cash flow analysis predicted that, under a given scenario with estimated probability 5 per cent, the company would breach its interest cover covenants in year 2. A 5 per cent probability may be deemed too high to tolerate, therefore the company may be prepared to pay its bank a fee for a committed facility. The total amount of the fee (at a rate, say, of 0.25 per cent per annum) depends on the amount of the facility. In turn, the size of the facility reduces the probability of the covenant breach. What needs to be done then is to balance this cost against various revised levels of assessed probability of breach until an acceptable level is found. If the overall costs were still considered too high, alternative sources of funding may need to be considered or other actions to alter the future forecast cash flows. But at the heart of the analysis must be a best guesstimate of the event probabilities.

Conclusion

Financial risk management, to be effective, needs to be based on quantified assessment of the risks. Risk cannot be expressed as a single number and there is no alternative but to adopt the language of probability distributions of returns and losses. The use of derivatives for hedging, or indeed for income generation, can be managed within the quantitative framework provided the precise nature of the hedging instruments are well understood under different stressed scenarios, so that nasty surprises are avoided.

Once the probability distribution framing of risk management is accepted, there needs to be clarity on which area of the distribution is being managed. Expected and unexpected loss management relates to pricing, cost control and profit performance management. In this area of the curve, the analysis of relevant historic data may be a solid basis for actions. However, when analysing and managing the risk of catastrophic adverse events there needs to be an open minded acceptance of the possibility of extreme scenarios, some of which may never have occurred in the past. In this situation, using only past events as a guide to the future is unsound.

Ultimately, it is the board of directors, or equivalent governing body, of each organization which bears the responsibility for managing risk, including financial risks. Given the increasing focus on this whole area of management in the light of financial scandals, risk policies need to be clear, workable and closely monitored and enforced by the board. Furthermore, boards need to take a hard look at their collective competence to supervise and control financial risk management and ensure they are in a position effectively to hold executive decision-makers to account.

References and recommended reading

Board of Banking Supervision (1995) *Report into the Circumstances of the Collapse of Barings Bank*. London: HMSO.

Bobker, D S (2002) *Risk Tolerance*. London: Gee Business Risk Management Bulletin.

BP website. See: http://www.bp.com/onefeedsection.do?categoryId=773&contentId=2002459

Cox, J C and Rubinstein, M (1985) *Options Markets*. Englewood Cliffs, NJ: Prentice Hall.

Federal Reserve Bank of New York (2005) USD/GBP 1993–2005. See: http://www.ny.frb.org/markets/fxrates/historical/home.cfm

Financial Services Authority (2001) *Integrated Prudential Sourcebook*. Available at: http://www.fsa.gov.uk

Great Britain (1986) Insolvency Act 1986. London: HMSO. [Section 122(1)(f).] See also: http://www.insolvencyhelpline.co.uk/insolvency-act/p04c6_2.htm#122

Hull, J C (1993) *Options, Futures, and Other Derivative Securities*, 2nd edn. Englewood Cliffs, NJ: Prentice Hall.

Jorion, P (2000) *Value at Risk, the New Benchmark for Managing Financial Risk*, 2nd edn. New York: McGraw Hill.

Kelvin, Lord (1891–1894) *PLA – Popular Lectures and Addresses (1891–1894)*, 3 volumes. See: http://zapatopi.net/kelvin/quotes.html#sci

Lowenstein, R (2000) *When Genius Failed: The Rise and Fall of Long Term Capital Management*. New York: Random House.

Ong, M K (1999) *Internal Credit Risk Models, Capital Allocation and Performance Measurement*. New York: Risk Books.

Platt, R B (1986) *Controlling Interest Rate Risk, New Techniques and Applications for Money Management*, 2nd edn. New York: Wiley.

US Treasury Bill rate 1954–2005. See: http://research.stlouisfed.org/fred2/series/DTB3/downloaddata

Vose, D (2000) *Risk Analysis, A Quantitative Guide*, 2nd edn. New York: Wiley.

Wilmott, P (2001) *Quantitative Finance*. New York: Wiley.

5

Business Continuity Management

John Sharp

Evolution of business continuity management

Business Continuity Management (BCM) is a relatively new management discipline. The concept of business continuity was developed in the mid-1980s as a new way of managing business risks. The basis of BCM is that it is the key responsibility of company directors to ensure the continuation of business functionality at all times and under any circumstance.

BCM grew out of the requirements in the early 1970s to provide computer disaster recovery for information systems. Traditionally disaster planning had been concentrated on the restoration of facilities after a major incident such as the loss of computing or telecommunications, or of a building or plant through fire or flood. The responsibility for these plans had been dispersed to various functions within a company. Typically these were the IT, estates and security departments. Disaster recovery plans in general are written on the basis of recovery after an event.

In 2003 the British Standards Institution published a publicly available specification, *Guide to Business Continuity Management* (PAS 56), which drew together the best practice in BCM and has been adopted by many organizations throughout the world. The principle on which the guide is based is that:

> Business Continuity Management establishes a strategic and operational framework to implement, proactively, an organisation's resilience to disruption, interruption or loss in supplying its products and services. It should not purely be a reactive measure taken after an incident has occurred. BCM requires

> planning across many facets of an organisation, therefore its resilience depends equally on its management and operational staff, as well as technology, and requires a holistic approach to be taken when establishing a BCM programme. (PAS 56:2003)

In 2006 the British Standards Institution published a new standard for BCM – BS 25999-1. This is a Code of Practice for BCM and incorporates the best practice from PAS 56, the BCM guidelines which support the UK's Civil Contingencies Act and other sources from around the world. In 2007 BSI will publish Part 2 of the new standard which will provide a Specification for BCM against which organizations may be certified.

Unexpected events do not simply happen; quite often they are created by the organization itself. Every organization has inherent weaknesses: faulty IT systems that are 'worked around', informal communication channels, lack of operator training, disconnects in structures and local process variations. Examination of the causes of most major disasters has found that there are several incidents or circumstances that combine together which lead to the eventual disaster.

BCM is about prevention, not just cure. It is not just about being able to deal with incidents as and when they occur and thus preventing a crisis and subsequent disaster, but also establishing a culture within the organization that seeks to build greater resilience in order to ensure the continuity of the delivery of products and services to clients and customers.

Business continuity management is about anticipating that things are beginning to go wrong and taking planned and rehearsed steps to protect the business and hence the stakeholders' interests. It is about maintaining their confidence in the management's ability to handle a crisis and to prevent disasters occurring, thus protecting the brand, reputation and image of the organization as much as the physical infrastructures and its employees. BCM goes beyond recovery from a disaster to establishing a culture that seeks to prevent failure and crisis.

Research undertaken by Knight and Pretty of Templeton College, Oxford in the mid-1990s (Knight and Pretty, 2000) has shown that the effect of disasters on shareholder value can be serious. They discovered that it is the lack of confidence in the ability of senior managers and directors to act quickly and professionally at the time of disaster that drives down share values. Effective BCM integrates with crisis management to ensure that, if a major incident does occur, not only is the organization able to maintain continuity of operations but that it is able to reassure the stakeholder community that it is in control.

The business drivers

Accepted as it is that the protection of brand, reputation and image of the organization is paramount for any organization, there are other external drivers which are having greater influence over the introduction of business continuity management (see Figure 5.1).

Industry regulations and legal requirements are having an increasing effect in driving organizations to establish BCM. There is an increased awareness by the regulators that organizations should have effective BCM in place for the protection of customers and the community. Since 9/11 finance regulators across the world have set out conditions for BCM that they expect the firms they regulate to follow. In some cases these conditions are mandatory, in others they provide strong guidance.

In the UK the Civil Contingencies Act 2004 requires local government bodies and emergency services to put in place effective BCM to ensure that they can continue to perform their functions in the event of an emergency. They have to ensure that they can mobilize the functions they need to deal with the emergency, minimize the impact on the responder's day-to-day activity and maintain vital services for the community at an appropriate level. In addition local authorities have the responsibility to promote business continuity to business and appropriate voluntary bodies in support of the concept of a resilient community.

Insurance companies are having an increasing influence. It is not the physical loss that causes the greatest pain for any organization but the loss of customers. Business interruption insurance is seen as a way of covering the revenue lost whilst the facilities are rebuilt. Until relatively recently the insurance market linked business interruption insurance to the building insurance. More recently they have sought to sever this link as business interruption losses have increased dramatically. Underwriters are looking for evidence that effective business continuity management is in place to reduce risk exposure of business interruption. If BCM does exist it can influence the level of cover offered or the amount of excess that is applied to a policy.

One of the most significant drivers today is that of corporate governance. Across the world regulation and legislation in this area is increasing. In the UK, the revision of the UK stock exchange listing rules places greater emphasis on internal controls to manage the principal risks facing a company.

When the Turnbull Committee guidance for directors on internal controls was first published in September 1999 (Turnbull *et al.*, 1999) the chair of the committee, Nigel Turnbull, stated:

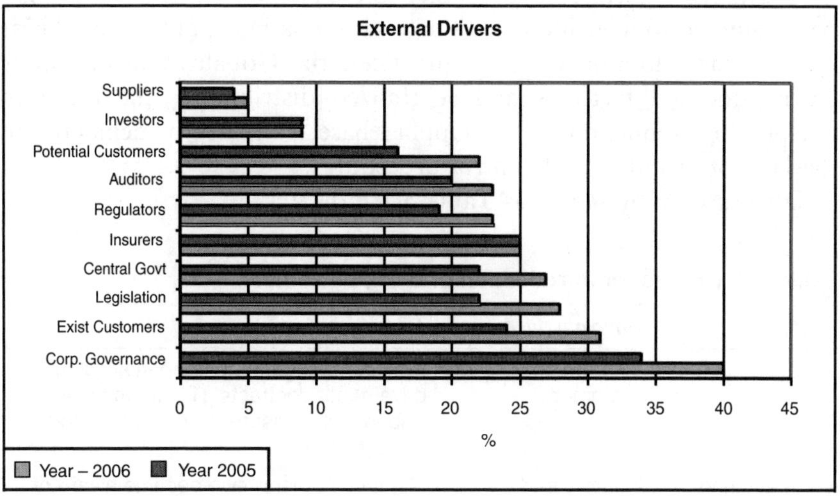

(from Chartered Management Institute BCM Awareness Research 2006)

Figure 5.1 External drivers for introduction of BCM

> The Guidance sets out an overall framework of best practice for business, based upon an assessment and control of their significant risks. For many companies, Business Continuity Management will address some of these key risks and help them to achieve compliance. (Nigel Turnbull, personal communication)

Another group that is acting as a key external driver are auditors who look for evidence of effective BCM being in place to meet regulations and legislation. Previously they asked if business continuity plans existed. The current approach is to look for evidence that plans are rehearsed and that BCM has been promoted within the organization.

Motivated by these external drivers, and the need to manage principal risks, organizations have identified that they are often dependent upon key suppliers for their own continuity. As a result the pressure for BCM has started to flow down the supply chain from customers. Just as major customers have insisted that their suppliers have quality and project management processes in place they are now demanding that BCM be established to ensure continuity of supply. This is driven not only by their need to achieve regulatory compliance, but also by the need to maintain their market share. The need for better management across the supply network was highlighted by the UK fuel crisis of September 2000.

A number of factors have emerged in the last decade or so that might be considered to have increased the level of risk in supply chains. These include: the adoption of 'lean' practices, the globalization of supply chains, focused factories and centralized distribution, the trend to outsourcing, reduction in the supplier base, volatility of demand and the lack of visibility and control procedures.

Drivers vary by sector as Table 5.1 indicates.

Table 5.1 Drivers for introduction of BCM, by sector

Sector	*Principal drivers*	*Comments*
Construction	Insurers and customers	Project management and penalty clauses drive major contracts. Health and safety issues high – insurers looking for good management.
Manufacturing	Insurers and customers	Major customers have become aware of their supply chain vulnerabilities – insurers are keen to reduce business interruption risks.
Distributors	Insurers, auditors and customers	Major players in the supply chain logistics.
Retail/ wholesale	No major drivers but customers and auditors have a degree of influence	Retail outlets drive the wholesalers but the outlets themselves have many customers who individually have no voice.
Finance	Regulators and auditors	Highly regulated industry and subject to a variety of audits.
Leisure	Insurers	Insurers are keen to reduce business interruption risks.
Utilities	Central government, regulators, insurers, auditors and customers	Critical infrastructure regulated companies who have major customers. Subject to a variety of audits.
Public authorities and emergency services	Central government and auditors	Many now subject to legalization under the Civil Contingencies Act.
Education	Auditors	Funding bodies auditors.
Health	Central government and regulators	Health services are a principal focus for government and also covered by the Civil Contingencies Act.
Professional services	Customers	
Business services	Insurers and customers	Insurers are keen to reduce business interruption risks.

(from *Business Continuity Management*, Research)

The drivers also vary with company size as shown in Table 5.2.

Table 5.2 Drivers for introduction of BCM, by company size

Company size	*Principal drivers*	*Comments*
Up to £1 million	No major drivers	Smaller companies are way down the supply chain.
£1 million–£10 million	Insurers and customers	The pressures at this level have started to appear from these two groups.
£10 million–£100 million	Insurers and auditors are main drivers	Insurers are keen to reduce business interruption risks with this size of company where they have greater exposure.
£100 million–£500 million	Central government, auditors, insurers and customers	This group includes many local authorities and plcs.
Over £500 million	Central government, auditors, regulators, insurers and customers	Listed and highly regulated companies. Critical organizations in UK economy.

(from *Business Continuity Management*, Research)

Future drivers may include investors and banks who would wish to see that continuity is built into business plans, trade and professional bodies and the public in general via the media and pressure groups.

Time has become a key driver for business continuity management. The speed of business has changed and there is very often little time to allow for a gradual recovery. The emergence of e-commerce and the lack of loyalty amongst customers have changed the need for recovery to one of availability. Organizations for whom this is key have to ensure that their services are available 24/7/365. The BCM process includes an assessment on availability and how the BC plan should be structured to meet customers' expectations.

It is the time dimension that has created the move to BCM and is the principal differentiator between risk and continuity management. It is argued that business continuity should not be considered subordinate to risk management. There is a risk management function that sits within business continuity. There may also be a separate risk management activity outside of this function, but not above, that deals with the day-to-day risk of conducting business. This will vary from organization to organization.

Introducing business continuity management to the organization

In seeking to establish business continuity management within an organization it should be 'a fit-for-purpose, business-owned and driven activity that unifies a broad spectrum of business and management disciplines in the public, voluntary and private sectors, including crisis management, risk management and technology recovery' (Sharp, 1999) and should not be limited to information technology disaster recovery (IT DR) (see Figure 5.2). BCM forms an important element of good business management, service provision and entrepreneurial practice. BCM ought now to be regarded, not as a costly planning process, but as one that adds value to the organization (BS 25999-1:2006).

Business continuity management is a continuous process that can be represented by Figure 5.3. It is generally agreed that an organization undertaking the introduction of BCM for the first time will start with understanding the business. However, it may be that a degree of continuity planning has already been undertaken and another point on the cycle would be a more appropriate entry point.

What must be clearly understood by the executive management of an organization seeking to introduce BCM is that it is a continuous process that requires ongoing management and high-level commitment. Organizations change and the environments in which they operate will change. To be effective BCM must become part of the 'day-to-day' management process reflecting these changes.

Creating the BCM structure

Executive management sits at the heart of effective business continuity management, regardless of company size. All new management processes introduced to organizations require champions at a high level. This may be the managing director of a small company, a director of a major plc or a group of executives within a local authority who demonstrate their ongoing support for the initiative. A clear demonstration of this high level commitment must be made at the very outset and must be always maintained.

There should be a clear statement of policy from the executive together with the allocation of appropriate resources to manage the process. Like quality management, a BCM coordinator should be appointed, reporting directly to the executive, to ensure that the organization has a uniform BCM policy or approach and that continuity resources are appropriately allocated across activities.

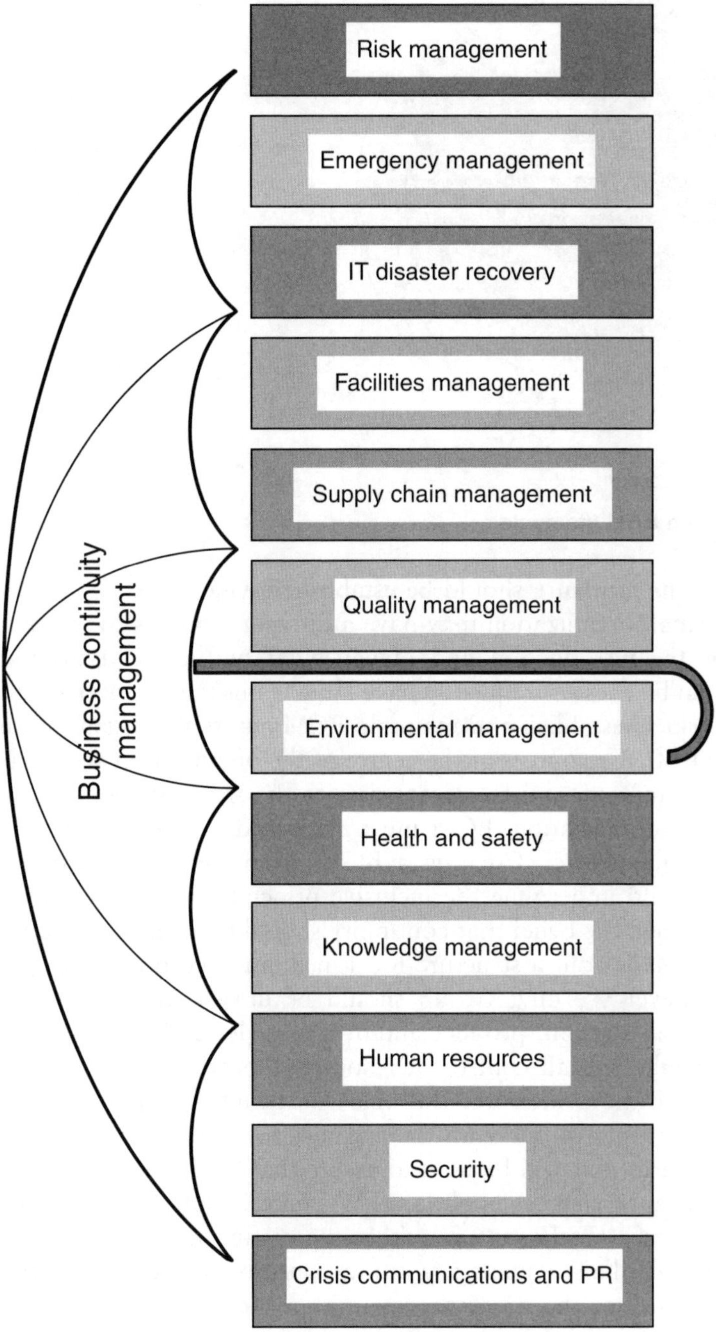

Figure 5.2 BCM as a unifying process

(from Sharp, 1999)

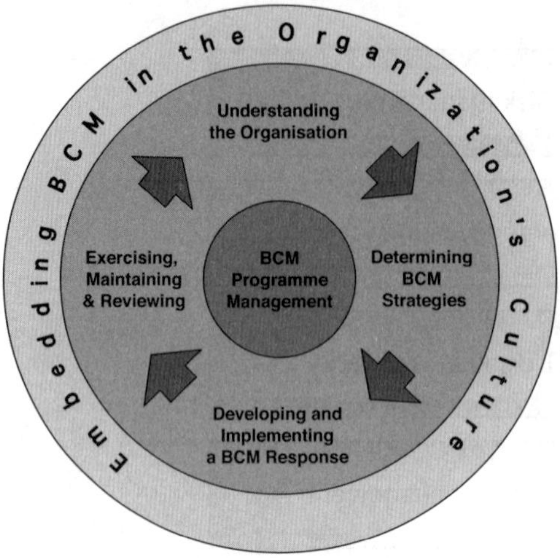

(from BSI 25999-1: 2006)

Figure 5.3 The BCM life cycle

An appropriate structure should be established which suits the organization. A small organization may have a director who has the responsibility for the introduction and management of the BCM process. International businesses frequently have large teams that work throughout the world to establish and maintain BCM across the organization. The level of BCM resources at the centre of the organization should be kept to the minimum and be appropriate to the size and geographical spread of the organization. BCM must be owned by the organization at the operational level. Creating a BCM department will enforce a 'silo' culture and undermine the inclusive principle that BCM tries to establish through the belief that continuity should be part of everyone's job. Figure 5.4 sets out a structure for a medium-sized organization.

A High Level Working Group should be drawn from the senior management at division, product and/or service level. The role of the group is to take overall control of resource allocations, set priorities for the organization, interpret the board's attitude towards risk, set continuity strategies in line with the organization's mission and establish the measures that will be used to assure the BCM process is fit for purpose. The approach the High Level Working Group takes will have a strong influence on the culture within the organization.

The divisional liaison managers are responsible for the introduction and maintenance of the BCM process within their area of operation. Very often these individuals have BCM added to their area of responsibility rather than be solely dedicated to the process.

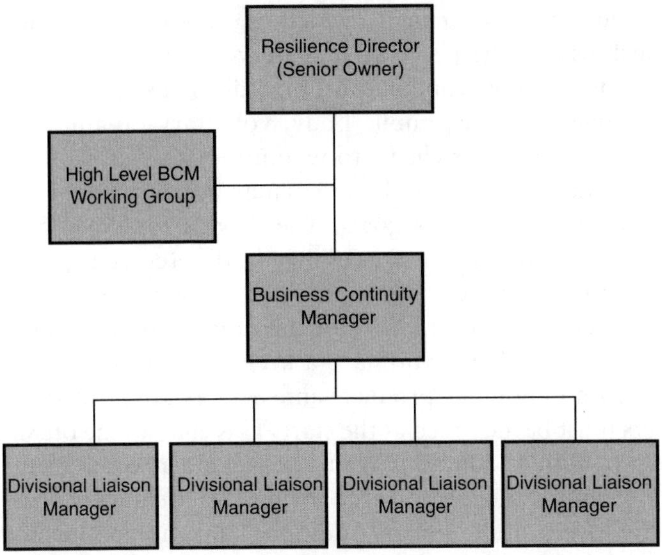

Figure 5.4 Possible BCM structure

Organizations that have successfully introduced BCM have used a 'matrix' management approach. A team of managers who understand the business and are able to appreciate how the workings of function and resources of the organization would be assembled. Such teams may have representatives from the executive, operational management, legal, finance, technology (ICT), facilities, purchasing, security, HR, suppliers, etc. Their role is to advise the High Level Working Group throughout the BCM process.

The first steps

Having established the policy, structure and measurement of the process the work can start on introducing BCM to the organization. Many organizations start by developing continuity plans against perceived risks, loss of IT or a building. This is the traditional disaster recovery approach that, whilst delivering a degree of comfort to senior managers that something has been done to protect the organization, has an inherent problem in that it might overlook critical activities outside of these facilities and services.

The direction that BCM has now taken is based on ensuring the continuity of critical activities and processes that deliver key products/ services of the organization to clients and customers. This is more aligned to total quality management, which is based on supplier/customer relationships and the processes that serve them.

Every organization has inputs and outputs regardless of size, sector or type, i.e. a commercial business, public body, voluntary organization or charity. All have customers or clients to whom they deliver products or services. Some of these products and services may be considered to be key to achieving the organization's goals. The drivers for the organization to deliver these products and services may be different, e.g. profit, community service, legislation, regulation, etc., and will vary from sector to sector and be dependent upon the size of the organization. In addition there are many stakeholders who have a keen interest in what the organization delivers and how the products and services are produced.

All stakeholders must be identified at the start. This enables the organization to consider continuity solutions against stakeholder requirements and perceptions. Some stakeholders are obvious: shareholders, customers, clients, employees and suppliers. Additional stakeholders include regulators, financial investors (banks), insurance companies, auditors, professional bodies, trade associations and government departments. Some are less obvious: competitors, the community and the environment in which the organization operates, media and protest groups. The latter two can have considerable influence on the public's perception of the organization.

The next stage is to clearly define the critical activities that enable the organization to deliver its key products and services. An approach must be taken which breaks the traditional functional view of the organization. One commercial approach is to consider what activities are involved from 'quote to cash'. That is to say, what is needed to get into a position to quote against a tender, win the business, deliver to the customer's satisfaction and then invoice for the goods and to receive payment. It requires an 'end-to-end' view of the organization and its activities. Consideration must also be given to any third party's role in these activities. Third parties include suppliers, outsourcers and intermediaries.

Michael Porter's 'value chain analysis' (Porter, 1998) provides a useful methodology to assist in the understanding of how an organization works. The activities are broken down to ascertain where value is added. This provides a starting point in understanding how the organization works. Many senior managers make the assumption that they know how 'it works around here'. This is not the case as the investigation into many disasters has clearly shown. If it is not understood how the organization works 'normally' then there is little chance of keeping it running at the time of a disruption.

Impact vs risk

The traditional risk management approach would now consider what are the threats/risks to the activities and what could stop them. Business continuity management, on the other hand, adopts an approach based on impact and time. It looks at the impact on the organization if the activity is interrupted; it looks at effects rather than the causes. Whilst we can predict many threats recent occurrences have shown that the unexpected will always happen, for example, fuel shortages, foot and mouth disease or 9/11.

BCM requires the organization to consider what the impact would be on itself and its stakeholders if the delivery of key products and services and their supporting critical activities are disrupted. This process is known as Business Impact Analysis (BIA). Measures of impact may be financial loss, the effect on service delivery, embarrassment/reputation, personal safety, personal privacy infringement, failure to meet statutory or regulatory obligations, effect on project objectives and schedules. The measures must also take into consideration time; how soon will the impact of the disrupted activity impinge upon the organization? Measures chosen must be appropriate; those for a commercial organization may be different from those for public bodies.

Consideration must also be given to incidents that occur outside the organization. The UK fuel shortage was an external event for most organizations but the impact was felt within. The 2005 product recall of over 500 food lines from UK shops containing Worcester sauce which was contaminated with Sudan 1 (a carcinogenic food colouring) affected the sale of Lea & Perrins Worcestershire Sauce despite this product containing no artificial colouring. Name association in the public perception depressed demand and increased customer calls to the Lea & Perrins helpline.

It is at this stage that the BCM High Level Working Group should be consulted to gain agreement on the level of impact against time that would be experienced by the organization if the delivery of key products and services and their supporting critical activities are disrupted. Agreement on which key products and services, if disrupted for any reason, would have the highest impact on the organization helps to focus where business continuity resources should be applied initially.

A complex organization may have many products and services, and whilst all are important, some are more critical than others. For example, one UK county council delivers 170 services to the community.

Following the BIA process it was established that 37 of these services were critical. With this knowledge the council was initially able to concentrate their BCM activities on the most important areas for the authority.

Process mapping

Having gained the High Level Working Group's agreement as to which are the key products and services the next stage is to identify the critical activities that support these products and services.

These critical activities will be supported by processes, some formal, some informal and established overtime. These processes draw upon the resources of the organization and of third parties. The next stage is to map these activities, processes and resources.

The mapping starts with the high level processes, e.g. handling customer complaints (see Figure 5.5).

The next level down is then mapped (see Figure 5.6).

There may be further levels of processes below that also need to be recorded. The system used to record the processes may be paper based or an appropriate software package.

The individuals who operate the processes should be involved in helping to map the way they work and the resources they use. Because

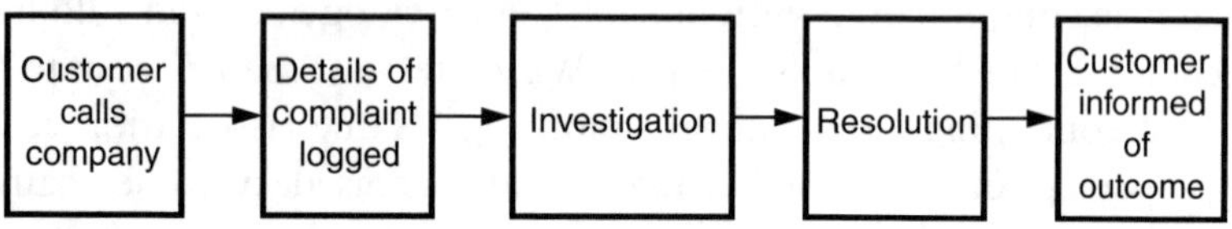

Figure 5.5 High-level process mapping example

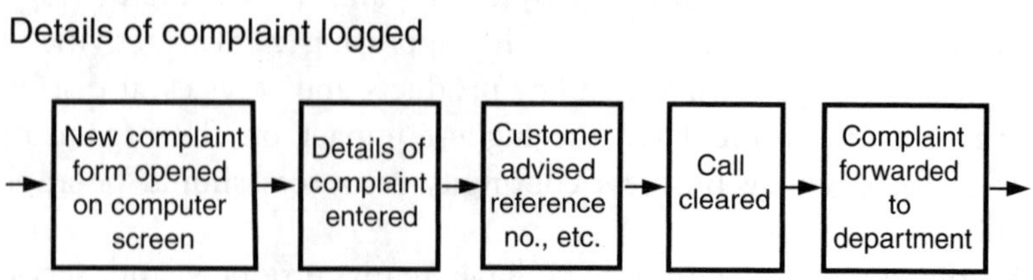

Figure 5.6 Detailed process mapping example

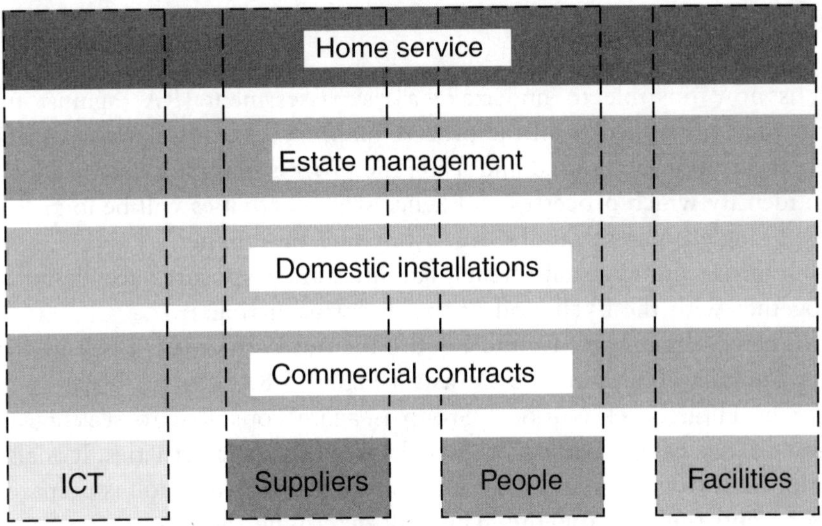

Figure 5.7 Mapping resources to critical activities

people work in different ways and informal processes develop over time it is useful, where possible, to work with several people who are involved in operating the same process.

As the mapping is being completed for the processes that support the critical activities it becomes possible to identify all of the resources that are used to support these activities, as illustrated in Figure 5.7.

The inputs and outputs are recorded together with the time-scales and the resources used to complete the task. The resources are recorded against the individual process elements. It is important to recognize that some activities are seasonal and that the use of resources may vary throughout the year, e.g. Christmas mail requires temporary staff and additional facilities.

The key resources used to support the processes may be people, information systems (ICT), data, facilities and suppliers. The numbers, location, skills, roles and responsibilities of the people required should be noted. The systems that support them must be logged, e.g. computer hardware, software applications, telecommunications and the information (data). It should be noted what facilities in terms of premises, plant, machinery and materials are required. Very often third parties have a major role to play in critical activities as suppliers of goods and services, as outsourcers or as agents between the organization and its customers/clients. Their part in the process must be recorded.

Risk assessment

It is now possible to undertake a risk assessment (RA) against the resources identified from the process mapping. Traditional risk assessment techniques are used and using the process mapping data it is easy to identify which processes and hence which activities will be impacted by a single point of failure, e.g. a building or supplier.

Internal and external threats, liabilities and exposures are identified together with the likelihood of the threat occurring.

The results of the BIA and RA are then used to create a risk matrix for the critical activities as shown in Figure 5.8.

The High Level Working Group is again consulted to seek agreement of the categorization of the risks to the critical activities. It is also important to understand what level of risk the organization is prepared to accept: the risk appetite. This will determine the level of resilience required and the amount of delay that is acceptable before continuity of operations is achieved.

From the risk assessment matrix in Figure 5.8 it can be seen that there are a number of options that can be applied to the critical activities, including accept, plan, manage or contain, and reduce or prevent.

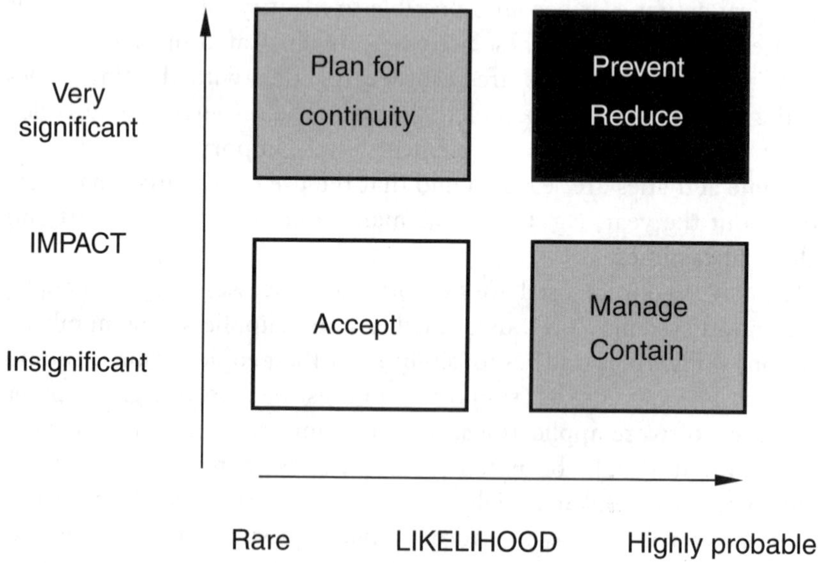

Figure 5.8 Example of a risk matrix

- Where the impact is insignificant and the likelihood of failure is rare then the High Level Working Group may decide to accept the risk and do nothing. This is a perfectly acceptable course of action and is driven by the risk appetite of the organization. The risk appetite may be influenced by the type and size of the organization, the sector, the stakeholders and the senior management's own approach to risk.
- Where the risk of failure is rare but the impact would be high it is essential that consideration be given to continuity and incident management plans that could deal with such a situation if it should arise. An example would be the classic case of a group of key staff winning the National Lottery and all failing to report for work.
- Where the risk level is high but the impact on the critical activity is low then the option is to mitigate the risk, that is to say to manage or contain the risk. If the risk of power failure is high then the provision of a standby generator and uninterrupted power supply will minimize the impact on critical activities. If the use of a single supplier would stop the activity then a second supplier would provide appropriate resilience to minimize the risk.
- Where the likelihood is very high and the impact would be considerable on the organization then urgent action will be needed. If it is not possible to reduce the risk then a decision may be taken to cease the activity. This may not be possible if it is a statutory requirement, e.g. to fight fires. Alternatives are to change or re-engineer the processes that support the activities or to transfer to an alternative location where the risk may be lower.

Insurance is often seen as a way of offsetting the consequences of some threats if they should occur. Although insurance can compensate for loss of facilities and earnings it will not protect brand and reputation. As customer loyalty to brands has weakened in recent years, organizations will have to consider how they will continue to service clients and customers whilst facilities are being rebuilt.

Business continuity planning is an element of the BCM process that is designed to ensure the organization can continue to deliver its products and services to clients and customers. The depth of planning applied depends upon the level of risk and impact on the organization of a disruption and the risk appetite of the organization's executive. The risk appetite will vary according to the size and style of the organization, the stakeholders and their interests, the sector in which it operates and the behaviour of competitors.

Once the High Level Working Group has agreed their approach to the risks associated with the delivery of the key products and services and the levels of continuity required if disruption should occur then it is possible to move to the next stage of the BCM process – strategy development.

Business continuity management strategies

The organization's approach to determining BCM strategies should be to implement appropriate measures to reduce the likelihood of incidents occurring, and/or reduce the potential effects of those incidents. In addition it is important to take due account of the resilience and countermeasure options already present within the organization in order to avoid the development of duplicate controls. The chosen strategies should provide continuity for the critical products or services of the organization during and following an incident (BS 25999-1:2006).

There are a range of BCM strategies that can be adopted to ensure continuity is achieved at a level and within a timeframe that is appropriate.

Full availability is provided where disruption to the activity cannot be tolerated. Examples would be 999 emergency call answering, e-banking activities or the A&E department in a hospital. Duplication of the activities and the resources that support them is the most appropriate way to achieve full availability. This may be the provision of a second online computer facility on a separate site running in parallel to the prime site served by a duplicated telecommunications network.

Where resumption of the activity can be phased over a period of time then it is possible to agree levels of resumption at fixed points in time. Consideration of the impact on the organization of the disruption over time will set the parameters for this approach, e.g. 25 per cent (critical point objective) to be available in two hours (critical time objective), 50 per cent in two days, full service in one week.

Examples of solutions which meet this approach are standby offices equipped with PCs and telephones where staff delivering critical activities can be accommodated at short notice, alternative suppliers or buffer stocks, the use of interim managers to fill critical posts, reciprocal arrangements with a similar organization.

There will be cost implications for each strategy chosen. Wherever possible these must be set against the cost of disruption. It must be appreciated that in some cases financial costs cannot be applied to the disruption of the activity. It may be that the greatest impact would be the damage to reputation or embarrassment for elected representatives.

In developing the BCM strategies it is important that they cover people, premises, technology (including ICT), data and supplies, and stakeholders. Consideration should be given to protecting the interest of the organization's stakeholders when the strategies are developed.

The decision on what level of resilience and continuity are to be applied within the organization falls to the executive and the High Level Working Group. They must sign off the strategies to support the critical activities, acknowledging the cost implications, before any planning activities can commence.

It is important to agree the priorities for the critical activities; these must be acknowledged by the individual owners of the activities. If this is not achieved then there will be conflict at the time of a disruption as managers seek to gain restoration of their activities first.

Business continuity planning

Experience has shown that organizations can be disrupted for many reasons. Business continuity planning has traditionally been based on known threats: loss of IT, loss of a building through fire, flooding, etc. In recent times, however, the UK has experienced some unexpected disruptions, including a widespread outbreak of foot and mouth disease, extensive disruptions to the rail network and a national shortage of oil-based fuels. In most cases existing business continuity plans (BCPs) did not cover these disruptions and the impacts they had on organizations.

Effective BCPs are written on the basis of recovering the key products and services and their supporting critical activities of the organization whatever the cause of the disruption. BCPs should provide a framework against which restoration can be achieved. The plan will list the critical activities with their previously agreed recovery point and recovery time objectives and the resources and processes that are used to support these activities. They will detail what actions must be taken and by whom to achieve continuity. As the plans are used under challenging and stressful circumstances they should be concise, simple and easy to follow.

Plans should provide answers to basic questions, such as:

- What is to be done?
- When?

- Where are the alternative resources located?
- Who is involved?
- How is continuity to be achieved?

A BCP may be part of a suite of interconnected plans covering emergency, business continuity, incident and recovery management. BCPs should be appropriate for the organization. A small organization, operating from one site, may only need a single document whilst larger organizations will need integrated corporate, divisional and business unit plans based on a common structure. Such plans must be synchronized to eliminate conflicts and ensure that agreed restoration priorities are achieved. A central BCM team or BCM coordinator must undertake this role.

The elements of a business continuity plan

The following paragraphs discuss the recommended elements of a BCP.

- *Roles and responsibilities.* The plan should clearly identify the roles and responsibilities of those who will be involved in delivering the plan to achieve continuity. It will identify the BC leader and key team members, and their deputies, to be assembled at the time of invocation. It will set out their levels of authority (including financial authorities) and to whom they must report their actions. It will also set out the point at which the responsibility for disruption management must pass to a higher level in the organization.
- *Invoking the plan.* The plan must indicate the circumstances under which it is to be invoked and who can authorize the invocation. It is essential that an organization moves at the speed of the incident if a crisis or disaster is to be avoided. The invocation of a business unit plan may need a lower level of authority to deal with a local incident. It is important that any invocation is flagged to senior management so that they are aware that an incident exists and can consider the wider implications for the organization. Instructions to that effect should be written into the plan.

  Call-out lists (call trees) should be included in the plan and details of where the team are to attend to manage the disruption (command centre). The command centre should be equipped with the appropriate level of communications and facilities to allow the incident to be managed effectively. 'Battle boxes' can be provided which include essential resources to assist the continuity team commence action.

- *Alternative locations*. Details of the standby locations should be included, together with maps, security arrangements to gain access, contractual terms and any other relevant information.
- *Recovery plans*. Small companies may include basic recovery plans within the BCP. These may be how to restore data or transfer telecommunications services to an alternative location. In larger organizations the recovery plans will be complex and will be separate documents owned by the unit responsible for providing the service, e.g. IT recovery plans for a major data centre. The BCP should identify the recovery plan owners and the key actions they will take.
- *Contact details*. The plan should include full details for internal and external contacts. These may include:
    - key senior management;
    - key operational staff;
    - emergency services;
    - local authority officers;
    - regulators and other compliance bodies;
    - suppliers;
    - key customers;
    - utility companies;
    - insurers.

  For external contacts it may be appropriate to include details of contracts, insurance policies, regulatory requirements, etc.
- *Vital documents and resources*. A list of vital documents and resources against each critical activity must be included and where these are located. Records of who is authorized to retrieve materials and security arrangements, e.g. passwords, will be required. Vital materials may include stationery, spare parts, specialist machinery and tools, etc.
- *Checklists and audit trails*. A simple checklist may be included to ensure the BC team completes mandatory tasks and provide a tracking process for task completion. With any major incident there will be a requirement for post-event inquiry and audit. It is vital therefore that a record is maintained of what actions were taken, why, when they were taken and by whom.
- *People issues*. Special consideration must be given to the needs of staff that may have been evacuated from the normal premises

without time to collect their personal belonging, e.g. money, credit cards, keys, identity cards, etc. There may be injuries or deaths and immediate family would have to be informed. The organization has a duty of care to their staff and these personal issues will need to be addressed as part of the BCP or a separate Emergency/Incident Plan.

- *Public profile.* Reputation and brand image are valuable assets for any organization, multinational or SME. Major disruptions will attract media interest in the organization who will judge how well it is handling the situation, exposing and exploiting any weakness or mistake very quickly to the wider world. An element of the BCP should be devoted to protecting the public face of the organization. Larger organizations may choose to have separate Incident Management plans that cover this area.

BCPs will be subject to change and therefore version control and configuration management must be applied. Each copy of the plan must be numbered and controlled distribution established. Where sensitive information is contained in the plan then it must be given the appropriate level of commercial confidentiality and security.

Plans may take various formats. They may be written as text or flow charts or produced by specialist software. They can be internet- and/or paper-based, held on a PDA or in a simple 'wallet' format. Within a large organization a common template may be used for the creation of BCPs. Whilst a template is useful as a guideline it must be recognized that no two organizations are the same and even locations within the same organization will have differences. The plan must therefore reflect the organization, not the organization be made to fit a standard template.

Ownership of the plan must be clearly identified. In larger organizations the business unit manager should be the owner. All plans must be regularly reviewed and signed off by the responsible owner.

Business continuity management as a culture

To be effective BCM must not be seen as a 'bolt-on' or another senior management 'passing initiative'. To be truly successful BCM must be integrated into the company culture. Before the process can start the Board or Executive team has to accept the importance and value of the BCM process. They need to encourage a management approach which contemplates the 'what ifs', or what might prevent them from delivering the organization's products/services. To be successful BCM must be 'owned' by everyone within an organization.

Many disruptions are caused by internal failures. Within many organizations there exists a blame culture that prevents people from flagging up problems. If the culture is about only wanting to hear the 'good news' then there will be a reluctance to draw attention to failings which may subsequently lead to disruptions.

All staff, including middle management, must be convinced that business continuity management is a serious issue for the organization and that they have an important role to play in maintaining the delivery of products and services to their clients and customers. It is essential that awareness and training programmes be established as part of the overall introduction of BCM.

Training must be given to all those who will be involved in the invocation of a plan. They must be familiar with the contents and the mechanisms that support it. The best form of training is exercising and rehearsing the plan; this is covered later in this chapter.

Raising awareness is done in two stages. The first is to ensure that all those in the organization are aware that BCM is being introduced and why. They will need to be convinced that this is a lasting initiative that has the support of the executive.

A technique which was used very successfully in the introduction of Total Quality Management in the 1980s was to hold team meetings at each level of the organization to introduce the concept and to ask the team to consider how they could improve the quality of their output. The same principle can be applied to BCM with the teams being asked to identify areas that prevent or impede the continuity of their area of operation. The key questions to ask such a group are the 'what ifs', since this style of question gets the group thinking about their contribution to continuity. Experience has shown that even at the lowest level employees are able to relate to the BCM concept and not only identify areas of potential disconnect but also possible solutions needed to maintain continuity.

Each organization will have a level of management that is particularly sceptical about the introduction of new initiatives; this is very often the middle management level. Particular emphasis must be given to gaining their support if BCM is to become part of the organizational culture. This management level will also have a large part to play in the initial charting of critical activities and processes, so gaining their support at an early stage is vital.

Once the BCPs have been produced it is important that all stakeholders are aware that the organization has BCPs in place to raise their level of confidence in the organization's ability to deal with disruptions.

Employees need to have confidence that their jobs will be protected whilst the disruption is being contained. It is critical that individuals know what actions they are required to take when the plan is invoked. When a recent large department store belonging to a major high street retailer caught fire the employees knew what to do the next day. Some went to previously designated alternative locations; others remained at home and rang a staff helpline for recorded advice. This contrasts with the example of a comprehensive plan that existed for a major UK government department where those people who were named in the plan were not aware that they had roles to play at the time of disruption.

New recruits to an organization must be made aware of the BCM policy and their part in the BCPs. This can be done by incorporating BCM material into the staff induction programme. Awareness of the overall BCM programme is maintained by using internal newspapers, emails, the organization's intranet, team meetings and broadcasts from senior management. These may highlight examples where the organization successfully managed an incident and praising those involved. It may also draw upon lessons learnt from external failures.

One major UK telecommunications company has included an element of continuity into management objectives and they have a comprehensive online training programme that all managers must undertake. A large UK local authority has included BCM objectives into their managers' performance related pay scheme. A forward-looking organization will include continuity in their mission statement, e.g. 'to continue to be the most successful supplier of . . . .' If the management's key objectives flow from such a mission statement they will also include continuity.

Stakeholders outside of the organization must also be made aware of the actions that will be taken at the time of a disruption. Customers will need to know how their supply of goods and services will be affected and when they can expect a return to normal working. Suppliers will need to know the alternative locations that they are required to deliver supplies to and also to have confidence that they will be paid. The banks and investors will need to have confidence that the management is handling the disruption effectively and that their investments are safe.

Regulators, legislators and others with statutory responsibilities will need to understand the alternative arrangements that are in place to meet the organization's statutory and regulatory requirements. The wider community may need to be informed of the actions that would be taken if the disruption could have a serious impact on their welfare, e.g. a chemical plant fire.

The purchasing department in the organization has an important role to play to ensure that key suppliers are made aware of the importance of BCM to the organization and the processes they should adopt to ensure continuity of supply. This applies to existing and new supply contracts. The publication of BS 25999-1 provides a useful basis on which to assess a supplier's BCM capability.

Those responsible for new product/service development should be encouraged to build continuity solutions into the design of the product/service and its supporting processes. It is easier and more cost effective to design-in continuity at the concept stage than add it as a 'bolt-on' after problems have arisen. One Australian bank will not allow a product to be launched onto the market unless an appropriate continuity solution is incorporated.

Exercising, maintaining and reviewing

BCM requires that effective plans be established to ensure an organization can respond to any incident. But the process does not stop at the planning stage. Plans are worthless unless they are rehearsed. Many examples exist where organizations have BCPs in place but the plans fail because they have not been rehearsed. In the UK research has shown that only 37 per cent of those organizations with plans test or rehearse them on an annual basis; 17 per cent never rehearse them at all (see Figure 5.9).

The rehearsal of plans is essential. There is not a plan created which will work first time; rehearsing ensures that disconnections and omissions within the plan are fixed before it is used in reality. 87 per cent of those that rehearsed found errors in their plans. It is far better to have found the errors at rehearsal than the first time the plan is invoked. Having found the errors it is essential that timed based actions are created to rectify the errors and omissions. Figure 5.10 shows the latest figures for UK organizations.

There are various forms of rehearsals but it important to test the systems, exercise the plans and rehearse the people.

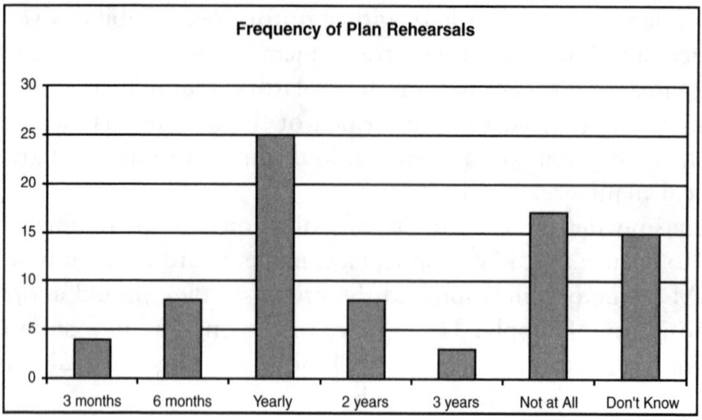

(from Chartered Management Institute BCM Awareness Research 2006)

Figure 5.9 Frequency of BCP rehearsals

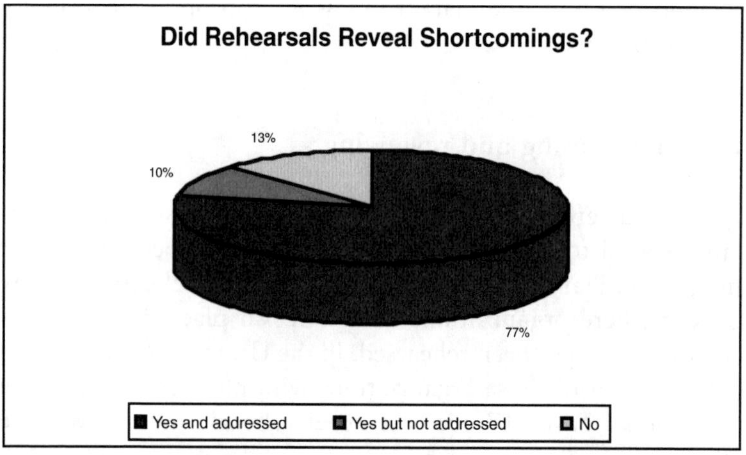

(from Chartered Management Institute BCM Awareness Research 2006)

Figure 5.10 Results of BCM rehearsals

Testing the systems may be ensuring that the standby generator starts when power is interrupted, that the data can be recovered from the backup source, that the telephone-divert arrangements do work. Testing should ensure that the technical systems work correctly and that the operating instructions are clear and valid for the equipment.

The tests should be as close to live working as possible, e.g. full load being taken by the generator.

Plans should be exercised to ensure they are comprehensive and realistic. The first exercise should be one to "prove the plan works' and should be sold as a learning exercise. It is not about 'pass or fail' but ensuring the plan is 'fit for purpose'. There are certain key rules to be observed with plan exercises. They should not 'risk' the organization, they must be practical and cost effective, be appropriate to the organization and designed to build confidence in the plan.

Exercises should be planned and observers appointed to note the way the BCM team handles the situation. Every effort must be made to gain full participation from those involved in the exercise.

There are various forms of exercise ranging from desk-top review, where the participants review and challenge the contents of the plan, through 'walkthroughs', where the interaction between players is assessed, to full plan test, where the site or building is shut down and a move undertaken to an alternative location.

Rehearsing the team players is vital. People demonstrate different characteristics when put under pressure. A real invocation will be a stressful situation and it is important to understand the strengths and weaknesses of the individuals concerned. In the UK the normal management culture decision-making is based on consensus with the maximum information being available to the parties. At times of plan invocation the management style may have to move to command and control, working with less than perfect information.

Different leadership styles are needed and it may be that the initial BCM team chosen may lack certain skill sets. Some of these can be acquired through training but often it will be necessary to change roles or even exclude people from the invocation team.

A log of all actions and outcomes must be made during the exercise and this must be reviewed as soon as possible after the event. It is a good idea that this review is carried out with the participants so they can express their own views on what went well or otherwise. The views of the independent observers should also be included.

A post-exercise report is completed which will include recommendations on actions to adjust the BCP. A senior manager of the unit in which the exercise was conducted should sign off the report and actions to be taken. This report will provide clear evidence to auditors that a BCM programme is being taken seriously within the organization. Fiqure 5.11 illustrates the various stages in an exercise process.

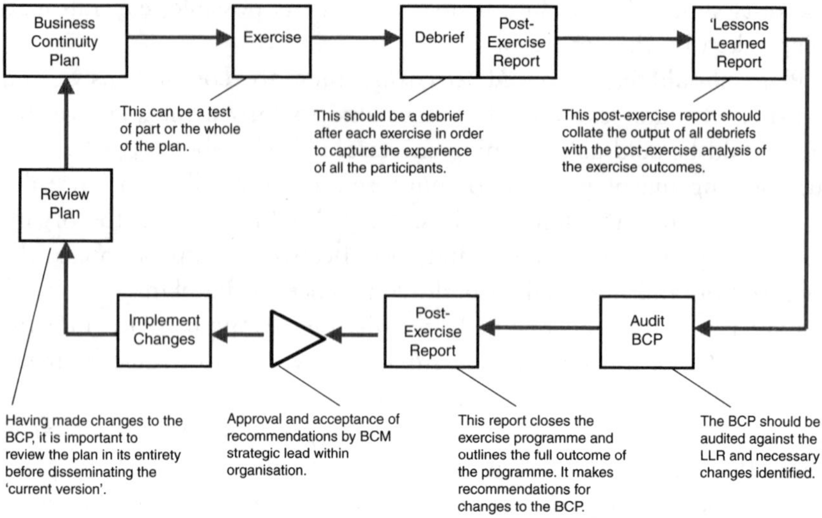

(from Emergency Preparedness 2005)

Figure 5.11 Business continuity plan exercise process

Maintaining the currency of the plan

Nothing stands still. Organizations are in a continued state of flux. Staff change roles and responsibilities, some will leave and new people join. Mergers, acquisitions, organic growth and downsizing means that structures and reporting lines will evolve. Suppliers and customers change, the regulatory and legal environments may be adjusted, political conditions in supply countries may become unstable. An outsourcing contract may change the responsibility for critical functions, e.g. IT outsourced to a third party. New products and services may be introduced, new sites opened or others closed. At the basic level contact details will always be changing.

Processes should be established in the organization whereby any changes that will affect business continuity are flagged up to the BCM coordinator or appropriate BCM lead. Adjustments to the BCP should be made if the changes are minor. If major changes have occurred it may be necessary to revisit the BIA to reassess the critical activities and supporting processes and resources. New continuity strategies may be required and the BCP changed. Any changes made to the BCM arrangements must be subject to the appropriate levels of 'sign-off'.

Notwithstanding any changes the BCM programme should be subject to an annual review to ensure that it is still current. An assessment should be made about the criticality of activities and their priority for recovery. Checks should be made to ensure that the supporting processes and resources are still correct. BCPs should be reviewed to ensure they are still appropriate and workable. An appropriate management level should sign off the reviews regardless if changes have or have not been made.

Appropriate staff will need to be made aware of any changes that affect the way continuity will be achieved in the organization. As mentioned before it is vital that version control is applied to BCM documentation and a process exists whereby updates are issued and old versions are withdrawn.

Reviewing the business continuity management process

The organization should, at appropriate intervals, review the BCM arrangements, to ensure they continue to be fit for purpose, adequate and effective. The results of the review may identify the possible need for changes to policy, strategy, objectives and other elements of the BCM arrangements. The frequency of the reviews is influenced by laws and regulations, changes occuring within the organization, the environment in which it operates or the requirements of stakeholders. The review may take the form of self assessment, internal or external audits.

It is critical that the BCM processes within an organization are subject to an independent audit to ensure that the processes are fit for purpose and effective. The auditors may be internal or external but must have an understanding of the basic principles and tenets of BCM.

The key objectives for the audit will be to:

- verify compliance with the organization's BCM polices, strategies and standards adopted by the organization;
- review the BCM solutions;
- verify that exercising of BCPs has taken place;
- verify that exercise reviews have been completed and actions taken to correct omissions and errors;
- highlight BCM deficiencies and issues and suggest resolutions.

An annual BCM audit should be made against agreed standards, guidelines or benchmarks. The British Standards Institution has issued a standard for BCM, BS 25999, that provides a useful framework for audit. The Civil Contingencies Act 2004 is supported by a set of guidelines which covers BCM and is appropriate for public sector bodies.

Conclusion

Despite the increased use of BCM in organizations there are still managers who continue to dismiss the need for continuity management, even in the face of such major disasters as September 11. Many have a strong belief that insurance will provide cover for any loss that they may suffer. This is not the case as losses are not restricted to material damage but include loss of revenues and customers. Research has shown that for every £30 of total loss incurred only £1 is recovered through insurance and the time between disasters and payments is considerable.

Organizations can be disrupted in many ways. Incidents including fire, flood, storm damage, internal and external vandalism or fraud, the failure of systems and loss of data, computer hacking, machinery breakdown or staff losses are only some examples. Added to this is the climate in which today's organization has to operate. The intolerance of customers and clients, their lack of loyalty and the demands of the banks for financial viability add considerable pressure at a time of disruption. If the organization is unable to manage a disruption correctly and quickly then it will rapidly turn to a crisis, then a disaster and the organization may well fail. The SME community is at greatest risk, yet they are the first to ignore the benefits of BCM.

As recent disasters around the world have demonstrated, it is not possible to predict all the events that can seriously disrupt an organization's ability to maintain the continuity of its key products and services. Because the unexpected will always occur there is a clear need to protect organizations by forward planning. Business continuity management is seen as a vital tool to achieve this.

References and recommended reading

Bland, M (1998) *Communicating out of a Crisis*. London: Macmillan Press.

Business Continuity Management 2006 (2006) London: Chartered Management Institute.

BS 25999-1: (2006) *Business Continuity Management – Part I: Code of Practice*. London: British Standards Institution.

Department of Trade and Industry (2005) *Operating and Financial Review*. See: http://www.dti.gov.uk/cld/financialreview.htm for details of current passage through Parliament into full legislation.

Great Britain (2004) Civil Contingencies Act 2004. London: The Stationery Office.

Hiles, A (2004) *Business Continuity: Best Practices*. Brookfield: Rothstein Associates Inc.

Knight, R F and Pretty, D J (2000) *The Impact of Catastrophes on Shareholder Value*. The Oxford Executive Research Briefings. Oxford: Templeton College, University of Oxford.

PAS 56:2003, *Guide to Business Continuity Management*. London: British Standards Institution.

Porter, E M (1998) *Competitive Advantage*. New York: Simon & Schuster.

Preparing for Emergencies, Guidance on Part 1 of the Civil Contingencies Act 2004 (2005) London: UK Cabinet Office.

Sharp, J (1999) *The Unifying Process*. Caversham: The Business Continuity Institute.

Turnbull, N *et al.* (1999) *Internal Control – Guidance for Directors on the Combined Code*. London: Institute of Chartered Accountants in England and Wales. Available at: http://www.icaew.co.uk/internalcontrol

6

Reputational Risk

Arif Zaman

Context

Much of the current material on reputation tends to concentrate exclusively on 'reputation management'. Too often this is completely synonymous with two areas which have negative connotations and are more about value destruction than value creation:

1. 'crisis management';
2. 'loss prevention'.

Reputational upside means that reputation risk can also be seen in terms of opportunities to be seized and value to be created. Innovative companies view risk through the lens of opportunity rather than just internal control and compliance, i.e. they see risk as both upside and downside, as an opportunity platform as well as a safety net. Implicit in this is moving from a reactive to a more proactive approach.

In fact the biggest reputational risk that a company may face is to deny that it has one.

Current approaches to reputation are neither 'strategic' nor integrated. Often there is a superficial and weak understanding of either reputation or risk (and often both). There are two reasons for this, one obvious, the other less so:

1. the use of both terms by so many people across functions and disciplines;
2. the way in which the meaning of language changes over time. Both 9/11 (highlighting the political/safety aspects of risk) and Enron/Andersen (highlighting the fragility of reputation when trust is lost) show how events can give rise to new twists on familiar words.

Post-Enron, regulators have stressed that

> the basic goal for directors should be the success of the company in the collective best interests of shareholders, but the directors should also recognise . . . the company's need to foster relationships with its employees, customers and suppliers, its need to maintain its business reputation, and its need to consider the company's impact on the community and the working environment. (Department of Trade and Industry, 2002)

This touches on three elements (Figure 6.1) that are integrally and increasingly linked and, when combined with understanding stakeholder expectations, form the key to unlocking the meaning of reputational risk for an international publicly quoted company – whether for the fund manager, board director or public regulator. Today no company concerned with value creation for its key stakeholders can ignore – or have knowledge gaps – in these areas.

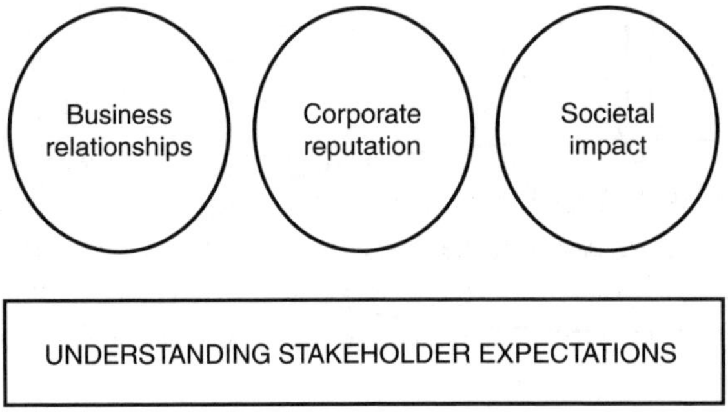

Figure 6.1 Stakeholder expectations

First, it is important to consider demand-side drivers. Fresh business challenges are demanding higher levels of trust across *all* stakeholders, as shown in Figure 6.2.

Second, it is important to consider supply-side drivers. The World Economic Forum's 2003 meeting in Davos took as its theme, 'Building Trust'. In a global public opinion survey, it found that 48 per cent of people express 'little or no trust' in global companies, with 52 per cent expressing similar scepticism about large national businesses. Interestingly, trust is even low when it comes to NGOs, trade unions and media organizations. Trust in business executives is also low (see Figure 6.3) (World Economic Forum, 2003).

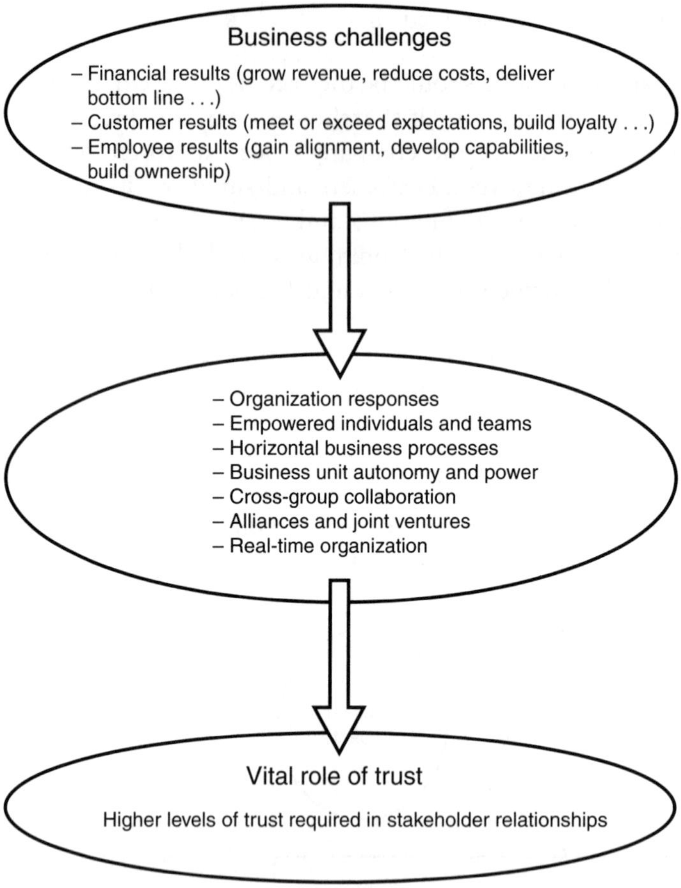

(from Shaw, 1997)

Figure 6.2 Business challenges

Loss of reputation is now the greatest risk facing most large publicly quoted companies and awareness of its importance is fast spreading to the public sector. The increasing complexity, competitiveness and internationalization of markets, coupled with a greater focus on issues of corporate responsibility, have placed the effective management both of business risk and financial risk at the very centre of a company's operations. Companies have found by experience that, if they lose the trust of a particular group of stakeholders, the costs can be very high, enduring beyond the economic life of a tangible asset.

To understand reputational risk, one must first understand reputation. Various definitions have been suggested:

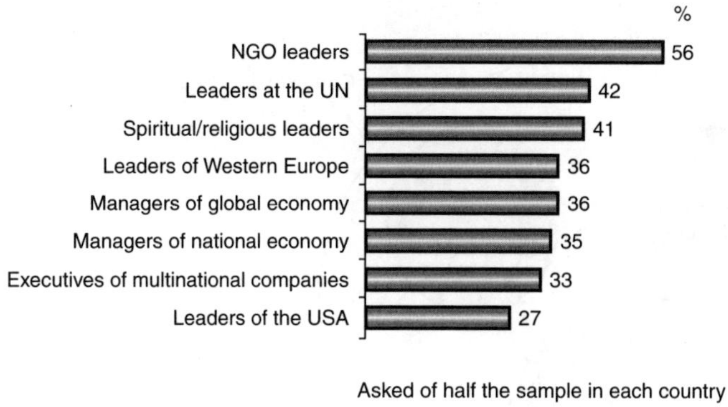

(from World Economic Forum, 2003)

Figure 6.3 Trust in leaders – percentage saying 'a lot' and 'some trust' (average across all 15 countries surveyed)

- a collective representation of a company's past actions and results that describes the company's ability to deliver valued outcomes to multiple stakeholders;
- the shared values of the company by its stakeholders that drive the trust, confidence and support an organization can expect from the reputation held by a person;
- how each stakeholder group experiences the company's brand through its operations and conduct in everyday situations; and
- how close these experiences are to what those same groups expect the company to do in the same situations.

The difference between them is a measure of corporate reputation. Thus:

reputation = experiences – expectations.

Based on their work with boards and senior managers over many years, researchers at Henley Management College have developed a framework which usefully focuses on three key elements:

1. experiences,
2. feelings, and
3. behaviours.

Figure 6.4 shows the interrelationship between these three elements.

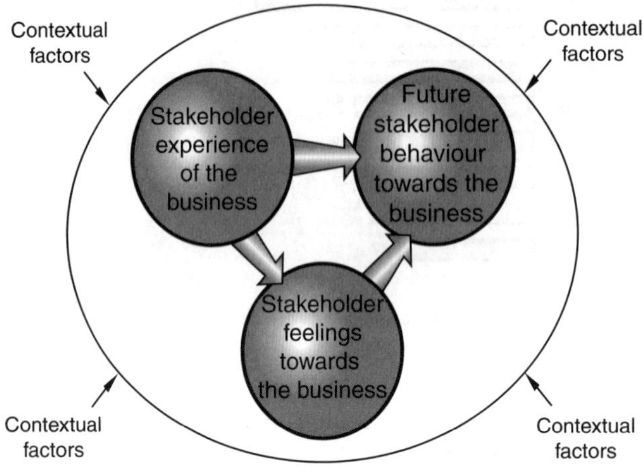

Business behaviour and reputation	A business's reputation is built upon the relationships it has with its stakeholders. Important relationship issues include the various kinds of benefits (tangible and intangible) offered to stakeholders and how stakeholders judge the past behaviour of the business.
Stakeholder trust and commitment	These lie at the core of effective relationships. These attitudes incorporate views of a business's reliability and dependability and whether these are likely to endure in an uncertain world. They also indicate whether stakeholders are willing to put effort into maintaining their relationships with the organization.
Long-term supportive relationships	These provide the basis for increasing the resources available to the organization, extending the scope of interactions with stakeholders, generating collaborative and innovative opportunities, seeking constructive solutions to problems and resolving potential conflicts.

(from MacMillan *et al.*, 2004)

Figure 6.4 A model of business relationships

All these definitions provide key elements (such as delivery against expectations through people's experiences) but the one used here is:

> *Corporate reputation is how key stakeholders perceive that your company or its employees behaves.* (Zaman, 2004)

This implies a short and simple focus on *key stakeholders*, any gap in *perception* (which is where the risk can exist) – whether this comes from emotion, attitude or experience – and, crucially, *corporate behaviour*. It also links corporate and individual reputation, whether this applies to the CEO or the front-line customer service employee. As the Deputy Director at the DTI's Strategy Unit put it to me: 'Perception is a determinant of behaviour – both individual and corporate.' Individuals are never too small to be meaningfully involved. Companies are not faceless monoliths, leviathans or globalization monsters; they are made up of people who have values.

Reputational risks do not happen in isolation. They interact with processes that are psychological (our emotions), social (our networks) and cultural (our environment). It is this interaction that underpins how we experience risk, whether hard or soft.

Pressures on companies from key stakeholders are framed by reputational agents. As the World Bank, which first coined the term (Leechor, 1999), has noted:

> they include accounting and auditing professionals, lawyers, investment bankers and analysts, credit rating agencies, consumer activists, environmentalists, and media. Keeping an eye on corporate performance and insider behaviour, these reputational agents can exert pressure on companies to disclose relevant information, improve human capital, recognise the interests of outsiders, and otherwise behave as good corporate citizens. They can also put pressure on government through their influence over public opinion.

The influence of NGOs, especially after the riots at the Seattle WTO meeting, the growth of the media in an electronic age and the power exerted by the rating agencies in assessing corporate health (highlighted by the collapse of Enron) are all evidence of how corporate reputation is framed and shaped for key stakeholders at least in part by these agents.

For some, risk assumed a fresh meaning after 9/11. What this means, with the breakdown of trust, is a need to understand what is needed to develop strategy under conditions of uncertainty. Companies need to move from a 'make and sell' mindset to one of 'sense and respond', as illustrated in Figure 6.5.

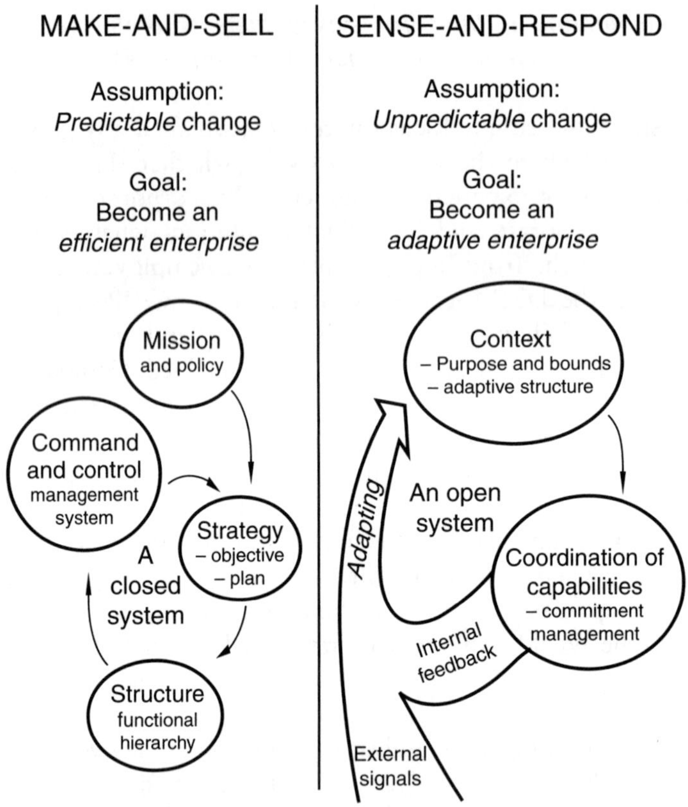

(from Haeckel, 1999)

Figure 6.5 Two ways to think about a business

But *how* can companies respond?

1. By making strategic investments (for example, in reputation-building areas and actions).
2. By actively monitoring various sources of uncertainty that can affect stakeholder expectations.

Taking a risk and being innovative are clearly linked and taking a risk to improve a corporate reputation is not in itself negative.

On one level the predominant approaches to risk are so narrow because it is often in the professional interest of the main protagonists (the insurance industry and communication consultants) to emphasize loss and crisis management, respectively. More constructively, this is because of a lack of balance in asking the right questions (whether for the board member or division head) by focusing on two areas above all else:

1. the upside as well as downside;
2. human/behavioural aspects as well as process and system driven approaches.

Significantly, both areas are central to reputational risk and value creation through understanding two associated areas that are key. This is illustrated in Figure 6.6.

> *Reputational risk is the comparison that key stakeholders make between how a company or its employees are expected to behave and how they actually behave.* (Zaman, 2004)

Key point: reputational risk can therefore be positive or negative.

Reputation needs to be seen as a source of risk in its own right and/or as a consequence of other risks occurring. However, what is

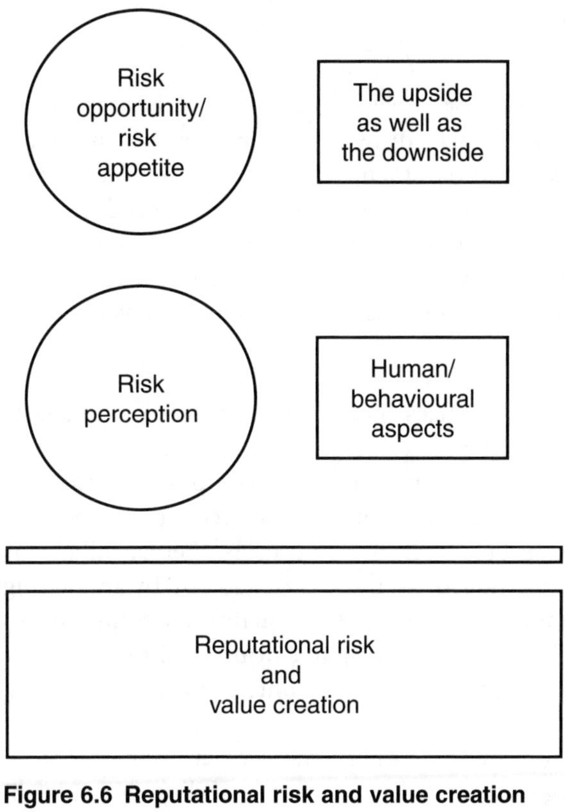

Figure 6.6 Reputational risk and value creation

striking is how definitions tend, coming mainly from the insurance industry or communications consultants, to take negative approaches synonymous with 'loss/insurance' and 'crisis'. A key reason may be a failure to focus on the definition of reputation and risk which sees reputation as being about the quality of relationships with stakeholders and risk as having an inherent upside. Moreover there is scarce recognition of the significance of emotional factors in framing expectations in key stakeholder relationships (i.e. amongst customers, employees and investors), set out below, which are not linked.

Reputational risk and key stakeholders

Reputational risk needs to be understood above all else in relation to an organization's key stakeholders (customers, consumers, employees and shareholders). If a company is able to do so, much of its efforts in the area of reputational risk will be productive and purposeful. This section addresses how key stakeholders might be affected by reputational risk.

Customers

If companies focus excessively on satisfaction, they run the risk of not understanding why customers feel drawn to return or the emotional meaning of the service experience to them. Moreover if customer service staff rely on customers to report when they have experienced negative emotional reactions, service providers run the risk of missing subtle emotional communications that may not be expressed verbally.

There are a number of common misconceptions about customers as stakeholders.

- 'Customer satisfaction influences business performance' – this only tells part of the story. Market-perceived relative quality is correlated with profitability. The term 'market' encompasses more than just customers; it includes all potential sources of revenue – customers, competitors' customers and non-users. 'Perceived' means quality as defined and judged by the customer, not by marketing planners or consultants. 'Relative' means quality as compared to the competition, a key differential in the firm's ability to attract and keep customers. 'Quality' in this context means exceeding customer expectations.
- 'Customer satisfaction means doing whatever it takes to keep customers happy regardless of the cost' – the ability to establish,

maintain and build customer relationships depends on the perceived value of the offering. Moreover customer budgets that are overshot in the first quarter do not provide the means to deliver customer value in the final quarter.

- 'Customer satisfaction leads to customer loyalty' – customer loyalty is best understood as a pattern of behaviour. It is the likelihood of staying with the main (i.e. most often used) service provider rather than switching to a realistic alternative.
- The primary drivers of loyalty in commoditized sectors are often expressed in comments like 'I tend to use the same shop/bank/airline/computer manufacturer without really thinking about it' or 'I can't be bothered spending time choosing between what different companies offer.' This does not build reputation. Drivers like 'I tend to stick with products/services I know and trust' minimizes the reputational risk and builds reputation.
- Secondary drivers may relate to convenience and choice where customers find it difficult to know the differences between what companies offer.

Two forces are at play in customer loyalty across business-to-consumer markets (BTC), for example, in BA's relationships with its passengers, and business-to-business (BTB) markets, such as in BA's relationships with its air cargo customers which is handled through business intermediaries such as freight forwarders or direct with large corporate customers themselves (see Figure 6.7).

Most marketing campaigns fail to acknowledge the growing importance of how an 'inert' mindset can often be the real cause of apparent loyalty – not brand benefits. This can increase reputational risk. One way to overcome this is to build strong perceptions of relative brand value.

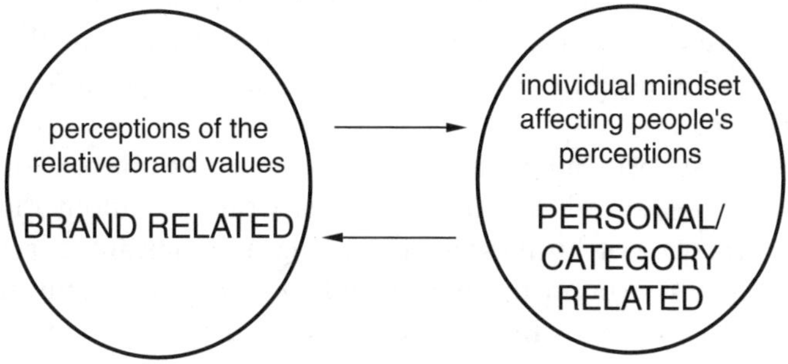

Figure 6.7 Customer loyalty across BTC and BTB markets

Different factors make different contributions in determining people's perceptions of the service they have received. The absence of some factors – for example, reliability – can have a strong impact on dissatisfaction levels. However, the presence of reliability may sometimes be taken for granted and hence increased performance may not lead to higher satisfaction levels. Moreover, people may be willing to tolerate small movements in some of these factors without any impact upon their satisfaction with a service.

Types of factors that affect people's perceptions of the service they have received are:

- Dissatisfying factors. If such factors are perceived to be inadequate, then dissatisfaction will result, but any increase in performance above adequacy has little effect on perceptions. For example, the presence of a dirty fork is likely to make customers dissatisfied, but a very clean fork is unlikely to add to satisfaction.
- Satisfying factors are those which, when improved beyond adequacy, have a positive effect on perceptions. When these factors are absent though there is little effect on satisfaction. For example, if a waiter does not remember you from your last visit to the restaurant you are unlikely to be dissatisfied, but if he does and also remembers your favourite wine, you are likely to be delighted.
- Critical factors are those where changes in performance affect both satisfaction and dissatisfaction ratings. In the example of a restaurant, slow service can cause dissatisfaction, while speedy service can increase satisfaction.
- Neutral factors: satisfaction is not responsive to changes in performance.

Empowered consumers are demanding ever higher standards in terms of quality and value for money. Consumers are more 'cash-rich, time-poor' than they have ever been. Some strategies for dealing with this that enhance reputation need to meet or exceed customer expectations, often not at great cost.

Consumers are also becoming more aware and active on a wide range of environmental, social and ethical issues. Concerns about the ethical working practices of businesses are having a significant effect on purchasing decisions around the world and the company's ethical approach must be in step with those of its valued customers. This is no substitute for a company being clear what it stands for and reputational risks can grow when gaps develop unchecked between how a

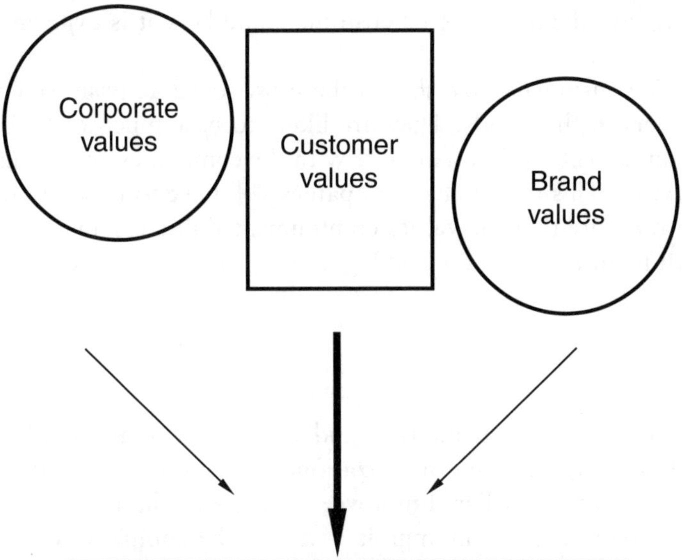

WHAT DO WE DO?	HOW DO WE DO IT?
Understand the value of time.	Minimize time-wasting on cumbersome processes.
Manage relationships through flexibility and problem-sharing.	Encourage a team approach by front-line customer service staff.
Identify opportunities to leave a positive customer experience.	Exceed expectations by adding surprise little touches in service delivery.
Do not lose sight of the value of personal contact.	Call centres are a prime culprit for this in the number of auto prompts required before it is possible to speak to a live person.
Fairness – a more flexible attitude to look for alternative solutions to problems.	Not telling customers there is only one way; focus on outcome not process.

Figure 6.8 Customer, corporate and brand values

company behaves in the minds of its customers and how it is *expected* to behave.

Generation Y consumers have shown the most social activism since the baby boomers in the 1960s. They are likely to base much of their consumption on the values they associate with the companies providing goods and services. This means that companies will have to make a far greater effort to ensure that the values communicated to consumers are consistent with its internal values (see Figure 6.8). If it is not, they will be exposed.

Employees

There is a close link between internal and external reputation. This reflects the relationship between organizational and corporate identity that has been referred to earlier. Employees' images of the reputation of the company represents an intangible asset for the company which needs to be nurtured if performance is to be maximized. This is the 'employer brand' equity in the minds of its employees, just as the awareness of, attitudes and behaviours towards a product brand such as Shell is the brand equity of Shell.

Employees' perceptions of the organization builds up over a sustained period. Even so, business history's value as a business tool for management development is often overlooked. It can be an extremely useful resource in a world where the labour market is becoming more flexible and many companies turn over their entire workforce in a regular cycle. Moreover corporate history can help us to learn from past successes and failures and avoid reinventing the wheel. Organizational memory and corporate amnesia matter to companies and affect employee perceptions and behaviour. Key elements are set out in Table 6.1.

Internal reputational risks increase when a focus on talent leads to a mindset which devises policies on individuals at the expense of teams and organizational systems. The 'war for talent' is to some extent a distraction from companies' real task of devising cultures and management styles that fully maximize human and intellectual capital, not just the skills and knowledge of an elite cadre.

Moreover 'war for talent' imagery overlooks the fact that often effective teams outperform even more talented collections of individuals, that individual talent and motivation is partly under the control of what companies do and that what matters to organizational success is the set of management practices that create a trusting culture. However, it is not just that the war for talent is the wrong lens through which to

Table 6.1 Organizational memory and corporate amnesia

Organizational memory	*Corporate amnesia*
Perhaps the most important constituent of any institution's durability.	When organizational memory disappears, the organization's ability to learn and develop naturally is interrupted, often with expensive consequences.
For the individual company, whose staff can today be displaced every five years, corporate 'memory' is increasingly other employers' experiences, which is not necessarily always relevant.	Is it greater for larger organizations?
Organizations have already paid for their memory at least once. If it is not to pass beyond reach, it needs to be managed professionally – just like any other corporate asset.	
It disappears through inherent short and selective memory recall, natural wastage when employees leave to join other organizations, the retirement of key individuals and/or redundancy, even through job rotation.	

see organizational success. Fighting the war for talent itself can cause problems.

Companies that adopt a talent war mindset often end up venerating outsiders and downplaying the talent already inside the company. This can in turn set up competitive, zero sum dynamics that makes internal learning and knowledge transfer difficult, activate the self-fulfilling prophecy in the wrong direction and create an attitude of arrogance instead of an attitude of wisdom. For all of these reasons, even fighting the war for talent may be hazardous to an organization's health and detrimental to doing the things that will make it successful.

Too many current and future leaders are poorly prepared for their roles. Some common failings include:

- to grow emotionally: the leaders who have high intelligence quotients (IQs) and low emotional quotients (EQs) are often clever and charismatic but destructive;
- to make creative connections: leaders who see the connections between A and B and B and C rarely see how A and C connect. They miss the more subtle patterns and ones that extend beyond the quarterly reporting period;

- to empathize: they often look at numbers or surface behaviour and lack an understanding of others' true needs and aspirations;
- to manage ego: deadly self-inflation, or hubris, frequently leads to derailment or nemesis;
- to overcome personal alienation and boredom: these leaders simply stop feeling the exhilaration of learning.

How can companies respond in ways that strengthen, not weaken, reputation and trust? They need to move beyond a product, service and distribution focus and elevate relationship building by:

- developing skills and values that lead to increased empathy and knowledge among all who would be part of relationship building;
- measuring and rewarding appropriate relationship-building activities.

They also need to acknowledge that feedback and relationship programmes are the most effective leadership development strategies.

The employer brand establishes the identity of the firm as an employer. It encompasses the firm's values, systems, policies and behaviours toward the objectives of attracting, motivating and retaining the firm's current and potential employees.

There is a need – especially in big, diversified companies – to convey unified, coherent brand messages in ways that are appropriate to different sites and cultures. Common risks are not starting branding efforts early enough, not making it intensive enough or senior management failing to give employee branding a high enough priority, in actions as well as words. Employee branding carries several reputational risks and these are set out in Table 6.2.

In the face of unexpected declines in hiring needs for entry-level talent, a number of US employers have recently been forced to rescind or defer a significant volume of campus job offers. Some of these companies have employed a variety of creative strategies (e.g. pre-employment severance packages, long-term start date deferrals) aimed at quelling the pain associated with such actions. From a strategic perspective, these tactics (and their accompanying publicity) represent an investment in employment brand – over the long term, such investments might mitigate potentially devastating levels of employment brand-erosion on key campuses. Perhaps most notably, these brand-building investments have been deemed valuable enough to survive waves of cost-cutting initiatives at many of these same organizations.

Table 6.2 Reputational risk and employee branding

Employee branding initiative	*Risk*
The brand the company creates says, 'we are a great place to work'.	But how does this broad claim differentiate the company not only from its competitors but from any other company offering the same brand message?
The brand is just the company's mission statement rehashed.	But how many mission statements really differentiate companies and how many express what is at the company's core? How many employees actually believe mission statements – and how many become empty statements, subject to employee derision.
Management (or consultants) create a brand for the company and 'parachute' it to the employees.	In such a situation it is questionable if employees buy into the brand – or even if they understand it.
The company creates a brand because the competition has created a brand.	The result is unlikely to capture the true essence of the firm. The brand will not be true or complete if it is drafted out of fear or only as a reaction or response.
The company creates its employer brand but it remains a separate effort – with a different message – from the marketing brand.	Effective brand efforts need to be unified and mutually reinforcing.
The company creates marketing and employer brands with the same message.	The connections between the two are shady at best and inexplicable to the employees.

Shareholders

Reputational risk in financial markets is driven in large part by market sentiment. There is, however, seldom any analysis of what market sentiment is, even less how it operates. Essentially market sentiment is a way of describing the central mood that drives individual share prices, sectors and the equity market as a whole. It is an emotional reaction to a piece of corporate or other stock-market related news. It can affect individual companies and sectors (for example, airlines after 9/11) and can continue for weeks or even months. Sentiment is a residual – the element in a share price that cannot be explained by reference to the fundamentals.

The best way to view market sentiment is as a pair of sunglasses which enable the market to view any announcement as always bad news or always good news. Thus the same two companies, one with a positive backing, a good feeling to it, a positive response, a positive branding image within the City, can come out with the same news item as a company with a weak corporate branding. Handling it well against handling it badly can see a share price increase 10 per cent instead of falling 30 per cent. What this means is the market either views one item of news as the glass being half full or as being half empty. An example would be current market conditions where, due to economic and geopolitical uncertainty, the market views everything as a glass half empty because it has bad news about the economy and the whole of the market. This can increase reputational risk for a particular company or sector.

This is made worse where there is the slightest doubt about a company's credibility, honesty, the opacity of its accounts – where even minor items hidden away can trigger more negative feeling towards a company or sector. This may relate to subsidiaries, franchises, finance leases – anything that will affect the company's reputation when people look at that side. If confidence is shaken, rumours will go round the City rapidly and people will not take the risk of buying after a profits warning even if the stock is cheap. The value of the company will then sink further and further and eventually may even disappear or be taken over. Thus market sentiment is important to manage to give each company a cushion against the fact that there will be unexpected bad news somewhere along the line.

A positive sentiment can often be viewed if a sector or company is perceived as well-run – when analysts do not have doubts about it or have questions about the honesty of the management. The attitude in the City is: 'So what if they've had a profits warning, I'll buy after the profits warning' and so it is the life jacket that enables the company to come up again and survive. This can increase reputational opportunity.

If everyone in the market knows the consensus estimate – the one the company has helped develop and fully expects to beat, if only marginally – they also know that the quarterly earnings report will offer little or no valuable information unless it is negative. The focus then turns to estimating how much the company's estimate will exceed the consensus estimate. This process is accelerated by the internet which has led to a proliferation of gossip and news easily available to everybody. Financial gurus of various sorts publish online the letters of privileged information that they used to address to their corporate clients. Even in a bear market and with greater regulatory scrutiny after an abuse of trust by several highly paid analysts, the 'whisper numbers' matter.

Availability of information, however, does not guarantee accuracy and whisper numbers themselves fall far short of being purely unbiased. Nonetheless academic research supports the view that whisper numbers are more important to market prices than consensus estimates. Nearly 70 per cent of companies that met the consensus estimate but failed to live up to whispered expectations saw their share prices drop over a five day period and more than 56 per cent saw it drop over a 24 hour period.

The key message is, although they are less influential than they were at the height of the internet bubble, whisper numbers still exist and companies need to acknowledge that a weak reputation in the market (e.g. in regularly revising profits forecasts) fuels their use. This matters because whisper numbers reinforce a short-term orientation and increase the amount of time and energy being spent just prior to the earnings announcements.

All this has made successful communication and management of people's expectations probably the number 1 or number 2 priority for a CEO. The Head of Equities Strategy for a big 4 UK bank has described how this works (Zaman, 2004):

> From the point of view of the share price in the short term and given the fact that chief executives tend to be pretty short these days, s/he may well be better managing expectations than managing the company. That suggests that it's a vital thing to do and if you look at the people who lose their jobs as chief executives it's almost invariably as a result of mismanagement of investment and financial expectations. That may well be, and almost invariably is, combined with a big push factor from underneath. Somebody who is mismanaging expectations has probably a) got a company that is disappointing and therefore there's bad news to bring forward and b) is trying to gloss over it and so is unpopular within his own business. But investors don't see that and they don't get into the depth of the business. They just see the chief executive or the finance director and so managing those expectations badly tends to end up with people losing their job.

When asked about the secret to British Airways success in its transformation from public utility to publicly quoted company, Lord King, BA's late Chairman, once confided that it was all down to a ruthless focus on cash flow (Zaman, 2004). We need to probe this to understand how it connects to expectations. The value of a company is the present value of the expected cash flows on the company and implicit in these expected cash flows and the discount rates used are investors' views about the company, the behaviour and credibility of its management and the potential for excess returns.

- *Risk is measured relative to expectations*: the risk in a company does not come from whether it performs well or badly but from how it does relative to expectations.
- *Good companies do not always make good investments*: it is not how well or badly a company is managed that determines stock returns but how well or badly managed it is, relative to expectations.

Managers can respond by:

1. *Focusing on information about the value drivers.* The requirements of the Operating and Financial Review (OFR) under changes to UK company law are a good place to start (discussed later in this chapter).
2. *Finding out what is expected of them.* If mangers are going to be judged against expectations, it is critical that they gauge what those expectations are. While this translates for many companies into keeping track of what analysts are estimating earnings per share to be in the next quarter, there is more to it than this. Understanding why investors value the company the way they do, and what they think its differential (rather than pure competitive) advantages are, is much more important in the long term. Central to this understanding is a strong relationship with investors where communication is trusted, open, clear and consistent.
3. *Learning to manage expectations.* When companies first go public, managers and insiders, abetted by their PR consultants, sell the idea that their company has great potential and should be valued highly. While this is perfectly understandable, managers have to change roles after they go public and learn to manage expectations. Specifically they have to be brave or humble enough and less macho in talking down expectations. This may be when they feel that their company is being set up to do things that it cannot accomplish. Again, though, some companies damage their credibility when they talk down expectations incessantly, even when they know the expectations are reasonable.

4. *Not delaying the inevitable.* No matter how well a company manages expectations, there are times when managers realize they cannot do this any more, because of changes in the sector or the overall economy. While the temptation is strong to delay revealing this to financial markets, often by shifting earnings from future periods into the current one or using accounting ploys (which still persist post-Enron as the regulatory investigation into Ahold suggests), it is far better to have the courage to deal with the consequences immediately. This may mean reporting lower earnings than expected and a lower share price (to maintain trust) but companies that delay their day of reckoning tend to be punished much more.

The UK Company Law Review White Paper (Department of Trade and Industry, 2002) indicated that companies should provide more qualitative and forward-looking reporting, in addition to information that is quantitative (e.g. the balance sheet), historical (e.g. the financial results in the past year) or about internal company matters (e.g. the size of the workforce). Moreover information about future plans, opportunities, risks and strategies are seen as just as important to users of financial reports as a historical review of performance.

How does all this link with reputational risk?

Best practice is emerging fast and from interesting quarters. Listed public companies in Australia will now have to report annually on their corporate governance procedures in relation to certain principles and will have to identify and explain any divergence from them. Specifically corporate governance guidelines state that the board's risk oversight and management policy should include a focus on 'reputation risk – the potential in loss or gain from changes in *community* expectations of corporate behaviour'.

This is not quite leading edge thinking – as it restricts the term to community. As we have seen, reputational risk is a much more powerful creator of corporate value if seen in relation to an organization's key stakeholders – customers, employees and shareholders (without which a commercial organization will have no resources or capabilities to deliver anything of value to the community). What is useful though about the Australian Stock Exchange's Listing Rules is that for the first time a major or probably any stock exchange/regulatory authority uses the language of *expectations of corporate behaviour*.

The role of the non-executive director is under more scrutiny than ever before. Codes of practice from the Cadbury and Hampel committees (Cadbury *et al.*, 1992; Committee on Corporate Governance,

1998), along with increasing pressure from institutional investors and judicial requirements and most recently the Higgs review (Higgs, 2003), have brought about a focus on the changing role of the non-executive director and the expectations attached to that role.

Non-executive directors (NEDs) are required to have a view of the company's affairs which is independent from that of the executive directors. They are expected to get sufficiently close to the business to understand its risks in some detail while maintaining both a strategic and monitoring position. They now have three problems in particular:

1. There is a danger that, as a result of recent events, NEDs will be expected to become all things to everyone. For example, whilst they have a monitoring and watchdog role, they are not auditors and neither do they have the resources ostensibly available to auditors to investigate independently or to verify all the information which management provides them.
2. They have time constraints which are often not adequately compensated for. On the whole, most NEDs are expected to spend around 24 days a year working for their companies. This means that it would take them around 10 years in the business to work the same number of days as a full-time employee works in each year of employment.
3. The recent decision of the Board of Equitable Life to sue its former directors has highlighted the financial risk which NEDs take on in addition to the reputational risk of which they should be aware (though Higgs made several suggestions on director liability to address this).

Relying on management to provide enough information to enable the non-executive directors to carry out their role is not sufficient and directors must know the right questions to ask to ensure they have the information necessary to carry out their duties efficiently. In this the role of the chairman is key. This includes the promotion of constructive relationships, management of the discussion processes, encouraging challenging and effective contributions in board meetings and ensuring appropriate information flows. The building of trust between all members of the board will also be part of this process and will enhance board performance.

The Higgs review (2003) acknowledges that corporate governance provides the architecture of accountability – the structures and processes to ensure companies are managed in the interests of their owners.

But architecture in itself does not deliver good outcomes. The review therefore also focuses on the conditions and behaviours necessary for non-executive directors to be fully effective.

There are several specific references to reputation.

1. 'Directors' duties are to act for the success of the company for the benefit of its shareholders as a whole. In determining how best to promote the success of the company, directors must, where relevant, take account of "material factors." These include long as well as short term consequences of their actions, the need to foster business relationships, including with employees, suppliers and customers, impact on communities and the environment, *business reputation* and fairness between different shareholders.' This is consistent with the changes in the Company Law Review in the White Paper (Department of Trade and Industry, 2002). It also matches the relationship-driven view of corporate reputation in relation to an organization's key stakeholders.
2. 'The composition of a board sends important signals about the values of the company. A commitment to equal opportunities which can be of motivational as well as *reputational importance* is inevitably undermined if the board itself does not follow the same guiding principles.' Diversity amongst NEDs for women and especially for ethnic minorities is now a reputational risk for companies. This is because they need visible practices as well as paper policies to demonstrate corporate commitment to equal opportunities as a tangible expression of their values. Moreover, given the weak position of many companies in this area, action on diversity provides a reputational opportunity and can increase motivation amongst current and potential executives and NEDs.
3. 'At a time when the perceived risks associated with being a non-executive director are growing . . . encouraging greater provision of [directors' and officers'] insurance, while it might reduce the personal exposure of directors, would not remove [their] *reputational risk* and paradoxically it would mean that there would be more to gain financially in taking action against directors.' NEDs have to live with a reputational risk that is individual as well as corporate. This could go with them and could apply in their membership of other Boards (perhaps one reason why Higgs recommends a maximum that 'a full time executive director should not take on more than one non-executive directorship, nor become chairman, of a major company' and that 'no individual should chair the board of more than one major company').

Long-term fiduciary duty also extends to being clear about behaviour with specialist advisors. One area where companies are increasingly vulnerable is in their relationships with remuneration consultants, who have a vested interest in designing ever more lucrative pay schemes for companies. Often they are hired directly by the management benefiting from such schemes rather than by independent board remuneration committees. BP and Diageo are amongst the very few FTSE 100 companies that have appointed consultants who do not also advise the management.

Globalization, international relationships and responsibilities

Political risk is usually understood to be something to do with regulatory risk, country instability, security consultancy and insurance. This is of limited value in the context of companies and reputational risk. It also ignores the fact that, as a result of globalization (and the backlash to it), political risk is becoming defined in broader ways. These include societal drivers and the actions of non-governmental players (though not necessarily NGOs but also trade unions, think tanks and academia). Moreover political risk needs to be seen as both the actions of legitimate government authorities but also as events caused by factors outside the control of government. This definition clearly implies that companies' political risks are increasingly subject to societal conditions and societal expectations.

There are two ways companies can respond.

1. The first – and more obvious – is more internally driven and deals with the areas over which companies can still exert some control even at times of increased geopolitical risk. This takes a more transaction and quantitative-based approach: increase investment in security, ensure meticulous compliance to corporate and government safety and security measures are in place. In fact the more effective approaches will be those where this is seen simply as part of the culture and the way that people behave.

   Two examples of how companies need to respond to supply chain risk – in goods and services – show this in action.

   An example for manufacturing companies is where US Customs are now expecting companies that import and export products to be aware not only of their own means of security, but that of their clients. The logic is that, should there be another attack on the US, only members of the partnership would be able to move cargo across the borders or through US ports.

An example in the service sector is anti-money laundering. Since 9/11 there have been a great many changes in the anti-money laundering laws and regulations in the UK, the US and many other jurisdictions. While some of these changes are a response to the corporate governance crisis, others owe more to the events of 9/11 or merely the natural evolution of anti-money laundering laws. Money laundering law now encompasses the proceeds of any crime, no matter how insignificant the crime or the proceeds and no matter where the crime was committed so long as it would have been a crime if it was committed in the UK. Moreover money laundering regulation is being expanded to encompass the insurance industry, law and accounting, property and dealers in luxury goods.

2. The second response is more externally driven and takes more of a qualitative and relationship-based perspective. It also implies that this is not something that companies can solve on their own (or even should) but that, through working with others, there is more chance of success than failure. This recognizes that action in Afghanistan may have dealt with 'the symptoms' of terrorism but it does not reduce the need to tackle the causes of that outrage. This has been well put by Maleeha Lodhi, twice Pakistan's Ambassador to the US (the last during 9/11), currently the Ambassador in the UK and the first woman editor of an Asian newspaper, who said: 'We must ensure that the root causes of terrorism are also addressed and ultimately for this war against terrorism to be sustainable, we must win the hearts and minds of people.'

   The second response asks: 'How can society respond – and what part can business play in this process?'

It is naive to believe that global trade relationships – such as giving local farmers access to international markets – will of itself reduce terrorism but it is similarly simplistic not to acknowledge that economic relationships can help to undermine an ideological message built on ignorance, fear and hate. Rising levels of foreign direct investment, poverty reduction and minimizing political risk are increasingly becoming connected, for example, in China, India, Vietnam and Pakistan. As Vietnam's Deputy Prime Minister recently told this author, his Government is not just expecting the country's poverty challenges to be taken up by international financial institutions, development agencies and NGOs but increasingly wants to know from foreign companies, using Vietnam as a pool of low cost labour, how they can help too (and this need not be financial 'philanthropy').

Distrust of the foreign company and national in some emerging markets has increased as 'think global, act local' and cultural sensitivity assumes a new urgency after 9/11. The war against Iraq has increased the political risks for US and UK corporate brands.

Managing corporate social responsibility risk

Corporate Social Responsibility (CSR) risks do not look like traditional risks.

1. They are of concern to a company's stakeholders:
   - Sometimes they are out of a company's arc of vision but important to its stakeholders.
   - Often based on cherished ideals (not necessarily acted on by promoter).
   - Stimulated by a distrust of business and its practices.
   - Resonate with personal experience and concerns.
2. . . . they are volatile:
   - Subject to shifts in nature and perception.
   - Emotive in nature, stimulating passionate responses.
   - Move quickly from fringe to mainstream.
3. . . . easy to communicate:
   - Relatively simple to communicate and media friendly.
   - Supported by vocal or influential champions or opinion formers.
   - Topical issues are particularly powerful.
   - Clear call to action – e.g. 'Don't buy Brand X'.
4. . . . and they do not exist in isolation:
   - Risks can also be compounded by other events, some of which may be similar in nature but others which are not at all linked.
   - 'Creeping catastrophe' identifies how initially an event may have no impact, but that as additional problems occur they can tip the balance to create a catastrophe. This can be seen in the problems which beset Barclays Bank, Shell and Monsanto.

The focus is on the processes *of identification, prioritization* and *implementation* of CSR risk and reflects on how these can be integrated into a current risk management framework.

An integrated programme of social and ethical risk management really begins when the entire risk assessment process is consciously supplemented by sensitivity to the attitudes of all significant stakeholders and their expectations of corporate conduct in any situation.

Learning from the experiences of apparently unrelated industries may also prove to be as important as assessing issues arising in one's own. Some 'left-field' risks will always prove impossible to anticipate. This does not diminish the value of a systematic process to identify all other known or predictable risks to reputation and performance.

Corporate social responsibility (CSR) is 'the commitment of business to contribute to sustainable economic development, working with employees, their families, the local community and society at large to improve the quality of life of all their stakeholders' (World Business Council for Sustainable Development, 2005). CSR or 'corporate citizenship' has now moved beyond local philanthropy (sometimes

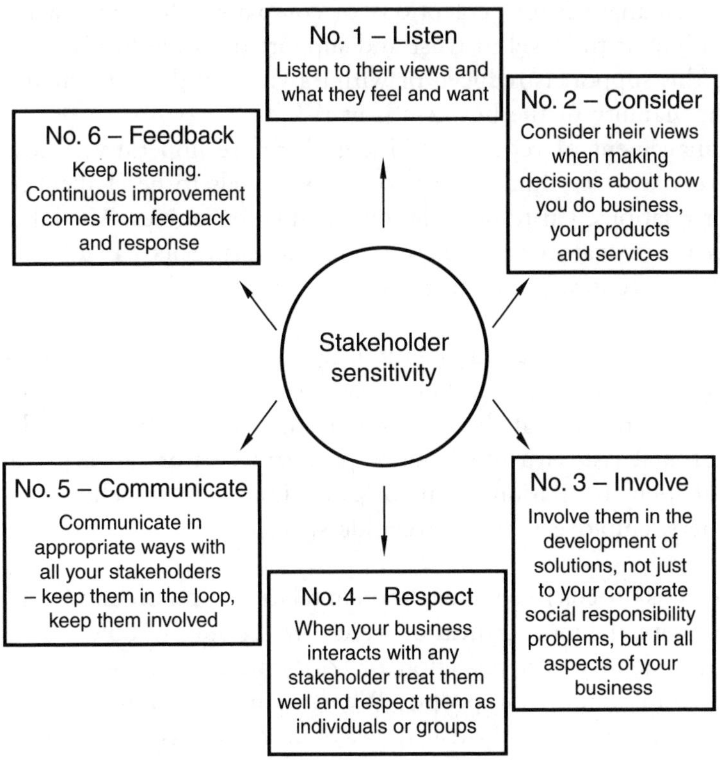

(from Social and Ethical Risk Group, 2001)

Figure 6.9 The six components of stakeholder sensitivity

associated with the term 'corporate social responsibility' or, more accurately, 'corporate social investment') and now encompasses the whole way that a company operates and its effect on all its stakeholders. In implementing effective CSR programmes to mitigate the damage of social and ethical risk, sensitivity to the opinions and expectations of stakeholders is essential. However, embedding sensitivity, particular to external stakeholders, has a number of 'components', as shown in Figure 6.9.

Summary

Managing risk has always been a natural part of day-to-day business, but the increasing complexity and internationalization of business, coupled with a greater focus of corporate responsibility, has now made reputation risk an explicit component of corporate governance. Reputation risks emanate from perceptions of company behaviours which threaten to impair the level of trust and support from the firm's stakeholders. If this support is reduced or withdrawn, then the performance or even the viability of the business is at risk.

The management of reputation risk is therefore imperative. However, the very way we think about companies needs to be challenged.

Investor relations. Customer relations. Human resources. The labels companies use to categorize functions and departments can obscure them from two central points in managing reputational risk:

1. Reputational risk is about relationships – and these need to be managed beyond people in these areas operating in functional silos. This comes together at the executive leadership and board level.
2. Reputational risk is a much more powerful creator of corporate value if seen in relation to an organization's key stakeholders – customers, employees and shareholders.

Reputational risk needs to be understood in relation to an organization's intangible assets, the most critical of which are set out in Table 6.3.

Corporate identity is a reflection of corporate strategy – and this includes a strategy for your people. What is often overlooked – and perhaps was in the case of British Airways in its tailfins saga in 1998 – is that corporate identity is also about organizations' social context. Corporate reputation is also about organizational as well as corporate identity. If corporate identity is about the logo, slogan or livery,

Table 6.3 Reputational risk and intangible assets

Intangible asset	*Relevance to reputational risk*
Reputation and trust	Reputation and trust are at the heart of expectations by stakeholders of corporate behaviour.
Relationships	Effective relationships are key to identifying, assessing as well as managing reputational risk whether at the executive team level or at the front-line customer interface.
Culture and values	Reputational risk is not managed because consultants are brought in or because the CEO says it is important. Reputational risks relate to behaviour – both individual (values) and corporate (culture).
Leadership and communication	Reputational risk is a board issue but ensuring it is understood relies on communication that is both innovative and honest.
Knowledge	External awareness of how employees, customers and shareholders perceive the organization is key to reputational risk. Knowledge derives both from the application of tools and techniques (e.g. being developed at Henley Management College) but also effective market insight/intelligence (i.e. environmental scanning, filtering, analysis and communication to decision-makers).

organizational identity consists of the many ways in which members of an organization perceive, feel and think of themselves as an organization. Stories and corporate folklore are all part of this, especially in a service-based company where people have such a central role and word of mouth is a key way in which news is spread.

Key points in understanding how to manage reputational risk for differential advantage are:

1. Reputation and risk must be prioritized together, though this requires a deeper understanding of both concepts.
2. Reputational risk needs ongoing board monitoring and executive management.
3. It depends on managing key stakeholders' expectations of corporate behaviour such as customers, employees and shareholders.
4. It is arguably becoming more important for a CEO than managing the company.
5. Emotional factors affect perception and expectations and cut across all key stakeholder groups so that attitudes, feelings and experiences bind customers, shareholders and employees who have overlapping identities.

References and recommended reading

Blair, M M and Wallman, S M H (2001) *Unseen Wealth: Report of the Brookings Task Force on Intangibles*. Washington, DC: Brookings Institution Press.

Cadbury, A *et al.* (1992) *Report of the Committee on the Financial Aspects of Corporate Governance*. London: Gee and Co Ltd. See also: http://www.ecgi.org/codes/all_codes.htm

Committee on Corporate Governance (1998) *Committee on Corporate Governance: Final Report*. London: Gee and Co Ltd. Available at: http://www.ecgi.org/codes/documents/hampel.pdf

Department of Trade and Industry (2002) *Modernising Company Law*. UK Government White Paper CM 5553. London: The Stationery Office.

Fombrun, C J and van Riel, C (2004) *Fame and Fortune: How Successful Companies Build Winning Reputations*. Englewood Cliffs, NJ: FT Prentice Hall.

Gillen, S (2005) Long-term value? *Chartered Secretary*, October.

Haeckel, S (1999) *Adaptive Enterprise: Creating and Leading Sense-and-Respond Organisations*. Boston: Harvard Business School Press.

Higgs, D (2003) *Review of the Role and Effectiveness of Non-Executive Directors*. London: Department of Trade and Industry. Available at: http://www.dti.gov.uk/cld/non_exec_review

Leechor, Chad (1999) *Reviving The Market for Corporate Control*. Washington, DC: World Bank.

MacMillan, K, Money, K, Downing, S and Hillenbrand, C (2004) Giving your organisation SPIRIT: an overview and call to action for directors on issues of corporate governance, corporate reputation and corporate responsibility. *Journal of General Management* 30:2 Winter.

Shaw, R B (1997) *Trust in the Balance*. San Francisco: Jossey-Bass, Wiley.

Slovic, P (2000) *The Perception of Risk*. London: Earthscan.

Social and Ethical Risk Group (2001) Unpublished report. London: Shared View.

World Business Council for Sustainable Development (2005) See: http://www.wbcsd.ch

World Economic Forum (2003) Available at: http://www.weforum.org

Zaman, A (2003) *Made in Japan: Converging Trends in Corporate Responsibility and Corporate Governance*. London: Royal Institute of International Affairs (Chatham House).

Zaman, A (2004) *FT Executive Briefing – Reputational Risk: How to Manage for Value Creation*. Harlow: Financial Times Pearson Education.

Useful websites:

DTI: http://www.dti.gov.uk/companiesbill/index.htm

Henley Management College: The John Madejski Centre for Reputation: http://www.henleymc.ac.uk/henleyres03.nsf/pages/jmcr

ICAEW: http://www.icaew.co.uk

Marketing Leadership Council: http://www.marketingleadershipcouncil.com

Reputation Institute: http://www.reputationinstitute.com

Turnbull: http://www.icaew.co.uk/cbp/index.cfm?aub=tb2I_6242

7

Risk-assessed Marketing Planning

Terry Kendrick

Managing marketing performance is increasingly being thought of as an important element in managing business risk. In the US a risk management style approach to business is now mandated through Sarbanes-Oxley corporate governance legislation. SEC (Securities and Exchange Commission) filings form 20f requires a company to provide a list of business risk factors which usually includes a number of factors traditionally in the domain of marketing management. In addition, the new draft COSO Enterprise Risk Management Framework which appeared in September 2004 mentions the word 'customer' 71 times and the word 'marketing' 11 times. Marketing and risk are ever closer in the US with quality and risk management approaches such as Six Sigma now being applied to marketing management environments there.

In the UK the spirit of the Turnbull report (Turnbull *et al.*, 1999) would encourage similar, if not the same, approaches. After April 2006 (for reporting year 2005) the DTI Operating and Financial Review will bring an approach of potentially similar rigour and transparency to that of the US. The draft Statutory Instrument decrees that the review should include information about risks and uncertainties within the areas traditionally owned by marketing, such as key relationships with customers. However, although best practice will explicitly consider the risks there are, at present, no generally accepted standards for risk managing the marketing planning process.

This is an important area to manage. A Grant Thornton survey in 2004 (Grant Thornton, 2004) found that less than 40 per cent of UK respondents had a contingency plan to meet the loss of key customers. Risk is fundamental to marketing management and, with marketing often claiming to own customer relationships, the marketing function has a role in reducing business cash flow vulnerability and volatility.

In our increasingly competitive market-places customer needs and demands just won't stand still long enough for a business to create the compelling offer that is bound to succeed. Only a proportion of new products will become successful. Marketing risks have to be taken and be well managed. Indeed, they *should* be taken because standing still is risky in these times. A person does not drown by falling in the water, he or she drowns by staying there.

When the late Chairman of Fiat, Gianni Agnelli, said: 'I fear that Fiat is too big for Italy and too small for the world' (Popham, 2002) he was highlighting a key strategic marketing issue: there are significant risks in strategic marketing choices. Good choice and implementation make the right product for the right market at the right time – bad choices and implementation result in the wrong product for the wrong market at the wrong time.

The business world has become riskier, markets change rapidly, product life cycles, particularly in technology driven products, have reduced considerably. Given that, in many markets, business breakthroughs are no longer a source of sustainable competitive advantage but simply short-term gains until copied by competitors, the marketing advantage often arises from being able to risk-manage the value creation process and sustain it within a business.

Even a continuous innovation approach thrusts a company into risky areas where both customer and shareholder value need some degree of risk management. Marketing often has the responsibility to capture the value to be won from changing technology and consumer tastes and, as such, is a prime candidate for the application of risk management tools and techniques.

Risk in strategic marketing

Strategic marketing planning is a particularly important business function in uncertain environments where growth cannot be assured for all competitors. Even in markets where growth is assured for all competent players marketing is important to ensure that the company has some of the best, most profitable, customers in the industry and not simply those customers that competitors do not want.

Traditionally, management response to uncertainty and risk in market-places has been to try to reduce that uncertainty and risk.

However, more modern approaches recognize, and demonstrate, that formal strategic planning has difficulties in uncertain times and that, in any case, reducing uncertainty is not always a good strategy. The trick is to manage uncertainty, recognizing the positive opportunities that risk can bring, whilst ensuring that the value that marketing hopes to bring is not compromised.

Marketing risks include the following:

- market-place conditions or industry characteristics (e.g. competition, political, social, economic, technological, legal risks, changing customer buying habits and preferences);
- characteristics of the organization's decision-makers and the way in which they make decisions (risk attitudes in the marketing team and organization);
- process of achieving marketing objectives (the way marketing is implemented as an 'end-to-end' project);
- marketing resource base, infrastructure, inter-functional relationships and culture (are the right things in place to make sure that marketing can deliver?).

These four types of risk (adapted from Palmer and Wiseman, 1999) exist at each and every stage of marketing planning – goal setting, situation review, strategy development, strategy implementation, monitoring control and feedback. A partial checklist of key risks at each stage is offered in the appendix to this chapter.

Senior marketing managers experience a number of types of uncertainty in their market-places:

- predicting what is going to happen out there in the market-places in which the organization competes;
- often it is difficult to predict the impact, or effect, of changes in the external marketing environment on the organization and marketing management decision-making;
- there is often an inability to predict what the marketing response options are, together with the value of each possible marketing initiative in terms of achieving desired organizational objectives.

However, some future circumstances can be predicted, from current trends, with a degree of confidence. For example, demographic and technological trends can help to picture the scene in future market-places. Other uncertainties can, through scenario planning, be tied into a range of expected outcomes which can then be managed for overall profit. There are, of course, some truly random events but not so many as popular conversation around the marketing department would have you to believe.

Clearly, in all of the above, the risks and uncertainties are a potential source of competitive advantage if we can manage them better than competitors. It is important to recognize that business risk is not solely about the adverse characteristics of risk, but also about the risk of not identifying or adequately exploiting good business opportunities.

Marketing has a part to play in addressing or exploiting the full range of organizational risks:

- Strategic risk – Does marketing effectively and efficiently support and deliver the goals and objectives of the organization? Or does it position the organization in an inappropriate way?
- Reputational risk – Does marketing deliver strong brand values and reputation or does it tarnish the organization's image?
- Operational risk – Are the risks to effective and efficient marketing implementation considered and monitored? Or does it work on a 'We've got good people, it's bound to happen OK' basis?
- Compliance risk – Does marketing activity put the company at risk of non-compliance with laws and regulations (e.g. anti-trust)?
- Environmental – Does marketing take account of the environmental impacts of its actions?
- Financial risk – Does marketing ensure that the most attractive and profitable business is obtained? Is the customer portfolio made up of some of the more profitable and secure customers or has marketing delivered a customer base which is made up of some of the worst customers in the industry?
- Information risk – Does marketing protect the organization's proprietary knowledge and data it holds either through its simple transactional data or existing customer relationship management (CRM) system?

The risks in marketing planning

A marketing planning process is often the backbone for sustained marketing activity undertaken at the strategic (choices of products and markets, positioning, etc.) rather than tactical level (campaigns, project plans, etc.). Such a process should be driven by formal planning structures yet remain hospitable to emerging trends and improvisational, risky, approaches.

Strategic marketing planning processes usually implement corporate objectives by considering where the organization is now with its products and markets, where it hopes to take them, the marketing objectives it wishes to achieve (usually in terms of value, volume, market share or margin) and how it intends to achieve such objectives. Finally, an action plan will be created and monitoring and control procedures set in place to ensure effective implementation and a feedback loop into the following year's planning round. Although seemingly very linear, a strategic marketing planning process such as the one illustrated in Figure 7.1 is, in best practice, very iterative and includes feedback loops to reflect on learning.

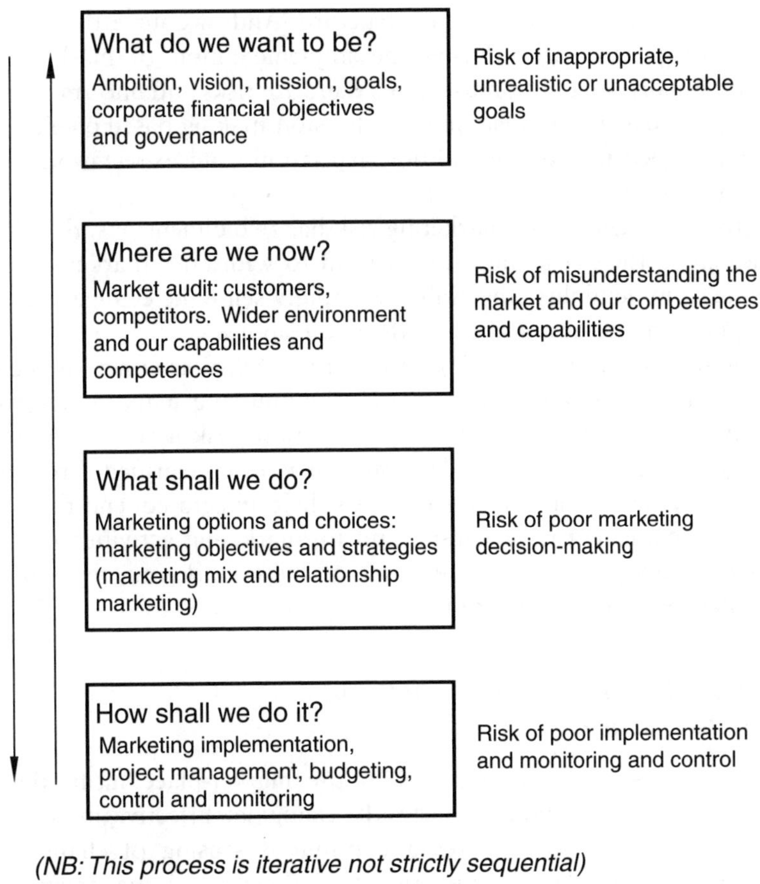

Figure 7.1 The marketing planning process and risk

Clearly, to ensure a valuable output from such a process there are a significant number of risks to manage along the way whichever marketing planning model is used. At the highest level there is the risk of setting a mission and goals which, although seemingly beneficial, do not reflect the opportunities in the market-place both overreaching or too soft. Risks abound in the situation review phase (Where are we now? – everything from market-place turbulence, political risk, social and technological change related risks through the potential for inappropriate customer segmentation, to competitor activities).

There are significant risks and uncertainties associated with all elements of marketing strategy development and the marketing mix – product and market risks, pricing risks, supply chain and distribution channel risks, and reputational and other risks associated with promotional campaigns. There are risks associated with overall strategic marketing planning and marketing structure. And of course there are project management risks during the implementation of marketing initiatives. Finally, in addition to all this there are risks and uncertainties in just how managers will react in their decision-making based on either their own propensities or the culture, aspirations and expectations of their organization.

Effective management of marketing risk has two dimensions: robustness (designing the marketing organization to withstand market-place turbulence) and flexibility (the ability to rapidly sense the change in the market-place, create and make an effective response).

Risk management in marketing can be approached as either an end-to-end activity or the application of risk thinking and management to specific parts of the process. Many organizations risk-manage part of the function (e.g. new product development is often clarified through a series of 'gates') but few have an explicit integrated end-to-end approach to managing risks within, and to, marketing activities.

The following section looks at some of these marketing risks and their management in more detail.

Risks arising from market-place conditions or industry characteristics

Uncertainties, risks and ambiguities in the market-place mean that opportunities and threats are constantly changing. Effective management of such instability requires a continuous sensing of changing industry and market-place characteristics: in effect, a risk management exercise.

When traditional prescriptive strategic planning processes appear too rigid to manage uncertainty scenario planning often emerges as an excellent risk management tool to provide a structure for the management of such conditions.

This tool develops from an initial descriptive picture of the market-place (often presented as a political, economic, social technological, legal, etc., analysis – sometimes referred to as a SLEPT, PEST or STEP analysis), an industry forces analysis (such as that suggested by Michael Porter in his Five Forces model – an industry analysis of buyer power, supplier power, potential new entrants, potential new ways to provide the value required by the market, and the push and shove of the usual suspects who compete in the market) and an overview of strengths and weaknesses in the market-place with their implications for future business (a SWOT analysis, covering strengths, weaknesses, opportunities and threats).

The resulting scenarios are descriptive narratives of plausible alternative futures. Rather than rely on a single 'most likely' forecast, they allow an organization to compare and contrast alternative opinions on how an industry or customer group may evolve. Since it is externally oriented, scenario planning is very effective at identifying growth strategies as well as potential downside risks in market positions. As such it reflects modern risk management practice which sees risk as having both an upside and a downside. Scenarios can also help identify the specific external industry changes that provide the first sign that there are emerging risks to cash flow, market share, value proposition or margins.

Other key elements in any scenario approach to risk-managing the external market environment will include the legal and regulatory environment, technological changes likely or possible, social and cultural shifts (including work patterns, religion and social expectations) and financial and economic conditions, trends and forecasts.

As well as legal risks associated with corporate governance and employee law, marketing is potentially in conflict with anti-trust law, data protection law and other regulatory and public policy issues. Technological risks, ranging from changing product features to health and safety, need to be understood and managed. Climate can be a source of risk and uncertainty in some, particularly agricultural, market-places.

For a marketer looking at territory options, political risk is a key factor. Political risk is the risk that a sovereign host government will unexpectedly change policies or attitudes towards business activity, usually through instability in the host country's government. Strategic alliances can be a response to such market-place uncertainties and risks even if alliances bring their own risks.

In addition to political risk, international market risk includes competitive rivalry, cultural differences, market demand, the differences in marketing infrastructure, customer buying habits, management experience in developing international markets and general risks around industry structure. In high risk markets organizations often choose the non-equity/export entry mode. In moderate risk markets joint ventures are often most appropriate and in low risk international markets the most likely entry mode would be a wholly owned subsidiary.

Product portfolio risks

Perhaps the most famous application of risk thinking to marketing planning is Igor Ansoff's matrix of product and marketing strategy options (Ansoff, 1957). This helps marketing planners to understand the relative risks of competing in existing markets when compared with entering new markets in the context of the existing range of products versus the development of new products.

Ansoff suggested four combinations of product and market strategies: market penetration (selling existing products to existing customers); market development or extension (selling existing products to new customers); product development (selling new products to existing customers) and diversification (selling new products to new customers).

It is clear, for instance, that to take the diversification route is very risky – taking this route puts an organization into areas where it probably has very little understanding of the new customer base or the new products it wishes to sell – uncertainty upon uncertainty, risk upon risk!

There may be instances where diversification is appropriate (e.g. where growth ambitions cannot be met by simply selling more of what we have or where there is no scope for new product development for existing customer types). However, in recent years, in an effort to control risk, many organizations have recognized the low risk potential in the market penetration box – existing knowledge of both customer needs and how the product works is likely to be good and the chances of success here are correspondingly higher. Hence many organizations have focused on a customer retention strategy. This often involves both cross- and up-selling together with, as appropriate, new product development or customization.

In reality, of course, the best risk-managed portfolios of customers and product/market sets are likely to be a combination of two or more of these quadrants. Where new products are part of the strategy there are a number of key risks to their survival: competitive environment, the organization's internal environment, the new product development process and the existence or otherwise of the product's competitive advantage.

Portfolio approaches to product and market options are useful tools for risk management. The Boston Consulting Group and General Electric matrices are classic examples. Real options is now emerging as a way to value risky propositions where the traditional discounted cash flow methodology appears to undervalue the opportunity. A real options approach applies financial options theory to non-financial assets and encourages managers to consider the value of strategic investments in terms of risk that can be held, hedged or transferred.

Collaborative technological development for new products brings its own risks: employee turnover, breach of secrecy, other firm's research staff and management. The Risk Diagnosing Methodology (Halman and Keizer, 1994) is a process of identifying and evaluating the risks in product innovation. As development schedules shrink and technology moves on apace such processes are important in managing risks in product innovations.

Pricing risks

Uncertainty and risk have a major part to play in pricing decisions and bargaining. Although price and risk are often thought of in an economic context there is a marketing context as well. There are significant risks to making a sound choice of price points if the customer's perception of real value has not been understood by the marketing department.

In marketing a consumer has a 'consideration set' of brands between which he or she will make a choice based upon a utility comparison or cost–benefit trade-off before making the final decision. Frequently purchased products usually have frequent price promotions and this provides the consumer with significant uncertainty about the prices of brands.

Some industries such as IT suffer from severe market turbulences and developing a long-term pricing strategy in such an industry is a difficult, though worthwhile pursuing, task. However, to lengthen product life cycles in an area of innovation can be a potentially risky marketing strategy for any individual organization.

Inventory changes, integration, forward selling, niche marketing and brand development, supply chain management, and using financial derivatives as hedging approaches, are all ways to undertake price risk management.

Distribution and supply risks

Risks to relationships with key suppliers who provide products and services to a company's core competences or products and services which differentiate the buyer's product in its market-places can have severe damage potential.

An effective risk management approach (although often not explicitly called that) in logistics and supply develops flexible and responsive delivery capabilities based upon postponement principles and supported by upstream supply chain coordination. This reduces inventory and demand forecasting risks. Uncertainty can be reduced by cutting lead times which shorten the forecasting horizon and lower the risk of error. Postponement is now recognized as a viable strategic option in managing supply chain and logistics risk.

Approaches such as supplier certification and quality management programmes are often in place but this is clearly not enough for a risk assessed approach.

Promotional and sales risks

Promotional activity may be said to be a way to reduce the uncertainty in a potential customer's mind as to whether a purchase should be made or not.

Money-back guarantees and demonstrations are two examples of important risk reduction tools in this area. Money-back guarantees are effective in reducing uncertainty when consumers have only a small amount of product knowledge, where it takes considerable time to understand and evaluate the product, where consumers need feedback from others and when consumers are contemplating an impulse purchase. Demonstrations can be effective when customers have high product knowledge or are able to learn quickly and when return costs are high. Both reduce uncertainty and risk in the customer's mind.

Risk behaviour within sales force activities is an important element of marketing planning. In most market-places sales representatives have a choice of going for low or high risk prospects. Low risk prospects may be existing, or highly compatible, customers who can offer small amounts of incremental business and high risk customers can be those who offer potentially large sales but will require significant effort and expenditure to win and develop with very uncertain chances of success.

Common sense requires sales force reward systems to be compatible with the risk context. If the marketing strategy is to focus on large contracts from a small number of 'relationship' or 'key account' customers (i.e. risky business in the sales force's collective mind), this will require a different reward structure from a marketing strategy which intends to meet objectives by generating small amounts of sales from a large number of customers to generate market share increases (much less risky in the sales force's perception).

Customer perceived risks

Many researchers have found consumer perceived risk to be context specific, hence difficult to manage. Perceived internet shopping risks, for instance, include credit card misuse, fraudulent sites, loss of privacy, delivery problems and product failure. Emotion is also now recognized as an important element in consumer perceived risk: negative emotions create a threatening consumption situation for consumers and lead to perceptions of risk about the product; positive emotions (e.g. about products capable of providing enjoyment) are associated with an accompanying sense of diminished risk.

Within organizational buying risk situations customer perceptions of risk (in terms of purchase importance and task uncertainty) have a significant influence on the way buying decisions are made. Understanding these suggests the need for adaptive selling: the ability to adjust sales behaviours in response to particular customer situations. A buying decision can be taken as an instance of risk taking and buying behaviours can be thought of as risk handling or management strategies.

Buyer–seller cooperation and uncertainty is an important issue. Relationship marketing requires cooperative exchange between buyers and sellers. The issue of 'customers at risk' is key to companies committed to a Customer Relationship Management (CRM) approach.

Relationship, brand and reputation risks

Brand is traditionally seen as a way to reduce risk inherent in a consumer's purchase, particularly through brand extensions for new products. A failed brand extension may well undermine the customer's relationship with the whole brand, not just the extension.

In recent years the business world has witnessed reputations (for example, WorldCom and Enron) falling overnight. Risk to reputation is high on the corporate agenda. Academics and practitioners have begun to work together to create measures and approaches to managing corporate reputations through the creation of a 'reputation index' (Cravens *et al.*, 2003) which could accompany the financial statements much like a bond rating summarizes the overall risk associated with investing in a company.

Reputation can be thought of as one of a company's greatest assets, if not, indeed, its greatest asset. There are compelling reasons to consider good ethical practice as an important risk management activity.

It is clear that there are a number of dimensions to reputational risk (as discussed in Chapter 6). Perhaps the most important risk is that customers misunderstand the organization's intentions and defect to competitors for ethical or other reasons. Investors may lose confidence or decide to make other investment choices. Suppliers and other business partners may not feel able to work with the organization and refuse to enter into a business relationship. Regulators may find the organization to be non-compliant. Activists may encourage boycotts or direct action against the organization's assets. The wider community may feel alienated from the organization and not wish to have it amongst them. Finally, the media may expose unattractive elements of the organization.

Corporate Social Responsibility (CSR) is set to become an increasingly important context for marketing activity. In a survey of the 1,500 delegates (most of them business leaders) attending the 2004 World Economic Forum meetings, fewer than one in five of those responding said that profitability was the most important measure of corporate success. One in four saw reputation and brand, both of which are at least partly influenced by the marketing function, as the most important measure (World Economic Forum, 2004).

How do marketing decision-makers deal with risk?

Many marketing risks cannot be formally assessed because they are embodied in the skills, experience and personality of the marketing managers in the risky situation. There are two key approaches to understanding this: risk taking by individual personalities (studied by psychology and decision theory) and organizational risk (studied as part of cultural theory).

Total perceived risk has been identified as a function of personal character, experience and circumstances. This of course means that, when thinking about individual marketing decision-maker attitudes, risk is very context dependent (and in this way similar to consumer risk perception as noted above). Whilst an expert snowboarder might see a certain mountain slope as a relatively low-risk proposition, an inexperienced person might consider it very risky. Similarly, a marketer who had been through several major rebrandings with other companies may perceive this as less risky than his or her board which had not been through such a process before.

Clashes of risk perception and propensities are not uncommon in marketing. In advertising, for instance, there is often a clash between the creative work of advertising agencies and the reluctance of advertisers to take risks. There can be significant risk of 'collateral damage' in advertising strategies and campaigns. The effective or poor management of creativity and risk will result in increasing shareholder value or the destruction of such value.

Managing risk in the process of achieving marketing objectives

Achieving marketing objectives requires a set of processes and skills that together work positively to manage uncertainty and risk in such a way that the progress towards objectives is not derailed sufficiently to result in failed objectives.

Intuitively, the achievement of marketing objectives will not stand or fall on one risk factor. Superb risk management in new product development, for instance, will not be sufficient to ensure overall marketing success. It will, for instance, be necessary to have diverse project risk management skills in place to ensure full and effective implementation of new product decisions. Furthermore, many critical risks will be cross-functional so a cross-functional approach to identifying and managing them is the logical approach.

In recent years there has been a long running debate between 'rational design' and 'emergent process' schools of strategy, both corporate and marketing. The perceived increased levels of environmental and organizational uncertainty and risk has led some to herald the demise of strategic corporate and marketing planning. In effect, there is a belief that change is too rapid and uncertainty too unmanageable to make planning effort worth the time it takes.

However, this is oversimplistic and for many companies the appropriate response is a process of 'planned emergence', or, in other words, planning systems hospitable to change and uncertainty.

Essentially, strategic marketing planning is a project and should be risk assessed and managed as such. Strategic marketing planning is vulnerable to crisis because it is often aggressive, looking to the future, and margin or cash driven. This can cause an organization to ignore its exposure to large-scale calamities – Exxon's poor response to the Exxon Valdez tanker spill is an example of this. This broad area of risk management can include risk assessment, crisis management and business continuity.

At present individual parts of many marketing processes have their own risk management approaches with varying degrees of rigour. However, there is the opportunity to risk-manage the whole process as a project and not simply pass over the implementation of strategy to project managers to risk-manage. By then it may well be too late and the fatal flaws in the plan may already have been missed or ignored. If marketing planning is to be seen as a project then project managers need to be involved at the strategy development phase of the process.

Customer portfolio issues are also important in the process of achieving marketing objectives. The higher the risk (volatility) associated with a customer the higher return required by the company to create value for its shareholders. There is a need to manage the risk of the overall customer portfolio as well as the returns from individual customers (Ryals, 2002). Various marketing strategies are possible to manage such risk – one would be to aim to reduce the risk of customers, particularly those who earn less than the cost of capital. Another would be to identify low risk customers who are value creating rather than value destroying. Customer risks can be either the risk of losing the customer or the risk of making losses on the relationship or the risk of supporting customers with resources which could support a better return from another set of customers.

A good way to start thinking about the risks in the customer portfolio is to consider which customers are most at risk of no longer needing the product or service or at risk of defecting to a competitor (either because of a poor offer or a competitor's increased quality offer). This can be considered in the context of their lifetime values (i.e. how much each customer is worth – turnover or profit – over the length of their time as a potential customer) and it is possible to be able to get a quick feeling for how exposed the organization is in the process of achieving its marketing objectives.

The matrix in Figure 7.2 can help to structure thinking and prioritize action.

If, on reflection, the highest lifetime value customers are also the least likely to stop buying the product or service in the near future then the organization is less at risk than if the matrix reveals that the highest

Probability of defection in the near future

		High	Medium	Low
Life-time value	High	Act now	Act soon	Monitor
	Medium	Act soon	Act soon	Monitor
	Low	Monitor	Monitor	Monitor

Figure 7.2 Addressing risks to the customer portfolio

lifetime value customers are likely to change the way they do things, thus not needing such services any more, or have grievances with the organization in a highly competitive market, thus increasing their chances of defection to another competitor.

If the organization is unable to even make sense of this matrix because it has no information on the key dimensions and has no procedures in place to understand these relativities within its customer base then it is time to worry and accept that it is at serious risk of ending up with a customer base which may simply be the set of customers other competitors were not willing to fight for.

Consideration of such risk issues often leads an organization to institute an approach to Customer Relationship Management (CRM).

Managing risks posed by organizational structure and culture

Many marketing plans fail because the planner did not assess whether the marketing organization was suited to implement the plan effectively.

Discussions often suggest that marketing activity should be cross-functional and integrated. Integration can be on two levels: integration of product, price, place and promotion; or integration of marketing strategies with the strategies of other departments within the organization. Within these two broad categories there are three strands of what integration means: interaction, collaboration or a composite of interaction and collaboration.

The interface between marketing and other departments is very important to the management of uncertainty and risk. For instance, integration between research and development and marketing personnel has regularly been found to be important in successful new product development. R&D/marketing integration is highly important to new product development success when technical and market environments are highly uncertain and less important when those environments are less uncertain.

Similarly, the integration of key decision areas between manufacturing and sales/marketing makes sense. More radically, benefits can accrue from supplier integration into new product development under conditions of technological uncertainty.

In summary, successful marketing planning requires interdependencies between marketing and other functional areas:

- manufacturing;
- R & D;
- physical distribution;
- technical support and after sales service.

Roadmapping is an attempt to reconcile the need to risk-manage the development of new products in ever changing market-places. Recognizing uncertainty and risk this approach is a vision of the future (typically five years) which provides an interdepartmental shared insight and overview of the business in time.

If the relationships between external suppliers and internal departments lack either the ability or motivation to support the firm's strategy then the firm's ability to show flexibility (in risky times) in its customer relationships can be compromised. When uncertainty is high an organization benefits from a more fluid structure than when times are more predictable.

Most marketing plans and initiatives involve a process of change and change is extremely risky. Machiavelli is widely credited with the warning that there is nothing more dangerous and risky than to introduce a new order of things.

Risk-managing strategic marketing

Before any effective risk management can be undertaken by the marketing department some understanding of the organization's risk appetite must be communicated to the marketing managers. What levels of risk can be tolerated? In what areas can no risk be taken? In which areas can reasonable risk be taken if able to be managed? Remember that the market analysts are not so much concerned with the risks faced as they are with how convincingly they appear to be managed.

People talk of risk taking or risk averse companies but often the reality is that different parts of the organization, quite reasonably, have different risk appetites. For instance, it is not unusual to see companies take risks to protect their core competences but to be very risk averse in straight financial matters. Reflect upon risk appetite and communicate this to the marketing planners. Such advice will probably not be a simple 'Don't take risks!' or 'Take risks!' Such timidity or 'gung-ho' attitudes are unlikely to be the best approach to long-term sustainable competitive advantage.

Marketing needs to be subject to a risk management approach which assures:

- risk planning context;
- risk identification;
- risk analysis, estimation and evaluation;
- risk response;
- risk monitoring.

It is important to do this without creating unnecessary bureaucracy, as discussed in the following sections. Although each stage is vital to effective management, once the risk planning context is agreed, the emphasis should be on the analysis, estimation and evaluation phase. Many organizations are very able to identify risks and have response mechanisms in place (e.g. insurance): the real difficulty in many organizations lies in understanding the risks and identifying upsides as well as downsides.

Risk planning context

Before any detailed risk identification takes place it is important to establish just what is to be risk-managed and develop an indication of the threshold for acceptable risk. How does the organization define strategic marketing planning? Who are the stakeholders within the process? When does a risk become unacceptable?

Further questions arise. What is to be risk-managed? How deep is the risk management activity? Simply a check to see if everything is being done as planned and risks to such functional processes have been identified and addressed? Or a more pervasive approach where strategic marketing planning is seen as a major source of customer and shareholder value – with the consequent requirement to risk-manage the value creation process rather than simply the specific tactics associated with the implementation of strategy? Put another way – is the risk management activity to be specific to the marketing department or the value that marketing creates (or destroys!)? If the latter then the marketing risk management context extends well beyond the marketing department.

The strategic and organizational contexts must be agreed and, to avoid scope creep, this initial stage should be completed with a clear outline of the boundaries of the risk management activity.

Risk identification

Marketing risk identification begins by looking at the process of marketing. How does it really work? Where can things go wrong? Where might they go wrong? Where are the most critical risks based upon the complexity of the organization's risk appetite? Where does marketing create or defend value for the organization? What could put that value at risk?

It is useful to create a risk register, perhaps utilizing a hierarchical structuring of project risks known as a Risk Breakdown Structure (Hillson, 2003b). The appendix to this chapter gives a start. The risk register should include both internal and external risks – strategic risks, reputational risks, operational risks (including project risk), compliance risks, environmental risks, information risks, etc.

Risk analysis, estimation and evaluation

Having identified the risks it is time to analyse and evaluate to determine the acceptability of a given risk. The main task of this part of the risk management process is to develop adequate, organization-specific, tools for dealing with complexity, uncertainty and ambiguity.

There are three ways in which risk can be evaluated, as follows.

1. Through quantitative approaches with numerical thresholds. This will often be a probability (or frequency)/consequences matrix (see Figure 7.3).

   Risk management matrices will inevitably have some degree of subjectivity and bias. In most marketing situations risk is a personal and social construct as well as a scientific construct. Also, such quantitative approaches require information which is not always available when the matrix is being completed.
2. Precautionary principle approaches. Such approaches suggest that if there is any doubt about the effects of potentially significant risks

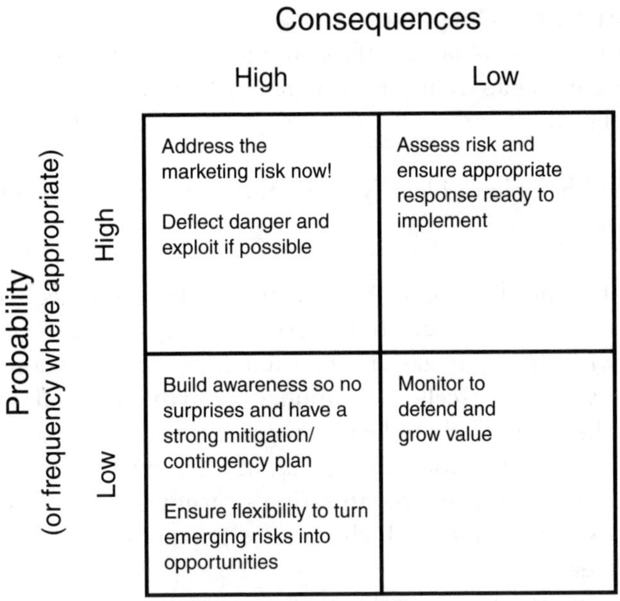

Figure 7.3 A probability and consequences matrix for marketing planning

they should not be accepted. In other words, the principle of 'better safe than sorry'. By being so cautious it is easy to avoid negative calamities but the downside for the organization is that such an approach is likely to put the organization at risk of falling behind in rapidly changing market-places. The precautionary principle is more popular in Europe than in North America.

3. Standards created as a result of focus groups, roundtables, deliberative rule making, mediation or panels. These have the benefit of being very company-specific and thus able to reflect what risk really means for the organization. In addition they can take into account the softer non-quantitative aspects of a marketing risk situation, which is not quite so easy to do as part of a quantitative approach.

The criteria for evaluating marketing risk include:

- How significant is the risk-opportunity or the risk-threat?
- How often, or likely, is it that this risk-event will occur?
- Is this risk confined to a part of the organization or does it fully impact directly on the organization's ability to meet its marketing objectives?

- Is the risk short term or long term?
- If the risk turns into an issue can the consequences be reversed?
- Is the risk, if becoming an event, immediate in its impact or is there a long-term delayed effect?

Most companies will be able to identify marketing risks in each of the following categories:

- Low probability and high extent of damage. For instance, a customer who has been successfully served for 15 years, who is very happy with the organization, does not expect to change its processes and who has excellent continued growth potential in its growing markets is unlikely to leave – the risk event is low probability (though not impossible). However, if that one customer accounts for 50 per cent of the organization's turnover there is, to moderate the low probability, a high damage potential if the low probability risk event occurs.
- Probability of occurrence is largely uncertain. In the 1980s and 1990s many oil companies took the financial risk of investing in China based on the marketing need to be in the frame if the Chinese market opened up to outsiders. Although it seemed possible that the markets might open the probability was uncertain.
- Disaster potential high and relatively well known. A children's charity accepting sponsorship from a company using child labour in another country would be taking high risks with its reputation.
- Both probability of occurrence and extent of damage remain uncertain. Developing a new territory for a regional product might be a risky marketing activity both from the point of view of acceptance afar and loosening of regional identity in the core market. But it might not.
- Dangers which can only be seen once the event has happened. Hindsight is a wonderful thing and marketers often wish they had it!

After such risk identification, analysis and evaluation it would seem time to move on to other activities confident that the issue of risk has been addressed. Unfortunately risk never sleeps. Risk and uncertainty management is part of all decisions and should form a component of all evaluations and decisions made during the currency of the project. Not all the risk variables are always identifiable at the project outset, and the probability of occurrence (or any of the other risk evaluation factors above) may shift as the move towards marketing objectives progresses, requiring, in best practice, real time, ongoing, risk management.

Risk response

Risk responses (Table 7.1) should recognize inherent opportunities as well as inherent threats.

This table highlights exactly where marketing planning can achieve superior returns even in difficult markets. Risks in the wider market-place are there to exploit as well as avoid. Many companies would have avoided the risks inherent in the Russian oil market. BP exploited this risk and since September 2003 has been in a joint venture as TNK-BP. Whilst risks still abound in such a market-place BP appears to be managing them well at present.

Risks can be shared rather than transferred. Strategic alliances enable difficult product or geographic markets to be developed for mutual benefit. And there are occasions when it might be appropriate to enhance the risks to increase the potential rewards from a relatively non-core part of marketing activities.

Financial risk management will often mitigate through insurance or hedging. Whilst this can be, if done well, a source of competitive advantage, there is some evidence to show that risk tends to migrate in the financial system with risk exposures simply moving elsewhere or transforming into a different type of exposure.

Risk response will often not be able to entirely eradicate the consequences of negative risk and some residual risk may be acceptable. All risk responses should be measured, practical, agreed and be managed by a risk owner.

Table 7.1 Responses to risk

Threat response	*Generic strategy*	*Opportunity response*
Avoid	Eliminate uncertainty	Exploit
Transfer	Allocate ownership	Share
Mitigate	Modify exposure	Enhance
Accept	Include in baseline	Accept

(from Hillson, 2003a)

Risk monitoring

Important elements in risk monitoring will include risk reporting, documentation and communication. Risk management is now firmly established as a board level responsibility and is an ongoing agenda item in many companies.

Given the difficulties in monitoring diverse risks within a company enterprise-wide risk management approaches are becoming increasingly common and the risk manager of the future will not only need technical skills but also an understanding of how risk relates to strategic and tactical marketing decisions. Some companies, recognizing this, have established the role of chief risk officer.

Strategic marketing risk management: create and defend value

Risk is ever present in strategic marketing planning applications and effective risk management of one part of the process does not necessarily mean that the benefits of strategic marketing planning can be guaranteed: excellent risk management of new product choices, for instance, will be compromised if the disciplines of risk management (risk identification, analysis, estimation, evaluation, response, monitoring) are not adhered to at the project management stage.

This recognition has been spurred in recent times by the need for marketing to show a return on marketing investment and confirm how it protects and enhances shareholder value. And, of course, corporate governance has also turned attention to risk management of both individual functions within an organization and integrated enterprise-wide approaches where appropriate.

Marketing often claims, with justification, to be part of the value creating activity of an organization and, as such, it is prudent to risk-manage the processes which create and protect that value. However, value is not created simply by, for instance, developing a 'killer application' but rather by the efficient and effective implementation of the whole marketing planning process: it is no good having excellent management of wider environmental uncertainty if the organization has a poor logistics implementation of the marketing offer; it is no good having great strengths to build on if the whole marketing show collapses when two key members of staff leave; it is no good strategizing until the perfect idea appears if the project managers are not there to add a sense of reality as to what might happen in practice.

Some organizations get lucky by remaining unaware of, or positively ignoring, risks whilst others, particularly in high reliability organizations, micro-manage all known risks. It is likely that most senior managers are only able to allocate a limited amount of resource to risk management in marketing. This suggests that it might be useful to start with the 80/20 rule of managing risk, looking for the 20 per cent of marketing activities that are responsible for delivering 80 per cent of the value that marketing creates or defends, and focusing risk management activities there.

Marketing planning without risk management is like scuba-diving without an air supply. One thing is certain about planning – things will not always go as planned so it is important to have a safe way back to the surface. The hope is that the things which do not go as planned are not critical to achieving marketing objectives or the development of customer and shareholder value. How well risk-managed is the organization's source of customer perceived value marketing planning? Risk taking cannot be completely avoided, nor should it be, but there is a need to create a culture of responsible risk taking.

It is likely that most senior managers are well aware of this potential problem and are committed to implementing at least some of the approaches outlined in this chapter. The major benefits of risk management in marketing come from looking at the whole process of creating customer value and subsequent shareholder value. There is a pressing need to ensure an integrated, ongoing, committed and reflective approach where marketing people are not afraid to discuss risk or feel that there is the possibility of being labelled as negative thinkers if discussions involve not just what is exciting but also what might go wrong.

The very marketing risks that might initially seem to be capable of stopping a company meeting its business objectives could just be the source of new customer and shareholder value in the future.

Appendix: A partial checklist of marketing risks to manage

Each phase of marketing planning is a source of risk to an effective strategic marketing planning process. These phases include:

1. goal setting phase;
2. situation review phase;
3. strategy development phase;
4. strategy implementation phase;
5. monitoring, control and feedback phase.

The following lists present some key risks which might occur at each phase of the marketing planning process.

1. *Goal setting*

- Unrealistic/unachievable objectives in the context of resource, infrastructure, cultural or current and anticipated future market conditions.
- Goals related to past and current achievements rather than goals related to future market and industry opportunities or constraints.
- Investors do not support marketing plans.
- Unclear risk thresholds/appetite.
- Vision not being shared by all stakeholders.
- Differing strategic reference points.
- Unstated objectives and priorities.
- Unclear objectives and priorities.
- Inappropriate risk propensity – averse, neutral, risk taker.
- Lack of foresight.
- Risk precipitated by various heuristics, biases and overconfidence.
- 'Short termism'.
- Lack of alignment between marketing and business plans.
- Risks to reputation arising from setting objectives unacceptable to some stakeholders.
- Poor KPI (key performance indicators) setting.
- Inadequate risk communication.
- Confusion over financial capital parameters.
- Risk of risks being hidden – cultural unwillingness to be open about risks at strategic level.

2. *Situation review*

- Lack of information on customers, an understanding of what value means to them and the relationships that they are willing to have with their suppliers.
- Lack of information on competitors and their likely response profiles.
- Data misinterpretation.
- Too little/too much/poor quality data.
- Inability to make senses of future trends/changing requirements.
- Poor analytical capability for SWOT.
- Risks specific to international or emerging markets.

- Risks posed by regulation and other legal factors – compliance risk.
- Biased risk estimates – influence of heuristics and overconfidence.
- Risks inherent in the tendency to review in terms of the past.
- Risks inherent in the tendency to review only in terms of current competences and capabilities.
- Information overload, disorientation by uncertainties.
- Inappropriate segmentation.
- Danger of looking for facts not indicators of customer value.
- Too blue-sky thinking way beyond the set of competences and capabilities that could be developed during the planning period.
- Risk of lack of involvement of non-marketing functions in creating the information base for strategy development.

3. *Marketing strategy development*

- Compiling customer, competitor, supplier and trend data that doesn't convert to information or intelligence for strategy decision-making.
- Political risks.
- Insufficient emphasis on the future market-place rather than now or the past.
- Groupthink, overconfidence and other heuristics and biases.
- Insufficient consultation.
- Lack of creativity and inflexibility.
- Being caught in the headlights – too many options.
- Increasing vulnerability or volatility of cash flow.
- Failing to consider all reasonable options.
- Inappropriate positioning (market, offering, competitive).
- Non-impactful value propositions.
- Inappropriate balance between relationship and transactional strategies.
- Not learning from the past.
- Inappropriate product, customer, segment, brand, supplier or channel portfolio.
- Risk of product recall.
- Inappropriate pricing strategy.
- Non-integrated marketing communications strategy.
- Mergers and acquisition risks.
- Underestimating competitor response.
- Inappropriate level of innovation.
- Inappropriate level of differentiation.

- Risks posed to reputation by our choices of strategy.
- Lack of cooperation to reduce risks where functions interface.
- Strategy not based upon existing resource or committed extra resource.
- Infrastructure building blocks not in place.
- Cultural change and other change elements inherent in the marketing plan not addressed.

4. *Marketing strategy implementation*

- Not enough feedback from the market as implementation progresses.
- Customer dissatisfaction.
- Customer defection.
- Underestimating the market and being too successful to cope.
- Incompetence.
- Inflexibility.
- Everyone does their own thing at implementation.
- Egos.
- Management has no crisis management skills.
- Lack of top management commitment.
- Lack of direct responsibilities for implementation.
- Lack of commitment amongst implementers.
- Insecurities, conflict and internal competition.
- Focus on process not outcomes – not knowing when to revise/dump the plan.
- Losing energy or direction.
- Confused ownership.
- Lack of a structured approach to identifying, assessing and prioritizing.
- No contingency plans.
- Change management risks.
- Risk of scope creep.
- Inadequate market testing.
- Risks posed to reputation/customer and suppliers' trust in the organization by the way strategies are implemented.
- Risk that things just won't go as planned.
- Lack of alignment of resource base, infrastructure, inter-functional relationships and culture.
- Clash of priorities.
- Lack of ownership.

- Inflexibility.
- Delays in implementation.
- Poor communication.
- Under-resourcing.
- Project management failure.
- Insufficient attention to detail.
- Inconsistent risk awareness and response, e.g. supply chain.
- Unintended consequences, e.g. environmental.
- Lack of resilience.
- Business interruption.
- Employee turnover/displacement/relations.
- Product or service quality issues.
- IT systems risks.
- Risk that issues cannot be resolved appropriately.

5. *Monitoring control and feedback*

- The monitoring process does not take account of changing market-place conditions or industry characteristics.
- Internal controls do not take account of changing market-place conditions or industry characteristics.
- Feedback from the market-place does not inform the planning process and cycle.
- Field staff (e.g. sales) are protective of the data they hold and do not share salient facts.
- Feedback from the market-place is distorted to reflect personal agendas or is ignored.
- Monitoring process does not regularly review risks to the process of achieving marketing objectives.
- Internal controls derail marketing value creating processes.
- The organization does not learn from feedback from the market-place.
- Monitoring process does not recognize the interdependencies between functions.
- Internal controls do not recognize the interdependencies between functions.
- Feedback from the market-place does not come from a broad base of functions.
- The organization does not learn from any problems identified in the marketing resource base, infrastructure, inter-functional relationships and culture.

References and recommended reading

Ansoff, Igor (1957) Strategies for diversification. *Harvard Business Review* **35**:5 113–124.

COSO (2004) *Enterprise Risk Management – Integrated Framework*. Washington, DC: The Committee of Sponsoring Organizations of the Treadway Commission.

Cravens, Karen *et al.* (2003) The reputation index: measuring and managing corporate reputation. *European Management Journal* **21**:2 201–212.

Department of Trade and Industry (2005) *Operating and Financial Review*. See: http://www.dti.gov.uk/cld/financialreview.htm for details of current passage through Parliament into full legislation.

Grant Thornton (2004) *International Business Owners Survey*. See: http://www.grantthorntonibos.com

Halman, J I M and Keizer, J A (1994) Diagnosing risks in product-innovation projects. *International Journal of Project Management* **12**:2 75–80 (RDM – risk diagnosing methodology)

Hillson, David (2003a) *Effective Opportunity Management for Projects*. New York: Marcel Dekker.

Hillson, David (2003b) Using a risk breakdown structure in project management. *Journal of Facilities Management* **2**:1 85–97.

Jagpal, Sharan (1999) *Marketing Strategy and Uncertainty*. Oxford: Oxford University Press.

Kendrick, Terry (2004a) Strategic risk: am I doing OK? *Corporate Governance* **4**:4 69–77.

Kendrick, Terry (2004b) Strategic marketing risk management: creating and defending value. *Executive Briefings in Risk Management* 2/04 May.

Kendrick, Terry and Fletcher, Keith (2002) Addressing customer myopia: strategic interactive marketing planning in a volatile environment. *Journal of Database Marketing* **9**:3 207–218.

McDonald, Malcolm (2002) *Marketing Plans: How to Prepare Them How to Use Them*. Oxford: Butterworth Heinemann.

Palmer, Timothy B and Wiseman, Robert M (1999) Decoupling risk taking from income stream uncertainty: a holistic model of risk. *Strategic Management Journal* **20** 1037–1062.

Popham, Peter (2002) Fiat, motor of modern Italy, crashes amid strikes and sackings. In *The Independent*, 19 Oct.

Ryals, Lynette (2002) Measuring risk and returns in the customer portfolio. *Journal of Database Marketing* **9**:3 219–227.

Turnbull, N *et al.* (1999) *Internal Control – Guidance for Directors on the Combined Code*. London: Institute of Chartered Accountants in England and Wales. Available at: http://www.icaew.co.uk/internalcontrol

World Economic Forum (2004) Corporate brand reputation outranks financial performance as most important measure of success. Available at: http://www.weforum.org

8

Operational Risk Management

Keith Blacker

Operational risk in context

Background to operational risk

Within the financial services industry, the term 'operational risk' was barely in use 15 years ago. One might, therefore, be tempted to think that operational risk is a new risk and yet nothing could be further from the truth. Power (2003), in his essay on the invention of operational risk, discusses how the Baring's rogue trader Nick Leeson may have been the true author and unwitting inventor of the *term* 'operational risk' but that the history of such operational risk incidents stretches back over many years. Operational risk is not new; it is an artificial construct which has been formulated to give some meaning to a group of risks which collectively can pose a significant threat to an organization. Within the financial services industry it is rapidly developing into a discipline in its own right. Within this discipline there is a growing recognition that there are two distinct areas to operational risk: operational risk management and operational risk measurement. Whilst both are fundamentally aimed at protecting the business, the former achieves this through the development of appropriate structures, processes and the training of people, whilst the latter achieves it through the calculation and establishment of an appropriate capital buffer.

The financial services industry provides the setting for this chapter and both the qualitative (management) and quantitative (measurement) aspects of operational risk will be examined. The focus will be on the qualitative aspects and, in particular, the issues surrounding people. Regulatory initiatives are driving forward the hard factors of operational risk management, the policies, processes and information flows, and such factors are slowly becoming well-established within financial services organizations. These mechanisms, however, rely on people. People must diligently carry out their duties and responsibilities, have an awareness of operational risk and how it may impact upon their day-to-day operations, all within the boundaries of an articulated and widely communicated operational risk appetite. People are not only at the heart of good operational risk management but, together with natural disasters, they are the root cause of operational risk management failures.

Definition of operational risk

In 2001, the Basel Committee on Banking Supervision published its second Capital Accord document (Basel, 2001), universally known as Basel 2. The working definition for operational risk derived from this Accord, which is now widely accepted by the financial services industry both in the UK and abroad, is:

> The risk of loss resulting from inadequate or failed internal processes, people and systems or external events.

Within the confines of this chapter it is not possible to explore other definitions but they are all variations on the above theme. As the above definition indicates, operational risk covers a broad area because it includes:

- *all* internal processes/systems;
- *all* people within (and arguably outside) the organization;
- *any* type of external event.

Before this definition appeared and began to be used, in the day-to-day parlance of the financial services industry it was frequently stated that operational risk is anything other than market risk and credit risk. Whilst this might conceptually be an easy way to think about operational risk, one of the reasons for having a definition is to attempt to give some focus to the measurement and modelling of operational risk. Basel 2 requires operational risk to be quantified; therefore it is necessary to state what it is rather than what it is not. Thus, for example, strategic risk is specifically excluded from the quantification work.

The definition of operational risk provides organizations with a template from which they can began to develop suitable and appropriate categories of risk (examples include IT, legal and outsourcing) which come under the operational risk umbrella. Blacker (2001) identified that organizations developed these categories to facilitate both a better understanding of operational risk throughout the organization and the aggregation of operational risks across business units. In some cases, the number of categories used can run well into double figures, thus allowing a high degree of granularity in the subsequent mapping of operational risks across the organization.

Reasons for growth in the importance of operational risk

The financial services industry has seen more than its fair share of scandals over the last 20 years. Many of these can be traced back to a failure in the management of operational risk. Common themes in disasters have been researched by a number of writers (see, for example, Turner, 1976) and an analysis of three rogue trader incidents in the past decade – Barings, Allied Irish Bank and National Australia Bank – show a pattern of management failings. If we are not to see a further rogue trader type incident then these management failings and common themes need to be recognized as alarm bells which, if they start ringing, require immediate action (*Financial Times*, 2004). The old adage that 'prevention is better than cure' is highly appropriate in the field of operational risk management.

These large-scale corporate failures have certainly been instrumental in stoking the operational risk fire, but there are a number of factors which have fuelled the growth in the importance of operational risk. These include:

- *Globalization* – there is an increase in risk exposure when a company leaves its home market and ventures into uncharted waters. Whilst companies can reduce the operational risks through joint ventures and strategic alliances the balance will be between the cost of the risk ('We're going to do this on our own') and the cost of the control ('We're going to play safe and share the risk with somebody else'). Dale (1994), for example, sees globalization in banking on a number of levels: the cross border delivery of financial services to foreign residents; the penetration of foreign financial markets; the transactions between banks from different countries. McConnell (1996), in his analysis of market risk, noted the increasing trend towards globalization with its 'attractiveness to customers'. This drive towards improved marketing economies leads to greater concentration and with it increased operational risk.

- *Outsourcing* – the trend towards outsourcing in financial services has been noted by a number of commentators and has been identified by the UK Financial Services Authority (FSA) as a key area of operational risk management. The operational risk implications of any type of outsourcing arrangements, whether they be strategic or tactical, need to be considered and understood as part of the decision-making process.
- *Information technology* – McConnell (1996) illustrated how the rapid developments in Information Technology provide the platform from which financial services companies can provide new and enhanced services to their customers. The reduction in transaction costs brought about by these developments has, over the last decade, seen new entrants into the UK banking market – supermarkets such as Tesco and Sainsbury and retailers such as Marks and Spencer. This is a dual edged sword in the management of risk since it requires new processes to deal with the new technologies (operational risk) and new strategies to deal with the competition.
- *Business climate* – more informed customers, new entrants and financial innovations, such as the growth in internet banking, lead to increased competitive pressures and a greater need to manage the resultant operational risks that emerge from dealing with these issues. Effective change management is almost a part of the daily routine for many managers. This, in turn, leads to quicker decision-making timeframes and stretches the ability of such managers to be well-informed about the consequences of their actions.
- *Regulation* – Basel 2 (Basel, 2001), and more recently the European Union Capital Requirements Directive (EU, 2004), are two of the main drivers behind the regulatory work being carried out by the FSA. Interpreting their non-prescriptive requirements (not just in relation to operational risk) is proving to be a challenge to many financial services organizations. In addition other guidance, such as Turnbull (Turnbull *et al.*, 1999), has placed more emphasis on (operational) risk management and the disclosure and reporting of (operational) risk management activities.

Operational risk management framework

Roles and responsibilities

Operational risk exists in every organizational procedure whether it be a simple petty cash system or a more complex strategic planning process and the organizational influence on operational risk is, therefore, widespread and covers all employees. Looking at operational risk from a people perspective requires a collective and integrated effort from the whole organization. The main players can be represented as the pieces of a jigsaw puzzle (as shown in Figure 8.1).

The key is making sure that the pieces fit together and no operational risk can fall through the cracks. Some of the drivers behind enabling a good fit include:

1. a coherent and widely used operational risk-mapping framework (discussed later);
2. a risk-based internal audit approach;
3. a willingness by management to use specialists to help them manage their operational risks;
4. good communication channels;
5. well-trained and risk-aware staff.

The operational risk function in the jigsaw is a recent development but in practice it can lead others in the organization to assume that risk is now under control. As Corduff (2003) noted the operational risk function is not a lightning rod that will attract and dissipate all unwelcome risk. It does not manage operational risk but facilitates the management of operational risk. Risk in general, and operational risk in particular,

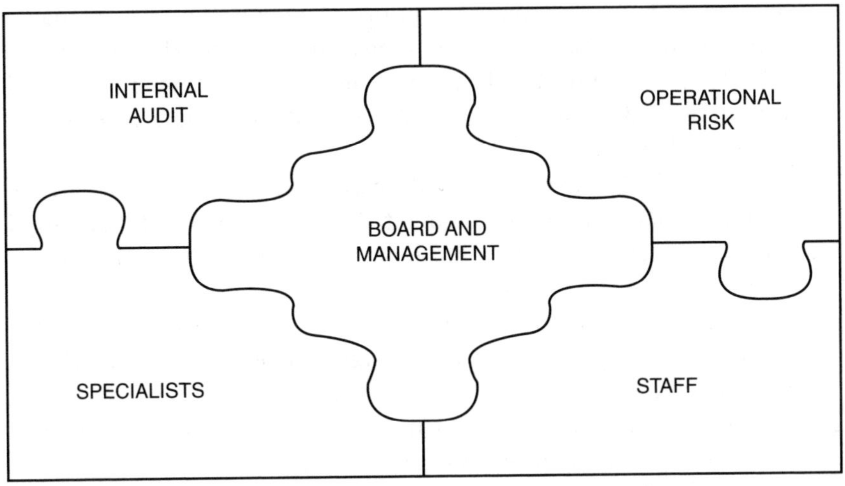

Figure 8.1 The jigsaw of operational risk responsibility

is an integral element of any business, and ultimate responsibility lies with the board of directors, since it is they who create the climate within which risk generally will be managed. Non-executive directors, in particular, have been cited as being in need of enhanced skills in the area of risk management (Higgs, 2003). Whether boards can cope with risk is beyond the scope of this chapter but it is not difficult to find in the litany of company failures a reference to boards not fully understanding the risks of the businesses which they are responsible for directing (see the Ludwig Report: Promontory Financial Group *et al.*, 2002). It is perhaps for boards to recognize that their challenge is not just to maximize shareholder (or stakeholder) value, but to protect it as well.

Operational risk management process

Fifteen years ago operational risk was being managed implicitly or informally with little in the way of documentation and no effort to be proactive or assign responsibilities for managing it. Today it is being managed explicitly or formally. An organization has to demonstrate that it is aware of its operational risks and what it is proactively doing to manage them. The question this poses is whether this formalization of operational risk management has led to a best practice in operational risk management? Work undertaken by the author (Blacker, 2001) suggests that whilst best practice may not (yet) exist, core practices have begun to emerge. Figure 8.2 illustrates a model of core operational risk practice.

The components of implicit or informal operational risk management are shown as shaded boxes along the horizontal line marked 'Phase'. These equate to the phases of a simple risk management model found in many risk management books: risk identification, assessment, mitigation and follow-up.

With the arrival of explicit/formal operational risk management, the core components have been augmented by a number of additional components which are represented by a further three horizontal lines:

1. process – the risk-mapping framework is now the driver behind the whole of the operational risk management effort and the phases are embedded within it;
2. elements – each of the phases has a number of distinct elements which act as the main drivers for that phase;
3. result – there is an explicitly stated current level of operational risk and a desired level of operational risk.

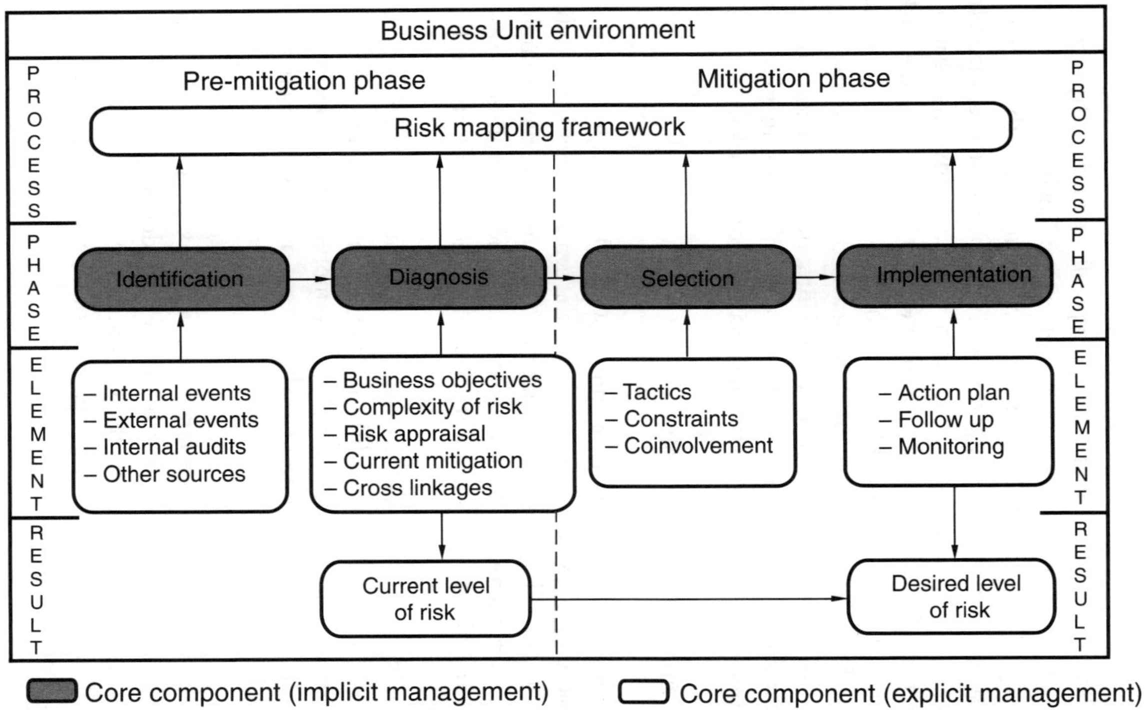

(from Blacker, 2001)

Figure 8.2 Core operational risk management model

The diagram illustrates that operational risk has to be managed within a particular context, in this case the business unit. Within that context, two main phases exist: the pre-mitigation phase and the mitigation phase. The pre-mitigation phase consists of:

1. *Identification* – operational risks are typically identified through the examination of internal and external events (incidents/losses), by the Internal Audit function and via a number of other sources (workshops, questionnaires, and so on) specific to the organization.
2. *Diagnosis* – the diagnosis represents the qualitative assessment, which provides management with the current level of the risk, normally assessed as the likelihood of occurrence and financial impact. There are a number of elements used to arrive at the diagnosis: the objectives of the Business Unit, the complexity of the risk, the initial risk appraisal, the current mitigants in place and the cross-linkages that the risk may have to other risks.

The mitigation phase consists of:

1. *Selection* – this is the decision phase when the manager examines the risk diagnosis and selects, from the options available, what action to take. There are a number of elements that will influence the decision, including the tactics available, the constraints imposed by the organization and the knowledge of who may be able to help to mitigate the risk.
2. *Implementation* – the development of any action plan (based on the mitigation tactic selected) and the use of adequate follow-up procedures, together with the ongoing monitoring of operational risk indicators, aim to reduce the operational risk down to its desired level.

This approach of reducing the large and complex area of operational risk management down to a few boxes in a model is not intended to trivialize the task ahead but merely to identify the building blocks from which a tailored solution to the organization's own particular circumstances may be constructed.

Incident databases

The use of operational risk incident databases across the banking industry has been developing over the last few years (Thirwell, 2003).

In other sectors of the UK financial services industry there have been calls for similar initiatives (The Giro Working Party, 2004) but it would be fair to say that most of the work done to date has been done at the individual company level rather than the industry level.

The basic aim of the database is to register events that take place either internally or externally which have an impact, or could impact the strategy, financial viability or capital requirements of the organization. Events, which may reflect an actual loss or near miss, are prescribed and fall within set boundaries such as:

- an issue that has resulted in a financial loss in excess of £x (where x is determined by the organization);
- a collection of issues, resulting from the same cause, that have together resulted in a financial loss of £x;
- a potential loss was prevented or substantially mitigated;
- a substantial amount of (normally unbudgeted) costs is likely;
- a latent impact, which may be difficult to quantify, may well occur.

Such events are not confined to operational risk events but events generally, although most would fall within the broad definition of operational risk. There is no standard *modus operandi* for establishing, using and maintaining an incident database. Figure 8.3 illustrates an example of the information flow of an incident database used in practice.

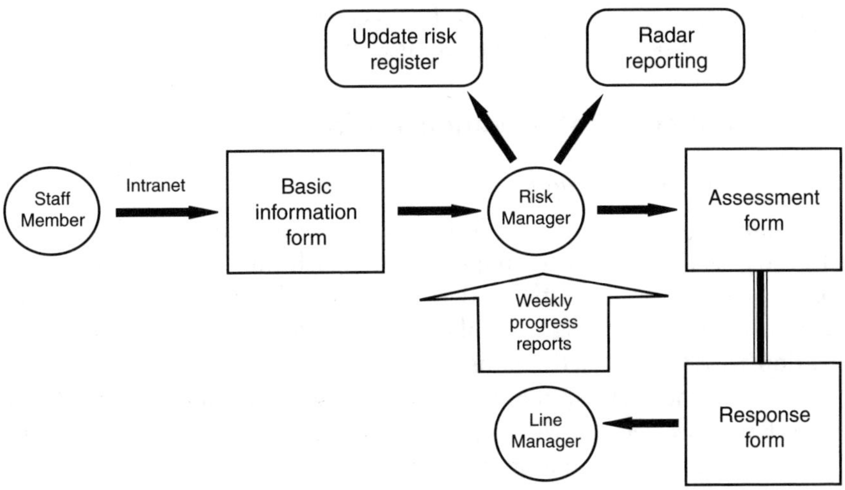

Figure 8.3 Information flow for an incident database

One of the key points to note in this example is that all members of staff have access to the incident database, reinforcing the point being made in the roles and responsibilities jigsaw that everybody has a part to play in operational risk management. Access and data input can be set up via the company intranet and with clearly articulated procedures; this approach is known to work well in practice.

Centralizing the reporting and recording of events in this way serves several purposes:

- Events can be used as a means to continuously improve the processes used throughout the organization in order that they fail less often in the future.
- Monitoring of events allows management to identify adverse trends within the organization in order to determine if resources are effectively employed.
- The process acts as a backstop to ensure that all risks are captured, thereby supporting risk management.
- It serves to improve the overall level of risk awareness throughout the organization and enable all members of staff to contribute to enhancing the risk management capabilities.
- It provides a source of data for assisting in the measurement of operational risk.

This last point is considered important for financial services organizations since it provides quantifiable losses that have been suffered by the business which may be used as a basis for predicting what future operational losses may occur. This in turn can be used to help calculate the operational risk capital buffer required by the regulators.

The measurement of operational risk

Why measure operational risk?

The short answer to this question is because within the financial services industry it is a regulatory requirement which aims to provide a level of stability in the industry and reduce the volatility of earnings. The argument is that having a regulatory capital buffer enables the organization to be cushioned against operational risks which, if they were to manifest themselves, might otherwise close the business down. Allied Irish Bank (see the Ludwig Report: Promontory Financial Group *et al.*, 2002) is a good example of this. Despite its $679 million rogue trader loss it maintained sufficient regulatory capital on its balance sheet (its overall capital ratio fell from 13.3 per cent to 10 per cent, still above the 8 per cent required), thus allowing it to continue trading, albeit with a somewhat tarnished reputation.

There are probably few who would disagree that looking at operational risk in purely quantitative terms could lead to a distorted view of a situation and so any resultant figures should be used with a degree of caution. One of the aims of calculating operational risk capital is to then use the techniques to allocate capital to business units within the organization. Internally this can then be used to reflect more accurately the business unit's cost of capital: the greater the operational risks, the higher the charge. This in turn will lead to a more accurate return on capital calculation for the business unit. Implementation of this type of approach, however, needs to be done taking due cognisance of some of the softer factors, such as getting business unit buy in, having performance measurement systems being linked to risk-adjusted rewards and incentivizing the business unit to lower their capital charge through better operational risk management.

Further issues arise with the different emphasis being placed by different regulators on which organizations should/should not be subject to the capital charge, which approach they should be using and whether this will achieve one of the stated aims of Basel 2, to create a level playing field internationally. Then there is the view of the rating agencies who are known to have always factored in risk management capabilities into their ratings and have produced a number of discussion papers on operational risk (see Young, 2003). Whatever point of view you take on this issue, it is clear that measuring operational risk can only provide a long-stop control. The best way to prevent operational risk occurring is through effective management not measurement.

Approaches to measuring operational risk

Operational risk measurement can involve a number of methods normally based on historical information, simulated information or a combination of the two. Basel (2001) offers three alternative approaches to 'valuing' operational risk:

1. Basic indicator approach – this calculates a value for operational risk capital using a single indicator as a proxy for an institution's overall operational risk exposure.
2. Standardized approach – this calculates a value for operational risk capital based on standard business unit lines using a broad financial indicator (e.g. income) multiplied by a beta factor (i.e. proxy for the operational loss experience).

3. Advanced measurement approach – this uses the bank's own internal loss data and a combination of qualitative and quantitative methods to calculate a value for operational risk capital.

The detail of these approaches is well documented in Basel 2 and Figure 8.4 illustrates how they fall within a spectrum. As one might expect the advanced measurement approach requires considerably more time and effort to calculate but, in theory at least, it should produce a lower capital figure. Basel 2 does not just deal with the calculation of operational risk capital. There are also approaches for calculating both market and credit risk capital charges.

The publication of Basel 2 was the catalyst for the development of a range of software tools to hit the market. Such tools cover both operational risk management and operational risk measurement, with a number offering an integrated package for those who are looking to use the advanced measurement approach. Concurrently, numerous conferences worldwide on operational risk measurement began to appear together with articles and papers both in practitioner and academic journals. The operational risk measurement bandwagon was rolling and nothing was likely to get it in its way.

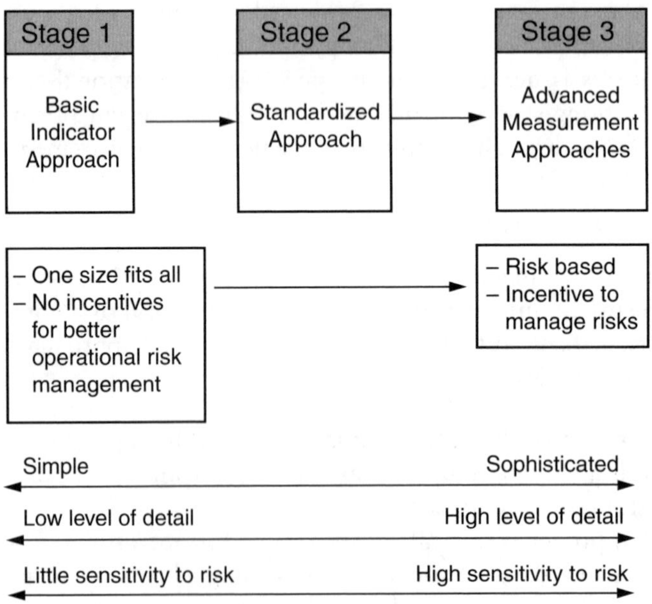

Figure 8.4 Approaches to measuring operational risk

As at the time of writing (April 2005) financial services organizations who have chosen to use the advanced measurement approach still have much work to do in adequately measuring operational risk exposures before the Basel 2 implementation date of December 2006. It may be that the application of a judicious approach to measuring operational risk will be sufficient for most organizations, but as one practitioner told me: 'You set aside capital for the unexpected and not the extreme', a view supported by Dowd (1998) who states that, whilst some operational risks may be easily quantified, others are 'clearly impossible' (Dowd, 1998, p 198).

Further examination of the advanced measurement approach reveals four key elements to be used in the calculation. All of these elements can be combined in different ways:

1. Historical data
   - Historical (internal) loss data – gathered from the incident database (see previous section).
   - External loss data – gathered from external loss databases such as the commercially available ORX and Opvantage.
2. Forward-looking data
   - Business environment and internal control factors – the risk mapping framework is used to capture and quantify potential future events that may affect the operational risk profile of the organization.
   - Scenario analysis/stress testing – Scenario analysis aims to capture and quantify high-severity events, drawing on the knowledge of experienced business managers and risk management experts. Stress testing is a way of affixing sensitivities to different scenarios, which carry different impacts, or different impact levels, of the same type of risk.

It is expected that organizations will start with scenario analysis and then migrate through the others as the data sets grow and the information becomes richer and the analysis more thorough. A template of the method being used in a financial services organization for scenario analysis, and also for stress testing, is illustrated overleaf:

Definitions

Scenario analysis looks at simultaneous moves in a number of risk factors often linked to explicit changes in the view of the world or specific events.

Stress testing estimates the impact on the organization if a particular risk factor moves in an adverse manner.

Details for each stress test/scenario analysis

Category

The category of operational risk.

Description

Details of the operational risk event.

Level

Company describes the area(s) of business within the organization that would be affected by the event.

Market describes how the event would affect other companies in the industry. This is only included if the effect on other companies would in turn influence the organization's finances or decision choices available to the organization's management.

Gross loss calculation

Rationale for establishing what a 1 in *x* (probability factor) year event would be and how the gross loss to the organization is calculated. The gross loss is the ultimate cost to the organization as a direct result of the event.

Knock-on effects

Details of the costs or savings to the organization due to effects triggered by the risk event, and how they are calculated. These are split into three categories:

1. *Company* – costs or savings to the organization as a result of existing arrangements.
2. *Market* – costs or savings to the organization due to the effect of the event on the market.
3. *Management* – costs or savings to the company due to management reaction to the event.

The net cost of the event is the cost after taking into account the knock-on effects.

Loss distribution

In order to model the effect of the risk event, a range of frequencies and severities is given for each risk.

Parameters

A brief description of how the risk event is modelled in the software program used by the organization.

The regulators will review the calculations that are used to measure operational risk in order to ensure that they are fit for the purpose and that there is a clear rationale for all the assumptions underlying the analytical framework in use.

The difficulties of quantification

The preceding brief comments and analysis of operational risk measurement do not do justice to the science of operational risk. Whether one agrees or disagrees with the idea of quantifying operational risk, and there are many people in both camps, is probably no longer the issue. Financial services organizations have always had an implicit capital buffer for operational risk. What they are expected to do now is make the calculation of that buffer explicit using one of the three methods. The issue then is not what needs doing, but what are the difficulties in doing it and what might be done to overcome those issues? The following are examples.

- Historical performance is no guide to the future – this type of warning appears on the promotion of investment products in the UK as a caveat to those who think that, just because a particular investment has historically yielded a good return, it will continue to do so. The same is true for historical internal risk incidents. Changes of management and risk appetite can influence the manifestation of future operational risk incidents. One solution would be to use the captured data in combination with forward-looking data and not to rely too heavily on historical events to calculate the operational risk capital charge.
- Shortage of skilled resource – evidence suggests that the skills required to undertake the type of detailed modelling work required are not in abundance. The actuarial profession is well placed to provide such skills but not every organization needs such skills to manage their day-to-day operations. Aside from adopting one of the two simpler approaches, the only other alternative is to use external resource to assist with the detailed calculation work.
- Recording of loss events – the recording of events in the incident database presupposes that all events will be recorded. The system is entirely reliant on people to own up and admit to making a loss but, as history has shown, this will not always happen: the three rogue trader incidents previously cited attest to this. In the author's experience, the best way to encourage people to own up is through

the development of an organizational culture which is seen as 'just' or 'fair' and which sees mistakes as an opportunity to learn rather than to blame. This is easier said than done!

- Getting regulatory buy-in – the calculation of operational risk capital is a new area also for the regulators. In the case of the UK, the FSA's non-prescriptive approach allows a certain amount of discretion to firms when calculating the operational risk capital charge (too prescriptive and it could introduce systemic risk). The regulators will want to make sure that organizations have used valid assumptions and robust data and not tried to force the figure that they wanted. Equally they will want to ensure that the end result looks reasonable in relation to all the other similar business that they have to regulate. Operational risk managers are likely to be in the front line of dealing with the regulators and will need to hone their negotiating skills in order to achieve regulatory buy-in throughout the process.
- Model risk – the use of modelling techniques to calculate the operational risk charge brings with it model risk, i.e. the risk that the models themselves may produce incorrect results due to incorrect programming, inappropriate assumptions or spurious data being entered. An organization must have good internal controls over the development and implementation of models, particularly where they are brought in externally.

It will be apparent that the development of forward-looking scenarios for modelling operational risk relies totally on people to establish the scenarios in the first place, and in doing so, people must restrict their thinking and vision in order to see what *might* happen. The issue here is that people are likely to suffer from risk myopia and be guided down paths which are familiar to them because of their backgrounds, prejudices, thinking processes, sensory perceptions, lack of imagination and inherent fears. Being able to anticipate events that might not happen is not just a matter of somebody switching on their internal radar and scanning as widely as possible. Inevitably, there are problems with this approach:

- *Range*: the radar screen is not big enough and, in an interdependent world, more things are causally connected than can be shown on the screen, e.g. the famous chaos theory butterfly flutters its wings in China, which triggers a complex chain of events that results in a tornado in Texas.

- *Depth*: the radar suffers from similar problems to geologists studying the deep underlying causes of a volcano erupting (or not), e.g. it is like trying to anticipate the macro area changes in the Japanese economy in 1990, the fall of the Soviet Empire and the Berlin Wall and a three year decline in the UK stock market.

Being able to spot remote-in-the-future threats and connecting them with current conditions and symptoms is an art and not a science. The art underpins the science and it always will. It is an inherent weakness in operational risk modelling that some of the data upon which the calculation relies is subjective and likely to be incomplete. Unfortunately, there is no known cure for this problem.

People risk

Understanding people risk

The previous sections have discussed some of the so-called hard factors of operational risk, all of which are necessary to facilitate the management and measurement of operational risk. The ongoing management of operational risk, as the definition implies, relies on the continued efficacy of the processes and procedures that are established by management as part of the overall risk governance system. All these mechanisms, however, cannot always guarantee to guard against the foibles of human behaviour. The correct operation of the mechanisms depends upon people and people are, again as the definition implies, a source of operational risk, and maybe *the* main source. Inevitably, therefore, when you are considering your approach to managing operational risk, it is necessary to consider people.

This focus on the people perspective looks at the behaviours of individuals in diligently carrying out their assigned duties and responsibilities and the bounds within which employees must themselves take risks with or without a clear understanding of their organization's tolerance of, or appetite for, operational risk. The following quote by Mark Lawrence, Chief Risk Officer of ANZ Bank at a risk management conference in Australia in 2003, summarizes the issue:

> People are somehow at the heart of this (operational) risk process and you only have to look at the Allied Irish Bank's experience a little more than a year ago and read the Ludwig report, which was distributed to the market. It was an 80-page

> or so litany of control failures leading to a near $700 million loss ... these control failures were really about either the absence of a policy or a control. Or, in most cases, human beings that were supposed to be doing something, not doing what they were supposed to be.

Further evidence to support the importance of people risk can be found in the UK Financial Services Authority's Consultative Paper 142 (FSA, 2002) which has a specific section (3A.4) covering people. It advises that a firm should maintain appropriate systems and controls for the management of operational risk that can arise from employees. This would cover such areas as:

- its operational risk culture and any variations in risk culture and human resource management practises across its operations;
- whether the way employees are remunerated causes an increase in operational risk;
- the extent of compliance with applicable regulatory and statutory requirements that relate to the welfare and conduct of employees;
- its arrangements for the continuity of operations in the event of employee unavailability or loss;
- the relationship between indicators of people risk (such as overtime, sickness and turnover levels) and operational losses and exposures;
- the relevance of all of the above to employees of a third-party supplier that are involved in performing an outsourcing arrangement.

People risk focuses attention on aspects of human error and how systems and procedures can be designed to either eliminate or alert the occurrence of such events. Work by Reason (1990) and Perrow (1999) has investigated the approaches to people risk within the ambience of high-risk/hazardous technologies and there is a body of literature in this area catalogued under the generic title of safety management. Much of the research has been directed towards engineers working in these high-risk/hazardous technologies where the margin for human error has to be reduced to as close to zero as possible because of the catastrophic effects that an incident may have (see Kletz, 1993; Petroski, 1985 and Reason, 1997 for examples).

There is little evidence in the literature of extensive studies being undertaken in the financial services industry, possibly due to the impacts being measured in 'monetary' rather than 'human' terms. If, as Reason (1990) asserts, modern technology has now reached the point where improved safety can only be achieved through a better understanding of human error mechanisms, then there is no logical reason why this should not equally apply to financial services. This dependence on technology, without which most of the global financial services market would cease to operate, must go hand in hand with the management of people risk. After all, it is people that develop and use (and in some case manipulate) the systems upon which the financial services industry so heavily depends.

People risk, as Mark Lawrence asserted above, also covers the deliberate, as opposed to accidental, actions of employees against the organization. The previously cited Allied Irish Bank $679 million loss, together with other well-known examples, serve to illustrate the potential scale of the problem both within and outside of financial services organizations. So, what do we mean by people risk? Blacker *et al.* (2004) proposed a definition as follows:

> The possibility that people will damage themselves, their organisation or the wider community either inadvertently or intentionally by deviating from best practice or prescribed rules for controlling risk.

People risk DNA

Risk taking is a fact of everyday life for all of us. Whether it be in a social or a workplace context people take risks, most of the time subconsciously, without even bothering to go through the stages of identifying and assessing a risk and then deciding on a course of action. We have all been trained by practice and experience in the management of risk and our perspective on, and perceptions of, risk result from our upbringing, our environment and our individual make-up (Adams, 1995, p 1). We all have our own 'risk DNA' which influences our risk-taking traits and the decisions that we make when faced with uncertainty. In an organizational context, we make decisions every day, some of which can have a profound effect upon the company we work for. Responding to a potential operational risk involves making a decision, even if that decision is to do nothing.

Recognizing the way that people behave in these types of risky situations does not mean we should move into the concepts and theories of popular psychology. The focus here is on operational risk and improving our understanding of what could cause people, or in some cases groups of people, to 'damage themselves, their organization or the wider community either inadvertently or intentionally by deviating from best practice or prescribed rules for controlling risk'. The causes of why people behave in this way can be simple or complex and may involve one or a number of the following.

- Not knowing what to do in a particular situation because people had not been trained or because the training they had was inadequate.
- Believing the world is a safer place than it is and thus failing to see the warning signals that something is about to go wrong.
- Being overconfident because of previous successes.
- Misunderstanding verbal or written communications.
- Relying too much on intuition rather than hard supporting evidence.
- Being stressed, tired, overworked, underworked or a combination of these.
- Being subject to environmental factors outside of work which may impair performance.
- Being influenced too much by 'group think' and/or the dominance of certain individuals in the group.

Hillson and Murray-Webster (2005) discuss in detail many of the drivers of risk psychology and the above list serves to provide an indication of some of the root causes of operational risk based on the authors' own discussions, experiences and research.

Another important people factor in operational risk incidents is to do with learning from past mistakes. Toft (1992), who has done extensive work in this area, describes how organizations, and the people within them, fail to use hindsight effectively by 'disregarding valuable information' and 'not recognising the isomorphic qualities possessed by incidents when they occur'. The rogue trader incidents at Allied Irish Bank and Barings had a number of striking similarities in the events that took place: the reporting lines and accountabilities of the rogue traders were blurred; the incidents took place at operations which were remote from the Corporate Head Office; both individuals were seen as star performers; both traders operated in volatile markets; senior management did not fully understand the products which were being traded. It would appear that organizations who want to ensure that they maintain effective control over operational risk must be prepared to learn the lessons not just from their own mistakes, but from the mistakes of others as well.

People risk in the workplace

One factor which needs to be taken into account in looking at people risk is the organizational setting. Much of this chapter has focused on financial services because that is where the term 'operational risk' is most commonly used. But, as Cooper (2004) pointed out, it is important to bear in mind that there are some important differences between an industrial and a financial services environment which could impact the propensity of individuals (and groups) to destroy value, either accidentally or deliberately. Table 8.1 illustrates the point.

This type of analysis could equally be carried out in other organizational settings.

People risk and organizational culture

Perhaps the greatest challenge for any organization which is looking to improve its people risk management and, in doing so, its operational risk management capabilities is creating the right culture and finding

Table 8.1 Comparison of people risk in industrial and financial settings

Industrial settings	*Financial settings*
'Errors' are mostly due to people reaching their physical limits.	'Errors' mostly arise when people reach their mental/cognitive limits.
The systems people are working in are relatively simple (e.g. manufacturing processes are built around linear, causal relationships). The environment is 'manageable'.	The systems are highly complex and widely distributed. This environment is, at best, only partly manageable.
Risk prevention is mainly concerned with physical safety and avoiding accidents.	Risk prevention is concerned with the security of value/assets.
Risk prevention is aimed at avoiding physical harm.	Risk prevention is aimed at avoiding financial loss.
The main incentive for individuals to make deliberate mistakes is malevolence or sabotage. Only a small proportion of people will have this incentive.	The main incentive for committing deliberate 'mistakes' is personal financial gain. This potentially represents an incentive for a larger proportion of the people and is an extension of self-interest.
Risk taking is not central to operations (the aim is to avoid disruptions to production).	Risk taking and risk management is a key skill in financial services – risk is of central importance and has a lot of meaning.

the most effective means of instilling desired core organizational values into the hearts and minds of each member of the organization. Shaping the way that people think, behave and respond to an operational risk is fine in theory but requires a consistent and continuous reinforcement of the core values, especially by those at the top of the organization. Operational risk is broad in nature and impacts across the whole of the organization. Imbuing an appropriate culture which heightens awareness of operational risk whilst at the same time recognizes and encourages the notion of taking risks is a challenge for any organization. Inevitably some will be better at it than others.

Organizational culture and its relationship to risk generally is a large subject area which has been reviewed by a number of authors (see, for example, Waring and Glendon, 1998). Based on the work of Blacker *et al.* (2004) there are a number of characteristics found in organizations where a general culture of heightened risk awareness exists:

1. *good organizational learning* – a culture that is willing to stimulate and encourage new ideas (taking risks) provides an environment for organizational learning to take place;
2. *high job satisfaction* – when employees have a real personal interest in their job and are rewarded appropriately and fairly, then this helps to engender a feeling of contentment and motivation;
3. *no witch hunts when things go wrong* – the 'just' or 'fair' culture previously alluded to appears to have a strong influence on the way that people behave by helping them to understand the boiling point of the organizational risk thermostat;
4. *a challenge process which is actively encouraged* – if this process is correctly managed it can help overcome the 'group think' attitude that is common and part of human nature;
5. *a board which is strongly committed to risk management* – everything about the culture of the organization will be driven down from the top;
6. *appropriate human resource practices* – this begins at the recruitment stage where employees are selected on the basis of their cultural fit within the organization;
7. *quality training in risk awareness* – neither the board nor management on their own can effectively manage risk. On a day-to-day basis they rely on the workforce to help them discharge this responsibility and training in risk awareness is a key factor in embedding an appropriate risk culture.

Inasmuch as the procedures of risk management must be backed by an appropriate culture, the implication for the chief executive is that it is they who must provide the leadership and nurturing support for such a culture. If it were asked what more could the chief executive do, the answer, for effective operational risk management, is as it would be for anything else to be effective – choose, retain and influence the right people for the right jobs.

Where is operational risk management heading?

Current tensions in managing operational risk

Operational risk in the financial services industry is taxing the minds and budgets of many organizations thanks largely to the expectations of Basel 2 and the growing realization that improving operational risk management can add value to the business and improve bottom line performance. That said, there is still some way to go before both operational risk management and operational risk measurement are firmly embedded into the organization, particularly where there are many business units which are both diverse in nature and geographically spread. The development of risk management standards (see, for example, AS/NZS 4360:2004; IRM *et al.*, 2002) has begun in earnest over the last few years with the most recent being the COSO framework for enterprise risk management. COSO stands for the Committee of Sponsoring Organizations of the Treadway Commission and its first framework for internal control, produced in 1992, had elements of risk management included. In September 2004, a framework for enterprise-wide risk management was published which aimed to establish a set of integrated principles, common terminology and implementation guidance for risk management (for more information, see http://www.coso.org).

Basel 2 does not prescribe any standards for operational risk management, stating merely that the framework that is implemented must be conceptually sound and integrated with integrity. Given the amount of time and effort that went into producing the COSO framework it was expected that the end result would provide (a) a solution to those who had not yet implemented a framework and (b) a benchmark for those who already had a framework in place. It is, therefore, perhaps somewhat surprising to find discussions taking place on why COSO is flawed and should not be used as a framework for operational risk management because it 'not only fails to help a firm assess its (operational) risks, it actually obfuscates the risk assessment process'

(Samad-Khan, 2005). McConnell (2005) takes a slightly more pragmatic view by recognizing that there are strengths and weaknesses in any such standards but that 'any good standard is better than no standard'. For those who were hoping that COSO might become the de facto standard for (operational) risk management this is clearly a body blow. Only time will tell if Basel 2 and COSO will converge and produce a document which is not only acceptable to all, but usable by all.

Another tension lies buried in the operational risk jigsaw puzzle. The roles of the operational risk unit and the internal audit function are, in most organizations, well-documented and articulated. However, in smaller organizations it is not uncommon to find these two roles combined under a Head of Internal Audit and Risk Management. Whilst the regulators expect to see an independent internal audit function, segregated from the operational risk unit, commercial realities will often dictate otherwise. This problem has been partly addressed by the Institute of Internal Auditors (UK and Ireland) who have published guidance on the subject (Institute of Internal Auditors, 2004) which identifies where the boundaries of responsibility lie from an audit perspective. This clarification will certainly help internal auditors and operational risk managers but it also needs to be explained to the front-line management and staff so that they clearly understand the roles and responsibilities of both internal audit and operational risk. This understanding applies even if there are two separate functions. It is my experience that line management and staff become understandably confused when they see two sets of people looking at the risks in their area and begin to question the added value from such activities. The answer lies in a constant reinforcement of operational risk's role in facilitating the management of operational risk and internal audit's role in providing independent assurance that operational risk is being managed effectively. The latter, of course, includes auditing the work of the operational risk unit.

A number of other tensions can exist in the development of operational risk which need to be considered in an organizational context. These include, for example:

1. operational risk lethargy setting into the organization;
2. boards and management abdicating their responsibility for operational risk management once the operational risk manager is appointed;
3. operational risk management not being fully integrated into operational risk measurement;

4. boards and management seeing operational risk management as purely a regulatory overhead and not an added value activity.

Raising the level of awareness of operational risk

The final section of this chapter discusses raising the level of operational risk awareness across the organization. Operational risk is a broad area of risk and it is imperative that people understand better how they are expected to contribute to the management, and in some cases the measurement, of operational risk. There is, however, a not-to-be-underestimated challenge in doing this. As will be apparent from reading this chapter, operational risk is concerned with looking at what could go wrong or managing the downside. But what about the other side of the risk management coin, taking risks? The words of the Arctic explorer, Sir Robert McClure spring to mind:

adventure = risk + purpose.

It is easy to see what he had in mind (for an individual) when he wrote this. If you have a *purpose* in life and are prepared to take *risks*, the net result will be your personal journey of *adventure*: the journey to *your* chosen destination. Take the risk out of the equation and your adventure and your purpose are the same. In other words, zero risk means no journey, no destination and not really much point in getting out of bed in the morning!

What McClure is pointing to in a business setting is that organizations have to take risks to grow, develop and achieve their goals. This is no more so than in the financial services industry where banks are in business to take risks, usually using other people's money; the trading activity is the often-quoted example of this. But it extends to developing and launching new products and services, acquiring new businesses and books of business, and establishing challenging sales targets. And this is where the challenge lies: raising operational risk awareness without stifling risk taking.

There is no doubt that formal operational risk management, and with it operational risk measurement, is here to stay. Driven by increasing regulatory demands and other corporate governance pressures, it makes good sense to utilize risk management proactively as a tool to manage the business, rather than merely accept it as just another bureaucratic overhead. Raising the level of operational risk awareness can only benefit the organization and will be welcomed and supported by the regulators. But we need to remember that the regulators do not spend too much time thinking about the effect that the regulations will have on the bottom line and shareholder value. This is the role of the board.

Even back in the 19th century, Robert McClure would have been well prepared before he set out on his adventures. He recognized that taking risks was necessary when venturing into uncharted and potentially dangerous waters. He knew he had to think ahead and (proactively) take precautions to manage potential risks that might arise as he journeyed towards his destination. His *attitude* to risk would have been one of the key factors in determining the success or otherwise of his adventure . . . and so it is for any organization which faces and wishes to manage operational risk.

References and recommended reading

Adams, J (1995) *Risk*. London: UCL Press.

AS/NZS 4360:2004, *Risk Management*. Homebush, Australia: Standards Australia; Wellington: Standards New Zealand.

Basel (2001) *New Basel Capital Accord – Consultative Document*. Basel: Basel Committee on Banking Supervision.

Blacker, K (2001) *An Investigation into Operational Risk Mitigation in UK Retail Banks*. DBA Thesis, Brunel University, October.

Blacker, K, Mills, R W and Weinstein, W L (2004) People Risk in the Financial Services Industry, *Henley Working Paper Series*, Ref. HWP 0403.

Cooper, D (2004) Comments on 'People Risk in the Financial Services Industry', correspondence with the author, November.

Corduff, B (2003) The importance of risk management in a corporate environment. Unpublished paper.

Dale, R (1994) Regulating investment business in the single market. *Bank of England Quarterly Bulletin*, Nov., 333–340.

Dowd, K (1998) *Beyond Value at Risk*. Chichester: Wiley.

European Union (EU) (2004) Capital Requirements Directive. Available at: http://europa.eu.int/comm/internal_market/bank/regcapital/index_en.htm#consultation

Financial Services Authority (FSA) (2002) *CP142 Operational Risk Systems and Controls*. Available at: http://www.fsa.gov.uk/pubs/cp/cp142.pdf

Financial Times (2004) Rogue traders are a risk that won't go away. 9 Dec.

The Giro Working Party (2004) *Quantifying Operational Risk in General Insurance Companies*. Presented to Institute of Actuaries, March. Available at: http://www.actuaries.org.uk

Higgs, D (2003) *Review of the Role and Effectiveness of Non-Executive Directors*. London: Department of Trade and Industry. Available at: http://www.dti.gov.uk/cld/non_exec_review

Hillson, D A and Murray-Webster, R (2005) *Understanding and Managing Risk Attitude*. Aldershot: Gower Publishing.

Institute of Internal Auditors (IIA) (2004) *The Role of Internal Audit in Enterprise-Wide Risk Management.* Position statement, Sept.

Institute of Risk Management (IRM), Association of Insurance and Risk Managers (AIRMIC) and National Forum for Risk Management in the Public Sector (ALARM) (2002) *A Risk Management Standard.* London: IRM/AIRMIC/ALARM.

Kletz, T (1993) *Lessons from Disasters.* Rugby: Institution of Chemical Engineers.

McConnell, P J (1996) *Information Technology for Market Risk Management in International Banks.* DBA Thesis, Brunel University, July.

McConnell, P J (2005) *A "Standards-Based" Approach to Operational Risk Management under Basel 2.* Available at: http://www.continuitycentral.com/feature0168.htm

Perrow, C (1999) *Normal Accidents.* Princeton: Princeton University Press.

Petroski, H (1985) *To Engineer is Human.* London: Macmillan.

Power, M (2003) The invention of operational risk. *ESRC Centre for Analysis of Risk and Regulation*, Discussion Paper no. 16, June.

Promontory Financial Group and Wachtell, Lipton, Rosen & Katz (2002) *Report to the Boards of Directors of Allied Irish Banks, P.L.C, Allfirst Financial Inc., and Allfirst Bank Concerning Currency Trading Losses.* March.

Reason, J (1990) *Human Error.* Cambridge: Cambridge University Press.

Reason, J (1997) *Managing the Risk of Organisational Accidents.* Aldershot: Ashgate Publishing.

Samad-Khan, A (2005) Why COSO is flawed. *Operational Risk Magazine*, Jan.

Thirwell, J (2003) Building and running an operational risk database. In: *Advances in Operational Risk: Firm-wide Issues for Financial Institutions.* New York: Risk Books, pp 197–207.

Toft, B (1992) *The Failure of Hindsight.* Available at: http://www.safety98.org/html/papers7/protected/a-16p.htm

Turnbull, N *et al.* (1999) *Internal Control – Guidance for Directors on the Combined Code.* London: Institute of Chartered Accountants in England and Wales. Available at: http://www.icaew.co.uk/internalcontrol

Turner, B (1976) The organisational and interorganisational development of disasters. *Administrative Science Quarterly* **21** 387–397.

Waring, A E and Glendon, A I (1998) *Managing Risk: Critical Issues for Survival and Success in the 21st Century.* London: Thomson Learning.

Young (2003) Moody's analytical framework for operational risk management of banks. *Moody's Investor Services*, Jan.

9

Project Risk Management

Stephen Ward

Recent years have seen a burgeoning literature on project risk management (PRM) processes and case studies of applications. Formal PRM processes and associated techniques are already widely used, and often highly developed. However, they are capable of much wider application than is currently the case. Most project management includes some risk management activity, but the scope and quality of this activity is often quite limited. While even limited PRM can be very beneficial, much greater benefits could be achieved from more extensive and more sophisticated effort.

PRM processes are of particular interest not simply because of the growing interest in project management *per se*, but also because PRM process issues in projects are generally pertinent to *any* organization context. The main reason for this is that most organizational activities can be thought of as a project, or part of a project. Depending on one's time horizon, projects can be short-lived, small-scale tasks; major organizational developments, perhaps involving component projects; or long-term projects such as the setting-up and continued operation of a whole organization.

This chapter offers an overview of what PRM is about, what it can be used for and what formal PRM processes involve. A key issue for achieving effective PRM is determining the scope of risks to be included in analysis and subsequent management. Partly this is a question of understanding what is meant by 'risk' in general, and partly it is about delineating the scope of risks that are considered to be project related.

Definitions of risk formulated by professional bodies and standards institutions have been surprisingly varied. Hillson (2003) and Ward (2004a) provide useful reviews. Most definitions refer to potential changes in performance measured in terms of particular performance objectives. In some definitions risk is the *effect* on performance although sometimes this is rather vaguely expressed as a 'combination' of the probability of an event and its consequence. Some definitions define 'a risk' as the *cause* of an effect on performance, or the *chance or possibility* of an event or something happening. However, such differences in focus are not particularly important for PRM as long as one recognizes the need to explicitly distinguish and address the sources or causes of possible variations in performance, possible consequences and the chances of different levels of variation in performance.

In terms of influence on PRM development, a key aspect of any definition of risk (as a source or its effect) is whether it relates to both positive and negative effects on objectives (performance) or just negative effects (Hillson, 2003). In the face of a general tendency for managers to set challenging objectives, a focus on threats and threat management is reasonable and can be very useful. For example, if a 'tight' budget for a project is set, then by definition this implies a preponderance of threats to keeping to budget over opportunities for coming in below budget. Unfortunately, PRM operating as threat management is often practised as an activity focused on reducing, or at best neutralizing, the potential adverse consequences of 'pure risks' – sources of risk that can only impair performance. The result is that potential opportunities to enhance performance by creatively managing threats are never even looked for, let alone evaluated.

To emphasize the desirability of a balanced approach to opportunity and threat management, the term 'uncertainty management' is increasingly used in preference to the terms 'risk management' and 'opportunity management'. However, uncertainty management is not just about managing perceived threats, opportunities and their implications. It is also about identifying and managing the sources of uncertainty that give rise to and shape perceptions of threats and opportunities.

Much good project management practice can be thought of as effective uncertainty management, clarifying what can be done, deciding what is to be done and ensuring that it gets done. For example, good practice in planning, coordination, setting milestones and change control procedures seeks to manage uncertainty directly. However, most texts on project management do not consider what a coordinated approach to proactive and reactive uncertainty management can achieve.

Sources of uncertainty in projects

Projects are a major part of all organizational activity, but they can be difficult to manage because of their novelty, limited resources and their temporary nature. Consider the following illustrative definition of a project: 'an endeavour in which human, material and financial resources are organised in a novel way, to undertake a unique scope of work of given specification, within constraints of cost and time, so as to achieve unitary, beneficial change, through the delivery of quantified and qualitative objectives' (Turner, 1992). This definition highlights the change-inducing nature of projects, the need to organize a variety of resources under significant constraints and the central role of objectives in project definition. It also suggests inherent uncertainty related to novel organization and a unique scope of work, which requires attention as a central part of effective project management.

An obvious aspect of uncertainty in any project concerns estimates of time, cost and quality related to particular planned activities. For example, we may not know how much time and effort will be required to complete a particular activity. The causes of this uncertainty might include one or more of the following:

- lack of a clear specification of what is required;
- novelty, or lack of experience of this particular activity;
- complexity in terms of the number of influencing factors and associated interdependencies;
- limited analysis of the processes involved in the activity;
- possible occurrence of particular events or conditions which might affect the activity.

Only the last of these items is directly related to specific events or conditions. The other sources of uncertainty arise from a lack of understanding of what is involved. Most definitions of (project) risk are limited because they refer only to potential events or conditions and their possible effects, not to uncertainty in a broader sense. Uncertainty is in part about 'variability' in relation to performance measures like cost, duration or 'quality'. It is also about 'ambiguity' associated with lack of clarity because of the behaviour of relevant project players, lack of data, lack of detail, lack of structure to consider issues, the working and framing assumptions being used to consider the issues, known and unknown sources of bias and ignorance about how much effort it is worth expending to clarify the situation.

Many significant sources of uncertainty that need to be managed are associated with the fundamental management processes that make up the project life cycle. A fair number of sources are implicitly acknowledged in lists of project management 'key success factors'. Potential sources typically identified in this way are listed in Table 9.1 against the various stages of the project life cycle.

In many projects, particularly large ones, formal use of PRM is usually motivated by the use of new and untried technology, where there are likely to be significant threats to achieving objectives. However, key performance issues are often less related to technology,

Table 9.1 Typical uncertainty management issues in each stage of the project life cycle

Stages of the PLC	*Uncertainty management issues*
Conceive the product	Level of definition Definition of appropriate performance objectives Managing stakeholder expectations
Design the product strategically	Novelty of design and technology Determining 'fixed' points in the design Control of changes
Plan the execution strategically	Identifying and allowing for regulatory constraints Concurrency of activities required Capturing dependency relationships Errors and omissions
Allocate resources tactically	Adequate accuracy of resource estimates Estimating resources required Defining responsibilities (number and scope of contracts) Defining contractual terms and conditions Selection of capable participants (tendering procedures and bid selection)
Execute production	Exercising adequate coordination and control Determining the level and scope of control systems Ensuring effective communication between participants Provision of appropriate organizational arrangements Ensuring effective leadership Ensuring continuity in personnel and responsibilities Responding effectively to sources which are realized
Deliver the product	Adequate testing Adequate training Managing stakeholder expectations Obtaining licences to operate
Review the process	Capturing corporate knowledge Learning key lessons Understanding what success means
Support the product	Provision of appropriate organization arrangements Identifying extent of liabilities Managing stakeholder expectations

(from Chapman and Ward, 2003. Copyright John Wiley & Sons Ltd., reproduced with permission) but rather are related to uncertainty introduced by the existence of multiple parties and the project management infrastructure. Such issues need to be addressed very early in a project and throughout the project life cycle, and should be informed by a broad appreciation of the underlying 'root' uncertainties. Chapman and Ward (2003) offer a six Ws framework for this purpose based on the following six questions about a project:

1. Who are the parties ultimately involved?
2. What do the parties want to achieve?
3. What is it that each party is interested in?
4. Which way (how) is each party's work to be done?
5. What resources are required?
6. When does it have to be done?

Understanding the uncertainty associated with each of these basic questions, and the implications of the interactions between them, is fundamental to effective identification and management of both threats and opportunities. Use of the six Ws framework from the earliest stages of the project life cycle can usefully inform development of project design and logistics by clarifying key sources of uncertainty. For example, failure to clarify stakeholder expectations and priorities at an early stage can cause major difficulties later in the project.

Another common source of difficulty in projects is a failure to carry out the design and plan stages thoroughly enough. Thus a project proceeds through to execution with insufficiently well-defined specifications for production. During execution this gives rise to difficulties necessitating additional design development and production planning, and consequently adverse effects on the performance criteria of cost, time and quality. This problem of 'premature definition' can be most acute in novel, one-off projects involving new technology, particularly when key stakeholders attempt to impose unrealistic completion dates or cost targets (Flyvbjerg *et al.*, 2003). In addition, some uncertainty about operating conditions and related factors outside the control of the project manager will always remain. Inevitably, judgments have to be made about the degree of detail and accuracy that is practicable in the design and planning stages. However, these judgments should be supported and informed by appropriate risk analysis that is undertaken no later than the end of the planning stage.

The allocate stage of the project life cycle is a significant task involving decisions about project organization, identification of appropriate agents by the project owner and allocation of tasks between them. Unfortunately, the introduction of an agent is prone to the three problems of adverse selection, moral hazard and risk allocation, and the uncertainties presented by these problems can be substantial. When agents are different organizations, these problems can be particularly challenging.

During the execute stage, the essential process issue is the adequacy of coordination and control procedures. Thus coordination and control ought to include risk management practices as 'good project management practices' which amount to:

- milestone management;
- adequate monitoring of activities likely to go wrong;
- ensuring realistic, honest reporting of progress;
- reporting problems and revised assessments of future issues.

A common issue in the execution stage is the introduction of design changes. Such design changes can lead to disruption of schedules and resourcing, and affect cost, time and quality measures of performance directly. A potentially serious concern is that changes are introduced without a full appreciation of the knock-on consequences. Apart from direct consequences, indirect consequences can occur. For example, changes may induce an extension of schedules, allowing contractors to escape the adverse consequences of delays in works unaffected by the change. Changes may have wider technical implications than first thought, leading to subsequent disputes between client and contractor about liability for costs and consequential delays (Cooper, 1980; Williams *et al.*, 1995a, b). Standard project management practice should establish product change control procedures which set up criteria for allowable changes and provide for adequate coordination, communication and documentation of changes.

In the plan stage, looking forward to the deliver and support stages, and developing appropriate responses for key sources of uncertainty, can reduce or eliminate potential later problems at relatively low cost. The key here is identifying which issues need this attention in the plan stage, and which do not.

Uncertainty management

Effective PRM needs to address uncertainty in a broad sense, with the early consideration of all sources of significant uncertainty and associated responses. PRM processes that adopt a focus on threats will not address many of the above sources of variability and ambiguity. PRM processes concerned with threats and opportunities will do better, but will still tend to be focused on uncertain events or circumstances. This does not facilitate consideration of aspects of variability that are driven by underlying ambiguity.

To address uncertainty in both variability and ambiguity terms, we need to adopt a more explicit focus on uncertainty management. To this end, it is more useful to define risk as an *uncertain effect* on performance, rather than as *a cause of (uncertain) effect* on performance. Such a definition of risk is: 'the implications of significant uncertainty about the level of performance achievable' (Chapman and Ward, 2003). Using this broad definition of risk we can then associate 'downside risk' with the *implications* of significant 'threats', or unwelcome consequences, and 'upside risk' with the *implications* of significant 'opportunities', or welcome consequences. Consideration of significant threats and opportunities then becomes *part* of uncertainty management.

Defining 'risk' as the implications of uncertainty about performance achievable, and 'source of risk' as a factor that produces that uncertainty, clearly links risk with how we define performance and associated performance objectives. This has the following four important implications.

1. *Setting objectives is part of risk management*
   PRM cannot be undertaken without reference to performance objectives of some kind. Defining performance objectives affects the nature of associated risk. For example, setting a difficult to achieve, 'tight' budget for a project makes the project more risky by definition, in the sense that the chances of exceeding the budget are increased. Conversely, setting an easily achievable, 'slack' budget makes the project less risky because the chances of exceeding the budget will be decreased. Consequently, selecting relevant performance attributes, formulating objectives for these attributes and modifying objectives should be regarded as important, even fundamental aspects of PRM.

2. *Performance and risk are multidimensional*
   Typically, in any given context, there is more than one performance attribute and associated attribute objective, often even a hierarchy of attributes or objectives. The implication is that variations in performance on each attribute are possible and measurable, and

hence that uncertainty exists in respect of each of these performance attributes. A simple example is the common presentation of project performance in terms of cost, time and quality related objectives. The cost attribute might be addressed in terms of capital cost or 'whole life' cost, and the quality attribute might be divided into technical specification, functionality, reliability and appearance, each of which may be 'at risk' to different degrees. Objectives may be set for each of these performance attributes and the project will be 'at risk' to different degrees with respect to each objective. Risk is multidimensional to the extent that the referent performance is multidimensional.

3. *Risk management should recognize trade-offs between performance objectives*
   Active management for performance usually involves making trade-offs between objectives because different courses of action involve different combinations of uncertainty in respect of the various performance attributes. Failure to recognize these trade-offs and articulate preferred trade-offs can result in ineffective and often inappropriate management of risk. For example, to ensure that a project is completed on time is it really sensible to adopt any course of action whatever the cost?

   In the extreme, performance attributes that are not readily quantified may be treated as inviolate constraints for management purposes. This may lead to neglect of uncertainty in these performance attributes and failure to manage associated risk, even though they represent important aspects of performance.

4. *Different stakeholders will adopt different approaches to risk*
   Most organizational activities involve more than one party working together, whether it be a team of individuals from the same organizational unit, cooperation between different functional units or inter-organizational ventures involving formal contractual arrangements. In any of these ostensibly cooperative situations, the different parties involved are likely to have different performance objectives, or at least different priorities and perceptions of objectives. As a consequence, different parties will have different perceptions of risks associated with these objectives, and consequently may wish to adopt different strategies for managing uncertainty. This divergence may be aggravated if different parties also have different knowledge and perceptions of the nature of the sources of uncertainty and different capabilities for managing risk (Chapman

and Ward, 2002, 2003). This suggests that in any PRM activity it is important to consider explicitly who the risk owners could be, and to make conscious decisions about how uncertainty and associated issues should be allocated to various parties.

Benefits of a formal approach to risk management

A formal approach to PRM is desirable because it provides structure and discipline that facilitates efficient and effective PRM. However, formality is not about the pursuit of a closely defined, inflexible procedure. It is about providing a framework that guides and encourages the development of best practice.

The degree of formality sought in using a given PRM process framework can be a key influence in achieving an effective and efficient approach. At one extreme a purely informal, intuitive approach could be adopted. At the other, a very high level of formality could be adopted, involving more cost, but potentially more benefits. Making the PRM process less formal involves less explicit structure, less formal documentation, less explicit articulation of objectives and deliverables, and fewer explicit phases. Part of the role of formality is clarifying the need for a richer set of motives, as well as helping the pursuit of that richer set of motives.

The essential purpose of PRM in organizations is to improve organizational performance via the systematic identification, appraisal and management of risks to that performance. However, Table 9.2 indicates four levels of the objective that might be held for PRM activity, focusing on process, application, performance and strategic capability. Process-focused objectives represent the most limited objectives; strategic capability objectives, the most extensive. Table 9.2 suggests potential objectives that correspond to each of these four levels. Many of the entries are derived from lists of benefits that are typically suggested as obtainable from effective PRM (for example, Association for Project Management, 2004, ch. 2; Office of Government Commerce, 2002, Appendix A). This presentation of benefits as objectives treats benefits as outcomes that need to be consciously aimed for if they are to be achieved. In general, potential benefits are not guaranteed; they will only be achieved if they are first recognized as such and then mechanisms for their achievement are built into PRM practice.

The bottom row in Table 9.2 relates specifically to four levels of objective that might be associated with documenting the PRM process.

Table 9.2 Levels of objectives for project risk management

1. Process objectives at a specific project stage	*2. Application objectives at a specific project stage*	*3. Performance objectives for all projects*	*4. Strategic capability objectives*
Define risky contexts	Crisis management	Demonstrate clear corporate governance procedures	Enhance culture of continuous improvement
Identify risks	Contingency planning	More reward for less risk	Good management distinguished from dumb luck
Size risk from various sources	Business continuity	Project objectives achieved more often	Bad management distinguished from simple bad luck
Determine the significance of sources of risk and likely effect on performance	Proactive control	Fewer surprises and crises	Enhanced competitiveness
Assess the appropriateness of performance criteria	Strategy formulation	More effective management of change	Enhanced corporate reputation via image of competence
Identify options for treating risk, assess these options, select appropriate options, and plan for implementation	More effective use of resources		Development of a RM culture where risk is welcomed as an opportunity and organization learning is commonplace
Monitor risks, assess the effectiveness of treatment, and review relevance of plans	Improved project evaluation and design		A culture of openness and teamwork generated
	More effective exploitation of opportunities		
Documentation of analysis	Clearer thinking Clearer communication Familiarization	A record of the rationale for decisions	A knowledge base to facilitate corporate learning A framework for data acquisition

(from Ward, 2004b)

Documentation is a key feature of all formal processes. This documentation is a key process output (a process-focused objective) but it also facilitates the operation of a formal process and it provides a means of assessing the performance of the process. Formal PRM processes require appropriate documentation for all these basic reasons, but documentation is especially important because of the need to deal with uncertainty in terms of both variability and ambiguity. This can include information in a wide variety of forms: describing activities, sources of uncertainty, possible responses, decisions taken, identified trigger points for action, and so on. Such documentation serves a number of useful purposes that can be worth pursuing in their own right:

- helps clarify initial thinking;
- makes for clearer communications and less misunderstanding;
- facilitates more rapid briefing of new staff;
- provides a record of the rationale for key decisions;
- captures knowledge to facilitate corporate learning;
- provides a framework for data acquisition and appreciation.

If only the first of these six purposes is of interest, limited documentation may be appropriate. However, the other purposes deserve careful prior attention, even if the design of the documentation has a fairly free format. The key underlying purpose of documentation, and a strategic capability objective, is to integrate the expertise of teams of people so they can make effective, collective decisions based on clearly articulated and consistent premises.

Process-focused objectives

Process-focused objectives pursued at a specific project stage are the most limited kind of objective because these are only concerned with achieving particular phases in a particular PRM process application. In crude terms, the PRM process might be described in terms of six phases: *define the context*, *identify risks*, *estimate risks*, *evaluate risks*, *treat risks* and *monitor and review*. As shown in column 1 of Table 9.2, the process objectives entries relate directly to achieving the output of these six phases. Given this correspondence, it is not necessary to complete a comprehensive PRM process to achieve one or more of the process objectives. For example, a given application of PRM might be primarily concerned with the identification of risks, and so stop the PRM process once the *identify risks* phase is complete. Such an approach to PRM would preclude pursuit of all the other process objectives listed in column 1 and, as a result, severely limit one's ability to pursue objectives in the subsequent columns of Table 9.2.

A central reason for employing formal PRM should be to guide and inform the search for favourable alternative courses of action. Central to achieving this is the concept of 'risk efficiency', which is concerned with the trade-offs between expected performance and risk that must be made in selecting one course of action or investment strategy over another (Chapman and Ward, 2003). In relation to risk efficient plans and trade-offs between risk and expected performance, risk analysis can help to:

- diagnose alternative risk efficient courses of action;
- demonstrate the implications of such alternatives;
- inform choices between alternative risk efficient responses.

In this way risk management can produce very much more substantial improvements in performance than a limited focus on merely 'keeping things on track'.

In principle, the process objectives in column 1 could be elaborated to reflect more sophisticated phase structure descriptions of the PRM process, and therefore more specific process objectives. Indeed, this is a primary motive for articulating formal process frameworks in more detail than the above six-phase characterization.

Application-focused objectives

Application-focused objectives in column 2 of Table 9.2 relate to the way risk is managed in a specific project stage. The first five application-focused objectives relate to the degree of anticipation sought in treating or responding to identified risks, starting with a largely reactive objective for PRM-labelled *crisis management* to a strongly proactive objective for PRM-labelled *strategy formulation*.

In its most limited form, a *crisis management* objective implies a concern for purely reactive fire fighting, that is, mitigating the effects of a serious and urgent problem or event. It also implies a concern to ensure systems can recognize crises quickly and respond rapidly and decisively. A more anticipatory *contingency planning* objective might involve planning for potential events by setting aside contingent resources, such as rapid response capability or backup operating facilities. A *business continuity* objective involves similar concerns, but implies more active management participation in attempting to change the probability of certain identified possibilities occurring as well as attempting to mitigate potential adverse impacts or exploit potential opportunities. A *proactive control* objective implies a wider set of concerns, subsuming crisis management and business continuity objectives, but also formulating or modifying performance targets where appropriate. Beyond proactive control, PRM might be applied to influence project strategy, including the evaluation and formulation of project strategy, and then seeking to influence the basic nature of the project.

The last three objectives in column 2 of Table 9.2 could be associated with pursuit of the first five application-focused objectives, but are likely to be achieved to a greater extent the more anticipatory the risk management application is. For example, PRM activity that has a strategy formulation objective is more likely to focus management attention on improvements in project evaluation and design than PRM activity that has a business continuity objective.

Performance-focused objectives

The performance-focused objectives in column 3 of Table 9.2 extend beyond the way risk is addressed in individual projects and relate to improved performance over a stream of projects and in corporate performance as a whole. Objectives in column 3 offer a practical way of measuring the effectiveness of PRM efforts.

Strategic capability objectives

Strategic capability objectives in column 4 of Table 9.2 imply a longer-term perspective of potential benefits from PRM than performance-focused objectives. Strategic capability objectives go beyond short- to medium-term improvements in organization and project performance in being concerned with fundamental qualitative improvements in PRM capability and related benefits. This includes the achievement of fundamental shifts in risk thinking, which make subsequent use and development of PRM easier, more efficient and more effective, thereby facilitating a virtuous circle of continuous improvement. For example, a complacent, risk-averse culture based on a widely held view that uncertainty and risk are negative issues, and that PRM is just more bureaucracy, should give way to a new PRM culture based on a shared view that uncertainty is the source of opportunities and that uncertainty needs to be understood in order to exploit opportunities effectively.

This kind of culture change can make an organization more exciting to work for and make going to work more enjoyable. This in turn can lead to higher quality staff wanting to join, and stay with, the organization and subsequent related improvements in organization capability and performance.

Links between levels of objectives

A shortcoming of much current practice in PRM is the lack of recognition given to the different levels of objectives for PRM in Table 9.2. This may partly reflect a failure to identify the full range of potential benefits. This may be due to a lack of clarity about how lower-level objectives (to the left in Table 9.2) contribute to the achievement of higher-level objectives (to the right in Table 9.2). Chapman and Ward (2003) discuss some of these links, but this is an area that would benefit from research with organizations that have been successful in pursuing level 3 and 4 objectives for their PRM activity.

Whatever the precise mechanisms linking achievement of objectives in one (lower) level with the next, it is certainly the case that limited attainment of process objectives will severely curtail performance in terms of higher-level objectives. For example, current PRM practice typically does not progress much beyond the fourth objective in column 1 of Table 9.2 (*determine the significance of sources of risk and likely effect on performance*). Often, this involves little more than plotting identified risk events on a probability impact grid, assigning notional priorities and then assigning responsibilities for managing these risks. More sophisticated analysis employs Monte Carlo simulation to progress to the next process objective (*assess the appropriateness of performance criteria*) to derive distributions of project performance in cost and time terms, although on its own this may not add a great deal.

The next process objective (*identify options for treating risk, assess these options, select appropriate options, and plan for implementation*) takes place in most PRM processes. However, this often involves no formal analysis to assess and compare the cost effectiveness of alternative treatment options. This severely limits progress that can be made in pursuing higher-level objectives and attendant benefits. Specifically, Chapman and Ward (2004) have argued that effective PRM should pursue risk-efficient approaches to project designs, plans and treatment of sources of uncertainty that evaluate trade-offs between risk and expected performance associated with alternative courses of action.

Nature of formal project PRM processes

Risk management process frameworks developed and promoted by professional organizations have an important role to play in the development of risk management best practice (APM, 2004; AS/NZS 4360: 2004; BS 6079-3:2000; CAN/CSA-Q850-97; CCTA – The Government Centre for Information Systems, 1995a, b; COSO, 2004; Godfrey, 1996; Institution of Civil Engineers *et al.*, 2005; IRM *et al.*, 2002; OGC, 2002; PMI, 2004). Among other things, such frameworks can bring together experts with different experiences, synthesize their experience and tailor general approaches to particular types of context or application.

In broad terms, there is a general convergence between different guidelines and standards in respect of generic PRM process frameworks. Most incorporate the basic phases of identification, analysis, evaluation and response selection, although the terminology used can vary, leading to sometimes subtle, and perhaps unintended, differences in emphasis and focus. At a more detailed level, comparisons between different process frameworks are not always easy to make. Different numbers of phases and labels for phases can imply rather different scope of activities, with more detailed frameworks facilitating the recognition and management of a wider range of issues than simpler frameworks. Another issue is the desirability of pursuing an iterative approach to individual applications of PRM, and what form these iterations should take between phases of the process (Chapman and Ward, 2003, ch. 4).

Some of the most developed risk management process frameworks focus on risk management applications in a project context. Examples include the UK Association for Project Management's (APM's) *Project Risk Analysis and Management (PRAM) Guide* (2004); the Project Management Institute's (PMI's) *A Guide to the Project Management Body of Knowledge* (*PMBoK®*) (2004, ch. 11) and the *Risk Analysis and Management for Projects (RAMP)* guide (Institution of Civil Engineers *et al.*, 2005).

In considering the development of PRM process frameworks, Chapman and Ward (2003, ch. 4) offer a process framework they refer to as the SHAMPU (Shape, Harness and Manage Project Uncertainty) process. Much of the content of this process is not new; rather, it represents a synthesis informed by issues arising in the design of other process frameworks. In particular, it has been informed by, and in turn influenced, the development of the PRAM process (APM, 2004). The SHAMPU process framework is summarized in Table 9.3 and illustrated in Figure 9.1.

Table 9.3 A nine-phase portrayal of the SHAMPU process

Phases	*Purposes and tasks in outline*
Define the project	Consolidate relevant existing information about the project at a strategic level in a holistic and integrated structure suitable for risk management. Fill in any gaps uncovered in the consolidation process, and resolve any inconsistencies.
Focus the process	Scope and provide a strategic plan for the RMP. Plan the RMP at an operational level.
Identify the issues	Identify sources of uncertainty at a strategic level in terms of opportunities and threats. Identify what might be done about it, in terms of proactive and reactive responses. Identify secondary sources of uncertainty associated with responses.
Structure the issues	Complete the structuring of earlier phases. Test simplifying assumptions. Provide more complex or alternative structures when appropriate.
Clarify *ownership*	Allocate *both* financial *and* managerial responsibility for issues (separately if appropriate).
Estimate variability	Size uncertainty which is usefully quantified on a first pass. On later passes, refine earlier estimates of uncertainty where this is effective and efficient.
Evaluate implications	Assess statistical dependence (dependence not modelled in a causal structure). Synthesize the results of the estimate phase using dependence assumptions which are fit for purpose. Interpret the results in the context of *all* earlier phases. Make decisions about proactive and reactive responses, and about refining and redefining earlier analysis, managing the iterative nature of the process as a key aspect of these tasks.
Harness the plans	Obtain approval for strategic plans shaped by earlier phases. Prepare detailed action plans. These are base plans (incorporating preventative responses) and contingency plans (incorporating reactive responses with trigger points) ready for implementation within the action horizons defined by appropriate lead times. Commit to project plans which are fit for implementation.
Manage implementation	Manage the planned work. Develop action plans for implementation on a rolling basis. Monitor and control (make decisions to refine or redefine project plans as required). Deal with crises (unanticipated issues of significance) and be prepared to cope appropriately with disasters (crises which are not controlled).

(from Chapman and Ward, 2003. Copyright John Wiley & Sons Ltd, reproduced with permission)

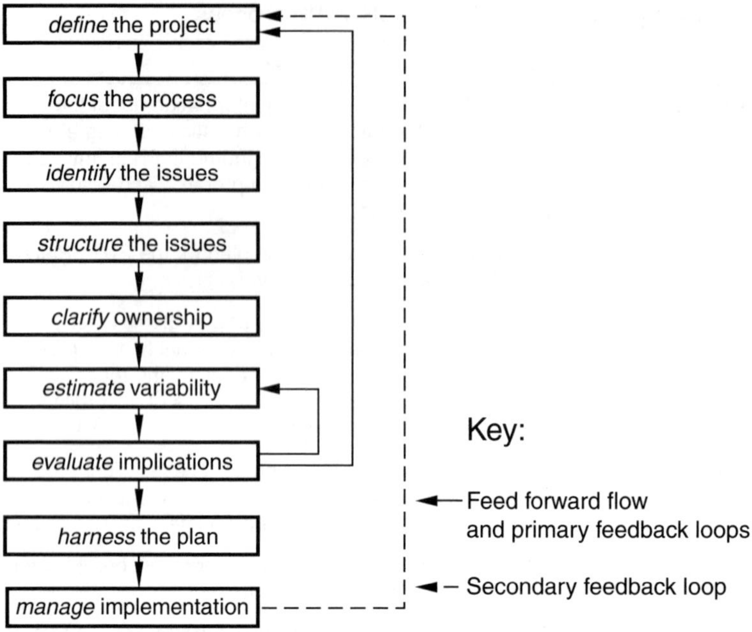

(from Chapman and Ward, 2003. Copyright John Wiley & Sons Ltd, reproduced with permission)

Figure 9.1 The SHAMPU process: flow chart portrayal

The SHAMPU process framework incorporates nine phases, including specific reference to 'define', 'focus', 'structure' and 'ownership' phases. These four phases broaden the scope of the process in comparison to simpler frameworks. In Table 9.3, the first two phases (*define the project* and *focus the process*) provide a basis for subsequent analysis. The next three phases (*identify the issues*, *structure the issues* and *clarify ownership*) involve qualitative analysis. The next two phases (*estimate variability* and *evaluate implications*) involve quantitative analysis. Together, these seven phases comprise the *shape* phases because they help to shape the approach to plans for managing project uncertainty formulated in the harness phase and implemented in the manage phase.

The following sections briefly consider the scope of component tasks that make up the PRM process. The discussion is structured around the component phases of the SHAMPU process framework in Table 9.3 because this provides a detailed characterization of the PRM process and facilitates comprehensive consideration of issues that need to be addressed to achieve efficient and effective PRM. Readers more familiar with other process frameworks should be able to relate the topics discussed here to these other frameworks without much difficulty. A more extensive discussion of each phase, including techniques, can be found in Chapman and Ward (2003).

Define the context

Any application of PRM takes place in a particular context to support a particular undertaking. The purpose of a 'define the context' phase is to consolidate relevant existing information about the context and its management in a suitable documented form. Without an adequate appreciation of context there is no basis on which to undertake PRM.

In principle, PRM could be usefully applied on a separate and different basis in each stage of a project's life cycle without the necessity for PRM in any previous or subsequent stages. For example, risk analysis could form part of an evaluation step in any stage of the project life cycle. Alternatively, risk analysis might be used to guide the initial progress at each stage of a project. In these circumstances, the focus of risk analysis is likely to reflect immediate project management concerns in the associated project stage. For example, risk analysis might be undertaken as part of the plan stage primarily to consider the feasibility and development of the work schedule for project execution. There might be no expectation that such a risk analysis would or should influence the design, although it might be perceived as a potential influence on subsequent work allocation decisions. In practice, many risk analyses are intentionally limited in scope, as in individual studies to determine the reliability of available equipment, the likely outcome of a particular course of action or to evaluate alternative decision options within a particular project stage. This can be unfortunate if it results in a limited, *ad hoc* 'bolted-on', 'optional extra', approach to PRM, rather than undertaking PRM as an integral 'built-in' part of project management throughout the project life cycle. Wherever it is carried out in a project's life cycle, risk analysis needs to be regarded as a contribution to PRM of the whole project. The opportunities for PRM include looking forwards and backwards at any stage in the project life cycle addressing all the issues indicated by Table 9.1 as appropriate.

A comprehensive and complete define phase should clarify all relevant aspects of the current project context, in a manner accessible to all relevant personnel. A single document achieving these ends is often held to be a key benefit of a formal PRM process, especially by senior managers.

Focus the risk management process

The focus phase recognizes that any systematic efforts at PRM must be carefully designed and managed to ensure an efficient and cost-effective approach. While generic process frameworks provide a phase structure for PRM, the precise scope and detail of analysis in each phase will depend on the context. In the case of PRM, context partly relates to the current stage of the project life cycle, as just noted.

There is no best way to pursue all risk analyses – much of the need to vary the approach taken hinges on why it is being undertaken. The reasons for undertaking PRM during a project can change significantly over the project life cycle, because the project itself changes, and because what is known about the project changes, sometimes in quite profound ways. This usually warrants some modifications and changes of emphasis in any PRM application. Failing to consider this issue is rather like operating a car hire firm that always offers a Rolls-Royce or a Mini, regardless of the potential customer's wallet or needs. 'If the only tool in your toolbox is a hammer, every problem looks like a nail', is a situation to be avoided. A requirement for effectiveness and efficiency demands that we design or select our models and processes according to our purposes.

Even in an organization with well-established formal PRM processes, decisions need to be made, consciously and regularly, about which models to use in individual applications. A 'model' in this context is the deliberate simplification of reality we use as a basis for analysis. The aim must be to avoid models that are too simple, obscuring important issues that should be addressed, but at the same time avoiding models that are too complex, involving effort that is not cost effective.

Identify the issues

Most PRM process descriptions emphasize a need to identify sources of risk early in the process, typically restricting this to potential events, and sometimes to just threats. As discussed earlier, effective PRM needs to address uncertainty in a broad sense, with early consideration of all sources of uncertainty and associated responses. As indicated in Table 9.3, the SHAMPU identify phase involves not only identifying sources of uncertainty, but also associated possible responses and secondary sources of uncertainty arising from these responses. For convenience, we refer to individual sources, their associated responses and secondary sources as 'issues'. It is these issues rather than sources of uncertainty that need to be identified and managed.

In terms of documentation, the identify phase involves the production of a list or register of uncertainties. The key deliverable is a clear, common understanding of the sources of uncertainty associated with the application context, and what can be done about them. Opportunities need to be identified and managed with the same resolve as threats as part of the same process. Often a PRM process is particularly successful because the process of generating and reviewing responses to threats leads to the identification of important opportunities, with implications well beyond the uncertainty that led to their identification.

Identification of sources of uncertainty and possible responses can be an individual activity or involve other people in a variety of ways, including: interviewing individuals, interviewing groups or various group processes such as brainstorming and decision conferencing (Hillson, 2003, ch. 4). A key concern is to stimulate imaginative thinking and draw on the experiences of different individuals.

Structure the issues

All the earlier phases necessarily involve some structuring of identified uncertainty management issues. The structure phase is concerned with reviewing and extending this earlier structuring. The objective is to improve understanding of the relative importance of different uncertainties given identified responses, to explore interdependencies between different sources of risk and their effects and to test the assumptions that were implicit or explicit in all earlier steps. This can lead to refinement of existing responses and prompt the development of new, more effective responses. Failure to structure can also lead to lost opportunities. For example, some responses to particular sources can deal with whole sets of sources, including sources that have not been identified. It is important to recognize the opportunities provided by such general responses.

Structuring involves reviewing and exploring possible interdependencies or links between context activities, resources, involved parties, sources of uncertainty and responses, and seeking to understand the reasons for these interdependencies. The most effective way to understand uncertainty dependence is to model it in causal terms. Two common approaches used in a system-failure analysis context are fault tree analysis and event tree analysis. Event tree analysis involves identifying a sequence of events that could follow from the occurrence of particular source–response configurations and then representing the possible scenarios in a tree diagram where each branch represents an alternative possibility. In fault tree analysis the process is reversed, working backwards from a particular event known as the top event, in an attempt to identify all possible sequences of events giving rise to the top event. Ishikawa or fishbone diagrams (Ishikawa, 1986) adopt a similar approach, showing necessary inputs to a particular final position.

A more versatile representation of causes and effects can be achieved with influence diagrams, as used in 'systems dynamics' (Forrester, 1958, 1961; Richardson and Pugh, 1981; Senge, 1990; Williams, 2002) and 'cognitive mapping' (Eden, 1988). One advantage of influence diagrams over tree diagrams is that much more complex interactions can be shown, including feedback and feed forward loop effects. The process of construction and interpretation of influence diagrams goes beyond identification of direct source–response and cause–effect relationships. It also assists in identifying potentially important links, such as the nature of source–response chains associated with vicious circles, or particular sources which influence many other sources either directly or indirectly. Increased understanding of cause–effect relationships can also prompt the formulation of additional responses.

Clarify ownership

The ownership phase draws attention to a central issue in PRM: the appropriate allocation of risk and associated incentives to manage it. It is basic good practice to make sure that every source of uncertainty and all associated responses have a manager and an owner. In practice, failures of PRM associated with ownership of issues arise because this activity is not recognized explicitly, or not given sufficient attention.

The fundamental reason for being concerned about who is responsible for what issues is that this will influence how uncertainty is managed and in whose best interests this will be. Part of the rationale for being clear about who owns issues before any estimation is to verify the feasibility of assumed responses and their effects. For example, in a project context, client-initiated redesign is a response that may invalidate all allocations of risk to a contractor, with knock-on cost implications that can be orders of magnitude greater than the cost of the redesign itself.

Estimate variability

The key deliverable of the estimate variability phase is the provision of a basis for understanding which sources and associated responses are important, based on numeric estimates of uncertainty associated with issues identified earlier in terms of cost, duration or other performance criteria. Some approaches to PRM suggest numeric probability distributions from the outset. Others suggest a non-numeric approach initially, using likelihood and criteria ranges associated with scenario labels such as 'high', 'medium' and 'low', commonly referred to as a 'qualitative assessment', with numeric measures later if appropriate (Hillson, 2003; Ward, 1999). However, qualitative statements of beliefs about uncertainty in this sense have significant limitations and are best regarded as a form of preliminary analysis.

Efficient estimating involves a first pass to size uncertainty, followed by further iterations to refine estimates of uncertainty where this is effective and efficient. A single pass approach is neither effective nor efficient. We want to minimize the time spent on relatively minor sources with simple response options, so as to spend more time on major issues that involve complex response options. To do this, a first pass with a focus on sizing uncertainty is needed followed by refinement of estimates where this matters.

Organizations which do not quantify uncertainty have no real basis for distinguishing aspirational targets, expected values and commitments that incorporate realistic contingency allowances. As a consequence, single value performance levels are employed to serve all three purposes, often with disastrous results, not to mention costly and unnecessary dysfunctional organizational behaviour. 'The cost estimate', 'the completion date' or 'the promised performance' become less and less plausible, there is a crisis of confidence when the goal posts are moved and then the process starts all over again. Senior project managers involved when PRM processes were introduced by BP in the 1970s stated that the avoidance of this cycle was the key benefit of PRM processes for them. The ability to manage the gaps between targets, expected values and contingency levels, and the ability to set these values appropriately in the first place, is a central concern of PRM. A recommended basis for refining estimates of targets, expected values and commitments is developed in more detail in Chapman and Ward (2002, 2003, ch. 10).

Evaluate implications

The purpose of the evaluate implications phase is to combine the results of the estimate phase in the context of earlier phases and evaluate all associated decisions and judgments. The evaluate phase includes the synthesis of individual estimates, the presentation and interpretation of results, process decisions like 'Do we need to refine earlier analysis?' and management decisions such as 'Is plan A better than plan B?'

The deliverables will depend upon the depth of the preceding phases achieved to this point. Looping back to earlier phases in order to refine an evaluation is likely to be a key and frequent decision. For example, an important early deliverable might be a prioritized list of issues, while a later deliverable might be a diagnosed potential problem or opportunity associated with a specific contingency plan and suggested revisions to this plan to resolve the problem or capture the opportunity.

A central task of the evaluate phase is the portrayal of the net combined effect of identified issues and responses. Typically this integration task is carried out with the aid of computer software based on Monte Carlo simulation (Grey, 1995; Hertz, 1964). This makes it relatively straightforward to add large numbers of probability distributions together in a single operation to assess the overall impact of a set of issues. Unfortunately, this convenience can seduce analysts into a naive approach that assumes independence between issues and consequently underestimates the potential variability in performance. Effective use of simulation software requires appropriate recognition of dependencies between variables and the presentation of calculations that show intermediate stages so that final results can be properly interrogated.

Harness the plans

The harness phase is about taking the preceding analysis and converting this into action plans associated with the relevant context activities. In the define the context phase, the nature of the undertaking of interest will have been defined and this will include the nature of plans for future action. These reference plans will be modified by the subsequent risk analysis to form what might be termed a 'base plan', incorporating proactive responses to uncertainty, but not reactive responses. In addition, the risk analysis should give rise to contingency plans that are an operational form of recommended reactive response to uncertainty and potential risks. Such contingency plans should include decision rules and define the trigger points that will initiate the selected reactive responses.

As part of the base plan documentation, an uncertainty analysis report at an overview level should include, as a minimum, a comprehensive list of threats and opportunities, assessed in terms of implications given recommended proactive and reactive responses, along with an assessment of alternative potential proactive and reactive responses. Uncertainty analysis needs to be documented to back up associated recommended modifications to reference plans and to provide an explanation of the need for both proactive and reactive responses.

Manage implementation

Managing implementation involves four different tasks that have to be managed in parallel: *manage planned actions, roll action plans forward, monitor and control* and *manage crises*.

Translating plans into actions is seldom entirely straightforward. Excessive planning detail in a deterministic framework can be a serious handicap. A simply defined deterministic base plan embedded in even a simple understanding of the uncertainties involved can be much more effective. The key is insight about what might happen, as distinct from what we hope will happen, with particular reference to the motivation of the parties involved and a clear vision of what really matters and what does not.

Rolling action plans forward includes recognizing changes in priority and urgency of risk issues. Each time plans are reviewed, eliminating the issues which have now been realized or avoided, confidence band assessments should contract, unless new issues are envisaged. Plotting how this process is progressing can be useful, especially if some serious set-backs have been experienced but the chance of achieving commitments is stable or improving. However, this is an example of a relatively complex portrayal of the monitoring process, best used infrequently at high levels. The lower the level, and the more frequent the monitoring activity, the simpler the devices have to be.

In relation to the *monitor and control* task, the distinction between target, expected value and commitment estimates is of substantial importance. Managing the process of reconciling what actually happens to these three types of estimates is essential if the monitoring process is to facilitate an understanding of the implications of departures from base plans.

Managing planned actions can embrace the variations from base plans which do not warrant contingency plans and the management of variations via contingency plans. A major concern of formal PRM is to avoid nasty surprises that give rise to crises, which then require *crisis management*.

Efficient and effective processes

Undertaking any PRM process is not without costs, and a key concern is ensuring an appropriate trade-off between these costs and the effectiveness of the PRM process. Effective and efficient PRM processes require an iterative approach. Instead of just a single pass through each phase of the process, an iterative approach involves revisiting or looping back to earlier phases to develop, refine or reconsider aspects of the analysis undertaken to date. If a single pass approach to all phases in a PRM process is attempted, it is likely to be highly inefficient and seriously ineffective. Time will be wasted on issues which turn out to be unimportant, and not enough time will be spent on the important issues not anticipated when the process was started.

In particular, the way iterations between phases of the SHAMPU process listed in Table 9.3 are managed has a major impact on the effectiveness and efficiency of the SHAMPU process itself. Figure 9.1 shows possible iterative loops between phases as the SHAMPU process progresses. Figure 9.1 displays the two key iterative loops that need to be managed formally, but selective informal looping back to other phases might also be used.

As indicated in Figure 9.1, and noted earlier, an iterative loop which goes back from the evaluate phase to the estimate phase might be expected in order to refine estimates for issues that matter. Further, this might be followed by an iterative loop back to the define phase to refine or redefine the basis of analysis and the qualitative analysis for sources of uncertainty revealed to be important, initiating a second complete pass through the seven *shape* phases. This might be followed by further iterative loops of this kind. The harness phase provides a bridge between the *shape* and manage phases, and as Figure 9.1 shows, this is outside the looping structure of the *shape* phases. The harness phase has two aspects which should follow sequentially without iterations if iterations through the preceding phases have been effective: obtaining approval for the project strategy which emerges from the earlier phases, and preparing detailed action plans which are then approved. As Figure 9.1 indicates, iterative looping back to the define phase from the manage phase should be a planned part of the process, but at a much lower level of intensity than loops from the evaluate phase, because loops back from the manage phase are comparatively expensive.

In practice, stepping through the phases of the PRM process will often need simplification to meet the needs of a particular context, to provide *efficient* risk management. Simplification merely to economize on resources and the amount of time spent on PRM is *never* appropriate. What is *always* appropriate is ensuring that the available resources are used to operate a PRM process that is as effective and efficient as possible within the time available. What is *always desirable* is adjusting the time and resources available to an appropriate level, but sometimes this is not feasible.

Determining what can be simplified in a PRM process, and what it is appropriate to simplify, is not a simple matter. To address this problem, organizations might adopt generic simplifications to PRM process applications by using common guiding principles, or by making policy decisions that constrain the nature and scope of formal PRM processes. Such generic simplifications are most likely to be made when a PRM process is first established in an organization, but they ought to be informed by knowledge of what is involved in a comprehensive PRM process. Simply adopting a very specific, rigidly designed 'off-the-shelf' process touted by a consultancy, or 'borrowed' from another organization, is not advisable. Such processes often involve quite specific (and simplistic) 'tools' or prescribed methods of analysis which encourage a mechanistic 'paint by numbers' approach to PRM. The very well-defined, 'tried-and-tested' nature of these processes can make them very attractive and amenable to rapid implementation. However, they represent a serious risk to the ongoing development of an organization's PRM capability. In particular, they can prematurely constrain employees' perceptions of what PRM is all about and what can be achieved with it. They can be comparable to patent medicines sold at a fair to cure all ills without the need for any kind of professional diagnosis of the patient.

Conclusion

This chapter has offered a brief overview of project risk management (PRM) and, necessarily, the presentation of material has been selective. In particular, little has been said about the tools and techniques that are available to assist with risk analysis. This was a conscious decision in order to allow a focus on more important issues like the potential roles for PRM and the scope of formal PRM processes. The intention was also to provide an overview of best practice and recent developments, rather than current common practice. This called for a presentation of PRM as uncertainty management and a discussion of different levels of objectives that might be pursued with PRM. Some organizations have already moved in this direction, but many have not, and consequently they are missing a major opportunity to improve project performance.

In terms of future developments, more organizations need to:

- adopt an uncertainty management perspective rather than just pursue threat-oriented risk management;
- make more extensive and thoughtful use of PRM in earlier stages of the project life cycle than is typically the case;
- recognize the pivotal role played by uncertainty associated with project stakeholders and their objectives;
- carefully consider the objectives they wish to achieve with PRM and proactively work to achieve these;
- employ uncertainty management processes that are both efficient and effective in addressing key issues.

For a given organization, the selection of directions in which to develop PRM will be driven by organizational capability to undertake PRM. An important aspect of this capability is the available knowledge, experience and expertise of organizational personnel in respect of risk management and their motivation to develop PRM (Ward, 1999). However, the ability to develop PRM is also dependent on a supportive organizational infrastructure. In broad terms, this includes tangible aspects of infrastructure, such as the nature and quality of administration and information systems. It also includes more intangible aspects of culture, such as the degree of trust and openness that prevails, attitudes to risk and uncertainty, tolerance of mistakes and receptiveness to creative thinking.

References and recommended reading

AS/NZS 4360:2004, *Risk Management*. Strathfield, NSW: Standards Australia; Wellington: Standards New Zealand.

Association for Project Management (2004) *Project Risk Analysis and Management (PRAM) Guide*, 2nd edn. High Wycombe, Bucks: APM Publishing.

BS 6079-3:2000, *Project Management – Part 3: Guide to the Management of Business-related Project Risk*. London: British Standards Institution.

CAN/CSA-Q850-97, *Risk Management: Guideline for Decision Makers*. Mississauga, Ontario: National Standards of Canada, Canadian Standards Association.

CCTA – The Government Centre for Information Systems (1995a) *Management of Project Risk*. London: HMSO.

CCTA – The Government Centre for Information Systems (1995b) *Management of Programme Risk*. London: HMSO, ch. 2.

Chapman, C B and Ward, S C (2002) *Managing Project Risk and Uncertainty: A Constructively Simple Approach to Decision Making*. Chichester: John Wiley & Sons Ltd.

Chapman, C B and Ward, S C (2003) *Project Risk Management: Processes, Techniques and Insights*, 2nd edn. Chichester: John Wiley & Sons Ltd.

Chapman, C B and Ward, S C (2004) Why risk efficiency is a key aspect of best practice projects. *International Journal of Project Management* **22** 619–632.

Cooper, K G (1980) Naval ship production: a claim settled and a framework built. *Interfaces*, **10**:6 20–36.

COSO (2004) *Enterprise Risk Management – Integrated Framework*. Washington, DC: The Committee of Sponsoring Organizations of the Treadway Commission. See: http://www.coso.org

Eden, C (1988) Cognitive mapping: a review. *European Journal of Operational Research*, **36** 1–13.

Flyvbjerg, B, Bruzelius, N and Rithengatter, W (2003) *Megaprojects and Risk – An Anatomy of Ambition*. Cambridge: Cambridge University Press.

Forrester, J (1958) Industrial dynamics: a major breakthrough for decision making. *Harvard Business Review* **36**:4 37–66.

Forrester, J (1961) *Industrial Dynamics*. Cambridge, MA: MIT Press.

Godfrey, P (1996) *Control of Risk: A Guide to the Systematic Management of Risk from Construction*. London: CIRIA.

Grey, S (1995) *Practical Risk Assessment for Project Management*. Chichester: John Wiley & Sons Ltd.

Hertz, D B (1964) Risk analysis in capital investment. *Harvard Business Review*, **42**:1 95–106.

Hillson, D (2003) *Effective Opportunity Management for Projects*. New York: Marcel Dekker.

Institute of Risk Management (IRM), Association of Insurance and Risk Managers (AIRMIC) and National Forum for Risk Management in the Public Sector (ALARM) (2002) *A Risk Management Standard*. London: IRM/AIRMIC/ALARM.

Institution of Civil Engineers, Faculty of Actuaries and Institute of Actuaries (2005) *Risk Analysis and Management for Projects (RAMP)*, 2nd edn. London: Thomas Telford.

Ishikawa, K (1986) *Guide to Quality Control*, 2nd edn. White Plains, NY: Asia Productivity Organisation/Quality Resources.

Office of Government Commerce (2002) *Management of Risk: Guidance for Practitioners*. London: The Stationery Office.

Project Management Institute (2004) *A Guide to the Project Management Body of Knowledge (PMBoK®)*, 3rd edn. Newtown Square, PA: Project Management Institute.

Richardson, G P and Pugh, A L (1981) *Introduction to Systems Dynamics Modeling with DYNAMO*. Portland, OR: Productivity Press.

Senge, P M (1990) *The Fifth Discipline: The Art and Practice of the Learning Organisation*. New York: Doubleday.

Turner, J R (1992) *The Handbook of Project Based Management: Improving Processes for Achieving Your Strategic Objectives*. New York: McGraw-Hill.

Ward, S C (1999) Requirements for an effective project risk management process. *Project Management Journal*. (USA Project Management Institute), **30**:3 37–43.

Ward, S C (2004a) *Risk Management: Organisation and Context*. London: Witherby.

Ward, S C (2004b) Developing project risk management. In: Slevin, D, Cleland, D I and Pinto, J K (Eds). *Innovations: Project Management Research 2004*. Newtown Square, PA: Project Management Institute, ch. 27, pp 453–464.

Ward, S C and Chapman, C B (2003) Transforming project risk management into project uncertainty management. *International Journal of Project Management* **21** 97–105.

Williams, T (2002) *Modelling Complex Projects*. Chichester: John Wiley & Sons Ltd.

Williams, T, Eden, C, Ackerman, F and Tait, A (1995a) The effects of design changes and delays on project costs. *Journal of the Operational Research Society*, **46** 809–818.

Williams, T, Eden, C, Ackerman, F and Tait, A (1995b) Vicious circles of parallelism. *International Journal of Project Management*, **13** 151–155.

10

Environmental Risk Management

Simon Pollard and Peter Young

The environmental risk management challenge

Risk has become a familiar concept in the 21st century. The term is widely used and means different things to different people. All individuals live with risk – some risks are more controllable than others; some better understood than others – most are managed implicitly without any formal analysis of risk.

This chapter is about environmental risk assessment and management. The management of risk, from or to the environment, has developed into a systematic process for making better and more accountable environmental decisions. Risks are assessed so that they can be managed better – by focusing first on the problems that are of greatest concern. The analysis of risk usually reveals the key drivers of risk to or from the system under study. Because we all have different concerns, it is important that risk-informed decisions are influenced by a range of stakeholders, including those that bear the risk, and that decisions and the basis for them are communicated throughout the process (Pollard, 2005).

Very often the questions faced by environmental professionals are not those where data is plentiful, the mechanisms fully understood or society's demands clearly stated. In uncertain circumstances, risk assessment and management can help balance technological development and society's need to protect the environment from harm. It is generally assumed that risks to or from the environment arise as an undesirable 'by-product' of some function or process, and need to be weighed alongside the accompanying benefits that such processes offer. There are also situations where risks exist naturally – such as flooding – or because

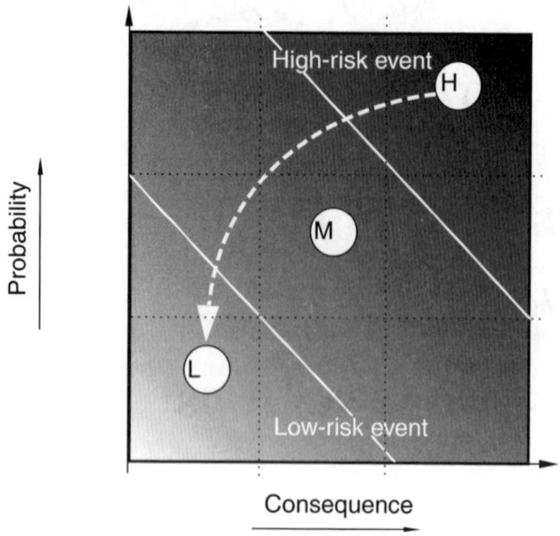

Figure 10.1 Fundamental concept of risk management showing regions of high (H), medium (M) and low (L) risk and objective of risk management (dashed arrow)

of human activities – for example, land contamination. In recognition of the risks inherent to these situations, regulatory and supervisory systems for their management have been devised.

Environmental risk assessment has developed into a management tool for organizing and analysing the available information on environmental problems. It has some aspects in common with other decision-making tools, such as environmental impact assessment (EIA) and strategic environmental assessment (SEA), though its explicit treatment of probability, consequences and uncertainty makes it ideally suited to distinguishing between the adverse environmental impacts (consequences) that could occur and the likelihood (probability) of those impacts actually occurring (Figure 10.1). This is the principal power of risk analysis and is a function not performed by EIA. This is an important methodological distinction for those charged with managing risk because separate strategies exist for managing the probability and consequences of environmental impacts.

Working definition and practice

What does environmental risk assessment involve? Put simply, assessing the likelihood and consequences of events that impact on the environment. That is, understanding what consequence(s) might happen as a result of an activity and how likely it is to happen – and then making judgements on whether to be concerned about this combination of consequences and likelihood (the risk) and how, and in what order, to manage unacceptable risks so they are no longer of concern (Figure 10.1). Risk assessment originated in the nuclear, chemical and oil industries where the language of risk was defined. For environmental applications, the most important distinctions are those between:

- a 'hazard' – a substance or an activity with a potential for harm; the 'harm' – the undesirable consequence or damage that results from exposure to the hazard; and the 'risk' – the likelihood of the harm being realized;
- the 'probability' of an event (that is, the likelihood of it occurring) and the 'consequences' if it were to occur; and
- the 'source' of a hazard, a 'receptor' (that which one wishes to protect) and the 'pathway' (the mechanism by which the receptor may suffer harm from the hazard).

The 'source–pathway–receptor' approach can be illustrated by imagining being on holiday in a caravan park on the banks of a river (Environment Agency, 2000). Under normal river flow conditions, this would be an attractive setting, but under extreme flood conditions there is a risk that the caravan park might be flooded and the caravans washed away. The *source* of the hazard is unusually heavy rainfall. The *hazard* associated with this source is potential loss of life or property damage. The *pathway* is the passage of water through the catchment, resulting in a rise in river level and the overwhelming of the flood defences. The *receptors* are the caravans and their occupants. If any one of these is absent, then *harm*, that is, actual damage, cannot occur. So, for a risk to be present there must be a source of a hazard, a receptor and a pathway between the source and the receptor and these must be connected during the event. Understanding risk in these terms is essential and helps inform risk management because we can manage risks by intercepting the source–pathway–receptor linkage. We may:

- remove receptors (steer development away from areas that flood; use flood warning and evacuation);
- block or alter pathways (install flood defences, alleviation channels or set up sustainable drainage systems); or
- address the source (difficult in this case for rainfall, but action on climate change may address the future severity).

Businesses need to take and manage risks to survive in a competitive market-place. Like all organizations, they have to manage risks from hazards such as competition; changes and quality within their supply chain; fluctuations in demand for their goods and services; skill shortages; and damaged reputations. On the environmental side, they may be exposed to risks from historical land acquisitions, inherited safety cultures or through non-compliant, albeit accidental, environmental releases. Risk 'profiling' across organizations has become essential to good corporate governance and a prerequisite for sound ethical, social and operational (including environmental) management. As a result, many large corporations have risk management committees that report periodically to the board, group risk managers whose responsibility it is to monitor risks across business functions and risk management systems that allow unacceptable risks to be anticipated and managed.

Environmental risk is a concern to organizations because of the liabilities that may accrue and the damaged reputation that can result from the potential or actual harm caused to the environment. Businesses operate in an increasingly regulated environment. Regulatory decisions about their actions are made by close reference to the statutory duties and powers of the regulator and the responsibilities of operators. One aspect of a regulator's work includes the issuing, drafting and enforcement of environmental permits allowing business to discharge to, or abstract from, the environment. This is where many environmental professionals first encounter the requirement for an environmental risk assessment; because the regulator often requires an assessment of risk to inform the siting (planning), or environmental permitting of industrial activities, it acts as a check on the operator's understanding of their own processes and can reveal specific vulnerabilities in systems that warrant close operational and regulatory scrutiny.

Best practice

A wide range of regulatory philosophies exist internationally on the implementation of risk assessment and management through environmental regulation. To different extents, individual countries adopt (i) quantitative and/or qualitative approaches to risk analysis; (ii) preventative or reactive approaches to risk management; and (iii) greater or lesser degrees of precaution with respect to the introduction of new technologies.

In the UK, the application of environmental risk assessment within pollution control has grown substantially over recent years. It now features as an explicit requirement of environmental planning and permitting within the requirements of European and domestic legislation. The environment agencies in the UK take a risk-based approach to regulating industry; that is, by targeting activities and operators posing the greatest likelihood of severe harm to the environment and public health. To assist risk-based regulation, regulatory risk ranking systems have been developed that distinguish between the inherent hazard associated with an industrial operation (e.g. operating a waste transfer station or a cement kiln) and the operator's competency in managing the risks posed by such an operation. The risk management capability of organizations is of increasing interest as many environmental regulators consider the implications of moving towards greater self-regulation.

What might one expect an environmental risk assessment to include? Regulatory expectations of environmental risk assessment in the UK were first published in 1995, in the then Department of the Environment's *A Guide to Risk Assessment and Risk Management for Environmental Protection*. These were revised and issued in 2000 as *Guidelines on Environmental Risk Assessment and Management* for England and Wales (DETR *et al.*, 2000). The Department for Environment, Food and Rural Affairs (Defra) re-endorsed their use in 2002 within the Department's risk management strategy (Defra, 2002). Good problem definition, use of a staged and tiered approach, the principles of proportionality and consistency of use, the explicit treatment of uncertainty and the need for presentational transparency are common themes in the revised Guidelines, colloquially referred to as 'Green Leaves II'. The guidance provides a generalized risk management framework (Figure 10.2) to which specific risk guidance, such as that for waste management regulation, genetically modified organisms, historically contaminated land, groundwater protection and major accident hazards, for example, can in turn refer.

Operators and developers of a wide range of programmes, plans and projects are required to submit environmental risk assessments to local authorities and the environment agencies in support of their regulatory and supervisory responsibilities. Risk assessments help regulators assess the significance of the risks associated with these and then identify, and prioritize, by reference to the risk, the risk management measures that are required to reduce risks to, and from, the environment and to human health. Regulators stipulate these measures as 'conditions' in their permits to develop land or operate plant. Preparation of the environmental risk assessment and implementation of risk management is usually the applicant's responsibility, in line with the 'polluter pays' principle. Because situations change and industrial processes develop

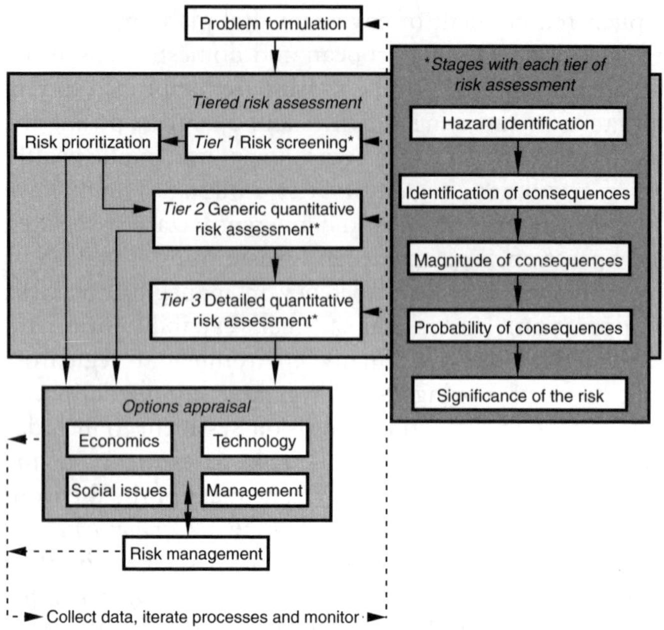

(after DETR *et al.*, 2000)

Figure 10.2 Framework for environmental risk assessment and management

over time, risk assessments are living documents requiring updating as and when modifications to an operation are proposed, or when new or additional information, relevant to the operation or local environmental setting, becomes available.

Not all activities necessarily require complex environmental risk assessment. For example, where the risk is undisputedly negligible or the impacts well understood, or where accepted mechanisms for effective control exist, a simple risk screening may be all that is necessary. For example, a risk assessment is usually required when there is concern about a known hazard and there is a sensitive receptor. A major chemical plant storing large quantities of hazardous bulk chemicals is an example of the former; residential housing close to a landfill site is an example of the latter. Sometimes an accepted approach to managing a well-recognized risk exists, such as bunding oil tanks or the use of wheel washes at waste transfer stations to avoid the release of mud onto approaching roads. In this type of circumstance, risk assessment may not be required, unless there is an intention to depart from the well-accepted solution.

As uncertainty increases and the likelihood of severe consequences becomes less clear, however, a formalized process of risk assessment assists in understanding the severity of the risk and how best to manage it. Advantages to risk assessment include:

- the distinction made between the consequences (impacts) and the likelihood of occurrence;
- a structured approach to assessing risk and thus establishing a logical basis for managing risk;
- providing a basis for the prioritization of risk management actions and the targeting of regulatory effort;
- the recording of decisions for future use; and
- ensuring decision processes, and their underlying logic, are transparent for others to appraise.

For operations and processes that impact on the environment, permits are required. Permit applicants use risk assessments to evaluate where pollution control measures are required and in turn to identify the type and level of financial investment (cost) required for risk reduction (benefit). The regulator has the role of technically reviewing the risk assessment in the context of the statute to inform its decisions on authorizing the specific activity, although it does not generally 'approve' the assessment as such.

In preparing these risk assessments, operators and their professional advisors are expected by the regulator to adhere to the general and specific guidance issued on environmental risk assessment and management. In reviewing an applicant's submission, the regulator evaluates it from a regulatory and technical perspective, assessing the quality and suitability of the submission, by reference to statutory requirements, the supporting science and relevant published guidance. On receipt of the risk assessment, and depending on the type of facility and quality of submission, the regulator will normally:

- conduct a technical and regulatory review of the submission, consulting internally and externally as required, and probing the submission for its technical soundness and completeness by reference to the legislation, available guidance and current state of the science base;
- request further work of the operator, if deemed necessary;
- consider the need for an independent review of the operator's risk assessment where there are reasonable differences of opinion or where a second opinion might prove valuable;

- consider the need for an independent risk assessment for any operation or proposal; and
- review the operator's proposed risk management measures, or those additional measures that should be considered, to mitigate the risks to an acceptable level of residual risk.

Risk assessments are therefore used by both parties to assess the magnitude and significance of the risk posed by the activity, identify the key drivers of the risk, prioritize risk reduction measures and assess the level of residual risk following application of these measures. Risk reduction is secured by applying conditions to the environmental permit, operating the process in accordance with the conditions as a minimum standard and by the regulator enforcing the conditions. Measures may range from technological interventions (e.g. the application of the best available technology) to a requirement for environmental management systems, training or even substitution of a product. Adherence to these measures is enforced through regulatory inspection and related regulatory mechanisms.

Whilst individual legislation specifies the use of environmental risk assessment for specific regulatory processes, the environment agencies have general duties and powers (for the Environment Agency, sections 4 and 5 of the Environment Act 1995) which they can use to request risk assessments of operators, permit holders and applicants. Furthermore, the adoption of various principles, tools and techniques for environmental decision-making feature in the Ministerial Guidance provided to the Environment Agency on its contribution to sustainable development (e.g. Defra, 2000). In short, the agencies may generally request a risk assessment for any activity that they regulate where pollution of the environment is suspected. The general expectations of environmental risk assessment work submitted for regulatory review are set out in the revised *Guidelines on Environmental Risk Assessment and Management* (DETR *et al.*, 2000).

The application of risk assessment in regulation

Individual statutory instruments set out the context and objectives of the legislation and usually state whether risk assessment is to be applied and for what purpose. Supplementary guidance, whether statutory or non-statutory will usually describe the detail on how risk assessment should be used and what the regulatory expectations are. Further technical guidance is sometimes developed in support of this. Some of the more common regulatory applications of risk assessment, the specific context and the guidance that supports their application are discussed in the following sections.

Environmental planning

For certain development projects such as waste management facilities (incinerators, landfill, hazardous waste facilities), it has become commonplace for applicants to submit a project-level environmental risk assessment as part of the environmental impact assessment required under planning legislation. Risk assessment offers greater resolution over EIA with respect to the relative likelihood of effects that the development may pose. It allows planners and their consultees the opportunity to scrutinize in detail the relative significance of potential impacts. With respect to the potential impacts of development projects on human health, the increasing application of health impact assessment (HIA) is seeing the outputs of project-level EIA, risk assessment and HIA converge.

Risk assessments submitted during planning may be refined, adapted or expanded upon at the environmental permitting stage contingent on the requirements of the permitting regime. At the permitting stage, the environment agencies have powers to require permit applicants to furnish additional information, within a specified period, for the purposes of determining the application.

IPPC and COMAH

Risks from the process sector were historically addressed through the Integrated Pollution Control (IPC) regime. The IPC approach was largely 'effects-based' and driven by the need to render releases from regulated processes to the environment 'harmless'. In risk terms, the approach used environmental criteria, and their exceedence, as a surrogate for assessing the consequences and probability of environmental harm.

Under integrated pollution prevention and control (IPPC) and the control of major accident and hazards (COMAH) legislation, risk assessment assumes a more formalized role. For COMAH, there is a requirement for operators to undertake an environmental risk assessment and to demonstrate that risks have been identified, and all necessary measures put in place, to prevent major accidents or to limit their consequences.

Each site is different and a systematic approach allows for the identification of the most important high-risk accident scenarios and the prioritization of resources, resulting in a transparent, proportionate approach to the management of major hazards from dangerous substances. As a general principle, IPPC requires that all industrial operators applying for authorization are required to assess the risk of accidents and their consequences and that necessary measures be taken to prevent accidents and limit their environmental consequences.

There is some element of overlap between IPPC and COMAH for certain sites and there is recognition that certain information required for both regimes may be interchangeable. However, the accident provisions for IPPC may fall beneath the threshold for COMAH classification. Whilst IPPC risk assessments may require consideration to be given to smaller incidents, these may still have significant impacts on the environment, individually or cumulatively.

Contaminated land

Risks from land contamination have historically been addressed on a 'suitable-for-use' basis with most sites being assessed for their future use under the planning regime. With the introduction of Part IIA of the Environmental Protection Act 1990 – 'the contaminated land regime' – in 2000, an increased awareness by regulators and industry has developed of the risks posed by historically contaminated land (DETR, 2000; Environment Act 1995).

Part IIA has made much more explicit the role of risk assessment in contaminated land decision-making. It firmly establishes the role of the conceptual model and the source–pathway–receptor relationship. A tiered approach to risk assessment is used with defined stages and roles for risk screening, generic and detailed quantitative risk assessment as well as formalized options appraisal for risk management. Technical guidance is available to assist regulators and industry to assess risks to human health, controlled waters and buildings. In addition, more general guidance covers the development of soil and groundwater sampling strategies and the communication of risk.

Planning and redevelopment of sites affected by land contamination still represents the most cost-effective and beneficial way of dealing with such risks in the longer term. One of the benefits of Part IIA is that its explicit approach to the assessment of risks is raising the standard of similar assessments under the planning regime, as its principles become more familiar among practitioners.

Waste management

Environmental risk assessment is fundamental to all phases of development for waste management facilities, from the strategic planning level through to the regulation of an individual facility. At the strategic level, risk assessment informs decisions about land use and underpins assessment of the environmental impact associated with the site location, considered through the development planning process. In the context of a permit, risk assessment is used to enable the operator and the environment agencies to identify whether, and what, risk management options, or mitigation measures, are required to adequately prevent, control, minimize and/or mitigate the identified risks to the environment from the facility. These measures are stipulated for waste management licences as licence conditions or in the working plan, and for pollution prevention and control (PPC) permits in the conditions or in the PPC authorization.

Under the 1994 Waste Management Licensing Regulations applicants for waste management licences submit site-specific risk assessments and previously, for landfill facilities, Regulation 15 (EU Groundwater Directive; see also European Commission, 2003) groundwater risk assessments in accordance with published guidance. Quantitative risk assessments, using the 'LandSim' probabilistic risk assessment tool (Environment Agency, 2001, 2003), for example, have represented good practice for many years for the assessment of hydrogeological risks from landfills. The risk management measures are subsequently addressed by specific licence conditions and working plan specifications. The complexity of the measures required depend upon the type and magnitude of risks that the operations present to the environment. Risk management measures may be relatively simple, such as operational procedures requiring simple action and documentation, or more complex, such as engineered systems with fully documented and quality assured stages of design, construction, testing and validation, operation and maintenance.

Some waste management facilities, including landfill facilities, now fall within the PPC Regulations 2000 as prescribed by Schedule 1, section 5. Under the EU Landfill Directive, all landfills are now required to adhere to new requirements regarding their design and operation, with waste management licences being replaced with new PPC permits that comply with the Directive's requirements. Under the Landfill (England and Wales) Regulations 2002, operators are required to demonstrate that necessary measures are taken to protect the environment and human health and to prevent accidents. The risk assessment requirements for the Landfill Regulations indicate the operator should have regard to:

- the generic Government guidance on environmental risk assessment and management;
- the specific technical requirements for landfills falling under the Landfill Directive;
- the European Commission's decision establishing criteria and procedures for the acceptance of waste at landfills pursuant to Article 16 and Annex II of the Landfill Directive; and
- the requirements of the Groundwater Directive; and hence
- Environment Agency *Guidance on Hydrogeological Risk Assessments for Landfills and the Derivation of Groundwater Control and Trigger Levels* (Environment Agency, 2002a).

The last document describes the framework for compliance with respect to groundwater for the above Directives and sets out the requirements for environmental risk assessment under the new legislative regime. The framework is supported by the quantitative risk models – 'LandSim v2', familiar to many practitioners, and now also the 'GasSim' model (Environment Agency, 2002b). In the future, the separate aspects of hydrogeological, human health and ecological risk, among others for waste management facilities, are expected to be drawn together within a single technical requirement.

Radioactive waste performance assessment

The Radioactive Substances Act 1993 provides the framework for controlling the creation and disposal of radioactive wastes so as to protect the public from hazards that may arise from their disposal to the environment. Regulatory guidance for disposal facilities sets down two criteria for assessment of the radiological safety of radioactive waste disposal facilities:

1. a dose limit for a facility's operational phase; and
2. a post-closure radiological risk target.

Post-closure, a radiological risk target is considered an appropriate protection standard because of the uncertainties inherent in assessment of future performance of a disposal system. The assessed radiological risk from a facility to a representative member of a potentially exposed group at greatest risk should be consistent with a risk target of less than one in a million risk per annum of a radiological health effect. Here, radiological risk is the product of the probability that a given dose will be received and the probability that the dose will result in a serious health effect, summed over all situations that could give rise to exposure to the group. Development of exposure scenarios and the conditions of institutional control (either by the operator or some successive regime) post-closure are essential aspects of risk analysis and management for radioactive waste management facilities.

If, for a chosen facility design, the assessed risk exceeds the risk target, the developer should show that the design is 'optimized' and that the radiological risk has been reduced (benefit) to a level that represents a balance between radiological and other factors, including social and economic factors (cost). This is consistent with the 'as low as reasonably achievable' (ALARA) approach to risk management. Where the risk is below the risk target and the regulator is satisfied that the safety case has a sound scientific and technical basis and that good engineering principles and practice are being applied, then no further reductions in risk need be sought.

Groundwater regulations

Activities likely to lead to the direct or indirect discharge of List I or List II substances, as defined by the Groundwater Directive, require prior authorization. Many activities authorized by the regulator under the Groundwater Regulations are intermittent agricultural discharges or disposals, and due to the large numbers of authorizations, a tiered system of risk assessment has been developed. This approach allows the regulator to match the scale of the operation with the complexity of the assessment. A simple risk screening system is applied to the bulk of the applications. This risk screening system (tier 1) uses several indicators that are readily ascertained from the application forms and readily accessible national data sets to score the application and determine whether the application for discharge can be: approved subject to standard conditions; refused; or needs to be supported by further data or a more detailed analysis of the risk.

A second level risk assessment tool for the land spreading of wastes (the majority of activities) has now been developed that relies on soil property data and a soil leaching equation. Other tools, such as the Environment Agency's 'ConSim' software package that takes account of processes within the unsaturated zone, are available for more detailed assessment of point source disposals.

The close relationship between codes of good practice and risk assessment is stressed. Many of the risk assessments are predicated on adherence to good practice, as noted in recognized codes, a number of which are now statutory. The assumption of good practice is reflected in standard conditions on authorizations and a system of site inspections to check for compliance with the terms of authorizations.

Tools and techniques for practitioners

A wide range of tools and techniques are in use for undertaking risk assessments. They range from straightforward examinations of the connectivity between the source of a hazard and the receptor, to sophisticated numerical packages for dealing with probabilistic analysis. In practice, many risk problems can be addressed, at least initially, using a qualitative analysis, providing the logic is sound and transparent. The ready availability of quantitative and probabilistic methods has driven an increasing trend towards quantitative expressions of risk estimates. However, given the extreme complexity of dynamic environmental systems, there is a continual need to ensure risk analysts do not 'overreach' with quantified risk estimates and infer more precision of their analyses than can be supported by their understanding of the system under study.

Complex environmental issues with significant consequences will invariably require a combination of qualitative and quantitative analysis, usually because certain aspects of the system are better described than others. Fitness for purpose is the rule. For example, in radioactive waste disposal, whilst the engineering features of a disposal facility can be described in quantitative detail, future exposure scenarios in thousands of years' time can only ever be represented by illustrative 'futures'. These types of complex assessments require formalized procedures for combining: experimentally derived data with elicited expert judgement; predictive and illustrative exposure scenarios; and qualitative with quantitative expressions of risk with their associated uncertainties, all set within a risk assessment framework. Problems of this type rapidly become specialist activities.

A tiered approach to risk assessment allows for risk screening, prioritization and, in general, a qualitative treatment in advance of quantification. Because there is often considerable uncertainty involved in assessing environmental risk, particularly in the assessment of environmental exposures and impacts, resources should be targeted accordingly, that is where risks or uncertainties are high, or where the costs of the assessment are justified by the benefits to decision-making. A simple 'risk screening' approach is used first to state clearly the issues of concern, establish the logic of the risk assessment and determine the key risks and priorities. If the decision cannot be made based on this approach then more detailed approaches are used, focusing on the key risks identified at screening. A further consideration is the type of risk being assessed. One may be concerned with:

- the risk of an initiating event, or combination of events, occurring that subsequently results in a release to the environment (e.g. the overtopping of a coastal flood defence by large volumes of sea water; the release of firewater from an on-site collection tank; a process plant failure; a landfill liner failure);
- the risk of an environmental receptor being exposed following a release (e.g. derogation of a drinking water supply by a leachate plume; grounding of a plume downwind of an incinerator stack; the incidental exposure to contaminated soil);
- the risk of harm resulting from exposure (e.g. risks to human or ecological health as a result of exposure to toxic/asphyxiant gases; damage to property following the entry of flood waters; harm to a wetland following over-abstraction or periods of drought; leaf damage to acid-sensitive trees following acid deposition).

Given these factors, experience has shown that it is invariably better to start simple and build in complexity as you need it. Sound guidance is to start simply by drawing out the problem as a diagram. Include aspects to be assessed and decide what aspects the assessment will and will not cover. Using the diagram (or conceptual model, Figure 10.3), write out possible source–pathway–receptor linkages; each linkage should have only one source, one pathway and one receptor. Ask whether, in each case, the source, pathway and receptor are linked or potentially linked; screen out those for which the answer is 'no'. Make simple but justifiable assessments (high, medium, low) separately for probability and consequence, for each linkage, recording the reasoning.

In comparing probabilities, consider the nature of the pathway – do direct or indirect routes (those requiring barriers to be overcome) exist between the source and receptor? In considering consequences think about the relative potencies of the source of the hazard and in comparing receptors, think about their relative inherent vulnerability (children or older people) and sensitivity to the specific hazard

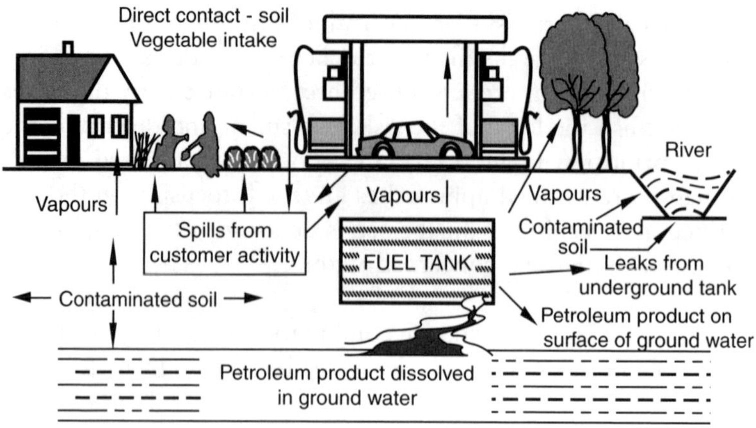

(© Energy Institute)

Figure 10.3 Example conceptual model showing potential environmental exposures at a petrol retail forecourt, illustrating sources, pathways and receptors

(immuno-compromised individuals, for example). Establish your assessment criteria and group source–pathway–receptor linkages accordingly; for example, those with high probability and high consequence, and prioritize those risks accordingly.

The type of risk influences the technique used to assess it. For example, event/fault tree analysis may be used to assess the performance characteristics of engineered systems and unit processes as there may be engineered safeguards to prevent the initiation or escalation of accident sequences (Figure 10.4). The event tree structure provides useful information by showing the combination of conditions required to achieve a particular undesired outcome. Additional value can be obtained by assigning conditional probabilities to each branch and quantifying the outcomes.

The quantification of environmental exposures following a release often relies heavily on distribution, including dispersion modelling, although event tree analysis can also be an important tool here. Understanding the risks of harm following exposure, beyond the reference to environmental criteria, requires a more detailed evaluation of physical, chemical or biological damage and reference to health-based assessment criteria that account for the toxicological consequences of exposure. Selecting the right tool, in the right circumstance and for the right purpose requires both:

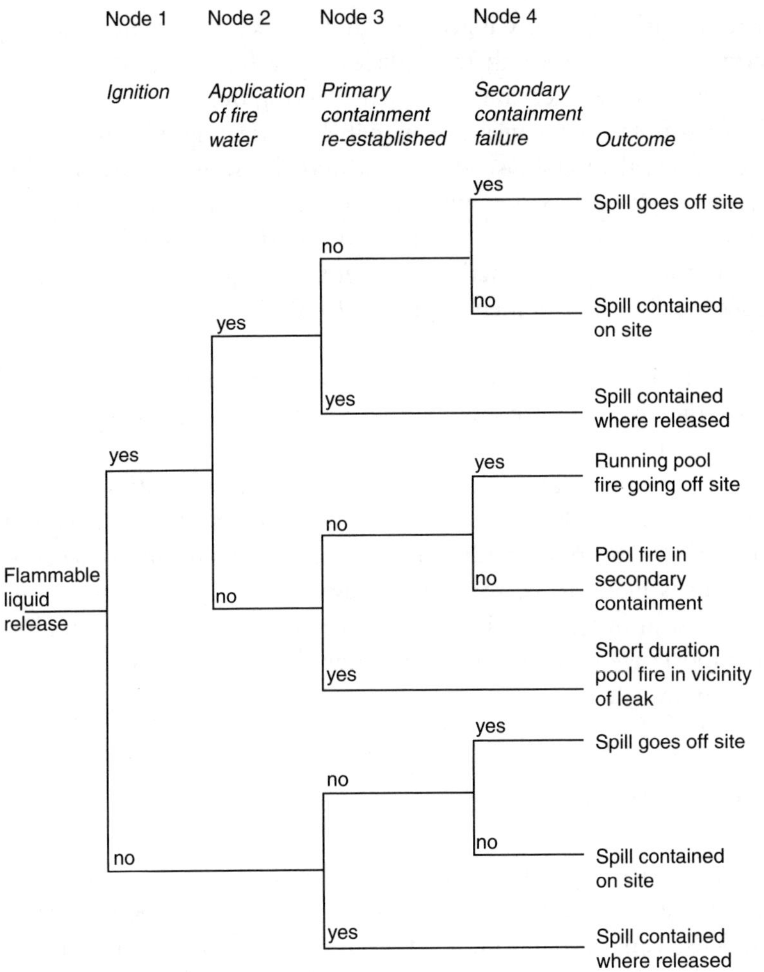

Figure 10.4 Example event tree for the release of flammable liquid from a process facility

- selection of the appropriate level (tier) of sophistication as needs, complexities, priorities and data allow; and, within this,
- selection of the appropriate tool with reference to the type of risk being studied.

Complex risks may require a range of tools at various tiers of sophistication in order to manage the uncertainties inherent to the problem. Often there is insufficient data to be certain about what one is dealing with. Models are inherently inaccurate and/or incomplete and one may not know what changes will take place in the future. It is important to be aware of these uncertainties when carrying out a risk assessment. A series of software packages are available for dealing with uncertainties in conceptual models, specific data and decision uncertainty, but in applying these and expressing risks quantitatively it is essential not to assume a level of precision in the analysis that cannot be substantiated. The following are practical pointers that can help when dealing with uncertainty (Environment Agency, 2000).

- It is best to concentrate on the 'big picture' before getting into the detail and to avoid a complex analysis of an issue unless you are sure it is important.
- Try to communicate where the greatest uncertainties lie. For example, you might be confident in the permeability of a landfill liner that is in good condition, but very uncertain as to whether the liner is likely to be torn or damaged.
- Be honest about uncertainties. Use 'what if' questions, to explore the importance of uncertainty to the final assessment of risk (sensitivity analysis).

Evaluating risk assessments

Many environmental professionals find themselves in the position of commissioning, evaluating or reviewing the risk assessment work of experts. This can be daunting in that they may feel in unchartered professional territory and the complexity of many assessments can often obscure the key aspects relevant to managing the risk. Below are some key principles.

- *Involve others.* The risk assessor needs to understand the context of the decision being made and the full range of factors that might influence it. There may be a variety of audiences for the output and both stakeholders and the public may wish to have the opportunity to help frame the questions the assessment addresses, and input knowledge. Involving the audience early on and throughout the process may assist in gaining acceptance for the approach and in getting a wider buy-in to the final decision, though it would be naïve to expect this as given.

- *Good problem definition is essential.* What is the environmental setting? What are the spatial and temporal aspects of the problem? Which aspects will the risk assessment address and which will it not address? This can often be set out schematically, or using a diagram often referred to as a conceptual model. Involving those with an interest in the risk assessment output at this stage is essential.
- *Taking a stepwise approach to the risk assessment is vital.* The identification of hazards, the assessment of exposures and the estimation of risk and the subsequent evaluation of the significance of the risk follow a logical sequence: What is at risk and what is it at risk from? What and how might it happen? How large will the consequences be and how probable are they? What criteria will be used to judge their significance? How significant are the probabilities and consequences and how certain is the assessment of probability and consequence?
- *Be prepared to review the analysis.* As the risk assessment proceeds, one often discovers new information that necessitates a revision of one's previous assumptions. Assessments that allow for iteration are useful because they facilitate review, may help avoid the incorporation of systematic bias and ensure that the risk assessment process is developmental rather than being treated as a 'black box'. In practice, all risks are dynamic in time and space, so changes to the 'risk profiles' of all operations should be expected.
- *Risk assessments should be fit for purpose.* Detailed quantitative work will not be required in every case and many potential risks can be screened out early on using a sound logic based on the 'source–pathway–receptor' concept. Allowing for different tiers of sophistication of analysis ensures that a sound logic is established before progressing to quantitative assessment and, consequently, that resources are focused on the higher-priority, more complex risks. An important aspect of 'tiering' is ensuring that a defensible justification is provided for risks screened out and that the remaining risks are carried over into the next tier of analysis. At any point, the assessor may need to revisit the justification for screening a risk issue out.
- *The assessment–management interface.* In practice, there is an iterative exchange of information throughout between risk assessment and management, simply because certain practical management measures may often be anticipated or known quite early on in the assessment. Some frameworks explicitly emphasize a distinction between the risk analysis and assessing the significance of the risk. Communicating with, and involving, others is essential throughout.

- *Practicality*. Risk assessments should not be overly complex, but guide the practitioner through the various steps and considerations. It should not 'force' a level of analysis that is disproportionate to the risk. Throughout, the assessor should practice an approach to risk assessment that is commensurate with the supporting science.

Hot topics and future trends

Future trends in the assessment of environmental risk are likely to see its continued expansion to more strategic levels of assessment (programmes and plans of activity) and to the comparative assessment of many risks within an individual assessment (comparative risk analysis). We can expect greater use of probabilistic techniques as these become more accessible and the current demand for greater openness in the process continues. With respect to technical developments, the practice of environmental exposure assessment continues to develop with an increasing interest in environmental exposures within the home environment. There is a growing awareness of the episodic nature of many environmental exposures whereas exposure has historically been often oversimplified as constant in space and time. There are important implications here for acute exposure and the potential overestimation of chronic risk.

Beyond methodological developments, issues receiving increasing attention include the practice of corporate environmental risk management and the maturity of risk management within organizations, the implementation of risk-based environmental regulation, the role of citizens in risk-based environmental decision-making and the relationship and tensions between risk management and the precautionary principle.

We have moved on a long way from where risk assessment was used as the basis for justifying a course of action, to recognition that assessing risk is a prerequisite to designing a good decision. Managing risk has become an essential business requirement. From embedding good corporate governance within organizations through to the management of individual projects and assets (Figure 10.5), the ability to understand, communicate, assess and manage risk is now a mainstream activity. Environmental risk management is playing its part in what is increasingly viewed as the integrated, enterprise-wide activity of business risk management.

(after Prime Minister's Strategy Unit, 2002)

Figure 10.5 The risk hierarchy from strategic to operational risk, applied here to the water utility sector

As organizations become more proficient in managing risk, their organizational capability develops. Corporate maturity in risk management may be reflected in accreditation schemes such as the environmental management systems series (EMS) 14001 and their recent updated versions (ISO 14001:2004 and ISO 14004:2004). Holding accreditations of these standards demonstrates a capability to pursue a 'plan–do–check–act' management loop and infers a capacity to implement institutional learning within a framework of continuous improvement. Researchers and practitioners are now investigating the use of 'maturity models', developed initially in the software industry, for assessing how far along the journey from novice to expert organizations have come in managing their business risks (Hillson, 1997). Initially these have been employed in the offshore industry, but the advances made in risk management capability maturity models more widely within health and safety regulation have direct application for the operation and regulation of land-based installations with environmental permits.

Environmental regulators are showing increasing interest in both risk-based regulation and self-regulation, under which the capability of operators to actively manage risk is being assessed with implications for the amount of regulatory attention given to sites and operators. Environmental regulators have an inherent interest in organizational capacities to manage risk where companies operate multiple sites at home and abroad. The plant level monitoring of risk management capability provides a valuable reality check on corporate statements on risk management. The operator pollution risk appraisal (OPRA) schemes introduced for environmental regulation of the process sector in the UK offer one example of how the inherent hazards associated with unit processes and operator performance at individual sites can be assessed to provide an overall risk profile for operators, process sectors and regions.

Within the stakeholder society, the risk assessments that support decisions on the licensing of new chemicals and processes find their way increasingly into the public domain, either through the regulatory process or through legal challenge. Historically, many of these reports would have been hidden from public view, but their recent accessibility has made available to many the complexities and uncertainties of environmental risk assessment. Risk assessment itself has become contentious, in part perhaps because some see its use as a means of justifying an action that may pose harm to the environment, rather than as a tool to identify what protection is required. Many have expressed unease over the number of assumptions used, the seemingly rigid approach adopted and the lack of opportunities for critique and broader engagement. New, inclusive paradigms for risk-informed environmental decision-making have been developed in response and participatory approaches to problem definition are being explored in the literature.

One of the key tensions recently has been the relationship between adoption of the precautionary principle and risk assessment, two approaches to decision-making that have erroneously been pitched against one another. In practice, the 'principle' requires an analysis of the significance and uncertainty of a hazard being realized, in order to inform the decision on whether to act now or defer action and monitor. It therefore requires an assessment of risk so that it can be applied.

Conclusion

Managing environmental risk is complex because the environment is dynamic, open and complex in its make-up and still relatively poorly characterized. One needs to be cautious, therefore, in applying risk analysis tools not to assume greater knowledge than one has available. This said, there is tremendous value to be gained in using environmental risk assessment to prioritize management action. Because environmental decisions invariably involve people and items they value (landscape, river quality, ecosystems), application of risk assessment and the setting of priorities will always be contentious. In a democratized decision-making environment, environmental risk analysts face the challenge of undertaking and communicating their analyses, whilst managing the demands for assessment processes to be more open and accessible to lay audiences.

References and recommended reading

Calow, P (1997) *Handbook of Environmental Risk Assessment and Management.* Oxford: Blackwell Science.

Cohrssen, J J and Covello, V T (1989) *Risk Analysis: A Guide to Principles and Methods for Analyzing Health and Environmental Risks.* Washington, DC: US Council on Environmental Quality.

Dahlström, K, Howes, C, Leinster, P and Skea, J (2003) Environmental management systems and company performance: assessing the case for extending risk-based regulation. *European Environment* **13** 187–203.

Defra (2000) *Environment Agency Financial, Management and Policy Review.* Available at: http://www.defra.gov.uk/environment/consult/eafman/03.htm

Defra (2002) *Risk Management Strategy.* London: Department for Environmental, Food and Rural Affairs.

Department of the Environment (1995) *A Guide to Risk Assessment and Risk Management for Environmental Protection.* London: HMSO.

DETR (2000) *Circular 2/2000 Contaminated Land: Implementation of Part IIA of the Environmental Protection Act 1990.* London: The Stationery Office.

DETR, Environment Agency and IEH (2000) *Guidelines for Environmental Risk Assessment and Management.* London: The Stationery Office.

Environment Agency (2000) *Introducing Environmental Risk Assessment.* Bristol: Environment Agency, HO-06/00 (reprint 2/02).

Environment Agency (2001) *LandSim Release 2: Landfill Performance Evaluation – Simulation by Monte Carlo Method.* R&D Publication 120. Bristol: Environment Agency.

Environment Agency (2002a) *Guidance on Hydrogeological Risk Assessments for Landfills and the Derivation of Groundwater Control and Trigger Levels.* Bristol: Environment Agency.

Environment Agency (2002b) *GasSim – Landfill Gas Risk Assessment Tool (Model and User Manual).* R&D Project P1–295. Bristol: Environment Agency.

Environment Agency (2003) *The Development of LandSim 2.5.* NGWCLC GW/03/09. Sept. Bristol: Environment Agency.

Environment Agency and Health and Safety Executive (1999) *Guidance on the Environmental Risk Assessment Aspects of COMAH Safety Reports.* Bristol: Environment Agency on behalf of joint Competent Authority. Available at: http://www.environment-agency.gov.uk

ESRC Global Environmental Change Programme (2000) *Risk Choices, Soft Disasters: Environmental Decision-making Under Uncertainty.* Brighton: University of Sussex.

European Commission (2003) Proposal for a Directive of the European Parliament and of the Council on the protection of groundwater against pollution. COM(2003) 550 final. Available at: http://europa.eu.int/eur-lex/en/com/pdf/2003/com2003_0550en01.pdf

European Communities (1980) Council Directive 80/68/EEC of 17 December 1979 on the protection of groundwater against pollution caused by certain dangerous substances [EU Groundwater Directive]. Luxembourg: EUR-OP. (OJ L 020, 26/01/1980 pp. 0043–0048.) See: http://europa.eu.int/

European Communities (1999) Council Directive 1999/31/EC of 26 April 1999 on the landfill of waste [EU Landfill Directive]. Luxembourg: EUR-OP. (OJ L 182, 16/07/1999 pp. 0001–0019.) Available at: http://europa.eu.int

European Environment Agency (1998) *Environmental Risk Assessment: Approaches, Experiences and Information Sources*. Copenhagen: European Environment Agency.

Fischoff, B (1995) Risk perception and communication unplugged: twenty years of process. *Risk Analysis*, **15** 137–145.

Great Britain (1993) Radioactive Substances Act 1993. London: HMSO.

Great Britain (1994) The Waste Management Licensing Regulations 1994 (SI 1994 No. 1056). London: HMSO.

Great Britain (1995) Environment Act 1995. London: The Stationery Office.

Great Britain (2000) The Pollution Prevention and Control (England and Wales) Regulations 2000 (SI 2000 No. 1973). London: The Stationery Office. As amended.

Great Britain (2002) The Landfill (England and Wales) Regulations 2002 (SI 2002 No. 1559). London: The Stationery Office.

Harrison, R M and Hester, R E (eds.) (1998) Risk assessment and risk management. *Issues in Environmental Science and Technology*, **9** 1–168.

Health and Safety Executive (2001) *Reducing Risks, Protecting People*. Sudbury, Suffolk: HSE Books.

Health and Safety Executive (2003) *Good Practice and Pitfalls in Risk Assessment*. Health and Safety Laboratory Research Report 151, Sudbury, Suffolk: HSE Books.

Hillson, D A (1997) Towards a risk maturity model. *Int J Proj. Bus. Risk Mgt*, **1**:1 35–45.

ISO 14001:2004, *Environmental Management Systems – Requirements with Guidance for Use*. Geneva: International Organization for Standardization.

ISO 14004:2004, *Environmental Management Systems – General Guidelines on Principles, Systems and Support Techniques*. Geneva: International Organization for Standardization.

Long, J and Fischoff, B (2000) Setting risk priorities: a formal model. *Risk Analysis*, **20** 339–351.

Ministry of Agriculture, Fisheries and Food (MAFF) (2000) *Flood and Coastal Defence Project Appraisal Guidance, Approaches to Risk: FCDPAG4*. London: MAFF.

OXERA (2000) *Policy, Risk, and Science: Securing and Using Scientific Advice*. Sudbury, Suffolk: HSE Books. Available at: http://www.hse.gov.uk/research/

Pollard, S J T (2005) Environmental risk management. In: Brady, J (ed.) *Environmental Management in Organizations. The IEMA Handbook*. London: Earthscan, ch 4.3, pp 212–226. ISBN 1 83383 976 0.

Pollard, S and Guy, J (eds.) (2001) *Risk Assessment for Environmental Professionals*. Lavenham Press, Suffolk: Chartered Institution of Water and Environmental Management.

Pollard, S J T, Yearsley, R, Reynard, N, Meadowcroft, I C, Duarte-Davidson, R and Duerden, S (2002) Current directions in the practice of environmental risk assessment in the United Kingdom. *Environ. Sci. Technol.*, **36**:4 530–538.

Presidential/Congressional Commission on Risk Assessment and Risk Management (1997) *Volume I, Framework for Environmental Health Risk Management* and *Volume II, Risk Assessment and Risk Management in Regulatory Decision-Making*. Washington, DC: US Government Printing Office. Available at: http://www.riskworld.com

Prime Minister's Strategy Unit (2002) *Risk: Improving Government's Capability to Handle Risk and Uncertainty*. London: The Strategy Unit. Available at: http://www.number-10.gov.uk/SU/RISK/risk/home.html

Royal Academy of Engineering (2003) *The Societal Aspects of Risk*. London: The Royal Academy of Engineering.

Royal Commission on Environmental Pollution (1998) *Twenty-First Report: Setting Environmental Standards*. London: The Stationery Office.

Scotland and Northern Ireland Forum for Environmental Research (SNIFFER) (1999) *Communicating Understanding of Contaminated Land Risks*. SNIFFER Publication SR97(11)F, Foundation for Water Research (FWR).

Stern, P C and Fineberg, H V (eds.) (1996) *Understanding Risk – Informing Decisions in a Democratic Society*. Washington, DC: National Academic Press.

USEPA (1999) *Integrated Decision-making in the 21st Century*. Peer review draft, May. Available at: http://www.epa.gov/science1/irp/

van Leeuwen, C J (1995) General introduction. In: van Leeuwen, C J and Hermens, J L M (eds.) *Risk Assessment of Chemicals: An Introduction*. Dordrecht: Kluwer, pp 1–17.

Vose, D (2000) *Quantitative Risk Analysis: A Guide to Monte Carlo Simulation Modelling*, 2nd edn. Chichester: John Wiley & Sons.

11

Legal and Contractual Risk Management

Anthony Cherry

A working definition of legal risk management

The law and lawyers impact on the risk management process in a number of ways. First, however you choose to categorize the risk facing a business, some of the categories will have a dominantly legal element. For example, the contractual obligations into which a corporation has entered create risks which are determined wholly by legal considerations. These contractual issues are so significant that they are separately addressed below. Governance, although outside the scope of this chapter, is also a purely legal issue.

Other categories will have obvious legal aspects, alongside operational issues. Employee risk or fraud would be good examples. Yet others, say reputation risk, seem at first sight to have little legal involvement, but on proper analysis do because, for example, of the way regulatory performance impacts on reputation. Therefore legal risk permeates any risk matrix which a business may construct.

Second, legal techniques are an effective solution for risk control and risk transfer. Much can be done through contracts, protocols and so on to reduce the downside in many risk categories. They are an important tool for balancing opportunity and risk.

Third, and perhaps less obviously, legal skills and legal considerations are relevant to the risk identification process itself, whichever specific hazard may be in issue. Whilst facilitation is a valuable tool in determining risk profile, experience shows that some forensic enquiry is also required to maximize the chance that the profile will be accurate.

In whichever sense we are talking about legal risk management, however, an active approach can play a crucial role in underpinning good corporate governance and promoting socially responsible practices. Good legal risk management cannot be proven to reduce the absolute chance that any particular contingency will occur, but as with other effective approaches it will reduce volatility and uncertainty about future risk.

Those who encourage legal and regulatory compliance by focusing on the spectre of personal financial liability or worse, imprisonment for directors and senior managers, are missing the point. There are no quick fixes. Protection lies in a commitment to good risk management practice and thorough implementation of sound techniques throughout the business.

Corporate manslaughter provides an excellent example of why this is so. The Government has been promising legislation on corporate manslaughter since 1997. Eight years later, there is still no increased prospect of anyone going to jail. A draft bill was produced in March 2005 [Corporate Manslaughter – The Government's Draft Bill for Reform, Cm 6497, Great Britain Home Office (2005)] to be followed by a consultation period and pre-legislative scrutiny of the proposals by Parliamentary Committee.

The difficulty of legislating for the liability of an individual within a complex organization to which commentators have pointed consistently over the years has not been, indeed cannot be, addressed. The bill focuses instead on making it possible to convict a company of manslaughter notwithstanding the impossibility of identifying a responsible individual.

Significantly the government failed to support the Private Member's Bill sponsored by Stephen Hepburn in March 2005 [Health and Safety (Directors' Duties) Bill (No. 22 of 2004–05)] which attempted to make one board member responsible for providing information to the rest of the board, who would then have had collective responsibility on the basis of that information. For reasons which are too complex to analyse here ministers must have decided, rightly, that this formulation would not work.

However, the important point here is that the risk identified is the risk that the corporation will, through its activities, kill someone. Irrespective of the criminal penalties which may be suffered, there are already a range of consequences for reputation, public confidence and the willingness of investors and bankers to finance the company. Readers will not need to reflect for long on, for example, the railway disasters of the last few years, to see that these risks were far from illusory for the companies involved.

Thus, by concentrating on what may be traditionally regarded as the pure legal risk, one could make a serious miscalculation about the resources which should be applied to, for example, preventing fatalities. Legal risk management, like any other type, delivers its real benefits through improved security of future revenue and profit, not through keeping the board out of jail.

The risk challenge

Whilst the major corporate scandals of recent years (Enron, Worldcom, Ahold and Parmalat, for example) may be widely interpreted as fundamentally financial in nature, because the companies concerned all misled investors about the extent of their revenue and profit, they nevertheless represent a significant element in the challenge facing legal risk managers.

First, consider the measures which have as a result either been initiated (the Sarbanes-Oxley Act of 2002 in the US) or been given more impetus and significance [Basel 2 for the Financial Services Sector (Basel, 2001) and, in the UK, the revisions to the Stock Exchange Combined Code (Financial Reporting Council, 2003) and the introduction of the Operating and Financial Review (DTI, 2005)].

The Sarbanes-Oxley Act was enacted in the US following the collapse of Enron to strengthen reporting requirements and provide protection for 'whistle-blowers'. It affects any company with a listing on the US stock exchange or with certain other financial interests in the US, so extends to many UK businesses.

The original Basel Capital Accord of 1988 (Basel, 1988) dealt with minimum levels of capital for banks. The new Accord (Basel 2) requires a risk-based approach and is due to be implemented on 31 December 2006. In order to give effect to Basel 2 and bring all credit institutions and investment firms within its ambit there will be a new EU Directive [Capital Adequacy Directive, CAD3 (2003)].

The Stock Exchange Combined Code controls many aspects of corporate governance for companies listed on the exchange. Throughout the 1990s there was a series of reports on corporate governance: the Greenbury (Greenbury, 1995), Cadbury (Cadbury *et al.*, 1992) and Hampel reports (Committee on Corporate Governance, 1998). At the request of the Institute of Chartered Accountants of England and Wales, Nigel Turnbull produced a guide to how the reporting requirements following these reports should be interpreted and 'Turnbull' became synonymous with risk-based corporate reporting (Turnbull *et al.*, 1999).

The Combined Code itself was amended following the Higgs review, the recommendations of which were largely to do with board organization, membership and responsibilities and are outside the scope of this chapter (Higgs, 2003).

The Operating and Financial Review was first proposed in the White Paper *Modernising Company Law* in July 2002. The House of Commons Trade & Industry Committee reported on the White Paper in May 2003. Draft regulations to implement the OFR were laid before Parliament on 12 January 2005. It will affect the next annual report filed by most large companies (Department of Trade and Industry, 2002).

All of these provisions require legal interpretation and legal support for implementation within organizations, so this is a prime example of legal and regulatory measures as part of the risk solution. All industries have the opportunity to embrace regulatory requirements in a way which goes beyond mere compliance and use the systems required to improve corporate performance.

It will require a new approach from lawyers to take this extra step and develop from giving pure compliance advice to delivering guidance on how compliance can be embedded in operational processes to benefit the business. There are some thoughts about how this may play out in the concluding section of this chapter.

Second, within the new environment created by revised governance requirements, particularly the obligation to report corporate risk and the protection offered to whistle-blowers, there is an opportunity for legal risk managers in the third sense, that is using legal forensic skills to support the reporting process, to reduce the opportunity for major distortions.

It would be foolish (and indeed dangerous from the point of view of the lawyer's own liability position) to suggest that the use of legal risk management techniques could eliminate the possibility of deliberate distortion of a corporation's performance. However, the forensic approach, used in a judicious blend with facilitative techniques, will improve the chances of avoiding this type of corporate failure in the future.

It is noteworthy that one of the risk categories which needs to be present in any system for reviewing risk is Deliberate Adverse Activity. Clearly a blunt request for information under this heading would be ineffective. However, a careful and more oblique enquiry into matters such as systems of incentive and reward and freedom to report suspicions outside an individual's direct management line can create increased levels of awareness and support a culture within which false accounting is less likely.

This illustrates why lawyers engaged in legal risk management must shift from an inward-looking focus on discrete areas of technical legal skill to an approach based on the client's business. In the process of risk identification and reporting it would not be necessary, in the above example, to have a detailed knowledge of how employment contracts should be organized to ensure protection for whistle-blowers but it would be essential to understand the governance requirements to have such protection. In contrast, where legal risk management is being used to provide solutions, the task is entirely one for the appropriate technical specialist.

Quite apart from corporate failures, legal risk management also faces challenges related to operational risk. A good example is the introduction of the General Product Safety Directive in Europe. Heavily regulated industries, such as pharmaceuticals and cosmetics, have long been accustomed to controlling product risk on a precautionary basis. They operate within well-established regimes of product testing and licensing with awareness and experience of reporting suspected issues and organizing the recall and withdrawal of products.

However, in other industries this expertise does not exist to such a great extent. Problems can arise in many ways. For example, a technology may be imported from another country where it has operated perfectly safely and cause problems because of different circumstances of use which were not anticipated. This effect has been seen with, for example, electric air fresheners where subtle differences in domestic electrical systems caused problems with fire risk.

In other cases, there may be a conflict between aesthetic design and functional safety. This can be an issue in the automobile industry, where there is an almost permanent tension between designers and engineers.

Most frequently of all, particularly with low margin goods, there will often be financial pressure to compromise on the cost of manufacture in a way that has implications for the safety of the product.

In all these circumstances and many more, legal risk management can only be effective to help control risk if practitioners adopt an approach which is based on reviewing the business as a whole. If one just answers the question 'How do we comply with the General Product Safety Directive?' in terms of to whom reports must be made and when, then it is unlikely that the client will gain any real benefit from the advice. If you look instead at the issue of how the introduction of the Directive should affect the way a business is run then there is an opportunity to make a real contribution.

Lastly by way of illustrating why there is a challenge to expand what is meant by legal risk management and what is done by those wishing to manage legal risk, there is an important lesson to be derived from what happens when, despite risk management measures, a disaster occurs.

This can easily happen in, for example, the chemical industry, where although excellent risk management has been in place for many years, environmental issues can arise with their origin in a different era, during or just after the Second World War, when standards and expectations were entirely different.

Figure 11.1, which is purely illustrative and based on experience of conflicting approaches but not on actual numbers, makes a point about how organizations should approach this type of crisis. There are few corporations today which would adopt the 'denial' model which is included in its purest form, although this approach was quite common in the not-so-distant past.

In this pattern of response, liability for the event which has occurred is wholly denied. A minimum of investigation and management of the problem is undertaken. Both regulatory enforcement agencies and civil claimants are turned away with the minimum level of engagement.

This is extremely economical at the outset and it continues to appear to work as the crisis develops. However, this is usually because the 'other side' (as in this model they are inevitably perceived) are quietly building their case in a way which is invisible to the company.

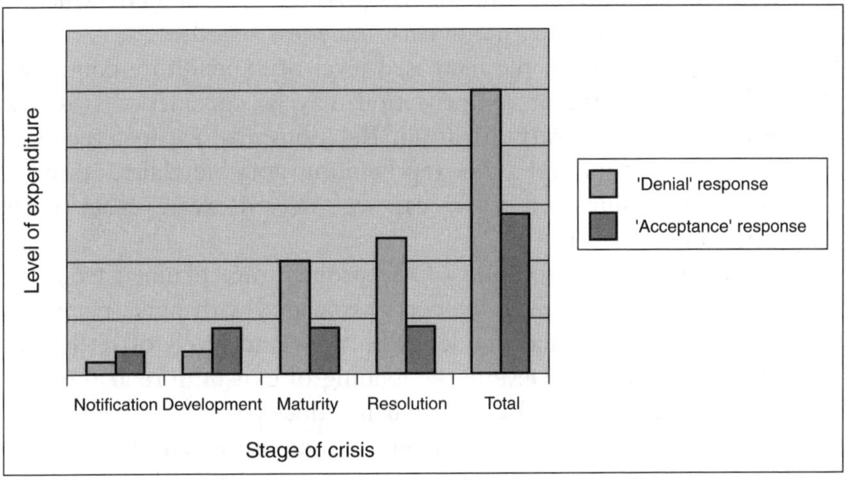

Figure 11.1 Illustration of crisis handling costs

Unfortunately the effect of this studied ignorance as the crisis matures is dramatic and disastrous. A prosecution, or civil claims, or both, are unleashed fully prepared on the business. Responses are required urgently and it costs far more in terms of management time and the cost of external advice to produce them in a rush than it would have done if planned at the outset.

Everything is done with backs against the wall and no quarter is given by opponents whose position has become entrenched. Documents cannot be found and organized. Witnesses cannot be traced. Settlements are only available, if at all, on adverse terms.

As the crisis moves to resolution this effect worsens. Both the cost of managing the crisis and the financial cost of fines and civil settlements are out of control. The total cost to the business is substantial despite the initial savings. Moreover, the financial reporting of the crisis during the early stages is likely to have been misleading and the ultimate cost much greater than predicted, leading to significant governance issues for quoted businesses.

Good legal risk management leads to a wholly different approach to the crisis, which can be called the 'acceptance' response. This does not necessarily mean accepting a liability, but it does mean accepting that, whether there is a liability or not, the event will have consequences which need to be actively managed.

In this approach more expense is incurred up front. The allegations are fully investigated technically and legally and an early assessment of liability is made. Public relations support is provided and there is a plan for communication with all the possible stakeholders, whether employees, local residents, politicians, the press or others.

As the crisis matures, the increased level of expenditure continues. A non-liability scheme of compensation may be considered to defuse concerns and avoid costly litigation. Relationships are fostered with potential prosecutors and those representing possible claimants who, through relationships of trust, can be steered away from more confrontational lawyers.

The maturity and resolution of the problem are planned from the outset and there are none of the costs associated with panic responses at this stage in the 'denial' model. Both fines and levels of settlement are substantially lower. Despite the loading of expenditure at the start of the crisis, the final total cost is much reduced.

Just as few businesses today would adopt an approach based on total denial, so it is unlikely that the 'acceptance' model will operate smoothly in every case.

Of course it is also true that, since any one crisis can only be handled one way, the financial benefits of the latter approach can never be proved empirically. What is clear, however, is that in terms of corporate reputation and corporate governance it has substantial benefits.

Again this approach involves managers of legal risk interacting fully with other risk professionals and understanding what they do in the context of the business as a whole. The common challenge, therefore, emerging from all these examples of legal risk is to generate a culture and a process within which good legal risk management can be practised.

Best practice process

Within the legal profession, when one mentions legal risk management and then outlines what is meant by it, the response is usually 'Well of course we all do that, it just means giving good, business-focused legal advice'. To some extent that is true and moreover it also reflects the perception of some clients. However, it misses the point about the value of high quality legal risk management in two fundamental ways.

First, as with many traditional legal services, legal risk advice given in the informal sense parodied here cannot be readily understood by the client in the context of their business because it lacks the structure and form which are required in order to:

- scale and prioritize risk issues;
- relate solutions to risk issues which are identified;
- track and measure progress on specific issues; and
- illuminate the interface with the other risk issues of the business.

Second, this type of advice is typically given in response to a particular problem and whilst all good lawyers will work outwards from that problem to analyse related issues, nevertheless the model remains one in which the consideration of risk expands from a narrow issue to fit the lawyer's perception of the client's business.

In an effective model, legal risk management starts from the top down, with an understanding of the client's business coming first, followed by the elimination from a comprehensive list of issues of those which are not relevant to the project in hand and a detailed forensic enquiry into those which remain. The report is thus able to put legal risk issues fully in the context of the overall risk profile of the business.

Not only does this approach deliver far greater value to the client but it offers a sound basis from which to approach risk reporting and in particular an attractive solution to the demands of Sarbanes-Oxley for companies with US regulatory requirements and the Operating and Financial Review in the UK (Department of Trade and Industry, 2005).

Significantly, it draws together the three senses of legal risk management outlined to produce a powerful argument for putting it at the heart of a modern approach to corporate risk.

In-house counsel, who are closer to the business process than most lawyers, are beginning to redefine their role in a way which addresses the second pitfall identified, that is focus on issues rather than on client need. General Counsel 100 Group (GC 100) was launched in the UK in March 2005.

Press statements from the Chair (general counsel at Barclays Bank) and joint Vice-chair (general counsel at National Grid Transco) make it clear that they see their role as moving from reaction to proactivity with a clear focus on risk (see *Financial Times*, 2005; *The Lawyer*, 2005).

However, this still does not address the first problem, the lack of a process designed to support this new 'top down' approach and to deliver scaled, reportable and measurable outputs. Indeed, in the same article, the Chair of GC 100 comments that one of the challenges of complying with Basel 2 will be to find a way of using lawyers to 'produce a way of measuring legal risks'.

The question of metrics for legal risk is a difficult one. There is no system in common usage which purports to provide objective measures of legal risk. Indeed, it seems likely that, granted the wide definition of legal risk which is necessary to understand the subject, it is unlikely that any such system could exist. However, that does not mean it is impossible to devise structures through which relative, as opposed to absolute, measures of risk may be derived.

Such textbooks as there are on legal risk management tend to be focused on the first limb of the definition adopted, approach the topic by looking at discrete areas of legal risk, such as competition, products or health and safety, and provide little guidance on how to put these issues in context and 'join up' the outputs so that conflicts and synergies can be clearly understood.

Against that background processes have been developed which draw heavily on the techniques and experience of enterprise risk managers to bring order and discipline to the reporting and understanding of legal risk.

There is a fundamental problem for anyone setting out to report on risk within a large organization. If you don't use some system for categorizing risk, then you can never make the first incisions into the body corporate and organize the resulting data flows in ways which can be ordered and comprehended. An attempt to profile risk without a system is like wrestling jelly and the result is equally messy.

Unfortunately, the instant you introduce any sort of structure there is scope for criticism of how that structure has been devised and where lines and distinctions have been drawn. The key point to understand is that the process is simply a tool to bring traditional legal skills to bear in a way which delivers valuable output to the client. It is not a strait-jacket and it is vital that creative energy is applied to relating data obtained across the categories used, not merely within each category.

One starting point for devising such a process would be the IRM/AIRMIC/ALARM joint standard on risk published in September 2002 (IRM *et al.*, 2002). The standard uses a basic and commonly understood division into strategic, financial, operational and hazard risks.

For a lawyer approaching a legal risk management project, this fundamental division is extremely helpful in taking an approach based on the business. It helps to understand, in order:

- what the business is setting out to do (strategic);
- how it will finance its planned activity (financial);
- how it will execute its strategy (operational); and
- against which unintended consequences it must guard (hazard).

Interestingly, the traditional concept of legal risk management would come into play almost entirely in the fourth of these major sectors, thus missing out on the whole point of the business to which advice is being given. In examples in the following section are illustrations of how taking the wider view benefits the client and transforms the contribution which lawyers can make.

The Joint Standard provides some suggested subcategories of risk within each of the major categories. It also recognizes that it is just a starting point which must be developed into a process suited to any given application. Before it can be used the subcategories suggested must be developed and expanded, from the experience of each project, to produce a list which can be used as a starting point for most projects in most organizations. An example of such an expansion is shown in Table 11.1.

Table 11.1 Example of expansion of subcategories of risk within each of the major categories

Cat Series No	*Category*	*Risk Series No*	*Description of Risk*	*Sub-division Series No*	*Sub-division*
1000	Strategic	1100	Board Composition		
		1200	Management structure		
		1300	Supervisory structure		
		1400	Organisational culture		
		1500	Reputation	1510	Corporate Reputation
				1520	Personal Reputation
				1530	Brand Reputation
		1600	Political, Economic, Social, Technical	1610	Political/ Public Policy
				1620	Economic
				1630	Social/ Demographic
				1640	Technical
		1700	Ownership/Control	1710	Past
				1720	Current
				1730	Future
		1800	Market and Industry changes		
		1900	R&D/Intellectual Property	1910	R&D
				1920	Intellectual Property
2000	Financial	2100	Deliberate Adverse Activity	2110	Self-Dealing
				2120	Contra-incentives
				2130	Property/ Information misuse
		2200	Foreign Exchange		
		2300	Credit		
		2400	Interest Rates		
		2500	Liquidity/Cashflow		
		2600	Fraud/Accounting Controls		
		2700	Risk Transfer		

Cat Series No	*Category*	*Risk Series No*	*Description of Risk*	*Sub-division Series No*	*Sub-division*
3000	Operational	3100	Customer Relations	3110	Customer demand
				3120	Customer organization
		3200	Supply and Outsource relations	3210	Supply chain
				3220	Outsource
		3300	Recruitment and HR		
		3400	IT systems		
		3500	Communication Processes	3510	External/PR
				3520	Internal
		3600	Distribution		
		3700	Competitors		
		3800	Regulations		
4000	Hazard	4100	Security and Public Access		
		4200	Employees		
		4300	Properties		
		4400	Product and Services		
		4500	Suppliers and raw materials		
		4600	Contracts		
		4700	Natural and Catastrophic events		
		4800	Plant and Equipment Non-IT		
		4900	Environment		

Of course the list as it stands is just that, a list. Behind it must go a series of first level questions which open up each category. A typical process which might support this expanded list is illustrated in a flow chart in Figure 11.2.

Once the scope and objectives of the project have been defined, irrelevant risk categories can be eliminated from the process, but it is important that this is done on the basis of project work, not assumptions. It is at this stage that it becomes necessary to consider the interface with other risk disciplines. Some of these interconnections with other risk professionals are considered below. They can improve legal risk management, but the vital point here is that, if the project demands the incorporation of other disciplines, then it must be recognized at the outset. Trying to retrofit two discrete processes once completed to make a meaningful whole will not work satisfactorily.

The most common problem is with projects which, whilst including a substantial legal element, also involve accountancy considerations. A good example would be a product risk profile for a financial services organization. Lawyers can get as far as determining that issues in the financial sector of the grid exist but should rarely go far beyond that, so a good working relationship with like-minded accountants is essential for this type of project.

It is tempting for lawyers to advocate their involvement on the basis that legal privilege might attach to some of the discovered and created data and documents. It needs to be clear that this is not, in fact, one of the benefits of engaging lawyers in this process. It is very unlikely that legal privilege will attach to anything created in the process and not possible for it to protect any existing documents which come to light.

However, it is part of the function of the lawyer engaged in this process to keep a very tight control over new documents which are created and preserved. There is no general requirement to preserve notes and drafts used to prepare the documents which comprise the formal record of the enquiry and only the formal record should survive. This does not, of course, apply to existing documents which may be evidence in relation to an actual or potential claim. They must not be destroyed.

The investigatory process which follows engages the traditional legal forensic skills. People may be seen in groups, where it may be appropriate to use some facilitative techniques to promote discussion, or as individuals, when specific enquiries are more easily pursued. At this stage risk issues can begin to be identified and graded according to criteria agreed with the project sponsor.

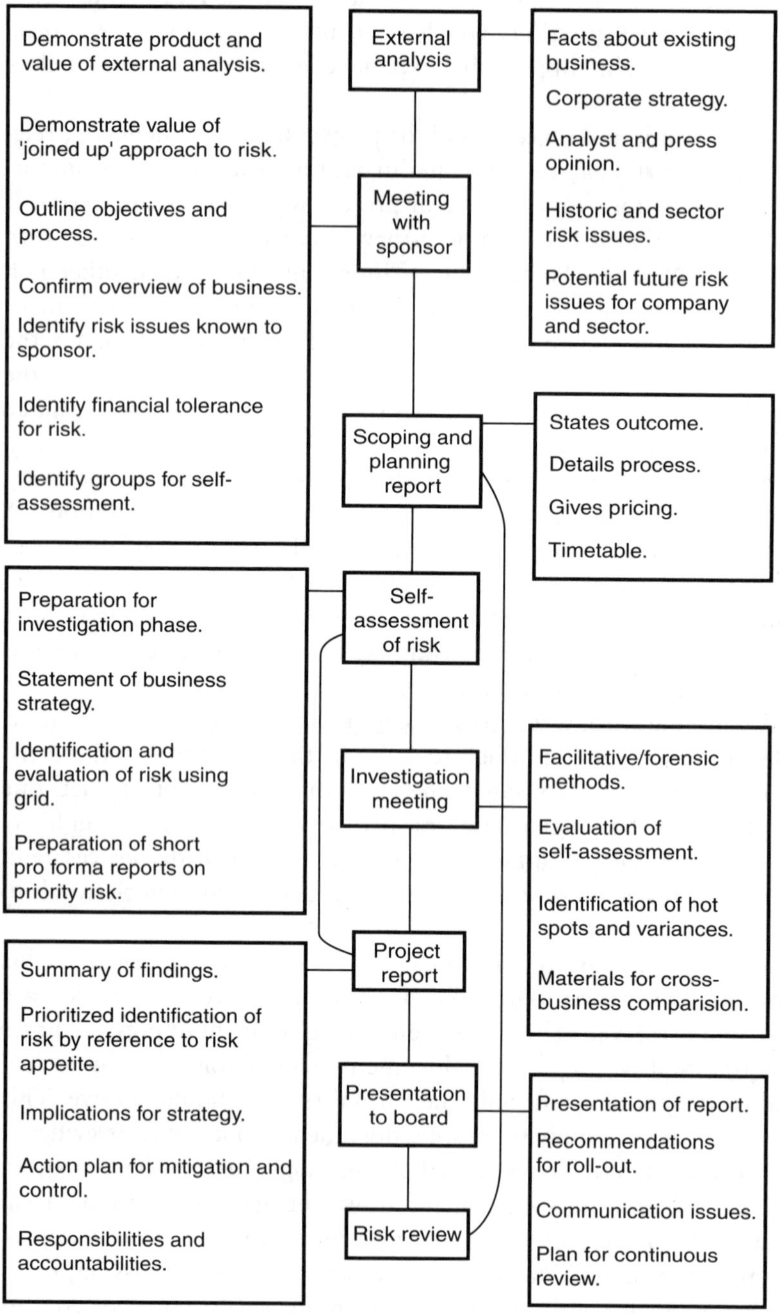

Figure 11.2 Typical process flow

A report is necessary at this stage and might be a combination of a spreadsheet showing risks, existing controls and suggested further work towards solutions, and a written report putting the tabular results in context.

It is probably unhelpful to use graphics or charts to suggest more measurement of risk than is actually present. Whilst it is essential that the output should be in a standard format permitting comparisons both between different risks at a given time and between manifestations of the same risk over a period of time, it is also vital that legal risk management remains a service rather than a product. The value comes from the thought and creativity delivered within the structure, not from the structure itself.

It is impossible to say in this developing field that the sort of process described represents best practice, but it certainly represents good practice as a means of delivering legal risk advice in a structured format.

How it works (case study examples)

Of course, unless we can confirm from experience that this type of approach offers better results than pure technical legal advice, or than legal risk management advice given in an unstructured way, then there is no compelling case for adopting it.

One good example concerns the sale of what might be described as 'semi-technical' goods. If you think of the way in which goods are expected to perform as a spectrum, then at one end you would expect to see very highly specified technical goods, say products for the aerospace industry. The risk exposure of the producer will not turn on whether the goods are of any particular quality, or even apparently in the case of some military hardware, whether they will work at all. It will be governed entirely by whether they comply with a very precise specification.

At the other end of this spectrum sit basic goods, say for example, a pencil, which generate very simple and precise expectations in consumers. Even in the wilder flights of consumerist fantasy it has not yet been suggested that a pencil (at least one intended for adult use) should carry a warning not to stick it in your eye.

In between, however, are shades of grey; goods that may or may not work in a particular application and here there is fertile territory for legal risk management. Examples would be chemical compounds known to work in cosmetic applications which may or may not be suitable for pharmaceutical use, or adhesives and sealants which could be transferred from one environment, say sealing windows into buses, to a related but different one fixing portholes into yachts.

In a traditional model of legal advice, it would generally only have been after the pharmaceutical caused an adverse reaction or the yacht lost its glazing at sea that a lawyer became involved. A lawyer giving risk management advice in a casual way might well suggest a review of the contractual protection against liability in such circumstances. There may be a recommendation for more control over representations made by the commercial sales force. If the lawyer has a good understanding of insurance then perhaps a review of risk transfer arrangements will be done, to make sure that, by giving advice on suitability for particular purposes, or on the method of application the business was not negating its products cover.

All these things would be good and right, but in both these cases, by taking an approach based on understanding the client's business and properly valuing the opportunity which these new markets represented alongside the risks involved, it will be possible to achieve more.

By considering the financial and cultural incentives driving the sales force in the direction of claiming that their product would perform in a particular application when they were not, in fact, certain that was so, it was possible to alter the context set by the companies concerned for this type of decision.

No amount of education and training will alter behaviours which are reinforced by reward systems that only measure revenue and fail to incorporate the cost of claims in the cost of sales.

The difference of approach can extend beyond the company too. In the sealants and adhesives example, review has led to a greater willingness to tell customers that work is needed to assess a given application and to work together to arrive at modifications and methods which solve the customer's problem whilst generating extra sales for the company.

In short, in these examples legal risk management made a real contribution to improved business process and sustainability of revenue and profit.

Another example concerns a risk profiling exercise undertaken as a precursor to the evolution of a business continuity plan. The core activity of the company was warehousing and distribution to members of a particular profession who also owned the business.

Some advantages were gained within the business continuity planning exercise itself. For example, using the wide-ranging approach described, problems were identified with HGV movements in the yard at particular times of day which, if injury or fatality were to result, could have led the Health and Safety Executive to impose a prohibition notice.

Since there had been established as a measure of the severity of risk the probability that service interruption for more than 48 hours would lead to severe loss of custom to competitors, this was an important matter to be dealt with as a preliminary to the business continuity plan. This type of hazard would not necessarily have emerged from a more facilitative approach to identification since it involved making a connection based on experience not possessed by the in-house participants.

However, the major benefits were in outputs from the enquiry process which, whilst not strictly relevant to the business continuity plan, were nevertheless reported to the client. For example, it was established that a common practice for gaining admission to customers' premises posed a very real threat to the security of those premises when temporary drivers were used. Another finding was that, whilst the fire hazards of some stored chemicals had been appreciated and appropriately controlled, the risk of harm to staff or others from the deliberate abuse of the same chemicals had not been recognized.

In all these cases, the businesses themselves took steps based on the findings. Sometimes the legal risk report is merely stating in a clear form things which at some level the organization already knew. In other places, it is drawing together pieces of information from diverse sources to create new knowledge about risk. It cannot be said that, without the system and process, these additional benefits would definitely not have accrued, but it would be difficult to argue that it would not have been a great deal less likely.

Interface with business process and risk management generally

It has been a recurrent theme throughout this chapter that legal risk management (as opposed to technical legal advice) can only add value if it is integrated with both the business process and with other risk disciplines.

Perhaps the most important aspect is the integration with business strategy and process, because it is this that brings balance to the exercise, by taking into account the opportunities which the business has. As with all types of risk management the danger is that otherwise it becomes seen as a purely negative exercise.

This is especially true of legal risk management because it is in the nature of the law that much of it is there to constrain and restrict some freedoms of individuals and corporations in order to protect the higher freedoms of others. Lawyers all too often find themselves telling their clients what they cannot do.

Bringing legal risk into play at an earlier stage and uniting it with business strategy provides a way to break these chains and increase the extent to which advice can be given in terms of how to do something with the minimum legal risk rather than why it cannot be done at all.

This means working hard to persuade commercial managers that both the attitude and the systems exist to transform not only the way legal advice is given, but also their perception of where it belongs in the chronology of a project.

The second key area of interface is with risk professionals using different skills but aiming for the same results. This chapter has referred on a number of occasions to a 'facilitative' approach to identifying and grading risk, meaning the type of approach in which the board and senior executives go on retreat with a facilitator, from within or outside the company, and brainstorm amongst themselves the risk issues facing the company.

This approach has many advantages and good results are reported. Unfortunately there are also some drawbacks. There are often one or two dominant individuals in the type of groups which are put together and others who have valuable insights can fail to put them forward. Moreover, the environment, especially if the facilitator is internal, may not be conducive to challenging received wisdom about important issues. If the group as a whole believes that the need for the company to do a particular thing is very great, then discussion about the risks associated with it may not be frank.

Equally, however the entire exercise cannot be run on the basis of cross-examination and challenge. Overt confrontation is just as likely to lead to failure to open up issues. Thus the aim is to work with professionals within the business to achieve the perfect blend of the two approaches. Those inside the business have the advantage of knowledge and trust, encouraging confidence in the process. Those from outside have independence and protection from the consequences of asking unwelcome questions. Experience suggests that getting this interface right is vital.

Third there are occasions when an investigation of a particular legal risk, or of risk generally with legal elements will involve expertise which lawyers do not have. As noted above, the most common example is where accountancy expertise is required. However, there are many other examples, especially where particular types of hazard risk, such as environmental risk or property risk are concerned, where other specific technical skills are required.

Fortunately, the development of legal risk management as a concept and as a service has happened alongside a greater appreciation that law firms can work increasingly with other disciplines according to pre-agreed protocols. Sir David Clementi published his report of the review of the regulatory framework for legal services in England and Wales on 16 December 2004 (Clementi, 2004), and this has opened up a wide debate about the future of the legal profession and multidisciplinary practice. This has led to a great deal of rethinking about working arrangements, short of formal partnership, which can work to the benefit of both the professionals and the client. These arrangements need investment of time and money, but once in place can make legal risk management much more effective.

Finally, there must be an interface in the field of risk solutions. Business continuity planning, as outlined above, is a good example. The outputs can also feed into media training. In the financial services, compliance issues require legal risk managers to work with appropriate consultancies.

Many of the skills required have traditionally been packaged within the risk transfer services provided by insurance brokers. There is a challenge in the market-place to provide these skills in a flexible way so that the process can be taken through to risk mitigation and control in areas where pure legal solutions are not enough. This is a vital part of the legal risk management proposition.

Contract risk

Another recurrent theme throughout this chapter has been contracts as both a source of risk and a solution for the control of risk. This apparent conundrum arises from the variety of ways in which contracts can be formed, from a simple oral exchange of promises for consideration to a complex written agreement governing every aspect of a relationship between two companies. It should be clear at the outset of this section that this is not a legal textbook. Legal concepts used in this section are explained only sufficiently to get to the points about contract risk which are made.

Almost everything which a commercial organization does deliberately will be subject to some contractual control. Because companies do not do much for free, there will at the very least be a simple contract governing how much it will pay or be paid for the activity.

Of course, like individuals, companies sometimes do things they did not intend. Liability for that type of activity is, broadly speaking, covered by the law of tort. The most common tort is negligence and is based on the concept that there are some circumstances in life where, although there was no deliberate contractual relationship, the parties were closely enough connected to give rise to a duty and the 'guilty' party ought to have foreseen that the damage which was done was possible.

Liabilities of this type are best controlled by effective risk management, but the only role for contractual risk management is to regulate between two parties how they will share liability for tort claims from other people (see below).

The simple oral contract has its place in commercial life. It would scarcely be economic to negotiate specific terms each time you need to order some more paper clips. However, this appearance of simplicity may be misleading. From the point of view of the paper clip supplier, that is their business and it may well be that there are terms about time of payment, etc., which they want to bind you to. So, most likely, when even the simplest supply is arranged you may well find printed on the back of the invoice which turns up standard terms and conditions of contract.

Whether those conditions bind the ordering company is a complex question. Broadly speaking, if the order was a one-off then probably not, as the contract was complete at the time of the telephone call. On the other hand, if you always order your paper clips from the same company and they always send the same invoice, then possibly the terms do apply. This is why when you order on the internet you will invariably need to 'tick a box' accepting terms and conditions.

The question is further complicated if it is the practice of the ordering company to print its own terms and conditions of purchase on the purchase order sent out to confirm the transaction from their side. There can then ensue a 'battle of the forms' in which it becomes critical to determine who saw what and when, relative to the completion of the agreement. Each case turns on its own facts, but all we need to understand here is that it creates uncertainty and thus risk.

So long as this issue is confined to the stationery cupboard, a legal risk manager can contemplate it with serenity, if at all, for though the chance of contractual uncertainty is high, the hazard is very slight. How much damage can a paper clip, or its absence, do?

Unfortunately, a similarly casual approach to contract formation can extend upwards into more business-critical functions and that is where a lot of contractual risk arises. In order to understand why, it is necessary to consider a few of the standard terms which will always be there, in one form or another.

Some of them will be fairly innocuous. They contribute to good orderly commercial life. Neither party will be surprised to see them. The party on the receiving end of the terms would have agreed them anyway if the contract had been negotiated. In this category, for example, fall terms about Force Majeure (unavoidable external forces), jurisdiction of the courts of the country where the contract is to be performed, provision for arbitration or mediation and so on.

Others, although important, are the things which will have been clearly understood by the parties, such as price, quantity and so on, so although there is scope for error and misunderstanding, again the risk is relatively small.

There is a further category, where the level of commercial understanding about what is normal is well established. Examples here would be provisions for when ownership in the goods passes, when the risk and thus the need to insure the goods passes and what happens in the event of default of payment. However, if the goods are valuable, then quite substantial risks can arise here, for example, that the goods will perish at a stage where the risk was with the purchaser, but it had failed to insure, believing risk to remain with the seller.

Finally there are terms which have a high probability of doing real damage if not properly understood. The most obvious of these are terms which seek to regulate liabilities between the parties and as against third parties if the goods or services are defective. Some terms are illegal, whether agreed by the parties or not, such as agreements to restrict or exclude liability for personal injury or death or for fraud. However, other restrictions or exclusions will be effective in a contract which has been specifically negotiated and effective if reasonable in one where standard terms have been imposed without negotiation.

Thus, if proper attention is not paid to the terms on which a business is contracting, actual liabilities and remedies for the default of others may be quite different to what would be expected under the general law. This is not just a theoretical risk. Much commercial litigation arises from precisely this type of misunderstanding.

For example, in cases where entrepreneurs are simply procuring and transporting goods which are required by their customer and manufactured by their supplier, deals are invariably concluded by a combination of telephone, email and possibly in some parts of the world still, telex. If terms of business have not been negotiated which will apply to all transactions, on both the purchase and the sale side of the deal, with individual supplies simply operating as 'call-offs' under that contract, then the uncertainties above can and often do lead to very substantial risk exposures.

Or, to take another frequently occurring commercial circumstance, suppose the purchaser of the goods requires specific machinery or equipment in order to use them, for example, a mixer or applicator. This machinery or equipment is often supplied by the supplier of the goods, but if the contract does not provide for that then there is uncontrolled risk on both sides. What happens if the machine malfunctions or the purchaser becomes insolvent?

In almost any business it will be possible to think of examples of this type of uncertainty and risk. Like any other risk, contractual legal risk can be controlled. Provided it is clearly understood who is responsible for what, quality assurance measures and other practical controls can be put in place to reduce the risk to a minimum. Risk transfer can be arranged to cover the residual risk.

Not only does care in contract formation allow for the agreed allocation of rights and duties to be documented, there is an allied benefit. The discipline of talking with lawyers to make sure that the contract is accurate forces the parties to consider the commercial benefits and costs involved.

This effect is especially clear where a business is providing a relatively low value component in a product which has a high value and creates significant risks in use. A good example would be the sale of basic equipment controlling the operation of seatbelts in automobiles.

It is important that both parties understand and agree how it would be reasonable to apportion liability for component failure having regard to the value of the contract and the profit made by each. If the component manufacturer cannot persuade the customer to accept a reasonable limitation on liability then they have to consider walking away from the opportunity.

If they take the opportunity and the risk, then their quality assurance must be excellent and their risk transfer provider must understand and accept the residual risk which is being transferred. The cost of that risk transfer must be fed back into the commercial decision whether to proceed. Used in this way the contract becomes part of the solution, not part of the problem.

Another class of contractual problem which causes frequent risk exposure is the warranty or guarantee. Requests for guarantees are frequently seen in the construction industry, where the length of the typical commercial lease (until recently almost always 25 years) means that developers are looking for assurance that the building will last until it is next likely to either receive a substantial renovation or be demolished.

Again, suppliers of quite small components in the building, with relatively little profit from the transaction, are often asked to warrant the performance of their goods. A warranty or guarantee means that the conditions which it promises will be met and that the recipient will have a remedy irrespective of the cause of failure. In some circumstances the benefit may extend to other entities than the original recipient.

Formal warranties can be a useful commercial tool, but warranties carelessly given in loose terms can create major unexpected and uninsured risks. Invariably, product liability policies exclude obligations contractually assumed and specific warranties usually fall foul of this exclusion.

First, the promise which is made should be clearly within the design capability of the product. If certain methods of using, storing or maintaining the product are essential to maintain its performance, then the warranty must be conditional on following those methods. These considerations mean that giving a warranty is not just a commercial or a legal matter, it is a technical one too – a good example of disciplines working together to control risk.

Second, the remedy offered should be proportionate to the potential gain from giving the warranty, i.e. the value of the contract to the supplier. The worst risk of all is to give a warranty without specifying a remedy, since the whole of the recipient's losses flowing from any breach may be recoverable. Whilst the risk control mechanism here is legal, the cost–benefit analysis is commercial.

Third, it should be clear whether the warranty is in addition to or in substitution for the general common law rights of the purchaser. Provided there is no attempt to exclude or limit liabilities which must not be limited or excluded by law (see above) warranties which replace the statutory warranties of fitness for purpose and satisfactory quality which would otherwise apply can be a very effective way of regulating liability between two properly advised businesses.

On the other hand, if the full range of common law remedies is left in place, the warranty is merely adding to the range of circumstances in which a claim may be made and by definition must increase the legal risk to which the company is exposed.

The examples given above are all about the supply of products, but the same principles apply in relation to all the dealings of a business. Whether looking at employment contracts, IT contracts, joint venture agreements or any agreement governing any aspect of what a business does, the same principles apply. Contracts entered into without preparation and on uncertain terms represent a significant risk to the business. Contracts which are related to the commercial aims of the business and properly drafted with regard to the risks which the business can and cannot accept offer one of the most effective solutions to controlling risk in an organization.

Future challenges

When considering the future, legal risk (in the narrowest first sense outlined) has an advantage over most other topics. Because legal and regulatory change is generally the subject of extensive consultation, the likely changes over the next two or three years are reasonably clear. However, whilst that is true taking the global view, it is not the case for any individual business, because actual legal risk is a combination of the external risk environment and the changing activities of the business. This relative certainty about short- to medium-term developments should never, therefore, lead to complacency about how they may affect a particular corporation. The principle of embedding legal risk management into risk management and business process generally remains crucial.

Viewed from the UK perspective, the biggest single source of future risk is the legislative programme of the EU. Particularly in the field of employment law there has been a steady stream of Directives affecting working time, discrimination and so on, supplemented by domestic provisions about minimum pay. Immediate risks for businesses include failure to understand and address issues of disability and age discrimination.

For example, it has been suggested that the entire HR policy of the IT industry will need to change. This may be difficult for the industry to accept granted the deeply ingrained culture of the primacy of youth – and somewhat ironic since it is failure of older people to cope with the pace of technical change which is usually stated as the reason for the unusually low average age of IT professionals.

Similarly, in the field of competition, product and environmental liabilities, the EU is the main driver. Of strong current interest is the way in which the Human Rights Act 1998, enacting the requirements of the European Convention on Human Rights, is being used to test the limits of domestic legislation. Whilst the primary current impacts of this are on governmental organizations, there is leakage into businesses providing outsourced services in sensitive areas, for example, transport of prisoners.

Contract law itself may be affected by EU developments in the next few years, as the need for standard pan-European terms for commercial contracts is debated. At present the International Chamber of Commerce provides standard terms known as *INCOTERMS 2000* (International Chamber of Commerce, 2000) for those who wish to use them, but there is no compulsion to do so.

Additionally there are the top-level policy developments such as the Capital Adequacy Directive linked with Basel 2 and the work of the high level experts on company law. The High Level Group of Company Law Experts was set up by the European Commission in September 2001 and published its report *A Modern Regulatory Framework for Company Law in Europe* on 4 November 2002 (European Commission, 2002). These detailed provisions fall within the scope of the chapter on governance.

Within the scope of this chapter it is only possible to observe that businesses must make sure they have systems, perhaps through trade organizations, for monitoring developments in European law in order to address future legal risk.

Second there are changes driven primarily by local UK political and social considerations. Formal legislation and regulation are the obvious indicators of legal risk, but generally speaking the risk exposure of the business arises long before formal regulation is in place.

The pressure to bring companies to account for causing fatalities is a good example. As discussed above, this argument has been played out mostly so far in terms of instantaneous, catastrophic death. However, the current debates about food quality and smoking in the workplace demonstrate that corporations must also consider how longer-term health issues will impact on their legal risk profile.

To take smoking, in January 2004, one of the leading trades union solicitors firms, in association with the pressure group ASH, wrote to the chief executive officer of every company in the catering and licensed trades advising them of the risks of passive smoking.

No doubt many of them took legal advice, but it is unlikely that all focused clearly on the risk issues. Whilst there was some risk of claims in the short term, there was little doubt that the principal purpose of sending this letter was to fix the date when the company received the letter as its date of actual knowledge about the risk. This date would be material if claims were brought, perhaps years in the future.

In all probability, many of the staff these companies employ are active smokers themselves, but how will that be proved if they sue in 10 years' time?

As we know from the history of asbestos claims, it is not safe to assume that any claims there may be in future will be met by insurance, so this issue does have the capacity to affect the sustainability of businesses in the leisure industry in the long term.

If the risks are properly identified and evaluated and suitable control measures are put in place a response could be designed which greatly reduces the threat. Only one listed company so far seems to have moved voluntarily, ahead of legislation. One might conclude they have had the best advice on this point.

So far as the nutritional value of food is concerned, again a combination of social and political pressures appear to have been the catalyst for change, but the risk of making people unhealthy has not changed in itself. Again a range of reactions can be seen across the fast food industry, but for the whole food sector this will be a major issue requiring attention in the next few years.

Examples of this type could be found in almost every industry sector.

Third, legal risk is affected by the decisions of the courts. The problem with judicial decisions is that they have the capacity to expand, by extrapolation from principle, to issues which at first sight are not affected by the case in question.

For example, the risks associated with asbestos exposure are well understood. One fairly common consequence of exposure to asbestos dust and fibre is the formation of scars on the pleura which lines the lung cavity. These scars, known as pleural plaques, cause no physical symptoms and a group of defendant companies recently pursued test cases to ascertain whether they should attract compensation. The decision of the Court of First Instance (*Grieves and ors* v *F T Everard & Sons and others* [2005] EWHC 88 (QB)) decided that physical injury was not a prerequisite for damages to be payable. There will be an appeal, but already commentators are considering other circumstances in which this principle may lead to awards of compensation where none would previously have been payable.

This type of legal risk is particularly difficult to assess and control, since new liabilities can arise from things which have already been done. Unlike regulation, the common law is retrospective.

Lastly there are international impacts. At first sight, the activities of the Attorney General for New York should not be very high on the list of priorities for legal risk managers in the UK. However, in the insurance sector this has proved not to be the case. On 14 October 2004, New York Attorney General, Eliot Spitzer, issued his first press release concerning an investigation into the commission structures applied by brokers in relation to commercial insurances. Whilst regulation here is the preserve of the FSA, the international broking businesses operating in the London market have already indicated fundamental changes to their approach to remuneration globally.

This particular issue will be significant for the insurance sector for the foreseeable future, but the key point is that business is global and legal risk is becoming so.

Conclusion

Substantial gains are there to be made if the mitigation of legal risk through regulatory and statutory compliance is seen as part of the business strategy, instead of just a bolt-on. The Operating and Financial Review represents the latest opportunity for corporations to use risk reporting to improve risk control.

When, following Turnbull, the Stock Exchange Combined Code first required a risk-based approach to company reports, legal risk management was widely interpreted as requiring the establishment of 'boilerplate' wording which would avoid any real disclosures of corporate risk whilst formally satisfying the requirements of the Code.

The Financial Reporting Council has organized a review of the operation of Turnbull. The general perception of risk professionals in other disciplines is that the role of lawyers in this process was fundamentally to frustrate the purpose of the changes.

There is a fear that, with the requirement for the OFR now in force, a similar approach will be taken. However, in the case of the OFR, the auditors will have to certify that the company has followed a suitable process.

The Accounting Standards Board issued an Exposure Draft in November 2004. The proposals work to a standard based on principles, whereby the OFR must reflect the directors' view of the business so that investors can assess the strategies adopted by the board and the potential for those strategies to succeed.

Since the auditors will not, by definition, be able to assist the board in the preparation of the OFR there is an opportunity here for legal risk management to prove it is not just about limiting the downside, but can be channelled to support strategy and the clarity with which strategy is understood. Whether or not that opportunity is seized will be a key indicator of whether legal risk management has the maturity to develop into an important element in forming business strategy.

References and recommended reading

Basel (1988) *Basel Capital Accord.* Basel: Basel Committee on Banking Supervision.

Basel (2001) *New Basel Capital Accord – Consultative Document.* Basel: Basel Committee on Banking Supervision.

Cadbury, A *et al.* (1992) *Report of the Committee on the Financial Aspects of Corporate Governance.* London: Gee and Co Ltd. See also: http://www.ecgi.org/codes/all_codes.htm

Capital Adequacy Directive (2003) *The New Capital Adequacy Directive, CAD3: The Transposition of the New Basel Accord into EU Legislation.* Available at: http://www.hm-treasury.gov.uk/consultations_and_legislation/cad3/consult_cad3_index.cfm

Clementi, D (2004) *Review of the Regulatory Framework for Legal Services in England and Wales: Final Report.* London: Department for Constitutional Affairs.

Committee on Corporate Governance (1998) *Committee on Corporate Governance: Final Report.* London: Gee and Co Ltd. Available at: http://www.ecgi.org/codes/documents/hampel.pdf

Council of Europe (1950) Convention for the Protection of Human Rights and Fundamental Freedoms, as amended by Protocol No. 11 [European Convention on Human Rights]. Rome. Available at: http://conventions.coe.int/treaty/en/Treaties/Html/005.htm

Department of Trade and Industry (2002) *Modernising Company Law.* UK Government White Paper CM 5553. London: The Stationery Office.

Department of Trade and Industry (2005) *Operating and Financial Review.* See http://www.dti.gov.uk/cld/financialreview.htm for details of current passage through Parliament into full legislation.

European Commission (2002) *A Modern Regulatory Framework for Company Law in Europe.* A consultative document of the High Level Group of Company Law Experts. Available at: http://europa.eu.int/comm/internal_market/en/company/company/modern/#framework

European Communities (2002) Directive 2001/95/EC of the European Parliament and of the Council of 3 December 2001 on general product safety [General Product Safety Directive]. Luxembourg: EUR-OP. (OJ L 011, 15/01/2002 pp. 0004–0017.) Available at: http://europa.eu.int

Financial Reporting Council (2003) *The Combined Code on Corporate Governance*. Available at: http://www.asb.org.uk/documents/pagemanager/frc/combinedcodefinal.pdf

Financial Times 11 April 2005.

Great Britain (1998) Human Rights Act 1998. London: The Stationery Office.

Great Britain Home Office (2005) Corporate Manslaughter – The Government's Draft Bill for Reform, Cm 6497. London: The Stationery Office. Also available at: http://www.homeoffice.gov.uk/docs4/con_corp_mans.html

Great Britain Parliament House of Commons (2005) Health and Safety (Directors' Duties) Bill (No. 22 of 2004–05). London: The Stationery Office.

Greenbury, R (1995) *Directors' Remuneration*. London: Gee and Co Ltd. Available at: http://www.ecgi.org/codes/documents/greenbury.pdf

Grieves and ors v *F T Everard & Sons and others* (2005) EWHC 88 (QB).

Higgs, D (2003) *Review of the Role and Effectiveness of Non-Executive Directors*. London: Department of Trade and Industry. Available at: http://www.dti.gov.uk/cld/non_exec_review

Institute of Risk Management (IRM), Association of Insurance and Risk Managers (AIRMIC) and National Forum for Risk Management in the Public Sector (ALARM) (2002) *A Risk Management Standard*. London: IRM/AIRMIC/ALARM.

International Chamber of Commerce (2000) *INCOTERMS 2000*. Paris: ICC Publishing. See: http://www.iccwbo.org/index_incoterms.asp

The Lawyer 21 March 2005.

Turnbull, N *et al.* (1999) *Internal Control – Guidance for Directors on the Combined Code*. London: Institute of Chartered Accountants in England and Wales. Available at: http://www.icaew.co.uk/internalcontrol

United States of America (2002) Sarbanes-Oxley Act of 2002. Available at: http://www.sec.gov/about/laws/soa2002.pdf. See also: http://www.sec.gov/spotlight/sarbanes-oxley.htm

12

Technical Risk Management

Tyson Browning

A project is 'a temporary endeavour undertaken to create a unique product, service or result' (PMI, 2004). Projects are unlike other business operations and their processes in several ways. Primarily, instead of doing exactly the same thing over and over, a project seeks to create something that has not existed before. Even if the project's stakeholders' expectations for this deliverable are clear, the path towards producing it is often ambiguous, especially if the deliverable is novel and/or complex. Creativity and innovation are required. Workers may start with a plan (hypothesis), find it deficient in several ways, learn more about the sub-problems and potential solutions through analysis and testing, and then change the plan. Workers learn along the way about what will and will not work. They create information and share it to increase their knowledge of and confidence in the planned design of the project's deliverable. However, a project is also finite in duration, so all of this planning and learning must converge to a satisfactory deliverable within a schedule and a budget.

A project's deliverable must conform to a number of '*technical*' requirements or quality characteristics, which for the purposes of this chapter will include *all requirements except those pertaining to the project's cost and duration* (or, from another point of view, the deliverable's price and lead time). While a project is in progress, uncertainty lingers about the actual ability of its deliverable to satisfy all of its requirements. Whether acknowledged or not, such uncertainty remains until the satisfaction of each requirement has been verified. Since there are usually adverse consequences of failing to satisfy requirements, this uncertainty implies some amount of 'technical' risk. *Technical performance (or quality) risk is the uncertainty about a deliverable's ability to satisfy its technical performance requirements and the consequences of any shortfalls.* Thus, in accordance with the standard definition of risk, there is some probability of failing to meet all the technical requirements, and there are some adverse consequences of any shortfalls.

Technical risk is just one of the many types of risk facing a project. Other major risk categories include:

- *cost risk*: the uncertainty about a project's ability to develop an acceptable deliverable within a given budget and the consequences of any cost overrun;
- *schedule risk*: the uncertainty about a project's ability to develop an acceptable deliverable by a deadline and the consequences of any schedule overrun; and
- *market (or customer) value risk*: the uncertainty about the anticipated value to the market or customer of the chosen project targets and the consequences of failing to meet the right targets.

Project cost and schedule risks are addressed in a separate chapter. However, it is important to note that each of these areas of risk is often mitigated at the expense of another. For example, product designers stereotypically prefer to refine and perfect a product endlessly, thereby lowering its technical risk but exposing the project to cost and schedule risks. Also, market value risk is lowered by choosing 'tougher' requirements (e.g. more or better features or higher performance levels) that are more likely to satisfy the market, but doing so increases technical risk (and forms the basis for tensions between marketing and engineering departments).

This chapter has two major objectives. First, it provides a high-level overview of the basic concepts and techniques of technical risk management, pointing the reader to several excellent sources of further information. Second, the chapter presents an emerging methodology, the risk value method, to complement the traditional techniques.

The technical risk management process

Traditionally, and contemporarily, the best practices for managing technical risks in a project involve following a basic process such as the one exemplified in Figure 12.1, which has its roots in techniques documented by the US Department of Defense in the mid-20th century (e.g. DAU, 1998; DSMC, 1983). The process involves project participants nominating a list of risks, analysing each and then prioritizing, resolving and monitoring them over the course of the project, regularly

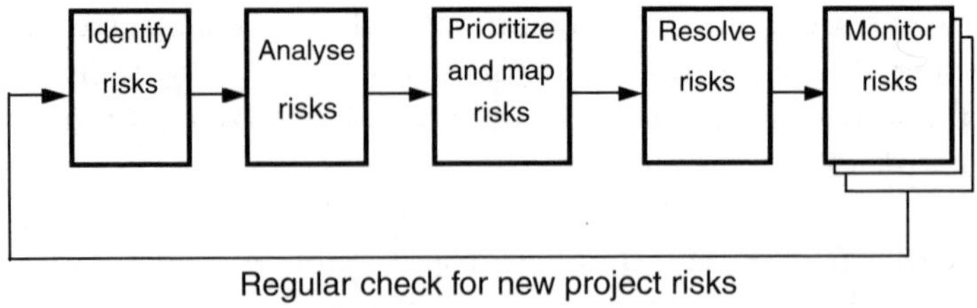

(adapted from Smith and Merritt, 2002)

Figure 12.1 Example of a traditional process for managing technical risk

checking for new risks along the way. Many excellent books (e.g. Hall, 1998; PMI, 2004, ch. 11; Smith and Merritt, 2002) well document versions of this basic process and add valuable lessons and insights. Many projects also use this basic process to manage cost and schedule risks. The following subsections further describe each of these steps.

Identify risks

Nominate a superset of all possible risks. Use checklists, historical data from other projects, expert opinions, stakeholder inputs and any other relevant sources of information. Most importantly, query project participants and have them participate in a brainstorming meeting. At this point, it is more important to err on the side of too many potential risk items rather than to rule them out prematurely. This step should be part of a project's initial definition and planning stage, along with budgeting and scheduling. The statement of each risk will probably need to be refined, since 'A risk event should precisely describe a happening that could occur, along with an associated time component or condition so that one can tell if the risk event has occurred' (Smith and Merritt, 2002). For example, instead of saying, 'The product design may not be able to achieve the weight requirement' – a statement that cannot be verified until the project is over – use a more helpful statement like: 'The product design may be judged to have a greater than 10 per cent likelihood of failing to meet the weight requirement by the penultimate design review.'

Each risk item should also have an associated impact, stated in terms of the total loss, such as: 'A greater than 10 per cent likelihood of failing to meet the weight requirement by the penultimate design review will force us to launch five weight analysis and reduction activities and switch to a lighter, more expensive material, at an estimated cost of £10,000 and two weeks to the project and £10 to the resulting product's per-unit cost'. Consequences may include (Browning, 1999):

- additional design iterations, which increase schedule and development cost;
- late-breaking performance improvement initiatives required for specific areas;
- customer or market rejects product (reduced demand);
- reduced reputation of firm;
- jeopardized future contracts and sales;
- other development, manufacturing, distribution, and support cost and schedule impacts.

The goal of this step is a *quantity* of risk items; quality (relevance) will be judged later.

Analyse risks

For each of the risks identified, gather additional information according to the standard risk model shown in Figure 12.2. Determine the factual drivers of the risk event and its impact and use these to estimate a probability of the event occurring and the probability of the event having an impact on the project *if it occurs.* (This latter probability could be 100 per cent. If the first probability is also 100 per cent, however, then the 'risk' definitely will occur and is therefore not a risk but a reality that must be dealt with.) It is important not to waste time arguing over specific probabilities. In fact, some companies limit the

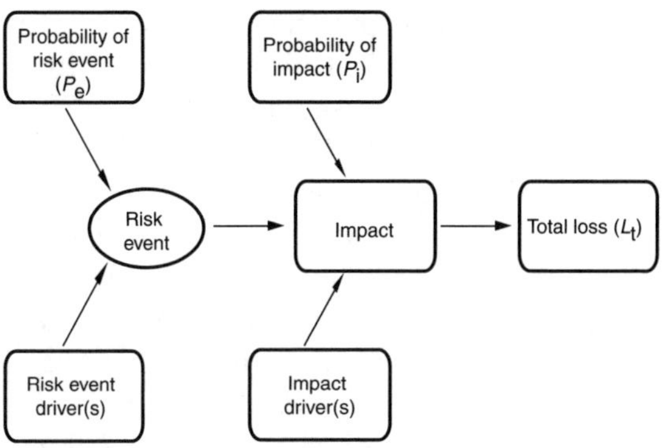

(adapted from Smith and Merritt, 2002)

Figure 12.2 Standard risk model

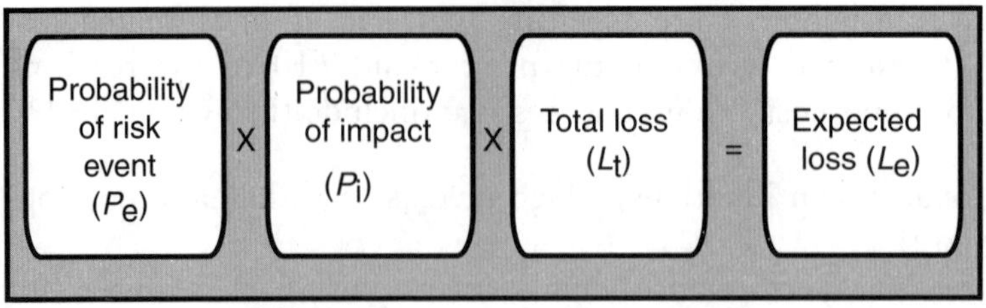

(from Smith and Merritt, 2002)

Figure 12.3 Expected loss formula

choices to 'low' (<10 per cent), 'medium' (20–50 per cent) and 'high' (60–90 per cent). Others use a 0–5 scale. These probabilities are then multiplied with the total loss from the impact identified with each risk item to determine the *expected loss*, as shown in Figure 12.3. Alternatively, some prefer the function $R = P + I - PI$ – where R is risk, $P = P_e \times P_i$ and I is impact (total loss, normalized on a 0 to 1 scale) – which gives greater emphasis to the high PI values.

Prioritize and map risks

Prioritize the risk items according to their expected losses. Risk items which are highly probable but which carry a small impact, as well as risk items which carry a large impact but are highly improbable, are subjugated to the risk items with moderate to high combinations of probability and impact. That is, while a project manager is uncertain about a great many things, the few critical uncertainties must get greater attention than the trivial many. Another helpful tool in this regard is a risk map like the one in Figure 12.4, which depicts regions of high, medium and low risk into which individual risks are mapped. While Figure 12.4 shows a 0–5 scale on each axis, a 0–1 scale is also common. The goal of this step is to select the highest priority risks for active management. The remainder should be monitored at a relatively low level of effort (passive management). The threshold for active management is a decision for the project manager to make. It depends on the number of risks implied by the threshold setting – since, as described below, an action plan must be created for each – and the project's attitude towards risk (risk averse, risk neutral or risk seeking). A long, complex or inherently risky project should expect to have to manage a substantial number of significant risks.

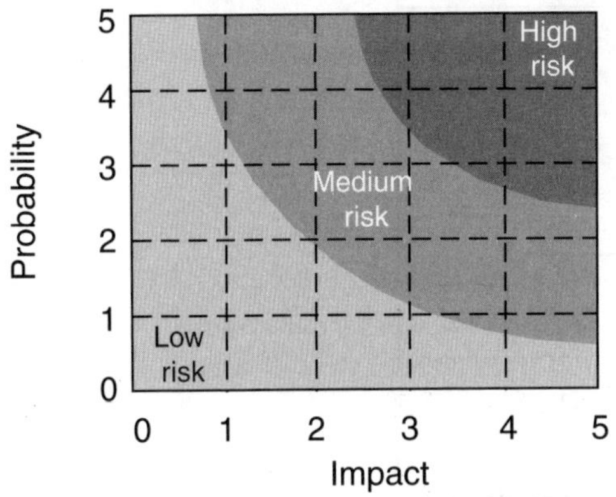

Figure 12.4 Risk exposure in terms of probability and impact

Resolve risks

Develop an action plan for each risk that will be actively managed. That is, add one or more specific activities to the project plan to address each such risk item. Plan, budget and schedule these activities just like any others on the project. The activities can involve *prevention* or *avoidance* of the risk item (actions to deter the risk event drivers), *transfer* of the risk event to another area (although it may not be possible to transfer the impact), *redundancy* (multiple paths to a solution), *contingencies* (prepared alternatives should the risk materialize; actions to decrease the impact drivers) and establishment of *reserves* (performance cushions in the project's deliverable). Certain actions can be thought of as hedging one's bets or buying insurance. Choose activities with the highest risk reduction leverage, i.e. the activities that provide the greatest reduction in expected loss for their cost. A common tool used in industry for planning the reduction of – and tracking the progress made in reducing – an aspect of technical risk is a risk reduction profile, also known as a 'risk step-down chart', 'risk waterfall chart' (Draves, 1993; Justice, 1996; SEI, 1996; Williams *et al.*, 1997), risk reduction chart (Huff, 1997) or Willoughby template. See the example in Figure 12.5, which shows how four planned activities reduce the assessed level of risk (measured on a [0,1] scale).

Monitor risks

Once the action plans are in place as part of the project's plan, schedule and budget, regularly reassess the risk event and impact drivers. Update probabilities and impacts. Check for new risk events. Re-prioritize risks.

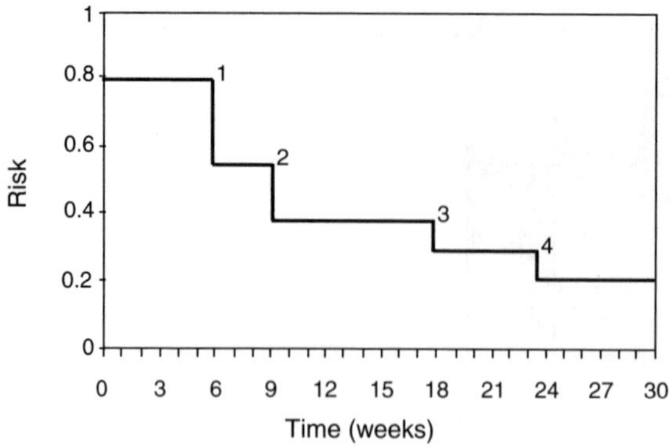

Figure 12.5 Example risk reduction profile

Add new resolution plans for any risks that become strong candidates for active management. These ongoing activities must also be planned, scheduled and budgeted into the overall project.

Failure mode and effects analysis

A particularly valuable tool for identifying technical risks is called failure mode and effects analysis (FMEA). Designers of complex systems have long used FMEA to systematically investigate the paths by which certain combinations of component failures could cause an entire system or critical portions thereof to fail. While designers endeavour to identify all such failure paths and combinations in advance, doing so is often impossible. For example, several US NASA Mars observers and landers, as well as the Space Shuttle Challenger, have experienced catastrophic failure modes that were not widely anticipated in advance. Projects should use the findings of previous projects as a starting point, in an effort not to repeat previous errors or oversights. Thus, organizational learning is a critical aspect of FMEA and technical risk management in general. See, for example, McDermott *et al.* (1996) for further information on FMEA.

Integration challenges

Despite their effective and growing use in a variety of projects, the technical risk management methods discussed above often suffer from a lack of integration with other project information. For example, the action plans for each risk item may not be well integrated into the overall project plan, schedule and budget at the *activity level*, i.e. a pot of 'risk money' may be kept separately, or the activities done to address the risks, since they may be seen as only being done 'just in case', may not be seen by everyone on the project as 'real work'. Moreover, risk items may not be tied well to the individual *performance attributes* of the project's deliverable that the project's stakeholders value. Since technical risk is all about the uncertainties and consequences of failing to meet requirements, it is important to have traceability between the risk items and the major areas of requirements. A third integration challenge is that project workers may not be used to accounting for uncertainty in their estimates of deliverable performance. For example, project participants often tend to speak of the final deliverable in exact and specific terms of its content, features, performance level, etc., rather than as a range of potential outcomes, each with a relative probability. Even if project participants recognize the uncertainties and assumptions behind statements that otherwise imply an inordinate amount of precision, their different perceptions of these uncertainties and assumptions are allowed to linger rather than getting put 'on the table' for discussion. Of course, as discussed below, discerning and reducing the lingering uncertainty adds value to the project.

Future directions: the risk value method

This chapter's second objective is to present an emerging method for project technical risk management that complements the traditional approach described above. The method stems from trying to address the integration challenges discussed above and several other observations about the way projects evolve towards their goal, their final deliverable(s). To reduce their uncertainty about the ability of the deliverable to satisfy all of its requirements, project workers need information that improves their confidence in the result's ability to meet expectations. Proposing, analyzing, evaluating, testing, experimenting, demonstrating, verifying and validating can create valuable information. Thus, when it comes to determining the value added or the progress made in a project, one wants to think about how much useful information has been created and how much confidence exists in the project's ability to meet stakeholder expectations. Conversely, one can think about how much risk remains that the project will fail to meet expectations. Over the course of a project, one would generally expect technical uncertainty and risk to decrease with an increase in useful information (Figure 12.6).

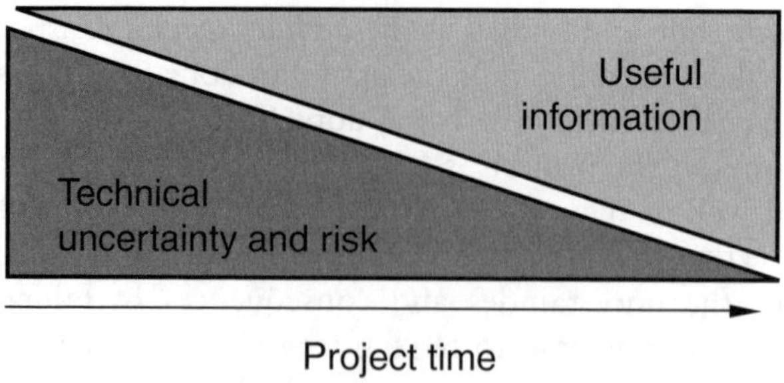

Figure 12.6 Risk decreases with availability of useful information

The approach presented here, based on the *risk value method* (Browning, 1998; Browning *et al.*, 2002), ties the areas of technical risk to be managed to the performance attributes valued by a project's stakeholders. It integrates several concepts and methods, including technical performance measures (TPMs), risk reduction profiles, customer preferences and uncertainty. The method is presented in steps and an industrial example, an unmanned combat aerial vehicle (UCAV), is used along the way to illustrate. The technique is useful for developing a plan and then for monitoring progress against that plan over the course of a project. The approach is prefaced by the introduction of several concepts, such as technical performance attributes and measures.

Technical performance attributes (TPAs)

The marketing literature often models a product or service as a vector of its key attributes – such as price, availability, features, quality and capabilities – aspects that customers and other stakeholders care about and express preferences for. Often, these attributes are determined and measured by a marketing function in an organization, which takes this information and uses it to help decide what kinds of products or services to offer and with what attributes and capabilities. When projects are commissioned for internal customers in an organization, effort is still made (hopefully) to understand the internal customers' wants and needs, desires and determinants of satisfaction. Thus, in general, the deliverable from any project may be characterized by a set of attributes pertaining to its capabilities, affordability and timeliness. Some of these attributes, especially affordability and timeliness, depend to an extent on the cost and duration of the project itself, but most of the attributes depend on the proposals and decisions made during the project about the design of the deliverable. This latter subset is referred to as *technical performance attributes* (TPAs). For example, the technical performance of a UCAV is based on attributes such as payload, weight, range, speed, reliability, stealth, noise level and altitude ceiling. Determining the TPAs is essentially like determining the 'whats' or 'critical-to-customer' characteristics in a quality function deployment (QFD) model (e.g. Clausing, 1994). Much of it depends on the 'voice of the customer'. Some of the challenges are to ensure a complete list of TPAs and to realize where they are interdependent. For example, the payload and range TPAs for the UCAV interact, because the available payload weight can be reduced by adding fuel tanks to increase range. The focus of this chapter is not on determining the TPAs, but rather on how to use them as a basis for deciding which technical risks require attention.

Technical performance measures (TPMs)

Each TPA must be measurable. For capabilities, such as the payload and range of an aircraft, this is relatively obvious. But other TPAs can be more difficult to measure. For instance, how does one measure quality? There may be several possibilities. Some TPAs are best measured in the aggregate, such as 'number of bugs' or 'number of non-conformances'. Some TPAs may be derived from other TPAs. For example, the payload and range of an aircraft depend largely on the aircraft's weight. While a customer may not necessarily care about the weight of an aircraft, this TPA has such a large impact on so many other TPAs – ones they do care about, such as payload and fuel efficiency – that they have learned to pay attention to it. Of course, aircraft designers know to pay attention to aircraft weight as the development project progresses. Thus, when trying to determine how to measure each TPA, it is important to involve experts who can help determine what characteristics of a project and its deliverable should be measured so that each TPA can in turn be measured. The goal is for each TPA to have at least one associated *technical performance measure* (TPM). TPMs are also known as figures of merit (FOMs), measures of effectiveness (MOEs) and other names in various companies and industries (although some give particular nuances to various ones of these terms).

Planning and tracking technical performance

The requirements, goals and objectives for a project's deliverable can be specified in terms of the TPAs and TPMs, and this is the preferred approach. This chapter refers to the required or desired levels of a deliverable's TPMs as *targets*, although some may prefer the term 'requirements'. Thus, each of the important attributes of a project's deliverable is (1) specified as a TPA, (2) measured by at least one TPM and (3) seeking to attain a target or required level of performance.

Early in the project, when the initial design of the deliverable is hypothesized, an initial estimate of each TPM should be made. Typically, the initial design is conceived to meet or exceed all of the TPM targets (or else why propose it?). However, further activities in the project serve to revise the initial estimates and confirm or disprove the hypothesis of meeting all the TPM targets (Thomke, 2003).

Many projects have used a tool called a TPM tracking chart to plan and monitor the evolution of each TPM. See Figure 12.7 as an example. A TPM tracking chart can capture predictions and actual estimates of a TPM relative to its target. Initially, experts with applicable project, deliverable and technology experiences may forecast a *planned* profile for the TPM. The profile is projected based on a number of factors, including technology risk, planned verification and validation activities, historical data, experience and expert opinion. Planned profiles integrate experts' experience, knowledge and opinions into a format that helps planners and managers make decisions. It is by no means a perfect situation – a good planner assumes the forecast is wrong. Yet, using TPM profiles – based on planned events in the project – presents the best information available in a helpful format. As the project unfolds, demonstrated measures and revised estimates are recorded periodically. Ideally, the *actual* profile will meet or exceed the target.

In Figure 12.7, the example UCAV preliminary design project spans 27 weeks. The target for the Effective Mission Range TPM is set at 2,100 nautical miles (nmiles) and is represented in the chart by the thick, horizontal line. Each circle represents a point *estimate* or measure of the *most likely* level of performance delivered by the design at various times. The high–low bars – showing the best- and worst-case estimates – convey the amount of certainty (or lack thereof) in the most likely performance level.

As the project unfolds, it is critical to track the measures of important TPAs relative to their targets. TPMs change as the project progresses, often in unforeseen ways. Each TPM may be estimated early

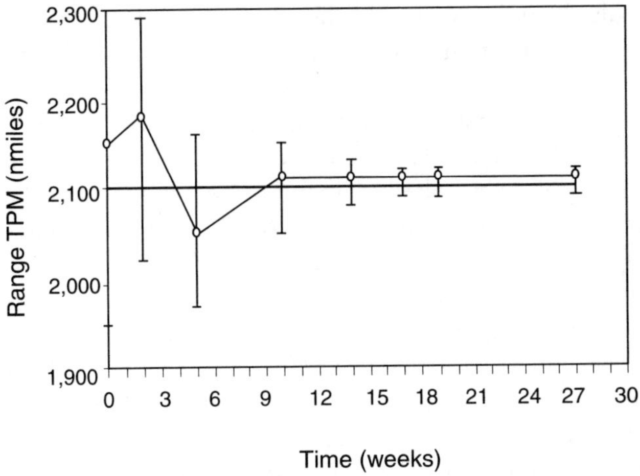

Figure 12.7 Example TPM tracking chart for UCAV mission range

in the project, when a baseline design for the project's deliverable is established, but initial estimates are very subjective and uncertain. As work is done, estimates are refined and become more objective based on information from other decisions, analyses, simulations, prototypes, tests, demonstrations, etc. When the project is finished, the TPMs indicate the level of performance provided by its deliverable.

Over the course of a project, predicting TPM behavior is difficult. TPM starting points depend on the quality of initial estimates. For many TPMs, their change over the interval t_i to t_{i+1} seems random. For example, Cusumano and Selby (1995, pp 318, 324) show defect (bug) TPMs for Microsoft Excel® 5.0 and Microsoft Word® 4.0 where the overall effect is a gradual decrease, but the localized fluctuation seems random. Other studies of engineering design projects have noted the 'design churn' effect (e.g. Yassine *et al.*, 2003), where the quality of the product design does not improve monotonically over time. While progress occurs in one area, other activities discover new problems. There is no guarantee that problems will be solved faster than they are discovered during any given interval. While global, composite performance may improve fairly steadily, local performance (represented by a single TPM) may seem more random. Thus, the latest performance estimates of a project's deliverable can be deceptive indicators of progress. When a baseline is proposed, it is put forward with the expectation that it will be able to satisfy requirements. The portfolio of TPM estimates will look good until a problem is revealed, at which point they suddenly degrade. Hence, using only the estimates or measures of the most likely level of performance for each TPM is a poor indicator of project progress.

However, the best- and worst-case performance estimates for each TPM – the high–low bars in Figure 12.7 – provide valuable information that is, unfortunately, often overlooked by many project managers. The idea that TPMs become more accurate as the project progresses relates to the reduction of uncertainty. Information produced by activities is used to reduce the uncertainty surrounding TPMs. Some activities (analyses, evaluations, reviews, experiments, tests) may not change the actual capability of the deliverable (the TPM levels), but these kinds of efforts are crucial for reducing its uncertainty (represented by the TPM uncertainty bounds). Notice how, in Figure 12.7, the estimate of the most likely level of performance jumps around, similar to an individual security in the stock market, but the uncertainty bounds tend to narrow over time. The uncertainty bounds deserve special attention, because they are the better indicator of progress and earned value regarding technical performance and risk reduction.

Risk in a technical performance attribute

Again, technical *risk* is the *uncertainty* surrounding the ability of a project's deliverable to satisfy its performance requirements *and* the *consequences* of any shortfalls. Thus, the amount of technical risk associated with a TPA depends on two factors: (1) the number of possible outcomes, cases or situations that fail to meet its target performance level, and (2) the consequence or impact of each such outcome. These factors will be addressed separately and then combined.

Technical performance uncertainty

When one is uncertain about the exact value of a variable, it is called a random variable and is represented as a distribution of possible values. In project management literature, normal, triangle, beta and gamma distributions are commonly used in quantifying cost and schedule risk. Here, a similar approach is taken for each TPM, using three data points – best case (optimistic), most likely and worst case (pessimistic) – to assume a triangle distribution of potential outcomes, as shown in Figure 12.8. While other-shaped distributions could also be used, the triangle distribution is simple and intuitive and makes minimal

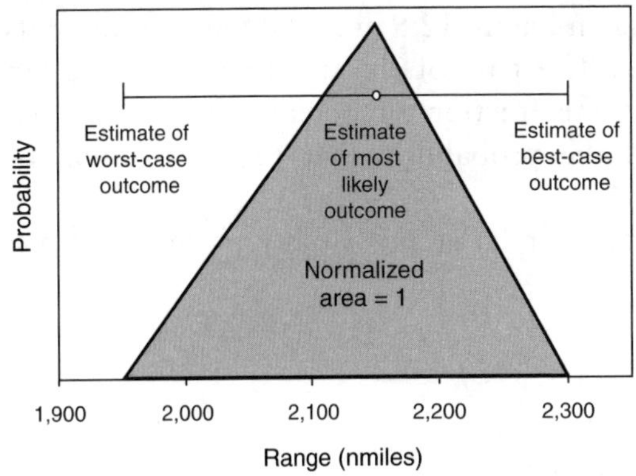

Figure 12.8 Conversion of week zero's three-point estimate to triangle distribution

assumptions beyond the small amount of subjective data available (the three estimates). The area 'under' the distribution is usually normalized to equal one, implying that the total probability of an outcome lying between the best- and worst-case estimates is 100 per cent. However, this area could also be assumed to equal some other amount, such as 90 per cent (to allow for a 5 per cent chance of an outcome worse than the estimated worst case and a 5 per cent chance of an outcome better than the estimated best case).

The triangle distribution in Figure 12.9 shows the relative likelihood of the example UCAV having various range capabilities, based on estimates made early in the project (i.e. in week zero; see Figure 12.7). The working design is estimated most likely to have a range of 2,150 nmiles. In the worst case, the designers estimate the design might provide a range of only 1,950 nmiles, and in the best-case outcome, a range of

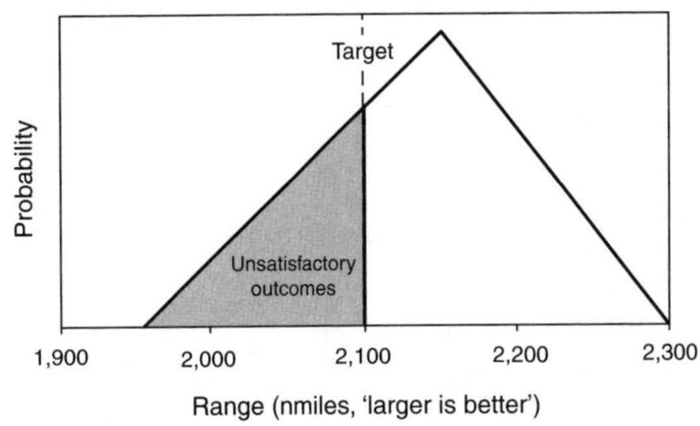

Figure 12.9 Triangle distribution function showing relative probability of various range TPM outcomes at project start

2,300 nmiles. The vertical line in Figure 12.9 at 2,100 nmiles represents the target performance level. The part of the distribution to the left of the target line represents the fraction of potential outcomes that fail to meet the target, i.e. the probability that the design will be unsatisfactory.

For a triangle distribution, the relative probability of any outcome, x, is given by the formula:

$$f(x) = \frac{2(x-a)}{(b-a)(c-a)} \qquad a \le x \le b$$

$$f(x) = \frac{2(c-x)}{(c-a)(c-b)} \qquad b < x \le c \qquad (1)$$

$$f(x) = 0 \qquad \text{otherwise}$$

where a is the worst-case outcome, b is the most likely outcome and c is the best-case outcome – for a 'larger is better' (LIB) TPM. This formula was used to plot the distribution in Figure 12.9. To calculate portions of the distribution, such as the probability of unsatisfactory outcomes, it is easier to use the cumulative distribution function (CDF), which is obtained by integrating Equation (1). The CDF for the range TPM at the time of the three estimates is given in Figure 12.10. Here, it is easier to tell that the probability of an unsatisfactory outcome is about 32 per cent, or roughly one-third of the area of the triangle in Figure 12.9.

Technical performance consequences

Project managers face many uncertainties, but not all uncertainties are equally consequential. The consequences of a project's deliverable

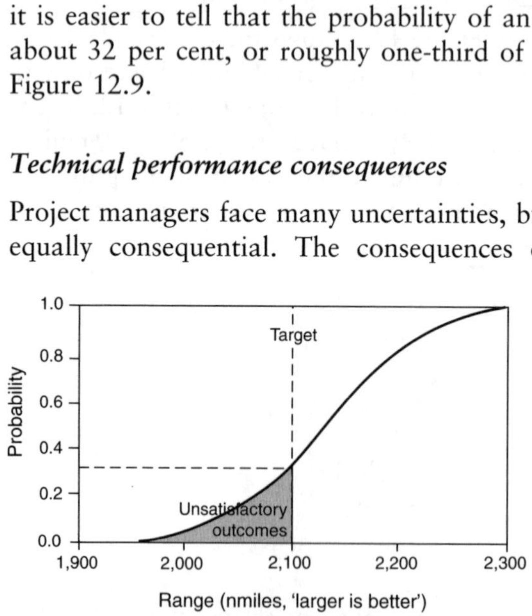

Figure 12.10 CDF for UCAV range TPM

failing to meet a TPM target may differ by (1) the TPA and/or (2) the magnitude of the failure. While some targets represent absolute thresholds, below which the entire deliverable is unacceptable, others represent stakeholder preferences, perhaps where more is better but less might be acceptable. To capture these possibilities for varying stakeholder preferences, utility functions (which have also been called preference or value functions) are adopted. Utility functions provide one helpful approach for quantifying customer preferences for various TPA levels.

Figure 12.11 shows an example (piecewise linear) utility function for UCAV range. The length of the x axis is chosen to span the continuum from disgusting to delighting the customer or market. The y axis is normalized from 0 to 1, where 0 implies disgust (minimum utility) and 1 delight (maximum utility). In this example, perhaps a military customer wants a UCAV for a particular mission that requires a 2,000 nmiles range. Nothing less will do. Slightly greater range is of marginally increasing value to the customer, to the point that a range of 2,500 nmiles is delightful. The utility function can be used to determine the consequence of various range capabilities in terms of customer utility or value.

An impact function, I_{TPM}, expresses the loss in customer utility or value for failing to meet a required level of performance:

$$I_{TPM} = \kappa_{TPM}|U_{TPM}(T_{TPM}) - U_{TPM}(x_{TPM})| \qquad (2)$$

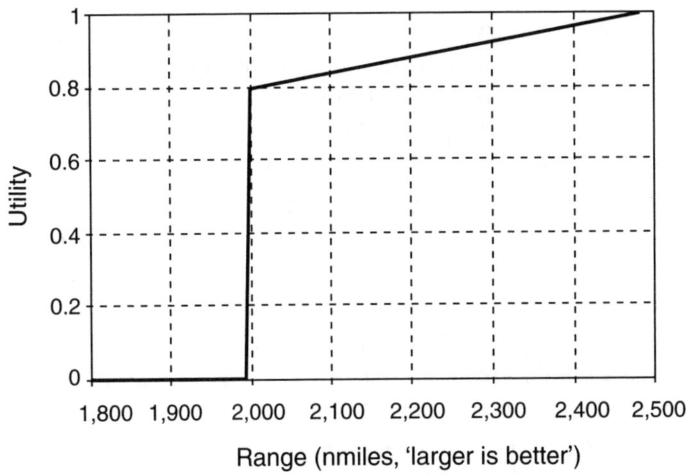

Figure 12.11 Utility curve for aircraft range

where T_{TPM} is the TPA's target performance level, $U_{TPM}(\cdot)$ is the utility function, κ_{TPM} is a conversion constant or function (discussed below) and the outcomes, x_{TPM}, are drawn only from the region(s) of adverse outcomes. That is, the impact of failing to meet a target is the difference between the utility provided by the target level of performance and the utility provided by the actual level of performance. Note that, if the utility function is flat in some region containing the target, the impact may be zero for some 'unsatisfactory outcomes' – meaning that a tolerance region exists around the target before impacts accrue.

For example, suppose the UCAV's range TPM is estimated to be 2,050 nmiles. While below the target of 2,100 nmiles, it is still above the 'cliff' in the utility function at 2,000 nmiles. Thus, the impact of being 50 nmiles short of the target is small in terms of utility. Using the function in Figure 12.11, $U(2{,}100) - U(2{,}050) = 0.84 - 0.82 = 0.02$ units of utility.

What is the consequence of a 0.02 drop in utility? Is this a little drop or a big one? Is this a cause for concern or not? κ_{TPM} can be used to convert one type of units, such as utility, into another type with greater meaning to the project, such as the expected sales or revenue. For example, suppose sales forecasts expect sales of zero units if the range is less than 2,000 nmiles, sales of 800 units if the range is 2,000 nmiles and sales of 1,000 units if the range is 2,500 nmiles. In terms of utility that is:

$$Sales(x) = 1{,}000(U_{Range}(x))$$

Thus, the 0.02 drop in utility in the example translates into (0.02)(1,000) = 20 fewer units sold. Furthermore, if the expected revenue per unit is £2 million, then κ_{Range} = (1,000 units)(£2 million/unit) = £1,000 million, and the 0.02 drop in utility translates into £20 million in lost revenue – probably a significant amount. While this number is interesting, of course it is extremely sensitive to the assumptions about market size and the relationship between utility and demand (which is not actually linear). Nevertheless, business cases regularly make assumptions about markets and demand, despite the problems with such forecasts. It simply makes sense to integrate and utilize the best information available from all parts of an organization when making project management and product or service design decisions. Furthermore, recognizing the value of having certain information, such as the impact of certain TPA performance levels, will encourage an organization that does not have good estimates of such things to put more emphasis on acquiring better ones. An organization with market savvy and historical data could calibrate κ_{TPM} to provide useful support for business decisions.

A variety of impact functions are possible. Utility functions provide just one approach. The key is to quantify the consequences of each unsatisfactory outcome, realizing that some adverse outcomes may be more consequential than others. If the impact of shortcomings in each TPA is measured in comparable units, such as lost utility, sales or revenue, then it becomes possible to compare the impacts of one TPA against another in a meaningful way.

Note that these impact functions are derived under the assumptions that 'all else is equal' and TPAs are independent. Of course, most TPAs are *inter*dependent. Thus, it is important to build impact functions by asking customers and marketing experts about a hypothetical product or service while varying only one of its TPAs at a time, with all the others held constant. For additional guidance on building utility functions, see, for example, Borcherding *et al.* (1991).

Technical performance risk

The technical performance risk for a particular TPA is the sum of the products of probability and impact for each unsatisfactory outcome. That is, since there is a range of 'unsatisfactory outcomes' between the worst-case estimate of a TPM and its target, one must account for each of these probabilities and impacts. Calculate a risk factor (expected loss) for each TPA by integrating over the probabilistically weighted impacts of all adverse outcomes:

$$\mathscr{R}_{\text{TPA}} = \int_{-\infty}^{T_{\text{TPM}}} f_{\text{TPM}}(x_{\text{TPM}})\kappa_{\text{TPM}} \left[U_{\text{TPM}}(T_{\text{TPM}}) - U_{\text{TPM}}(x_{\text{TPM}})\right] dx_{\text{TPM}} \tag{3}$$

where $f_{\text{TPM}}(x_{\text{TPM}})$ is the distribution of TPM outcomes, such as the triangle distribution given in Equation (1). That is, for each potential outcome in the range of unsatisfactory outcomes (determined by, for example, Equation (1) and the chosen target, T_{TPM}), multiply it by its impact [given by Equation (2)] and then sum these risks of individual, adverse outcomes to arrive at a single, scalar risk index representing all adverse outcomes. Equation (3) shows the formula for the case of a 'larger is better' (LIB) TPA such as aircraft range, where the adverse outcomes are those less than the target ($x_{\text{TPM}} < T_{\text{TPM}}$). For 'smaller is better' (SIB) TPAs, reverse the limits of integration. For 'nominal is best' (NIB) TPAs, two integrands, a LIB and a SIB, must be summed.

In practice, Equation (3) must be evaluated numerically, i.e. approximated by the summation of a finite number of discrete outcomes. [To minimize the error in this computation, it is helpful to divide the distribution $f_{TPM}(x_{TPM})$ or its cumulative distribution function (CDF) version into bins of size equal to the units of measure for the TPM, rounded to some reasonable level (e.g. whole number).]

For example, let us return to the project's initial estimate of UCAV range (Figure 12.9). The potential outcomes between 1,950 and 2,100 nmiles are unsatisfactory but, out of these, the ones below 2,000 nmiles are much more consequential. Thus, evaluate Equation (3) as

$$\mathcal{R}_{\text{Range}} = \kappa_{\text{Range}} \sum_{1950}^{2100} f_{\text{Range}}(x_i)\,[U_{\text{Range}}(2100) - U_{\text{Range}}(x_i)] \tag{4}$$

where $f_{\text{Range}}(x_i)$ is shown in Figure 12.9, $U_{\text{Range}}(x_i)$ is shown in Figure 12.11 and κ_{Range} = £1,000 million, as described above. Hence, $\mathcal{R}_{\text{Range}} \approx$ £35 million, which is the expected loss in sales revenue due to the uncertainty in the range capability of the UCAV design.

So, to summarize the UCAV range example: the UCAV design concept's range was estimated at a point in time in terms of best-, most likely and worst-case outcomes. These data were used to assume a triangular distribution of potential outcomes. Comparing this set of outcomes with a design target enabled calculation of a 32 per cent probability of unsatisfactory outcomes. Furthermore, the utility function established that some of these adverse outcomes (particularly the ones less than 2,000 nmiles) brought much worse consequences than others. Taking a weighted average of the losses from the adverse outcomes, using their relative likelihood as the weights, determined the expected loss (£35 million) represented by the current lack of certainty in the outcome.

Overall technical performance risk in a project

The overall technical performance risk for a project, $\mathcal{R}_P$, is a function of all the $\mathcal{R}_{\text{TPA}}$s. The function can take any of several forms, each with advantages and disadvantages. For example, a weighted average of m $\mathcal{R}_{\text{TPA}}$s is given by

$$\mathcal{R}_P = \sum_{i}^{m} w_{\text{TPA}_i} \mathcal{R}_{\text{TPA}_i} \tag{5}$$

where the w_{TPA_i} are weighting factors and $\sum_{i}^{m} w_{\text{TPA}_i} = 1$. The advantage of a weighted average is its simplicity, but it has the disadvantage of potentially allowing extremely poor performance in one TPA to have a minimal effect on the overall technical risk. More sophisticated techniques, such as a geometric mean or multi-attribute utility function, can also be used. These approaches solve some difficulties but create others.

The weighted average is suggested for simplicity, and because the individual $\mathscr{R}_{\text{TPA}}$ it combines are each a non-linear function that increases quickly as its worst-case value moves away from the target. Large individual $\mathscr{R}_{\text{TPA}}$ values will have a large influence on $\mathscr{R}_P$. This effect is helpful, since one would not want a single, high-risk TPA to be 'washed out' by a large number of low-risk TPAs when determining overall technical risk. For this reason, it is important also to pay attention to the single largest $\mathscr{R}_{\text{TPA}}$. Some even prefer to let

$$\mathscr{R}_P = \text{Max}(\mathscr{R}_{\text{TPA}_1}, \mathscr{R}_{\text{TPA}_2}, \ldots, \mathscr{R}_{\text{TPA}_m}) \tag{6}$$

Expanding the UCAV example, now consider four TPAs: payload, range, reliability (mean time before failure) and stealth. For each TPA at the beginning of the project, Table 12.1 shows the target, worst-case value, most likely value, best-case value, outcome distribution, utility function, κ_{TPM}, relative importance (weight) and risk level. The total $\mathscr{R}_P$ at this point is £28 million by Equation (5) or £56 million by Equation (6). Either number chosen is primarily useful in a relative sense: managers are interested in the reduction of this exposure over the course of the project. In fact, one might even want to determine the 'value added' or 'earned value' for the project in terms of its reduction of this amount.

Showing progress

Over the course of a project, its activities should be planned to create useful information that reduces technical risk. Thus, the risk calculations in Table 12.1 must be updated frequently over the course of the project. To illustrate improvement in the range TPM, consider the tracking chart in Figure 12.7.

Figure 12.12 shows the range TPM at weeks 0 and 14 with its uncertainties represented by triangle distributions. By week 14, useful information has been created that has reined in the uncertainty from week 0. While the probability of an unsatisfactory outcome has not changed much, especially poor outcomes with greater consequences have been eliminated. Thus, while uncertainty remains, risk has been drastically reduced for this TPA.

Figure 12.13 shows progress (solid lines) and risk level (dashed lines) for four TPMs over the 27 weeks of the example UCAV preliminary design project. (The purpose of the preliminary design phase is to do the background work necessary for preparation of a proposal to the customer, a defence agency. The designers must create enough information to increase their confidence in the proposed design to a certain level. After all, they must have reasonable confidence that in the next projects they can actually design [in detail] and build what they propose in this preliminary design project.) Note that the reliability TPM is only affected once, at week 17, and that stealth is not affected at all. This is because few or no activities are currently included in the preliminary design project plan to affect these areas. Thus, another value of managing technical risk on a project is in conjunction with other aspects of project planning. Project planners must somehow determine which activities to include in the plan and schedule. Knowing which areas of technical risk pose the most challenge to meeting stakeholders' expectations can help them identify, prioritize and schedule the appropriate activities. Figure 12.14 shows the overall risk profile over the 27 week project, as calculated with Equation (5). Here it is also clear which TPAs are contributing the most and therefore where additional efforts should be focused on reducing technical risk.

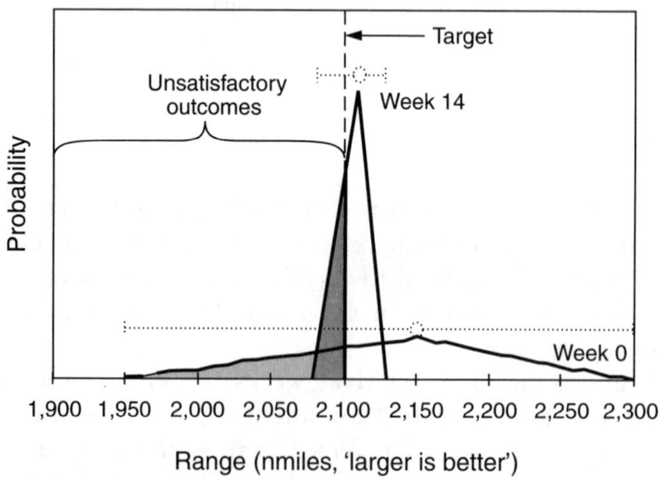

Figure 12.12 Reduction in unacceptable outcomes from week 0 to week 14

Table 12.1 TPM data and risk levels at the beginning of the UCAV project

TPA	Target	WCV	MLV	BCV	Outcome distribution	Utility function	K_{TPM}	w_i	$\mathscr{R}_{TPA}$
Payload	100 kg	95	110	120	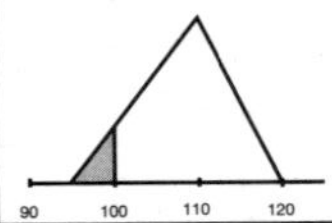	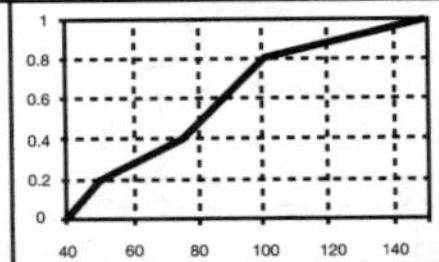	£1,000 million	.3	£1.8 million
Range	2,100 nmiles	1,950	2,150	2,300	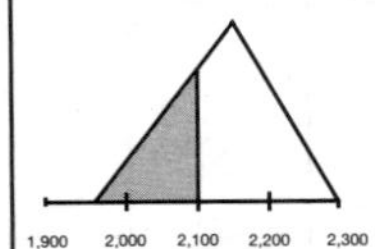	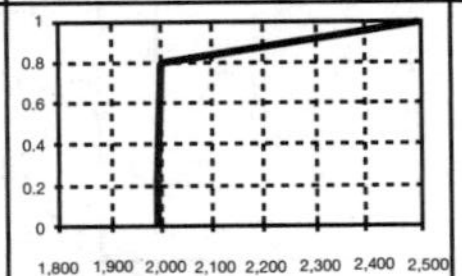	£1,000 million	.25	£35 million
Reliability	2,000 hrs	1,000	2,500	3,500	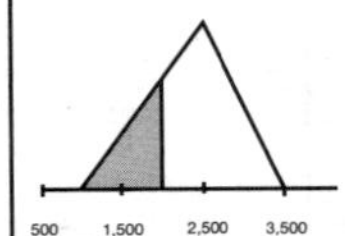	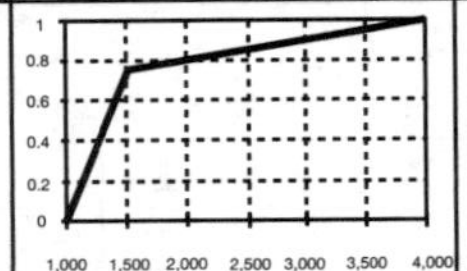	£1,000 million	.2	£24 million
Stealth	1.4 (ratio to previous baseline)	1.2	1.45	1.8	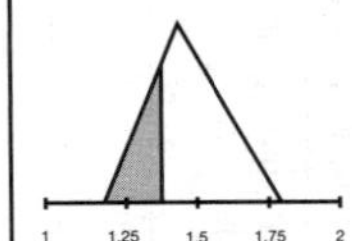	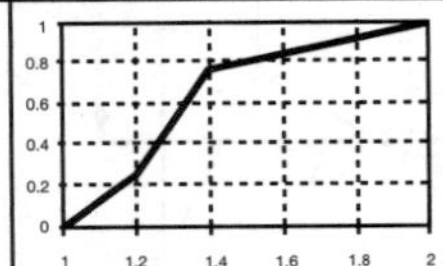	£1,000 million	.25	£56 million
								$\mathscr{R}_p$:	£28 million
								Max:	£56 million

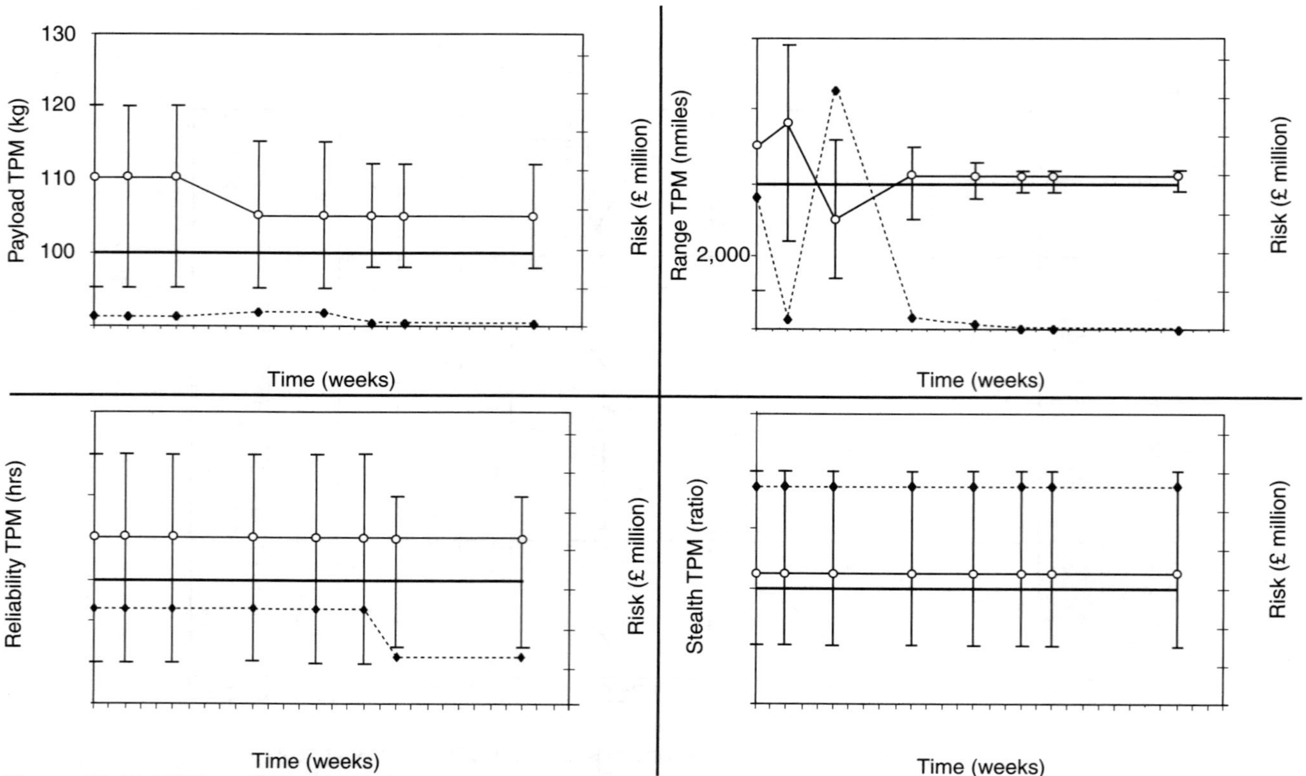

Figure 12.13 TPM profiles and risks during the UCAV preliminary design project

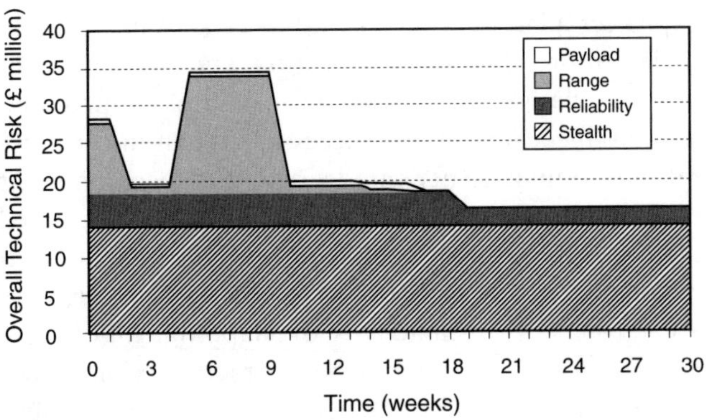

Figure 12.14 Overall risk profile for the UCAV preliminary design project

Insights

The approach to managing technical risk based on the risk value method spawns several insights. First, it focuses management attention on *choosing activities* that will reduce the risk that a project will produce an unsatisfactory deliverable. By tying this effort back to marketing metrics, the project participants have before them a constant reminder of the amount of jeopardy in which their project exists vis-à-vis customer preferences. Thus, not just project management's but everyone's attention is focused on reducing the most critical uncertainties facing the project.

The risk value method accounts for reducing technical risk via several avenues. First, a project may decrease its uncertainty about the performance level of its deliverable in a particular TPA, i.e. it may tighten the distribution of possible outcomes. Second, a project may seek to avoid any unsatisfactory outcomes with the worst consequences, i.e. it may shift the distribution in the direction of improvement. Third, a project may try to work with its stakeholders to relax the requirements or targets, i.e. it may shift the target away from the direction of improvement. Any of these actions will reduce the technical risk for the project. Management must determine which makes the most sense and is most feasible at a particular time.

The risk value method draws attention to the *uncertainty* connected with each TPM, emphasizing the importance of risk reduction and maintained flexibility. It emphasizes the importance of estimating each TPM early in the project, which helps ensure that risky areas are not overlooked during project planning. Then, initial risk reduction can be achieved by earlier, more directed verification and validation of uncertain aspects of the design and more appropriately timed and postured reviews. Maintained flexibility is necessary when uncertainty persists. Paying attention to uncertainty can decrease the focus on point solutions and increase the attractiveness of approaches such as set-based design and robust design. It can also enable projects to benefit from additional activity concurrency, since projects with fast uncertainty reduction receive greater benefits from activity overlapping. All of these advantages accrue when using the approach in practice. Companies that effectively manage and reduce uncertainty and risk should realize competitive advantages.

A salient aspect of the risk value method is how it can be used to link risk reduction to *particular activities* in a project. Advocates of activity-based management emphasize the activity as the common basis for cost, schedule and quality accounting. A number of models (e.g. Browning and Eppinger, 2002; Grey, 1995) already exist that evaluate cost and schedule and their risks in terms of activity networks. Now, the foundation is laid for models that consider trade-offs between cost, schedule and technical risks in a project (Browning, 1998). By comparing the contributions of each activity not only to technical risk reduction but also to project cost and duration, one can determine each activity's productivity or efficiency in adding customer value (Browning, 2003).

Furthermore, the risk value method supports post-project analysis and learning. By comparing planned risk reduction profiles to actual achievements, a firm can evaluate its project planning and control capabilities and improve its processes.

Practical limitations of the approach

Despite its advantages, the risk value method has some limitations in practice, especially those common to all measures and metrics. For instance, metrics can be 'gamed'. The project participants must exhibit proper attitudes towards TPMs and uncertainty if the estimates and measures will be meaningful. If workers merely pad uncertainty estimates to justify more activities to reduce uncertainty, then the project may not be able to clear a business case hurdle or win a contract. Furthermore, no metric is better than the data used to calculate it. The information about uncertainty and risk in a project is subjective.

Nevertheless, the risk value method integrates the most useful information available in a meaningful way to support decision-making. It facilitates trading off various TPAs to achieve a well-balanced deliverable. A strong argument for the risk value method, despite the metrics-related challenges, is that these same, subjective data – used in an *ad hoc*, unsystematic and unintegrated fashion – constitute the current state of practice.

Perhaps a more fundamental limitation of the approach is that many managers and workers do not think in terms of fuzzy values. Uncertain data are often exchanged in projects with no accompanying indication of their precision. Significant digits are often overstated or ignored. Project participants must think in terms of 'spread' and attend to the amount of uncertainty in their estimates and projections. Becoming aware of the drivers of uncertainty and risk in TPMs can help estimators discern the firmness of their data.

Finally, care must be taken to account for 'extreme events', i.e. events with a very low probability but catastrophic consequences. Because of the averaging across all adverse outcomes and again across various TPAs, these types of outcomes may be undervalued in the basic version of the approach presented in this chapter. However, the approach can be extended to account for such situations more appropriately. For a discussion of the risks of extreme events, see Haimes (1998).

Opportunity management

So far, the focus has been on adverse technical outcomes, i.e. situations when performance fails to meet targets. However, the uncertainties surrounding each TPM and the utility functions contain information useful for evaluating the 'upside' potential as well. This is called 'opportunity'. Opportunity is quantified similarly to risk, as the product of the probability of an outcome and its impact, except its impact is a reward. Thus, *technical opportunity* is the uncertainty about the ability of a deliverable to exceed its performance requirements and the rewards of doing so.

Prescribing an optimal project in terms of risk and opportunity requires an assumption about risk attitude. One manager may follow a conservative (risk- and opportunity-averse) strategy to minimize the probability of an outcome other than the desired one. A liberal (opportunity-seeking) manager may seek to maximize the probability of the best outcome. A typical but somewhat conservative strategy is to maximize the probability of an *acceptable* outcome. Should the goal of a project be risk minimization, opportunity maximization, or both?

The answer seems to be *both* – yet without mixing them, since this could allow opportunities to obscure risks. Hence, opportunity and risk, while calculated similarly, are not mixed directly. Areas of high opportunity often hint at ways to compensate for certain risks, but typically these must be negotiated with stakeholders. Also, opportunity is not merely the absence of risk. While some opportunities are merely the inverse of related risks (e.g. instead of having too short a range, a UCAV could have more), others are 'pure opportunities' unrelated to risks: uncertain events or circumstances which would produce real additional benefits or value, if they could be captured proactively and exploited (e.g. there may be an opportunity to sell to another customer or market segment, necessitating additional TPAs and TPMs). Readers interested in a fuller discussion of risk and opportunity are directed to Hillson (2003) and Browning and Hillson (2003).

Conclusion

This chapter has presented an overview of the traditional approach to managing technical risk in projects and a new approach based on the risk value method. These approaches are complementary: using both will help catch and manage technical risks more comprehensively than using either alone.

Both approaches are also related to broader project management methodology. The value imparted by a project as a whole (and of every activity within it) is based on the value of its result. During a project, activities contribute value by creating information that increases certainty about the ability of the design to satisfy requirements. It is crucial to plan, budget and schedule the activities that will make the greatest contribution to reducing the risk that the project will fail to meet stakeholders' expectations of value. Indeed, from a point of view, this is the goal of project management, unless perhaps it is more properly stated as '*to maximize the project's value to stakeholders*', thereby accounting for opportunity as well as risk.

In closing, consider the value of certainty and predictability, both to the project organization and to its customer. Certainty may be of direct value to a customer, i.e. it may itself be a TPA. Certainty also translates into an increased ability for project managers to establish and fulfil commitments and expectations.

It is also helpful to turn the problem around and consider the cost of uncertainty. Uncertainty has many costs during a project – e.g. costs of resource buffers, options, safety margins, etc. – and these costs are passed along to the customer in higher prices. Whether the customer considers certainty explicitly or not, product costs reflect the costs of uncertainty. The following are consequences of persisting technical risk in a project (Browning, 1999):

- required investment in backup plans;
- inefficient resource allocation (wasted time and money);
- cost and schedule risk;
- inability to prioritize activities or interfaces;
- inability to make commitments;
- 'fuzzy' decision-making; conservatism; misguided trade-off analyses;
- much higher required investment in project planning and management.

Thus, again, failure to manage risks properly in one area of a project increases risks for other areas.

References and recommended reading

Borcherding, K, Eppel, T and Winterfeldt, D von (1991) Comparison of weighting judgments in multiattribute utility measurement. *Management Science,* **37**:12 1603–1619.

Browning, T R (1998) *Modeling and Analyzing Cost, Schedule, and Performance in Complex System Product Development.* PhD Thesis (TMP), Massachusetts Institute of Technology, Cambridge, MA.

Browning, T R (1999) Sources of performance risk in complex system development. *Proceedings of the 9th Annual International Symposium of INCOSE.* Brighton, UK, June 6–11. pp 711–718.

Browning, T R (2003) On customer value and improvement in product development processes. *Systems Engineering,* **6**:1 49–61.

Browning, T R and Eppinger, S D (2002) Modeling impacts of process architecture on cost and schedule risk in product development. *IEEE Transactions on Engineering Management,* **49**:4 428–442.

Browning, T R and Hillson, D A (2003) *A Quantitative Framework for Multi-Dimensional Risk and Opportunity Management.* TCU Neeley School of Business, Working Paper.

Browning, T R, Deyst, J J, Eppinger, S D and Whitney, D E (2002) Adding value in product development by creating information and reducing risk. *IEEE Transactions on Engineering Management,* **49**:4 443–458.

Clausing, D (1994) *Total Quality Development: A Step-by-Step Guide to World-Class Concurrent Engineering.* New York: ASME Press.

Cusumano, M A and Selby, R W (1995) *Microsoft Secrets: How the World's Most Powerful Software Company Creates Technology, Shapes Markets, and Manages People*. New York: The Free Press.

DAU (1998) *Risk Management Guide for DoD Acquisition*, 5th edn. Fort Belvoir, VA: Defense Acquisition University Press.

Draves, J P (1993) *A Risk Management Process for Department of Defense Acquisition Programs Operating in an Integrated Product Development Environment.* Master's Thesis (Eng.), California State University, Long Beach, CA.

DSMC (1983) Risk assessment techniques: methods overview & technique descriptions (Ch. 4 and App. F), *Defense Systems Management College Handbook.* Fort Belvoir, VA: DSMC, pp. iv-1–iv-25, F-1–F-13.

Grey, S (1995) *Practical Risk Assessment for Project Management.* New York: John Wiley & Sons.

Haimes, Y Y (1998) *Risk Modeling, Assessment, and Management.* New York: John Wiley & Sons.

Hall, E M (1998) *Managing Risk: Methods for Software Systems Development.* Reading, MA: Addison-Wesley.

Hillson, D A (2003) *Effective Opportunity Management for Projects: Exploiting Positive Risk.* New York: Marcel Dekker.

Huff, D S (1997) Prophet™ – the engine for integrated risk management. *Proceedings of the 7th Annual International Symposium of INCOSE.* Los Angeles, Aug. 3–7. pp 737–743.

Justice, R (1996) Risk in the F-22 Program: a defense science board task force analyzes F-22 concurrency and risk. *Program Manager*, **25**:(Jul.–Aug.) 68–74.

McDermott, R E, Mikulak, R J and Beauregard, M R (1996) *The Basics of FMEA.* Portland, OR: Productivity, Inc.

PMI (2004) *A Guide to the Project Management Body of Knowledge*, 3rd edn. Newtown Square, PA: Project Management Institute.

SEI (1996) *Continuous Risk Management Guidebook.* Pittsburgh, PA: Software Engineering Institute.

Smith, P G and Merritt, G M (2002) *Proactive Risk Management: Controlling Uncertainty in Product Development.* New York: Productivity Press.

Thomke, S H (2003) *Experimentation Matters.* Boston, MA: Harvard Business School Press.

Williams, R C, Walker, J A and Dorofee, A J (1997) Putting risk management into practice. *IEEE Software*, 75–81.

Yassine, A A, Joglekar, N, Braha, D, Eppinger, S and Whitney, D (2003) Information hiding in product development: the design churn effect. *Research in Engineering Design*, **14** 145–161.

13

Managing Fraud Risk

Jon Finch

Whilst the practice of identifying and systematically managing business risk is becoming accepted as essential, it is surprising that the risk of losses through fraud remain amongst the least recognized.

Fraud losses can be of any scale from a few pounds sterling to an uncontrollable vortex that has the potential to wipe out a major corporation, as shown by the Enron, WorldCom and other recent disasters. It is estimated that some £40 million is lost to fraud each day in the UK alone. This is certainly an underestimate since it relates to discovered and reported fraud. Much fraud remains undiscovered. Even where identified, fraud is often unreported due to the desire to protect business reputation and expedite recovery of losses.

So, what exactly is fraud? As with the definition of risk, there are many variants and as many dissenting opinions, but one useful definition is:

> Obtaining dishonest gain through deception, covert action, misrepresentation or misuse of privileged knowledge or access.

This chapter offers an overview of practical considerations that surround the design and implementation of a viable fraud risk management process in a company. It has deliberately been written in a style that includes a number of true 'war stories' and examples.

Fraud comes in many shapes and sizes. Examples are:

- Breach of trust in any form. This may include the deliberate leaking of sensitive information to the benefit of a third party, particularly if the information is 'sold' for personal gain.
- Conflict of interest, where an employee sets up a company that trades with the employer's organization covertly, thus benefiting

from an inside track on orders and knowledge. Usually this is to the detriment of the company in terms of value for money.

- Employee malpractice generally, where company assets (including employee time) are used in furtherance of the employee's personal business objectives. A classic case of this occurred in an international project where a major contract was slipping steadily behind schedule despite the hard work and long hours of a good project team. The core problem was identified as the poor focus of the project director. He was starting up his own consultancy business and recruiting his own team, but using the office facilities. Over 40 per cent of his salaried time was supporting his own venture. His poor decision-making and grasp of the detail in managing the project contract and subcontractors almost cost his employers massive penalties. He was dismissed and replaced by a UK project director, who succeeded in recovering the schedule and delivering within time-scale and budget.
- Fraud that clearly constitutes a criminal offence. The rest of this chapter concentrates on this type of fraud, which may be the work of one individual or the result of a well-organized criminal conspiracy.

Specific standards for combating fraud

It is difficult to identify any cohesive formal standard in the UK for managing fraud risk. There are some good papers on fraud, two of which are referenced at the end of this chapter. Perhaps not surprisingly, the US accounting bodies, notably the American Institute of Certified Public Accountants (AICPA), have kick-started improvements to anti-fraud content in their guidelines post-2002. Specifically they now add the need for an emphasis on professional scepticism (not to believe all they are told); to include specific questions on fraud in discussions with management; to include unpredictable tests to cross-check areas of accounts that otherwise may not be tested; and to target instances of management overriding controls.

In the UK OFR (Operating and Financial Review) regulations, there are enhanced annual disclosure obligations that extend corporate governance requirements on major companies (Department of Trade and Industry, 2005). However, even under the formal statement of 'principal risks and uncertainties' there is no specific reference to fraud management.

So, despite a lengthy search, a well-founded *standard* against which fraud management can be measured is lamentably elusive. Or is it lamentable? One might ask whether it would perhaps be unwise to have a concrete standard for fraud risk. There is much good practice and experience that has been written down by various bodies and individuals in the form of *guidelines*, for example, the HM Treasury Guidelines referenced (Fennelly, 2003), but bearing in mind that fraud is usually an innovative crime that is best countered by *covert* risk management tailored to a company's needs, surely it could be counterproductive to enforce a standard for organizations to follow?

Therefore this chapter offers a further form of guideline (rather than a standard) from which companies may build, to intercept and implement a viable fraud risk management process that is right for them.

Differences between fraud risk and other business risk

Most business risk results from factors or risk drivers that are beyond the control of any single party, yet are capable of being analysed, understood and responded to with planned provision. Fraud risk may also be analysed and reduced with effective measures. However, fraud is the product of covert, deliberate and usually illegal action, making identification and deterrence more sensitive. Given that it is statistically shown that over 80 per cent of fraud results from illicit activities of a tiny minority of employees within organizations, it is a particularly delicate area to probe. There are examples of hitherto well-motivated, upbeat and effective workforces being left feeling untrusted and undervalued by insensitive studies into fraud risk exposure. Some company management teams even regard the impact of assessing their vulnerability to fraud as potentially worse than any likely losses.

Also, staff members in smaller companies tend to be personally known and trusted as a part of a hierarchical 'family'. It is sobering to remember that 90 per cent of fraudulent employees have been employed over 12 months, whilst 20 per cent of employees discovered committing fraud have been on the payroll over 10 years.

However, fraud affecting a company may not directly involve its staff, but be a type of fraud that has little reliance on employees. These fraudulent conspiracies exploit weaknesses in the external interfaces and outward facing procedures of an organization without employees being knowingly complicit.

As with all business risk, fraud *can* be countered safely and effectively. The approach has to be managed sympathetically but firmly, developing a culture of zero tolerance to fraud. An anti-fraud policy, together with good communication and leadership, is essential to promote an open and honest dialogue with all staff. The vast majority of the employees in any company will totally support measures taken to eradicate losses through fraud, provided that the approach is appropriate for that firm's culture.

Why worry about the risk of sustaining loss through fraud?

As with all unidentified business risk, fraud may continue to flourish undiscovered until it is too late to avoid a major loss. As already stated, business risk analysis and management can be undertaken fairly openly, whilst fraud risk has to be managed with privacy and discretion.

The impact of fraud does potentially extend well beyond the financial loss to a business. Many frauds start with a minor opportunistic act or misrepresentation by one individual. Having profited, whether through a flaw in the operation of processes or a blatant lie, the probability is extremely high that the activity will be repeated and expanded. Almost all undiscovered fraud grows in terms of the initial damage inflicted.

A minority of frauds will result from organized, well-planned and executed activity by a group who are professional in spotting gaps in procedural safeguards, often involving several companies in sophisticated transactions. The losses from such fraud are usually high.

Apart from fiscal loss, fraud that involves other organizations (suppliers or subcontractors, perhaps even customers) may seriously damage trusted relationships and the reputation upon which organizations trade. Reputation risk is fully discussed in Chapter 6 of this book, but should not be underestimated in importance as loss of reputation usually leads to loss of business and, if a listed company, may lead to rapid loss of shareholder investment.

Why does fraud happen in a company?

The short answer to this question is 'human greed'.

Before looking at the types of fraud that may occur, it is useful to explore *why* one company might be more prone to suffering fraud than another! An analysis of the generic shortcomings in companies of all sizes where fraud has occurred show:

- a failure to recognize the risk of fraud, let alone look for it;
- a lack of any understanding of fraud risk;
- a poor, complacent or demotivated internal audit function;
- an ineffective personnel department with unprofessional recruitment practices, especially in following up references, induction training, appraisal and ensuring supervision where the role is a trusted one;
- a misguided or poorly implemented strategy and practice for data security and integrity. This applies to paper records as well as computerized data;
- inappropriate authority levels for signing off transactions;
- poor procedural consistency and a tolerance of short cuts and breaches of process;
- a culture of general sloppiness.

However, even in the best-run company with excellent processes and well-motivated staff, fraud can take root. It is easily forgotten that systems that control the secure handling of assets are staffed by people; people who have detailed and unique knowledge of 'how it all works'. It only needs one of these staff to become corrupt and work to exploit the inevitable gaps in any control system for fraud to be almost certain.

Types of fraud

There are several recognized types of fraud, which may threaten a company. These are:

- asset theft;
- false accounting;
- insurance fraud;
- impersonation and identity theft;
- computer-based fraud;
- credit card fraud;
- investment fraud.

Each is summarized below.

Asset theft

This is usually associated with false accounting (see below) and can occur in many forms in a company, and be of almost any scale.

As a simple example of how asset theft through false accounting can cost serious money, the sales executive or support engineer who travels frequently between clients will be 'on trust' to his company to account for his business expenditure. Usually company processes employ a system whereby an employee makes his business expenditure within a framework of budgeted rates, probably utilizing credit or debit cards to settle the costs as they occur, before submitting a formal claim, backed by receipts, for management to authorize before reimbursement. The employee then receives the repayment from the company and settles his credit or debit card account before incurring any interest.

Several informal polls have shown that over 60 per cent of those asked if they have ever included a distorted item in one of their claims for expenses, answer in the affirmative. Asked why, it is deemed 'alright'; 'Everyone does it, don't they?' 'It isn't much'; even on several occasions 'The company works me hard without overtime, and they owe me'. Despite people's protestations or use of defensive euphemisms, this is still fraud. Not only is the company suffering loss, but so is the Inland Revenue since this (probably) regular 'income' is untaxed.

Whilst accepting that this is seen as a minor fraud, costing a few tens of pounds on each affected monthly claim, if ignored it *will* grow. If a company has 1,000 employees claiming regular expenses for travelling and subsistence, and 60 per cent are over-claiming by just £30 a month; then in each month 600 × £30 will be unnecessarily reimbursed. That represents £18,000 a month or £198,000 in the 11 working months in a full year, straight off the bottom line. Many large companies have well over 4,000 staff 'on the road' and unidentified false values *will* grow well beyond a notional '£30 a month' per claim.

As an example of how fraud escalates, some years ago a case arose where one employee of a company had developed a lifestyle dependency on the tax-free rewards of his fraudulent claims. He moved from just enhancing his travelling costs a little to claiming wholly unnecessary trips by private car, where the mileage rate was generous. Realizing that his authorizing manager was hardly reading the claims, he inserted plausible but entirely phantom journeys and was 'reimbursed'. After a while he graduated to the purchase of high value but unwanted project items. He resold the assets through auction and privately, including latterly through eBay. On some occasions he made photocopies of the receipts and claimed more than once. It was only when the company updated the expenses system to *automatically* claim back VAT on purchases outside the well-regulated purchasing system (which should have been used for asset purchases) that a failure to reconcile the relevant accounts resulted in a major internal audit going back through over three years of expense claims.

The agreed loss through this individual's fraud was eventually assessed as very significant. The authorizing manager was severely reprimanded. The fraudster was dismissed for gross misconduct and prosecuted, pleading guilty and receiving a shortened custodial sentence in return for his agreement to sell his house and reimburse the company from the profit realized.

Other examples of asset theft fraud are:

- The leakage, for personal gain, of secret information or intellectual property that is of value to a competitor. Such 'personal gain' may be financial, or perhaps an investment in a future benefit, for example, a rewarding position within that competitive organization.
- Stealing and selling highly sensitive commercial information, for example, costings of competitive bids or records of clients' dealings and prices paid for services, which can be used to advantage by the buyer of such information.
- Covering up and facilitating the direct theft or misappropriation of valued assets, for example, plasma screen televisions, hi-fi sound systems or computer technology, by forging authorizations, fraudulently downsizing purchase ledger, goods received and stock records to hide missing items.
- Demanding or accepting corrupt payments in return for promoting or procuring products and services from a supplier, where dealing with that supplier is not in the best interests of the company.
- Deriving benefit through creating fictitious 'employees' on the payroll and diverting the salary and other remuneration for personal gain. This fraud has regularly occurred over the years. In some companies it does require surprisingly few management and staff to accomplish and sustain this scam.
- Similar to the fictitious employee fraud, a 'ghost' customer is created within the company records, who makes some apparently small *bona fide* purchases, before using a line of company credit (usually set up with false or managed references) to 'purchase' and take delivery of valuable assets before vanishing. The complacency of many companies in not verifying references properly, or establishing

appropriate checks on addresses and financial status when an apparently 'good' new customer is in the early stages of trading, will facilitate this type of fraud.

False accounting

As we have seen, this is usually a key element of asset theft, but there are false accounting frauds that extend well beyond the cover-up of asset misappropriation. For example, the enhancing of a corporation's value such that those who benefit from the false valuation in enhanced share price or bonus payments receive benefit that is unfounded. The story of Enron, where a spiral of unsustainable year-on-year valuation was propped up by fictitious diversified company operations in the accounts until the lie became too big to hide, perhaps will always be the benchmark corporate fraud. When the bubble finally burst, the most tragic victims were the small shareholders and many honest employees who had invested their savings, pension rights and lives in the corporation.

Insurance fraud

This is often seen as a 'victimless crime', which is far from the truth. The insurance companies take premiums against underwritten levels of risk and they settle validated claims from their provisioned accounts. If the value of settled claims exceeds the budgeted level, the company will spread the deficit over enhanced premiums for their customers in future years, if the market-place will allow higher premiums to be competitive.

As an example from the 1950s, I personally knew an eccentric lady who habitually burnt a small hole in her living room carpet when she became short of cash, claiming on her insurance for a new one. The insurance company would pay up, never coming to inspect the damage, as coal fires then used gaseous coal and were notorious for spitting out hot embers. The damaged carpet would be patched or rotated so that the offending piece was under some heavy furniture and the payment would supplement the household income. No receipts were demanded, nor were the damaged items taken away.

The coming of VAT and increasing professionalism has largely forced this kind of slack dealing into history, but insurance fraud continues to be attempted, despite the increasing vigilance of the industry in managing their underwritten risk.

Companies, suffering in poor market conditions or through poor management, can be tempted to divest themselves of 'assets' that are neither saleable nor affordable by staging their loss, followed up with a full claim on their insurance.

Insurance companies, whilst having a reputation of paring down their settlements by maximizing the safeguards within the small print of their policy offerings, do have an obligation to settle covered claims unless they can prove fraud. However, insurance is a highly competitive industry and reputation for fair dealing is paramount. The loss adjusters will seek to ensure that claims are met fairly, using specialist investigators where they suspect there may be fraudulent intent. If proved that damage or loss results from a deliberate act of attempted fraud, not only will the insurance company refuse any payment but also they will initiate and support the criminal prosecution of the fraudster.

Perhaps the most famous case in recent decades was that of Lord Brocket, who whilst finding himself desperate for cash to support his ancestral home, could not bring himself to destroy part of his collection of classic vintage cars, so he conspired to have some dismantled and removed whilst reporting them stolen. He claimed £4.5 million before his conscience caused him to withdraw the claim. However, one of his co-conspirators broke ranks and confessed, leaving his Lordship to be prosecuted and imprisoned (Brocket, 2004).

Impersonation and identity theft

Impersonation has been a classic fraud for many hundreds of years. The modern variant in the form of 'identity theft' is dealt with under 'computer-based fraud' below, since such theft through modern impersonation of individuals and companies is largely facilitated by the use of online records and payment transfers.

Impersonation allows the fraudster to act in the persona of the victim, thus gaining control of assets and accounts, including receiving and diverting benefit to third-party accounts from whence the stolen value may be realized. Usually these interim accounts are then closed, leaving a broken trail for those pursuing the assets taken.

In the 18th, 19th and early 20th centuries, impersonating wealthy individuals, perhaps that had recently inherited substantial fortunes, demanded strong nerves, excellent research, intelligence and good acting ability as well as a passable family likeness. In the 21st century, where the fraudster usually never appears in person and misrepresents through the internet using stolen data, is quicker, less skilled and considerably safer.

There do exist elaborate 'long cons' or frauds involving constructing 'stings' to defraud greedy and unscrupulous individuals by meticulously staging scenarios involving impersonators with watertight false backgrounds. They manipulate the target through managed events at which the victim is progressively convinced of a failsafe opportunity for reward, before finally being enticed into parting with substantial assets. The fraudsters then vanish with their gains.

The best protection against this, and many other types of 'con' frauds, is to remember the old adage: 'If it seems too good to be true, it probably is'.

Computer-based fraud

This is a complex area, yet one that is increasing rapidly with the speed and ease of transferring funds around the internet, including between banks and their customers. The ability to do significant research online, with ever increasing access to many registers, census data and searches on individuals, has also facilitated identity theft and impersonation. Identity theft is currently the fastest growing type of fraud in the UK.

It usually results from the targeted theft of card and bank account details, lifted from discarded receipts, letters, cash transaction slips and invoices. Such data may come from fraudulent telephone calls or misrepresentation on the internet. These details, coupled with data gained from easy (largely online) research of public records (electoral lists, central registry records, etc.), allow a fraudster to mimic the original person sufficiently that goods and services can be financed straight out of credit card and bank accounts, whilst loans may be successfully applied for in the name of the victim.

For example, the standard 'security questions' from banks and credit card companies are 'What is your mother's maiden name?' 'What is your date of birth?' 'What is your home telephone number?' These details can be found by searching available registers on the internet, albeit for a small cost in fees. If you have the name and billing address of a cardholder, with these easily secured details, the genuine person can be imitated online to make purchases and even raise loans, the assets being conveniently redirected to a false address or temporary account.

If the target victim's personal email address can be discovered, with the researched personal details in a fraudster's hands, a password will often be obvious from combining names and numbers. With the ability to use the victim's email to subscribe to a credit reference agency online, a victim's total credit details, accounts and record are accessible. With such knowledge major transactions may be initiated.

In some cases, major financial benefit has been achieved through obtaining original signatures from discarded correspondence in waste bins and putting through secured loans on property. Without the ability to act remotely and fast through a computer on the internet, such frauds would carry a high risk of premature detection. Often scheduled to coincide with annual holidays, festive seasons, or where a victim is hospitalized for a long period and daily correspondence is largely 'on hold', the task of short-term impersonation by telephone and over the web is virtually risk-free until it is too late and the perpetrator has vanished with the rewards. Most likely to be targeted on a person rather than a company, but where a person is also a key member of a company team, such frauds may be successful in extracting value from an organization.

The best prevention against identity theft is to ensure that absolutely *no* sensitive information is discarded unshredded, that passwords are truly unguessable and that key accounts and email, telephone and all postal traffic is checked daily. Some more imaginative 'security details' by institutions would help too, such that the information is not a matter of public record.

Computer-based fraud sometimes involves the illicit programming of systems for reward.

A somewhat ancient example of this some 35 years ago involved a specialist in a consultancy who was an accomplished systems innovator. One morning the police quietly arrested him. He was sentenced to a few years' imprisonment for efficiently making money from randomly selected batches of bank transfers being cleared. He had inserted a randomizing routine in the control software (written in assembler code and Fortran) which, when triggered, would select a batch of payments a few seconds before midnight, adjust the electronic timestamp to indicate that the date of processing was the next day, thus post-dating the transaction. In those days of batch processing, interest on money in transfer between accounts was credited to the banks undertaking the clearance. By falsely adjusting the transfer records, all parties to each transfer in the batch *assumed* that the batch had been processed on a different day, the other party benefiting from the interest. The 'ghost' day's interest on a batch was actually diverted by the software to a suspense account which in turn was ultimately transmitted to a falsely named account, implying ownership by a private merchant bank. From this account, regular cash withdrawals were made and funds transferred to an overseas account. These days, security surrounding BACS

(Bankers Automated Clearance Services) would never allow any party to prosper in this way and indeed the whole basis of monetary transfer has changed since those very early days of computerized bank clearance.

This individual was caught mainly because his lifestyle was not supported by his stated income on Inland Revenue records. Suspicion, given his work on the clearing banks' software, started an investigation that lead to his discovery and arrest. At the time this was hailed as a clever 'victimless crime' as neither party realized that they had lost anything.

The modern explosion in computer-based fraud is a reincarnation of many of the oldest classical scams now powered by the speed of internet transactions.

Apart from identity theft, the main computer-based frauds are variants of the following:

- Illegal access to company or private data through hacking into systems and extracting value through intellectual property, commercially sensitive data or creating transactions to the benefit of the fraudulent intruder. Most of the asset theft described earlier can be facilitated by successfully gaining unauthorized access to computers supporting a company or individual. Ghost transactions, phantom employees and amendment of records to cover losses are possible, as are the bypassing of many standard cross-referencing systems that are designed to flag up discrepancies. The increasing use of 'secure' systems, firewalls, 'anti-spyware' and antivirus software, even on domestic systems, is having a favourable effect. That said, a professional hacker would still be likely to gain access to any normal commercial or personal system without undue difficulty. The best deterrent is to ensure that virus and security software is kept updated and run regularly across all files stored on a computer and that particularly spyware and key-logging software (which records and transmits key strokes to a third party) is detected and deleted. A firewall is essential if use of the internet is a regular feature of computer usage.
- Credit card and charge card scams are dealt with below, but the ability to make illegal transactions on the internet using just the number, expiry date and signature strip digits, coupled with the name and address of the account holder, can be quite straightforward given even a transient sight of the card (e.g. by a worker in a restaurant, pub or club) and some simple research already described above.

Credit card fraud

This comes in many forms. For example, one new scam involves a bogus 'company' setting up a website then taking the first 6 digits of the 16-digit card number (that identifies the bank, type of card and country) and then randomly assembling the last 10 numbers using a personal computer attached to high-speed broadband, using likely groupings of numbers. Transactions are initiated, targeting platinum and gold cards where high value transactions and credit limits are more commonplace. Most cardholders only realize there is a charge that is unfounded when their statement arrives (if then), by which time the fraudsters have removed their site and moved to another internet service provider (ISP), effectively vanishing. The banks are now beginning to trace such frauds with the cooperation of the ISPs that unwittingly host these sites.

Of course, better known are the many and various methods to steal and clone genuine cards for short-term gain. The present use of 'chip and pin' cards should make the fraudulent use of cards less attractive where there is an increased risk of being detected whilst using the stolen or cloned card. However, there are reports that thieves are already breaching this security by spying on card pin entry before stealing the card or by disabling the chip so that the more easily created magnetic backup strip takes over. In the meantime identity theft and fraudulent 'card holder not present' online transactions are increasing.

Investment fraud

This is a variant of trading fraud where highly attractive shares are offered, promising massive return on investment through dividends and enhanced share valuation. Usually backed by 'expert' evidence, these ventures purport to be solid and safe. It is rare, but not a new fraud.

In the last 200 years there have been several major frauds whereby the evidence to back 'get-rich-quick' claims has been manufactured from the outset. As shares were sold and word spread, the pressure for buying a share of the 'certain' riches raised the share value rapidly, leading many to overextend themselves to gain a part of the profit. Then, after a frenetic period of growth, the sponsors of the company vanish with the rewards, leaving the unfortunate servants of the company to deal with the often newly bankrupt owners of now worthless stock.

The 'South Sea Bubble' scam ruined many, whilst in the 1990s the Bre-Ex mining scandal broke after investors in a 'proven' rich goldfield in Indonesia discovered that the prospect samples had been deliberately falsified. The short-lived boom in stock values hugely benefited a few whilst many lost a fortune. The expert who had vouched for the value of the deposits fell from an aircraft to his death as the scheme collapsed.

Before concluding this section on the types of fraud, it must be remembered that the ideal fraud is one that secures a high return to the fraudster for a manageable amount of risk. The ultimately 'perfect' fraud is therefore one in which the victim doesn't know they have lost anything, at least for a considerable interval, therefore allowing the system used to defraud the company or individual to continue.

Fraud, a victimless crime?

With almost all fraud, there is an obvious loser. For example, with insurance fraud, the initial loser is the insurance company who will be forced to pay out a settlement sum unless the cause of the claim is proven to be outside the contract of insurance. The ultimate losers are the honest policyholders who pay increased premiums on renewal and the company who may lose a competitive edge in trading and reputation if the losses are large.

With false accounting fraud and asset loss through fraud, the situation may be hidden for a time, allowing the fraudster to plan his 'exit strategy'. In some cases, systemic fraud involving semi-automated processing by computers may continue to cause loss until some unrelated issue leads to discovery. Here the losers are the company owners or the employees who may lose bonus payments and job security.

Therefore fraud is *not* a victimless crime and often, as with Enron, the victims of company fraud will be people who lose their financial security through no fault of their own. Whether individuals or companies, beyond the financial assets lost, the cost in terms of stress, damaged health, relationships and quality of life is often immeasurable.

Exposing a fraud problem

The sad probability is that, at some level, most organizations have a fraud problem. The following are the most significant *indicators of fraud*:

- Instinct or 'sixth sense'. Particularly in small- to medium-sized businesses, where the cash flow, ongoing costs and rates of return on investment are intimately understood by members of the management team, any anomaly should trigger a suspicion that 'not all is as expected'. It is essential that any discrepancy be thoroughly checked until the reasons are understood. Even if not caused by illegal activity, it is probable that affected procedures and practices can be tightened as a result.

- A shortfall against profit expectation in a particular period whilst turnover, costs and revenue seem on or above target. This is a common sign of financial leakage, asset theft or possibly fraudulent trading. Indeed, one of the objectives of fraudsters is to cover their tracks by false accounting, so that their scam is able to continue for longer. Careful checking of actual cash and bank statements, including unannounced stocktaking of assets and reconciling cash flow against the book records, may find the only indicator in a carefully constructed fraud.

- Specific behavioural indicators by one or more staff members, particularly where their role offers fraud opportunity through access or authority abuse.

  These include:

  - Noting any employee who has a pattern of work that shows 'ultra-dedication' to a particular role. Such staff will regularly be first into work and probably last to leave; be rarely sick; tend to waive holiday entitlement and be reluctant to accept promotion where that would mean changing activities, locations, routine access to systems or authority for certain functions. A marked reluctance to delegate is another a key pointer justifying further checking.
  - Through line management, other staff and HR, be vigilant for significant lifestyle upgrades. Be aware of employees who are known to be in difficulty through debt problems, addiction to gambling, drinking or drug usage, especially who suddenly seem to have money available. Carefully ascertain where the apparent wealth has come from – it may be genuine! However, do not ignore the potential risk and run an opportunity assessment to identify the extent and area of any possible fraud that this individual might be benefiting from.
  - Be wary of new staff in sensitive positions who suddenly resign. Check their external relationships and dealings with suppliers or subcontractors. Covertly inspect their work records

and access to systems, preferably whilst they are still working notice.
- ○ Beware of any incidence of a supplier or subcontractor insisting on dealing with one particular member of staff, or any such internal preference being expressed between departments.
- ○ Watch for any employee who has an excessive disdain of security controls, procedures or system safeguards, especially where a constant complainer and unusually cynical.
- ○ Pick up any sign of an employee who, despite not having a high-pressure role, appears to be stressed 'without cause'.

It should be remembered that there are many staff members at all levels in most British companies who work extraordinary hours and put their job before many other personal priorities. It therefore becomes essential to evaluate such risk sensitively and usually covertly to avoid any prejudice or premature accusation until the evidence is obtained that proves the guilt of the person beyond any reasonable doubt.

- Be aware of any cause for concern within the company by stepping back and realistically checking for examples of 'slackness' in operating key processes or uncomfortable characteristics in management style.

  These may include:

  - ○ Gaps in accounting records, absent management accounts, poor controls on expenditure including cheque control, statement reconciliation and movements between the company's accounts. Absence of controls and effective audit trails.
  - ○ High stock levels with low turnover of stock, but with an increasing or disproportionately high activity in invoicing against the relatively static stock.
  - ○ Instability in the internal financial audit team combined with complacent external auditors.
  - ○ Follow up any instance of incomplete checks on new staff before granting access to systems, procedures and working practices.
  - ○ Beware of unusual areas of 'secrecy' relating to specific contracts, customers or supplier agreements that exceed the need for normal commercial confidence.
  - ○ Pick up any slackness in accepting photocopies rather than insisting on prime documents in authority process chains.

- Any unresolved lack of balance in accounts, or excessive adjustments and exceptional items to achieve balance.
- Any identified large payments to individuals or 'ghost' employees on payroll.
- Any identified instance of normal and proven controls or process being overridden by management.
- Avoiding approval thresholds by splitting up contracted work into packages in order to reduce approval level for business authorization.
- Poor support for internal audit by senior management. Withholding from the audit team of the necessary independence and authority to probe.
- Poor corporate governance implemented and/or weakly practised.

The chapter to this point has studied modern fraud and shown why it is so important to respond to the threat to both companies and individuals. Having described the problem, it is now possible to turn to its solution.

Essentially, as with any form of threat or risk, it is important to approach the issue in a sensible, orderly and professional manner. The methods adopted for successfully assessing and managing fraud risk are based on the well-honed cyclic risk management model familiar to most risk managers.

The remainder of this chapter is devoted to the management, reduction and potential elimination of fraud risk in an organization.

Fraud risk management

There is a clear distinction between the establishment of a process that will facilitate protection against fraud *and* the handling of specific cases of suspected fraud to eliminate further loss and to maximize recovery. Both facets of fraud risk management are important.

Operating a process that protects by making fraud less likely to succeed and to maximize early detection whilst not inhibiting the flow of the business is essential. On discovering fraudulent activity it is equally important to professionally manage the situation, ensuring that the suspected parties are prevented from inflicting further damage whilst evidence is gathered and assessed, ultimately achieving a beneficial outcome for the company.

The creation of a viable fraud risk management process includes thorough vulnerability assessment, effective preventive activity and management of identified fraud risk in a cyclic Fraud Risk Management Plan (FRMP).

In parallel the policy is prepared for handling identified fraud to achieve the optimal result for the business. The basis for enacting this policy is a Fraud Response Plan, understood by each line manager in the organization.

Taking as an example the preparation necessary for a company where little fraud protection is in place, working through each stage to achieve a viable fraud risk management and fraud response plan, most of the principles are in common with standard business risk management. However, as already indicated, fraud risk management has the additional need for high security, secrecy and meticulous care in dealing with each potential risk and every discovered case of suspected fraud.

There are specialist fraud risk service companies in the field, for organizations that wish to either import the skills or outsource the whole task. That said, most companies first wish to establish if they have a problem and, mindful of the adverse effect on confidence of any unwanted publicity, initially keep their response in house.

A summary of a typical fraud risk management process is shown in Figure 13.1.

The following sections address each of the process components illustrated in the diagram in turn.

Preparation

Establish a *fraud risk 'owner'* in the organization. This will often be a delegate of the chief accounting officer, finance director or equivalent. They should have all necessary authority and access to the company CEO, the audit committee (where present) or owners of the business.

It is essential that the management of fraud risk is a recognized responsibility of a senior accountable manager with appropriate personal attributes and positioning. As examples, in two multinational companies where the process has been implemented, one fraud risk owner is the corporate security manager, and in the other is the head of internal audit. Both report to the director of finance, with formal access and direct reporting lines to the audit committee, CEO and chairman.

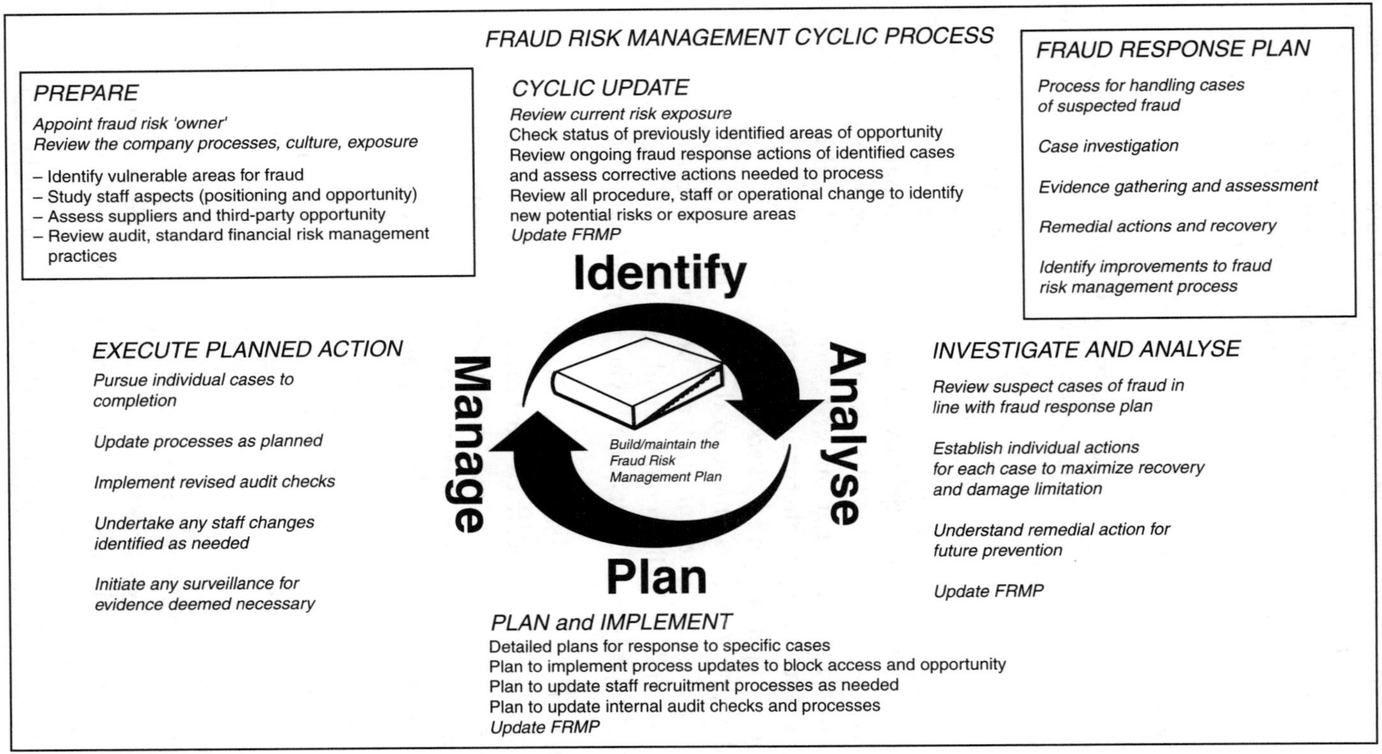

Figure 13.1 A schematic overview of the cyclic Fraud Risk Management Plan

Once an owner for fraud risk is appointed, a statement of the *company policy on fraud* should be produced and published internally. How this is done will depend on the morale, size and culture of the company, the objective being to achieve acceptance without demotivating or offending the majority of staff who would never consider committing fraud.

The policy should cover:

- a clear statement of the perceived fraud threat to the business, justifying a zero tolerance approach that will seek to protect the company and staff;
- stating that every employee, whether management or staff, has an obligation of trust to the company neither to commit any act of fraud nor to tolerate any fraudulent act by another person. The channel for any 'whistle-blower' or 'hotline' initiative should be advised where supported by the company senior management;
- identity of the senior manager responsible for fraud risk management and offering alternative contact points for questions or concerns (perhaps in HR/Personnel);
- making a closing statement to the effect that it is recognized that only a tiny minority of staff are potentially dishonest and even fewer would actually commit fraud, but that the policy is essential to safeguard the interests of all who play by the rules.

A confidential *fraud response plan* should be agreed, usually by the chairman, CEO and executive board directors, and promulgated to *just* those senior managers who need to know how to respond in the event that a suspected fraud is reported.

The contents of a fraud response plan should include:

- The process for reporting a suspected fraud. In most cases the perpetrator will be unaware of any suspicion and it is recommended that the process specifically ensure that senior management and appropriate line managers are briefed only on a 'need to know' basis.

  This is for a number of reasons:
  - The suspected person may be innocent. The situation of the suspect could become untenable if concerns were generally known.
  - Evidence is easier to collect when a fraudster believes they are in the clear.

  - By not unnecessarily alerting those around the suspect, including management, it lessens any damage should the suspect prove innocent; and it prevents alerting any of the suspect's colleagues or management in the event that they are accomplices.
- Process for formal logging of the basis for suspicion. Within a short time of a case breaking, the appointed fraud risk owner should review the facts together with the senior manager ultimately responsible for the employee(s) suspected, the organization's security manager and allow interviews (where appropriate) of the source(s) of the allegation. Actions to provide evidence will follow.
- The creation of the *FRMP* by a process of detailed vulnerability assessment (see below) supplemented by extraction of risk data from each discovered case of fraud, updating the FRMP accordingly.

An assessment of the organization's vulnerability to fraud should be undertaken as a matter of urgency, concurrently with the creation of the statement of policy and the fraud response plan. This will identify the exposure to fraud to form a starting point for detailed risk assessment. It will categorize key areas of concern within the FRMP.

The methods favoured for the initial vulnerability assessment are:

- Consider who could be targeting the company. Are they customers, suppliers, criminals, competitors or employees?
- A series of facilitated fraud risk workshops, attended by the management who really understand the company processes, staffing profiles and have access to specific staff files, IT access policy, procurement practice and asset management. This leads to workshop outputs including:
  - ranking of areas where fraud risk is highest;
  - identifying any specific processes that are vulnerable to fraud;
  - mapping sensitive processes against key trusted staff;
  - noting any concerns or suspicions voiced in the workshop for later follow up;
  - update of the FRMP.
- For each area of fraud risk, vulnerable process and concern identified from the workshops: assess the key drivers of the risk (i.e. the prime root cause(s) of the risk) and establish a plan and actions for refining and countering the risk threat. This detail should be entered into the FRMP.

From this preparation, the workshops, assessment reviews and discussions, the FRMP will emerge as a partially populated risk management plan. The FRMP has to be a highly secure document for the eyes of very few within the company, as it will inevitably detail vulnerable processes, staff positions, external transaction areas and suspect third-party companies and staff. It will also require consideration to ensure conformation to the Data Protection Act 1998, as access must be highly restricted. In all other respects, the FRMP is the equivalent of the normal Risk Management Plan as commended for every project or major operation, and which should be regularly reviewed, managed, updated and *acted upon*!

The format of the FRMP will vary greatly from company to company, but the content will in some form usually include the elements summarized in Table 13.1.

The cyclic Fraud Risk Management Plan (Figure 13.1)

The preparation stage will have resulted in the FRMP being populated by those areas of exposure identified by the vulnerability assessment. The FRMP will also contain any suspected fraud cases that are ongoing, including the analysis of how the frauds were perpetrated and any weaknesses in processes exposed.

In conventional risk management, the risk plan would be built and maintained with regular review of ongoing risk status being undertaken across the whole plan. With fraud risk, each element of the plan needs to be reviewed and updated on a 'case-by-case' or 'risk-by-risk' basis. However, at least quarterly the whole plan should be overviewed at an appropriate level to ensure no item is being left behind and that the overall priority assessment is still valid.

Cyclic Fraud Risk Management Plan update review phase

The accountable 'fraud risk owner' in the organization will normally appoint a company fraud risk manager who is one of the very few people to have access to the entirety of the FRMP. This appointee will prepare a shortlist of FRMP entries to be reviewed by a small panel of senior managers or their delegates, each entry being presented by the named owner for that risk.

The review panel will:

- be briefed on the status of the fraud risk plan entry, summarizing any key aspects that have emerged since the last review;
- check that all actions have been progressed and be updated on the current status;

Table 13.1 Sample FRMP content

FRMP entry	*Details of entry content*
FRMP reference	It is essential that entries in the plan have a reference that allows each incidence of suspected or potential fraud to be identified uniquely, linked to other cases as needed.
FRMP date	This is the date that the first entry for this risk or fraud was made in the plan.
Summary of the fraud risk or case	A narrative providing an overview of the actual or potential fraud, together with any identified gaps in procedures that may facilitate fraud to be committed.
Sources of information	The source of the fraud intelligence including any original statements.
Status	The current point to which the fraud risk has been investigated and remedied.
Priority	Usually one of 'low', 'moderate', 'high' or 'immediate' values. Depends on a realistic assessment of the threat level to the company. This value is normally a product of assessing impact and probability (see below).
Probability	Of the fraud occurring, continuing or repeating, assessed from the evidence and usually with values of 'low', 'moderate' or 'high'.
Impact	An assessment of the damage the potential or active fraud can do to the business. It should be remembered that a high impact risk, even with low probability, cannot be ignored, since if that risk triggers, the consequences of the fraud could be grave.
Actions	The summary schedule of the outstanding actions, with cross references to detailed action files.
Evidence	Summary of evidence with cross-reference to detailed files.
Fraud loss	An actual or estimated figure of losses on this fraud to date, and/or an estimate of potential losses from risk identified in vulnerability study.
Review date	The next scheduled FRMP review date for this item in the plan.

- receive any new information relating to the case represented by the entry;
- discuss and decide on the action required to remedy any fraud exposed;
- identify any secondary or further risk that arises from the analysis work undertaken;
- update the FRMP and set the next review date for that risk entry in the plan.

Cyclic investigation and analysis phase

Throughout the cycle, following the formal FRMP review, each case will be progressed according to the priority assigned. Usually one investigator or auditor, mindful of the need for security and gathering evidence, will execute the assigned actions on several cases or risk exposures reviewed. Urgent decisions will be referred to the review panel handling the case or threat, as they are already briefed. All progress, issues, decisions and events will be updated in the FRMP.

A vital part of this phase of the cycle is to identify any necessary change to processes to safeguard the company, or identify any individual who appears to be placed to act fraudulently due to the absence of independent controls.

It may be possible to effect a remedy quickly whilst within the cycle, this being agreed, authorized and executed pending FRMP update at the next due review date.

It may be that new evidence emerges of an ongoing fraud during this phase of the cycle, in which case the Fraud Response Plan will ensure that the appropriate actions are taken to set up the entry in the FRMP and manage the ongoing situation.

Cyclic planning and implementation phase

From the analysis work on each fraud risk, draft procedural change documents should be drawn up to remedy any identified weakness. In practice, these procedural changes have to be carefully planned and agreed with the process owners to ensure that the changes will not be in conflict. Most organizations, especially those conforming to corporate governance standards, will operate a process change control panel or equivalent. Where the reason for change relates to fraud prevention, the change validation and agreement work need not disclose that the processes are being updated for security purposes.

Cyclic plan execution phase

This last phase of the risk management plan cycle executes the agreed actions from the last review, introduces changed processes with the help of process owners, introduces any required training for those affected and initiates the agreed case actions to close off specific fraudulent acts.

At the end of this period, the next review phase will take place and the cycle begins again, each FRMP entry continuing until the associated fraud risk is closed.

The above, whilst being a generalized summary of a fraud risk management process, shows how a basic fraud risk management approach can work in most organizations. When reading this it is the principle that matters, rather than the detailed process, since that will (and should) vary from one company to the next.

Handling third-party fraud

This chapter has so far discussed the concept and reality of fraud perpetrated within a company by dishonest employees, usually alone but perhaps with a few colleagues. Where fraud is well planned to operate between companies it is more serious and difficult to isolate and remedy.

Where a company is externally targeted, it is often through a weakness in outwardly facing processes. It may be an inside fraud insomuch that one employee spots the opportunity and engages assistance from others outside the company to operate the fraud.

So, as an example of such a fraud, the following is an overview of a complex case, presenting just the key fraud points to show the way it worked and how it was countered.

This actual case involved conspirators in two companies, one a manufacturer buying in components and the other a company making and supplying these specialist products.

The manufacturing company had been trading with the supplier for over 10 years in a sound relationship. It was in a period of growth and fully expected that the annual profits would be proportionately increased. They were not.

The management undertook a detailed check on some suspect areas, seeking anomalies in the accounts rather than malpractice. Some minor errors in recording stock movements were noted, but nothing that could account for the level of losses suspected.

A classic vulnerability study was undertaken, which looked at:

- areas of operations where assets were handled, together with processes for recording movements;
- revenue processes, ordering, goods received, invoicing, follow-up and payment, bought and sold ledger entries;
- an analysis of departmental and trading accounts to understand where the greatest differentials between budget and actual figures existed;

- 'finished goods' and 'component' stores control processes and records;
- staff changes and movements over three years.

From the above, a FRMP was built, focusing on the supplier's data and invoice/payment patterns. Staff movements were also analysed.

Sufficient evidence emerged to create concern that there might be fraud operating within the company. This included employees in sensitive and directly relevant roles who were rarely absent, identifying that processes for accepting goods received and authority to pay invoices were weak and spotting that no overall stocktake had occurred for some years as reliance had been on a rolling stock check programme.

A review meeting on the FRMP decided to authorize a sudden unannounced total stocktake using a specialist team of external auditors over a four-day Easter weekend. Only the warehouse manager and the senior management team were aware of the audit. In parallel with this the company security team started a low profile investigation on the lifestyle of the authorized signatories and the store assistant. References and background checks were reviewed and revalidated for the newest recruits. The place of work of family members was established by local investigation. The European Convention on Human Rights is likely to make more difficult some aspects of such surveillance, whilst the Freedom of Information Act 2000 has tended to put more information into the public domain.

The outcome of this work was that significant discrepancies existed in the stock levels of components delivered by the supplier according to the goods received documents and the actual stock in the warehouse. However, invoices had been received from the supplier in line with goods received notes and had been paid to the supplier by cheque.

Further enquiries showed that the wife of one of the authorizing managers was working in her maiden name in the supplier as an account manager with authority to service orders from the manufacturing company. She also managed the invoicing, and was able to cancel orders and apply credit notes, preventing follow-up for unreceived payments. Whilst the relevant transactions had been deleted, security copies had been stored on backup data files.

It was found that payment cheques were being routinely intercepted after printing and removed. The supplier, being a small family company, carried the family name, suffixed by 'Ltd'. The supplier's database in the manufacturer had been changed so that cheques would omit the 'Ltd'. A personal account had been opened 18 months before in that name at a London branch of a high street bank, using the address of the couple's home.

Five people were in the conspiracy to defraud the manufacturer; the employee husband, his wife in the supplier, the stores assistant in the manufacturer, a clerk handling the printed cheques and a never discovered IT person who had amended the database using a privileged password.

In any fraud, once discovered and proved internally, the most difficult decision is to address the minimization of damage, whilst punishing those involved. Where more than one company is involved, that decision involves more parties, as it is necessary to synchronize the action taken.

The considerations are:

- the risk of loss of reputation in the market-place, since defrauded companies are often seen as inefficient;
- managing the employee morale such that the outcome is at least neutral, and even positive;
- the need for recovery of the lost financial assets. Once the police are called in, it is normally their priority to prosecute and achieve a conviction, not to recover the stolen funds.

In this case the police were asked to review the final stages of the analysis and to ensure that there was sufficient evidence before confronting the four known parties to the fraud. In fact, the four fraudsters readily admitted the scam once faced with the evidence, and to gain mitigation in sentencing against a guilty plea, agreed to return goods and assets worth around 90 per cent of the money defrauded. They received short and suspended prison sentences in return.

Both companies introduced new practices, which would make any repeat of the fraud unlikely to prosper.

A number of points arise from this example and are worth considering.

Cooperation of third parties

This cannot be relied upon and for commercial reasons it is very hard to request unless, as in this case, the relationship is very strong. Where a fraud involves a number of organizations, the most likely course of action to achieve success would be to learn as much as possible about the in-house fraud and find enough evidence to support the involvement of the other parties. At that point, convening a meeting of representatives of each company would usually yield a positive result, but may threaten the desire to keep the issue private until all evidence is analysed.

The police can open doors (for example, gain details of bank transactions and telephone call logs) but perform best from a body of good evidence that has already been gathered.

Keeping the fraud in-house

In many cases the fraud could be dealt with and stopped using internal disciplinary action, and not pursuing the criminal act in the public courts. Whilst this minimizes the major damage associated with reputation risk and may make voluntary recovery of lost assets more likely, it does leave the perpetrators unpunished in law and therefore without a criminal record. This may help them to do it all over again somewhere else.

Unpalatable though adverse publicity is, the prosecution of such people is the only way to avoid the risk of virtually becoming an associate in the fraud by suppressing the information.

Whistle-blowers

It is necessary to consider the issue of handling 'whistle-blowers' (staff who feel that management should know about activity that is not legitimate). Companies should, within their fraud policy, offer a secure and sometimes anonymous conduit for reporting any issue to the company. A majority of all employees are honest, hardworking staff and management who may have profit-related bonus prospects. If they discover a suspicious activity, then by offering a way of passing on their concern, it may lead to a major saving to the company. Sometimes reward for information that is subsequently shown to be valuable is offered as an inducement.

Summary

This chapter has outlined an effective process for cyclic fraud risk management, which relies on the trust and integrity of a few of the senior management team in a company. Fortunately it is very unusual for those in the top management of a company to become embroiled in fraud.

In recent years the greed (and ultimately desperation) displayed by a few executives in engineering corporate conspiracies to defraud their owners (their shareholders) by collusion with their bankers, external auditors and chosen senior employees has acquired infamy, ruining thousands of innocent lives. This risk (very low probability – hugely high impact) makes the operation of independent internal audit committees and external audit companies an important safeguard. With increasing focus on corporate governance and the need to ensure that the true value of a company is fairly stated in the market, it is perhaps a little surprising that fraud risk management remains the poor relation in so many UK companies.

References and recommended reading

Association of Accounting Technicians (updated 2003) *Fighting Fraud Guide*. Available at: http://www.aat.co.uk/docs/members/Guidance_notes_Fighting_fraud.pdf

Brocket, Lord (2004) *Call Me Charlie*. London: Simon & Schuster.

Council of Europe (1950) Convention for the Protection of Human Rights and Fundamental Freedoms, as amended by Protocol No. 11 [European Convention on Human Rights]. Rome. Available at: http://conventions.coe.int/treaty/en/Treaties/Html/005.htm

Department of Trade and Industry (2005) *Operating and Financial Review*. See http://www.dti.gov.uk/cld/financialreview.htm for details of current passage through Parliament into full legislation.

Fennelly, Richard (ed.) (2003) *Managing the Risk of Fraud*. London: HM Treasury. Available at: http://www.hm-treasury.gov.uk/media/42E/E2/Managing_the_risk_fraud.pdf

Great Britain (1998) Data Protection Act 1998. London: The Stationery Office.

Great Britain (2000) Freedom of Information Act 2000. London: The Stationery Office.

14

Counter-terrorism Risk Management

Richard Flynn

Risk and terrorism

There can be little doubt that terrorism and the consequences of protecting against it have affected many people's lives. Baggage checks at airports, security announcements at stations or counter-terrorism posters on buses: all act as reminders of the risks from terrorism and its continuous presence in our environment. In considering risk and terrorism definitions are of vital importance, although it is often difficult to obtain a consensus as to the meaning of the terms.

Any analysis of the concept of risk will quickly demonstrate that there are a multitude of approaches, both practical and theoretical to understanding risk. Renn (1998, p 50) notes that 'Talking about risks faces the immediate danger that everybody talks about something different. There is no commonly accepted definition for the term risk – neither in the sciences nor in the public understanding.' Although there is no internationally agreed definition of terrorism – notwithstanding a practical legal definition – this has not prevented effective action being taken and risks identified and managed. The commentators on risk, Douglas and Wildavsky (1983, p 1), have said: 'Can we know the risks we face, now or in the future? No, we cannot: but yes, we must act as if we do.' Although perhaps overstating the case it does represent a fundamental issue in the field of risk. Both natural and man-made risks require a response as part of our ability to survive. In fact, responding to a risk without a full understanding of its nature occurs frequently as a practical necessity.

Uncertainty and terrorism

Risk can be described generically as 'decision-making under uncertainty'. However, Ritchie and Marshall (1993, p 120) say: 'We think it useful to start with a statement of the blindingly obvious, viz, uncertainty is the opposite of certainty.' The statement although obvious is in fact more complicated than it first appears.

Certainty can be said to occur when a consequence can be unambiguously predicted to follow a specified event. The complication occurs with the meaning of uncertainty. Uncertainty is said to occur where the decision-maker has less than complete knowledge or information about a situation, and the consequences that result from such a decision made under such circumstances. In reality, decisions under uncertainty are made every day, but there are two types of uncertainty which are different. They are aleatoric uncertainty and epistemic uncertainty.

Aleatoric uncertainty arises from situations of pure chance, such as the rolling of a die where *ceteris paribus* the outcomes would be truly random. Epistemic uncertainty occurs where a problem needs to be resolved by the exercise of judgement. It is this second type of uncertainty with which this chapter will be concerned.

When looking to manage the risks posed by terrorism we are not simply dealing with random or pure chance events. If decision-makers in the real world were faced with complete uncertainty, they would be effectively powerless. However, expertise and understanding of terrorists and terrorism can be developed, thereby reducing epistemic uncertainty and increasing the ability to predict.

When there is significant epistemic uncertainty there is an increased requirement for effective information processing by the decision-makers. This may include using technology such as computer modelling, or involving groups of people (expert or otherwise) to express an opinion about the problem. Surowiecki (2005) has recently argued that perhaps people are programmed to be collectively smart, and that with large groups of non-experts, which exhibit four crucial characteristics, they can on average produce better decisions than expert groups. He argues that there are four conditions which need to be present for groups to be characterized as wise crowds. These conditions are:

- Diversity of opinion – each person should have some private information available to them. This is akin to the concept of subjective probability (see below).
- Independence – each person's opinion is not determined by those around them.

- Decentralization – each person is able to draw on their own local knowledge and has the ability to specialize.
- Aggregation – there must be a mechanism available to the crowd to translate private judgements into collective decisions.

When these conditions are met then it is likely that the group's decision will be accurate.

Ritchie and Marshall (1993, p 122) observe that in situations where the level of knowledge of outcomes and the mechanisms that produce them is incomplete, estimates are likely to be based upon subjective probabilities. A subjective probability is based on a personal judgement of the nature of the outcomes with the likelihood of their occurrence. They note that subjective probability will be based upon:

- the available information;
- the person's previous experience; and
- each person's cognitive functions, which synthesize both into a hopefully realistic future scenario.

The analysis of intelligence is very much within this category where the police and security services around the world have to constantly interpret and make judgements on the intentions and capabilities of terrorists, using all the resources highlighted by Ritchie and Marshall.

Risk and uncertainty

Frank Knight in 1921 first fully examined the distinction between risk and uncertainty. Knight believed that risk was measurable. The process of measuring risk is mediated by the theory of probability, which Knight believed could be determined in two ways. The first is an *a priori* probability of various outcomes. This approach works best in a closed system, for instance in games of chance such as poker or roulette where the probabilities are known, and it is simply a matter of mathematics. According to the father of modern probability theory, Jacques Bernoulli (1713), over time – in some cases a long time – the outcomes of an event will generally conform to *a priori* probabilities. This is known as the 'law of large numbers'. This method of calculating probabilities involves the collection and analysis of data over an extended period of time, which is not necessarily the most efficient way to reach decisions in the real world.

Alas, the reality of the world does not allow us to calculate accurately *a priori* outcomes in such a manner as events may be influenced in ways that are not always apparent. For example, cheating or the application of skill and knowledge can affect an outcome. We cannot rely upon simple *a priori* mathematical certainty when making decisions about risk events. As Boyne notes: 'What we can be clear about now is that there is no single purely mathematical route to the essence of risk. In even the simplest of cases, rationality and culture will mutually inform and deform each other.' (Boyne, 2003, p 6). A situation that led Knight to note: 'The business man himself merely forms the best estimate he can of the outcomes of his actions . . . ' (Knight, 1921, p 227).

Having considered the nature of uncertainty it is now necessary to consider the nature of terrorism.

What is terrorism?

To achieve an agreed definition of what constitutes risk is an enormously complex issue; risk like terrorism is a relative rather than absolute term, and its meaning is dependent upon context (Crenshaw, 1995). The modern view of terrorism is closely linked to an evolving understanding of other sources of risk that has occurred over the last 200 years, although terrorism has a longer history.

Terrorism is not a purely modern phenomenon; it has a long history dating from biblical times. The conquest of Canaan and the total destruction of the city of Hazor, where no one was spared from the sword and the city was razed to the ground, is cited as an example of the use of terror to subdue an enemy. In New Testament times the Zealots – a group of fiercely patriotic Jewish fighters opposing the occupying Romans in Judea – attacked both Romans and those in the Jewish establishment who supported the Roman occupation (Martin, 2003). Indeed, we still use the term 'Zealot' today to describe someone who is seen as an enthusiastic or excessively enthusiastic supporter of a cause or person.

It was around the time of the French Revolution that the term 'terrorism' began to be used in a context that is closer to our understanding of what we mean by terrorism today. Edmund Burke, the British philosopher, coined the term *terrorism* using it to describe the *regime de la terreur,* which was effectively state terrorism in furtherance of the revolutionary ideology of the French Republic. There is a vigorous ongoing debate about the nature of state terrorism and its relationship to more 'traditional' terrorism. State terrorism will not be considered in this chapter and the interested reader is referred to Schweitzer and Shay (2003).

Interestingly, during the same century as the French Revolution the word 'risk' began to find currency in English and there occurred a change in the meaning of the word. Lupton (1999) views the change as occurring with the emergence of modernity, beginning in the 18th century and evolving over the next 200 years. Using Giddens' definition of modernity: 'the institutions and modes of behaviour established in post-feudal Europe, but which in the twentieth century increasingly have become world-historical in their impact' (Giddens, 1991, p 14) – Lupton identifies that the meaning of risk widened from providence mediated through natural phenomena to events where the consequences of human decisions, both rational and otherwise, carried dangers to other individuals or groups. Consequently the concept of risk became one where ideology, politics and organizations themselves became sources of risk, and where outcomes were the consequence of human action rather than 'expressing the hidden meanings of nature or ineffable intentions of the Deity' (Giddens, 1990, p 30). This has led, in the modern era, to populations being terrorized in the pursuit of political, ideological or religious causes. It has been described as the new terrorism and is characterized by:

- loose cell-based networks;
- potential acquisition of weapons of mass destruction;
- politically vague, religious or mystical motivations;
- asymmetrical methods – these are methods of conflict that do not use previously accepted or predictable rules of engagement.

This is in contrast to the characteristics of traditional terrorism, which are (Martin, 2003, p 5):

- clearly identifiable organizations or movements;
- explicit grievances championing specific classes or ethno-national groups;
- relatively 'surgical' in their selection of targets.

However, these are descriptions of terrorism and not definitions. Terrorism is an emotive term and often applied, sometimes indiscriminately, by different interested parties in any situation where violence has been used. The phrase 'one man's terrorist is another man's freedom fighter' is often cited and neatly encapsulates the relativity around the term. This relativity in terminology requires that we move away from expedient and often politically motivated labelling, to analysing what we mean by terrorism. Can there be criteria that can be used to judge whether an act is one of terrorism? Crenshaw (1995) argues that we need to transform 'terrorism' into a useful analytical tool rather than simply a polemical one.

As with the defining of risk, there are many definitions of terrorism. Although estimates vary, the most exhaustive survey in this area cites over one hundred definitions of terrorism (Scmid and Jorgman, 1998). Any analysis of terrorism if it is to fulfil Crenshaw's aspiration must be able to:

- identify the core characteristics that make an act one of terrorism;
- distinguish terrorists from freedom fighters or guerrillas.

In relation to the first criterion, Martin (2003, p 6) argues that the layperson's understanding of what it means would probably include the following:

- politically motivated violence ...
- usually directed against soft targets ...
- with an intention to affect (terrorize) a target audience.

This reflects a reasonable attempt to map a layperson's understanding of what we mean by terrorism. Unfortunately, the issues that lay behind the defining of the term are far more complicated. As Whittaker (2004) points out, even today we do not have an acceptable international definition of terrorism, although international law places a duty upon the state to prevent, within its own borders, political terrorist activities being directed against another independent state. Indeed, there is a long history of international conventions and declarations against terrorism, going back to the 1937 League of Nations Convention for the Repression of International Terrorism (League of Nations, 1937).

A definition of terrorism should not only appear intuitively correct, it should also allow for academic rigour, thereby becoming a useful tool in understanding and differentiating between different forms of violent action. Martin (2003, p 32), after looking at many of the definitions provided by terrorism experts, identified a number of common features among them:

- the use of illegal force;
- sub-national actors;

- unconventional methods;
- political motives;
- attacks against 'soft' civilian and passive military targets;
- acts aimed at purposefully affecting an audience.

The second criterion is perhaps a more difficult one to meet as it is very much linked to the perspective of the viewer of the violent action. Whittaker (2004, p 4) has attempted to distinguish between the terrorist, freedom fighter and guerrilla. He sees the defining and differentiating characteristics as the choice of target and mode of activity. He contrasts the three in their use of violence in the following ways:

- The *terrorist* targets civilians.
- The *guerrilla* goes for military personnel and facilities.
- The *freedom fighter* conducts a campaign to liberate his people from dictatorial oppression, gross disarmament or the grip of an occupying power.

From Whittaker's perspective what distinguishes a terrorist from the others is not the degree of violence used, since all are capable of using great violence; it is the choice of target and the methods employed. Although all of this comes with an important caveat; as Whittaker acknowledges the descriptions often change with time and circumstances. Those who were in the past viewed as terrorists may become respected leaders of their communities and act upon the world stage – such is the nature of politics.

Aside from the academic thinking on terrorism, there is still a need to ensure that terrorists are prevented from carrying out attacks, caught and face due process of law. It is the law that effectively provides us with another way of defining terrorism by the use of legislation. In the UK the Terrorism Act 2000 provides us with a definition of terrorism which gives an interesting perspective on managing the risk. The legal definition is shown diagrammatically in Figure 14.1.

In common with many criminal offences, terrorism is made up of two important legal concepts. They are:

1. *Mens Rea* – this is the intention to commit the offence and this intention will be adduced from evidence.
2. *Actus Reus* – this is the act itself, the intention put into action.

The large central circle of Figure 14.1 contains all of the components of the intention. The carrying out of an action or threatening to do so with the intention of influencing government or intimidating the public,

What is Terrorism?
Section 1(1), (2) Terrorism Act 2000

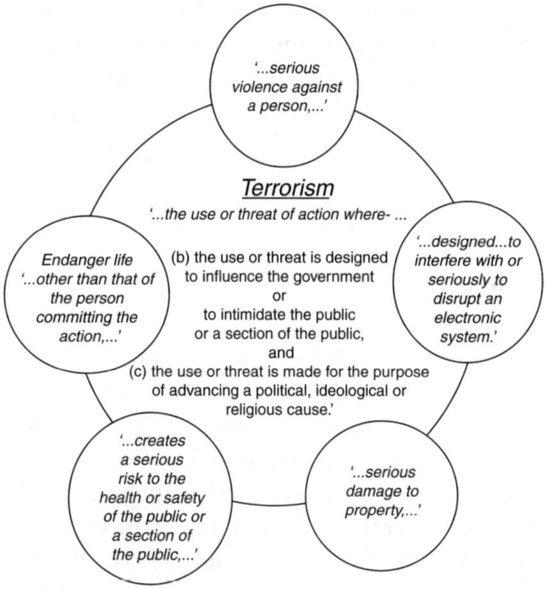

[Section 1(1), (2) of the Terrorism Act 2000 is reproduced under the terms of Crown Copyright Policy Guidance issued by HMSO]

Figure 14.1 Legal definition of terrorism

or a section of it, in order to advance a political, religious or ideological cause is the heart of the offence. This is the *Mens Rea* of terrorism. In addition some form of action needs to be carried out in order for the offence to be complete (*Actus Reus*). Consequently, if one or more of the following actions (the smaller circles) are carried out the offence is complete.

- Serious violence against the person – assassination or bomb explosion.
- Designed to interfere with or seriously disrupt an electronic system – electronic attack, such as viruses or denial of service.
- Serious damage to property – bomb explosion.
- Create a serious risk to the health and safety of the public or a section of it – the release of chemical, biological or radiological material.
- Endanger life other than that of the person committing the action – suicide attacks.

This is an important and extensive piece of legislation, and it needs to be, since it has to take account of all of the risks the UK faces immediately from terrorism and those it might face in the future. It is often stated that the law lags behind societal changes and is too slow to reflect contemporary life. Terrorism legislation cannot afford to be in that position. The legislation is effectively a risk map, trying to identify and capture the risks from terrorism and ensure that powers exist to deal effectively with them.

Who is at risk from terrorism?

Through an examination of terrorist attacks from around the world the types of targets terrorists select can be discerned. From the data in Figure 14.2 one group that can be clearly identified is the business community that makes up the largest single discernable group targeted by terrorists. Although the largest category is 'other' it includes many different venues, which show no overall predominance. Consequently it is more difficult to be precise as to their specific nature as a target.

Why should terrorists target the business community? The definition of terrorism under the Terrorism Act 2000 suggests that the business community is an important contributor to the social and economic fabric of any community. By attacking and destroying business targets the terrorists not only succeed in killing innocent civilians (one of the defining criterion for terrorists according to Whittaker) they also imagine that their actions will put pressure on governments to accede to their demands. This is at the heart of the legal definition of terrorism where the terrorists aspire to influence government by their actions.

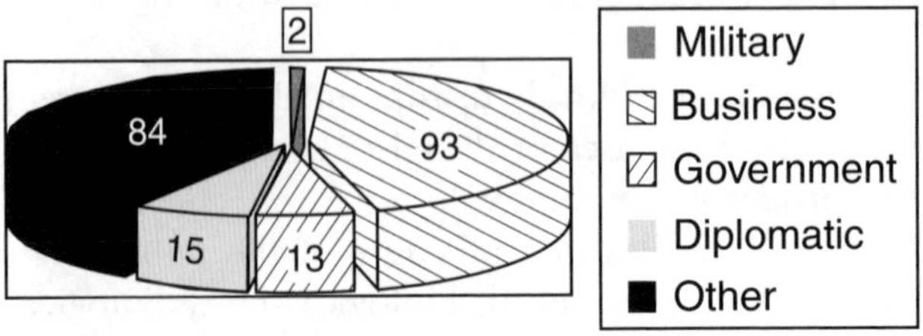

(US Department of State, 2004)

Figure 14.2 Terrorist attacks worldwide – by sector

The risks from terrorism

The Director General of the Security Service recently addressed the Confederation of British Industry (CBI) on the issue of terrorism and the need to manage the risks associated with it. It is worth highlighting two parts of that speech (Manningham-Buller, 2004). The first relates to the nature of the threat, and the second to the way that thinking needs to change about how businesses protect themselves from the threat of terror.

> There is a serious and sustained threat of terrorist attacks against UK interests at home and abroad, including against the business community ... my message is to broaden your thinking about security issues. A narrow definition of corporate security including the threats of crime and fraud should be widened to include terrorism and the threat of electronic attack.

From an examination of the social and economic consequences of the 11 September 2001 attack, it is clear that the devastating impact not only affected New York City but also the United States as a whole and the world economy.

- Property loss and insurance costs at the site: $21 billion.
- Total cost to world insurance market: $25 billion – $50 billion.
- Estimated job losses in Lower Manhattan area: 100,000.
- Estimated job losses across the US by the end of 2002: 1.8 million.
- Estimated rise in commercial insurance premiums to cover the risk of terrorism between 2002 and 2004: 50 per cent (Cabinet Office, 2003).

In view of these consequences, how can business organizations manage the risks associated with terrorism, and why does it make good business sense to be a resilient business?

Terrorism as a business risk

Businesses are generally well versed in the management of risk. A burgeoning business and scientific literature is developing, looking at how organizations identify, perceive and manage risks. Carey (2000) argues that, unless a business has a clear vision of its objectives, it cannot realistically assess the risks it might face. He also believes that its objectives must be framed in concrete and specific terms if a business is to identify its real areas of risk. It is likely that there will be a number of different risks that need to be considered and taking a holistic approach to their management is the most effective strategic approach to take in managing them. When examining the top 10 risks that concern business (see Table 14.1) it can be seen that terrorism is not at the top of the list.

In reality a business is much more likely to suffer the effects of an information technology failure or fire than from a terrorist attack, and sensible businesses would be wise to plan for such events. The problem with planning for a terrorist attack is that many businesses do not see themselves as being at risk. Surveys from London First and the London Chamber of Commerce indicate that larger businesses are much more likely to prepare for a terrorist attack, especially if they are a global business, whereas small and medium enterprises (SMEs) are much less likely to plan for such an eventuality. Indeed the smaller the business the less likelihood there will be of planning (*London Business Crime Survey*, 2004; *London First Business Survey*, 2004). Why should this be?

Table 14.1 Top 10 threats and disruptions to business

Potential threats and disruptions	*2005 (%)*
Loss of IT	70
Loss of telecommunications	64
Fire	56
Loss of skills	56
Loss of people	55
Loss of access to site	53
Terrorist damage	53
Damage to corporate image/reputation/brand	48
Negative publicity/coverage	44
Employee health and safety incident	35

(adapted from *Business Continuity Management*, 2005)

The media and terrorism

It has already been noted that people tend to make their own subjective judgements based upon information that is either externally available to them or personal. Generally, people do not think about the range of risks they are exposed to and only think about the risks when they are brought to their attention. It is often through the media that people have their attention drawn to the risks they might face. These can range from the inappropriate selling of mortgages and suspect food additives, to crime and terrorism. Research indicates that the media play an important role in the way that risks are framed and explained to the public (Boyne, 2003). For instance, with regard to terrorism there is evidence to support the view that the media play a crucial role in forming business people's perceptions of the risks posed by terrorism. The bar chart at Figure 14.3 shows the sources of information about terrorism that businesses access.

It is clear from the chart that three sources of information predominate: newspapers, television and the police. These three sources are

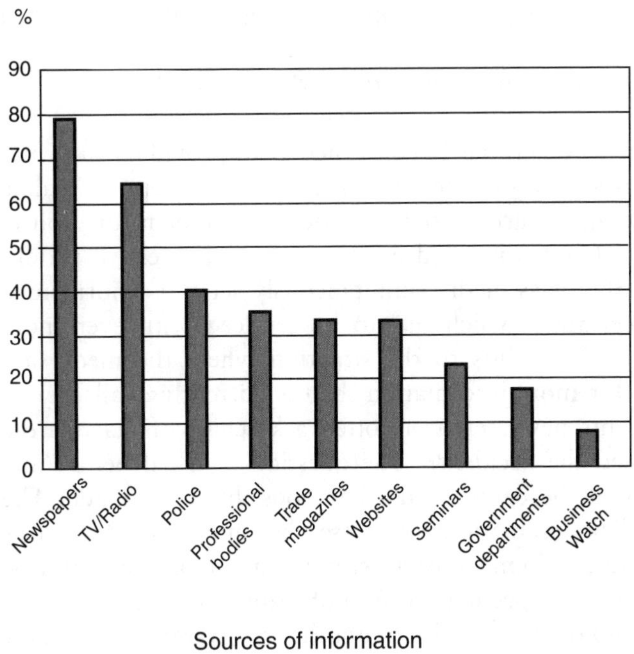

(from *London First Business Survey*, 2004)

Figure 14.3 Sources of information about terrorism

consistently present across the broad range of businesses of differing sizes. Larger businesses can employ experts in security and business continuity and they can develop plans to help protect the business against terrorism and general crime. They can also improve the business's ability to recover from an emergency. Many security managers in large businesses often have either police or military backgrounds and this often assists them in their dealings with the police and government departments since they can tap into their networks.

Smaller businesses have less capacity to employ their own experts so often have to rely on information from the media. They do not have access to the knowledge networks available to larger businesses. The SMEs are the most unprepared sector of the business community in relation to the risks from terrorism. There are dangers associated with relying upon the media for information on terrorism, especially when it is presented as a news item. Sometimes information, which is designed to relieve existing risks, actually increases alarm.

Ritchie and Marshall (1993) believe that this situation generally occurs because:

- the original risks were not fully appreciated by the affected people; and
- the proposed remedies were not properly understood.

The mass media are not primarily concerned with providing information to assist businesses in their management of risk, except for public information campaigns carried out by the Government or police. Luhmann (2000, p 11) has pointed out that 'in the process of producing information, the mass media simultaneously sets up a horizon of self-generated uncertainty which has to be serviced with ever more information'. This often leads to the situation where the media are constantly asking for more information than is currently available.

At major incidents news reporters often ask senior officials at the scene: 'What caused the accident?' The question is asked before any proper assessment of the causes could have possibly been made. The reporters seek to elicit speculation which itself becomes grounds for further speculation and development of the story; even though there may be no basis in fact for such speculation. As Luhmann (2000, p 11) notes: 'Each programme holds the promise of another programme. It is never a matter of simply representing the world at any one given moment.'

This situation is exacerbated by the need to provide 24-hour news coverage. As Boyne (2003, p 41) states: 'What matters is the success of the news item in getting our attention, in making sure that we watch and listen, in creating the possibility of follow-up items . . . This is quite a distance from the mode of communication required for a rational discourse on risks.' The challenge is to ensure that the business community receives risk information in a form that they can use, and which allows businesses to manage a wide range of risks, including terrorism.

Managing the risk of terrorism

Power (2004) notes that there are a wide variety of risks that are processed by different government agencies within what he calls the 'government of risk'. It would perhaps be surprising if there were only one approach to managing risk. As Power observes, there are different problems, functions, public perceptions, moral frameworks, institutional arrangements and, of course, the nature of the risk itself which provide infinite variety (Power, 2004, p 18). Within the business community there is a wide range of risk-based activity which needs to be managed. These areas of activity have traditionally been subdivided into two main classes:

1. financial risk management; and
2. operational risk management.

Financial risk management (see Chapter 4) deals with risks associated with financial matters, such as the use of money or other like assets such as bonds, shares or other financial instruments. There is a highly developed mathematical modelling ethos within this area of risk management which assists businesses in making decisions about investments, spending and general fiscal management.

Operational risk management (see Chapter 8) deals with risks of a non-financial nature, such as crime, brand protection as well as the management of non-financial assets. This clearly covers a wider range of disparate risks manifesting themselves within an increasingly complex and fast moving business environment. Consequently many businesses are now facing wider risk exposures than ever before and are looking for approaches that enable them to manage these as effectively and efficiently as possible.

Neville-Rolfe (1997) has put forward three principles for effective risk management within an organizational environment. These have proved to be very useful first principles for businesses seeking to manage the risks they face in an effective and efficient manner. The three principles are:

1. Think small first – small businesses or the lowest common denominator within a large business should be able to implement the risk control measures.
2. Proportionality – the costs of the risk control measures should be commensurate to the risks.
3. Focus on the goal – do not be too prescriptive and allow businesses to achieve the goal in their own way.

Whether managing the risks from terrorism, crime or some other operational risk, following these three principles can provide businesses with a number of benefits. These include:

- Businesses of all sizes can do something to manage risk. The difference is largely one of scale. Generally a smaller business will require simpler measures to be implemented than its larger more complex counterpart.
- In managing risks, it is necessary to consider the costs. It makes no sense to spend a large amount of money, or invest time and resources, into protecting an asset that is either of low value or is not critical to the business. There may be activities that can be carried out with little or no cost. Tightening up on existing procedures or improving general housekeeping may be all that is required. However, it is necessary to ensure that adequate resources are allocated to protect the critical assets within a business. In short, the cost of protection should be commensurate to the risk.
- Often the best solutions to a problem are those that businesses develop for themselves. Because there is such a diversity of business activity in the UK a wide range of risk management strategies will necessarily reflect this diversity. Having diverse risk management approaches within the UK economy is strength in terms of protecting it from terrorist attack. Where vulnerability is exploited within one risk management approach this vulnerability will not broaden the risk exposure, because the other management approaches operate in a different way depending on the nature of a particular business sector or the unique nature of individual businesses.

Despite the diverse nature of UK business activity it is still possible to develop a generic model of what a resilient business should look like.

This is a business that is able to detect, manage and recover from the risks that it might face.

What does a resilient business look like?

Figure 14.4 presents a schematic model of how a resilient business might look. This is made up of three components:

1. using and sharing information;
2. protective security;
3. business continuity.

In order for a business to be resilient and to be able to manage risks effectively it must have these components in place, and crucially they must be as far as is possible integrated. In essence it is enterprise-wide risk management (ERM).

Each of the components are examined below, followed by the question of integration.

Using and sharing information

The best risk management decisions are those based on knowledge, experience and the ability to apply expert subjective judgements which can be augmented by the use of technological tools that assist in the decision-making. All of these are used to help reduce as far as possible the degree of uncertainty. Naturally, the better informed the decision-maker is about a situation, and having an understanding of how others have dealt with similar situations in the past – whether successfully or not – can help improve decision-making. Very often communicating

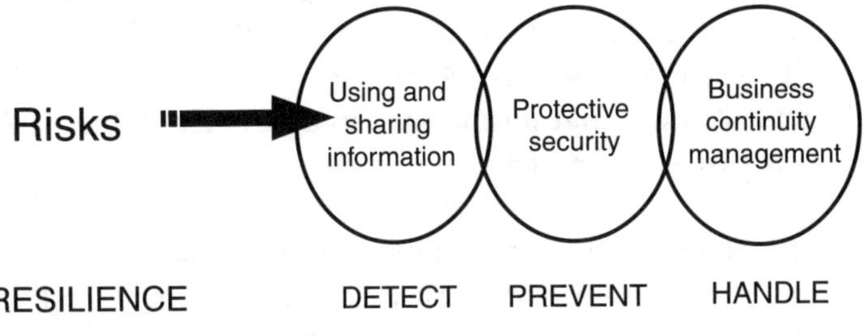

Figure 14.4 The components of a resilient business

with others can help businesses to appreciate risks that perhaps they had not previously considered, or to better understand the nature of those risks and the consequences of them for their business.

There is very often much knowledge residing within businesses and individuals, who may not consider that they are experts in risk, but who do have a thorough understanding of their business. The challenge is to capture this knowledge, recalling Surowiecki's assertion that the 'wisdom of the crowds' in certain circumstances can yield better decision-making than that obtained from a few experts. Improved communication both within businesses and between them is of vital importance. This is not to downgrade the role of the expert, but as Surowiecki has shown they do not always get it right and he provides a number of notable examples. 'We're all familiar with the absurd predictions that business titans have made: Henry Warner of Warner Bros. pronouncing in 1927, "Who the hell wants to hear actors talk?," or Thomas Watson of IBM declaring in 1943, "I think there is a world market for maybe five computers".' (Surowiecki, 2005, p 32).

The problem is that there are often too few opportunities for businesses, especially smaller businesses, to speak to one another about the risks they may face and having access to experts, especially in relation to the risks associated with terrorism.

One of the major issues to come out of the 11 September 2001 attack is that there was a clear lack of information sharing across different government agencies, with rivalries between city, state and federal agencies leading to vital information being missed or not accorded the importance that it should have warranted (GAO Report, 2003). Likewise, within the business community, businesses are often reluctant to share, on a formal basis at least, some of the lessons they have learned in dealing with business-related risks. The key message, not only for government but also for the business community, is that they have to be more willing to share information about risks and also share knowledge about effective ways in which these risks can be managed. The result will be that all businesses will benefit and the resilience of the UK economy will be increased.

There are practical things that businesses can do to help reduce their vulnerabilities. For instance they can:

- contact other businesses in their neighbourhood, trade associations that represent their business interests. Can they provide advice tailored to the particular line of business? Do they provide advice on dealing with the risks the business faces?

- make use of information relating to threats from crime and terrorism. They can improve appreciation of some of the threats that your business may face. Useful UK government websites include: http://www.crimereduction.gov.uk, http://www.businesslink.gov.uk and http://www.homeoffice.gov.uk/terrorism;
- become an active learner: when viewing or reading a news report on a crime, or terrorism, they should ask themselves: 'What could I have done to help prevent or reduce the impact of such an event if my business was affected?'
- keep up to date with current affairs (quality newspapers and television). Remember, attacks by terrorists in faraway countries might lead to a better understanding of the risks that the business might face.

Protective security

Sir David Veness, the recently retired Assistant Commissioner for the Metropolitan Police Service, often said: 'Good crime prevention is good counter terrorism'. By this he meant that the way crime risks are managed, by being vigilant, security minded and having good security measures in place, will also help protect businesses from terrorism, or at least make the work of the terrorist more difficult. This synergy is important; the message is that terrorism should not be treated as a risk that is difficult or impossible to manage, or as somehow different from other risks that a business manages on a daily basis. Terrorism is a manageable risk and the activities that businesses are carrying out now to protect themselves against crime will serve them equally well against the threat of terror. It is not only at the practical level that this synergy is being identified. Academics are also looking at the theoretical frameworks used for understanding crime and developing methods of control. They are discovering that these also work well in explaining terrorism and how it can be managed (Roach *et al.*, 2005).

However, a problem arises in assessing the risks from both crime and terrorism using the traditional business risk management tool, the risk matrix. An example of a risk matrix is shown in Figure 14.5.

The risk matrix is used as a way of assessing the risks that confront a business. This technique provides a score that is the product of the impact that a risk will have on the business and the likelihood of it happening. In the matrix shown below if the product is one, then the impact is deemed insignificant and it is unlikely to happen, while a

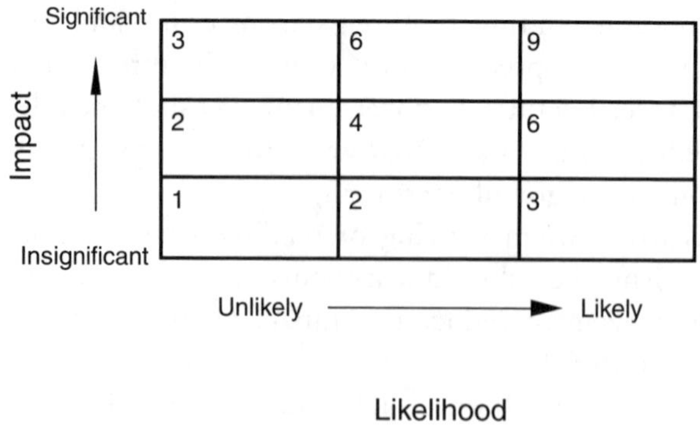

Figure 14.5 The risk matrix

score of nine indicates the risk will have a significant impact and it is likely to happen. So in the former case a business may decide to do nothing, while in the latter case the prudent business would put measures in place to prevent or mitigate the consequences of the risk.

However, there is a problem in using the risk matrix when assessing risks associated with crime and terrorism. The problem is highlighted in the following quote: 'There is no point in trying to be precise about the likelihood – this is not a mathematical assessment of probability, (although it is frequently referred to as probability) but rather a considered and informed view . . . ' (IMS Risk Solutions Ltd, 2003). As has been shown the formation of subjective probabilities does rely upon having a well informed view. The problem with using the risk matrix in relation to crime or terrorism is the fact that the intentions and methods used by criminals and terrorists are often hidden and unanticipated. Consequently, a different way of thinking about the risks posed by crime and terrorism needs to be considered. It should take fully into account both the knowledge (intelligence) about criminals and terrorists and the vulnerabilities of their victims. With this approach risk is seen as the product of a threat and vulnerability, as follows:

threat x vulnerability = business impact

Table 14.2 presents some examples of what is meant by the terms 'threat', 'vulnerability' and 'business impact'.

The threat is made up of the intention and capability of those that pose a threat. These judgements are usually made by the police or the Security Service and are obviously of a confidential nature. However, a prudent business will take steps to inform itself of the nature of the threats from the many open sources of information. This can be

Table 14.2 Some examples of threat, vulnerability and business impact

Threats (can be external to the business, or can come from within)	*Vulnerability* (a weakness that can be exploited by a threat)	*Business impact* (the cost resulting from a vulnerability successfully exploited by a threat)
Computer viruses	Do you regularly update your software virus protection?	What might happen: You lose client records and pass the software virus on to your customers. This wastes time, loses money and damages your reputation as a reliable business.
Theft of company Information	Do you check your new staff records adequately?	What might happen: Commercially sensitive information is stolen and given to a competitor. This delays the launch of your products and projects.
Terrorism	Have you noticed suspicious behaviour towards a neighbour? Although the behaviour is odd, you don't want to bother the police.	What might happen: Later, a bomb explodes outside that neighbour's business. You are unhurt because you are away, but others are not so lucky.
Disruption to supply chain	Do you check whether your critical suppliers have business continuity plans in place?	What might happen: Critical suppliers being unable to provide vital services. You lose two weeks' business as a result.

achieved by speaking to the police, keeping up to date with current affairs and talking to other businesses or bodies that represent their business interests. With crime and terrorism becoming increasingly important business issues, many business organizations are developing their own guidance in this area. There is also information available from the Security Service website at http://www.mi5.gov.uk which considers the threats businesses might face and countermeasures they can take to protect themselves.

By removing the threat or a vulnerability there will be little or no business impact. Although businesses might not be able to tackle the threats directly – that is the role of the state – they can do a lot to reduce their vulnerabilities. It is here that businesses can help by remaining vigilant, being security minded and having good basic security measures in place. Often the business itself is in the best position to identify its own vulnerabilities and how they might impact upon it.

A number of options are open to businesses in the way that they manage security risks. Their decision-making will often reflect their particular businesses' 'risk appetite'. The PAS 56 business continuity specification defines risk appetite as 'willingness of an organization to accept a defined level of risk. Note: Different organizations at different stages of their existence will have different risk appetites.' (PAS 56:2003) This risk appetite is often linked to the culture of the business, reflecting its commercial attitudes and values. Taking this into account a business needs to make a decision about how to deal with security risks. Generally they have four options available to them:

1. Put security measures in place to remove or reduce vulnerabilities. It is not possible to remove or reduce all security threats to a business, but vulnerabilities can be removed or reduced. Management is already managing the vulnerabilities to the business (competitors, products, customer base), but every business needs to think more carefully about the risks from crime and terrorism
2. Transfer some or all of the vulnerability (insurance). Transferring some of the vulnerability by insurance might provide some financial recompense, but it cannot replace lost information or fully recover lost business and reputation. It is best to consider insurance for some security risks in conjunction with good security measures.
3. Do nothing. Doing nothing will leave a business dangerously exposed and it is likely that sooner rather than later a threat will bring the business to a halt or seriously disrupt it.
4. Terminate the risk. Some risks are best avoided either by terminating a relationship or changing the way that business is conducted.

A prudent business would want to prevent or mitigate a security risk, since although doing nothing might be a legitimate option, it is also a very risky one.

Business continuity

The final component that makes up a resilient business is business continuity management, which has been defined as 'an holistic management process that identifies potential impacts that threaten an organisation and provides a framework for building resilience with the capability for an effective response that safeguards the interest of its key stakeholders, reputation, brand and value creating activities.' (PAS 56:2003).

Business continuity is dealt with in Chapter 5. Here business continuity will be considered as a vital component of a resilient business, and as an important new technique in the counter-terrorism armamentarium. Good security and robust and connected information sharing are necessary but not sufficient conditions to ensure that businesses remain resilient. Having a business continuity plan is effectively a fall-back position for businesses should their security fail. But there is a problem in that not enough businesses are taking business continuity seriously and are therefore leaving themselves exposed. The Business Continuity Management Survey (*Business Continuity Management*, 2005) has shown that just over half (51 per cent) of the businesses surveyed had a business continuity plan, although the overall trend shows year-on-year increases in the number of businesses developing business continuity plans. Much work still needs to be done to persuade smaller businesses of the need to have a business continuity plan which will enable them to deal with the consequences of terrorism.

It is one of the greatest strengths of business continuity that it is concerned with the consequences of a risk and how these affect the business, rather than the nature of the cause. Looking at security risks, security personnel try to understand the nature of the risk and its source. They then put measures in place to try to prevent the risk affecting the business. With business continuity the cause is not the primary concern. The most important issue for the business continuity planner are the consequences that flow from a risk and its effect on the business.

Within the resilient business the synergy between security, seeking to identify and prevent the causes of the risk, and business continuity seeking to mitigate the consequences of that risk, form a powerful strategic approach to managing the risks posed by crime and terrorism. This is important because the effects of terrorism can be far reaching, as seen by the social and economic impacts on business and civic communities following the 11 September 2001 attack. There are often two foci in any terrorist attack, the primary target and secondary gains. The primary target is the site or sites that the terrorist action is intending to destroy. In destroying the primary target, especially if it is a significant business or even business district, the trading and supply chain relationships the business or district had with other businesses will be severely disrupted. Like the ripples that emanate from a stone being thrown into a pond, the potential for disruption could spread throughout the supply chain, having an impact on all the businesses within it. These secondary gains need not be constrained by geography. In a world of global trading, events in other parts of the world can have a direct impact upon businesses in the UK. Business continuity provides us with the ability to reduce the secondary gains for terrorists by ensuring that the social and economic impact of this secondary disruption can be minimized.

Integration and the future

In order to manage the risks posed by terrorism and the wide range of other risks that businesses face there needs to be less 'silo working' within organizations. A more holistic approach to managing risks is required. There is a need to ensure that security, business continuity and risk professionals, together, start to map out the risks that businesses might face and develop responses that support each other and hence the business community. The effective use and sharing of information underpins this process and it is vital for its success.

In summary:

- The threat from terrorism is now global.
- The business community is in the front line.
- Terrorism will be a long-standing menace.
- Working in partnership will frustrate and eventually defeat the terrorist.
- Terrorism is a risk that can be managed like other business-related risks.
- Security and business continuity has a vital role to play in mitigating the wider social and economic consequences of a terrorist attack.

The future management of the risks from terrorism requires better integration between different disciplines and more effective sharing of information. George Wald in *Philosophy and Social Action* (1999) summed up the situation well when he said:

> We already know enough to begin to cope with all the major problems that are now threatening human life . . . Our crisis is not a crisis of information; it is a crisis of decision of policy and action.

The time for action is now.

References and recommended reading

Bernoulli, J (1713) *Ars Conjectandi.* Basle.

Boyne, R (2003) *Risk.* Milton Keynes: Open University Press.

Business Continuity Management 2005 (2005) London: Chartered Management Institute.

Cabinet Office (2003) *The Costs of the September 11th Attack.* London: Cabinet Office.

Carey, A (2000) *Learning to Thrive. Business Continuity. A Directors Guide.* London: Institute of Directors.

Crenshaw, M (1995) *Terrorism in Context.* University Park, PA: Pennsylvania State University Press.

Douglas, M and Wildavsky, A (1983) *Risk and Culture.* San Francisco: University of California Press.

General Accounting Office of the United States (2003) *Homeland Security. Efforts to Improve Information Sharing Need to Be Strengthened.* GAO-03–760.

Giddens, A (1990) *The Consequences of Modernity.* Cambridge: Polity Press.

Giddens, A (1991) *Modernity and Self-Identity.* Cambridge: Polity Press.

Great Britain (2000) Terrorism Act 2000. London: The Stationery Office.

IMS Risk Solutions (2003) *Risk Management for Good Governance.* London: British Standards Institution.

Knight, F H (1921) *Risk, Uncertainty and Profit.* Boston, MA: Houghton Mifflin.

League of Nations (1937) *Convention for the Repression of International Terrorism, International Conference, Geneva, 1–16 Nov.*

London Business Crime Survey (2004) London: London Chamber of Commerce and Industry.

London First Business Survey (2004) London: London First.

Luhmann, N (2000) *The Reality of the Mass Media.* Cambridge: Polity Press.

Lupton, A (1999) *Risk.* London: Routledge.

Manningham-Buller, Eliza (2004) Speech by Director-General of MI5 to the CBI Annual Conference 8 Nov 2004. See: http://www.mi5.gov.uk

Martin, G (2003) *Understanding Terrorism. Challenges, Perspectives, and Issues.* London: SAGE Publications.

Neville-Rolfe, L (1997) Good regulation: weighing up the risks. In: *Science, Policy and Risk.* London: The Royal Society.

PAS 56:2003 *Guide to Business Continuity Management.* London: British Standards Institution.

Power, M (2004) *The Risk Management of Everything. Rethinking the Politics of Uncertainty.* Demos. Available at: http://www.demos.co.uk/catalogue/riskmanagementofeverythingcatalogue/

Renn, O (1998). Three decades of risk research: accomplishments and challenges. *Journal of Risk Research*, **1**:1 40–71.

Ritchie, B and Marshall, D (1993) *Business Risk Management.* London: Chapman & Hall.

Roach, J, Ekblom, P and Flynn, R (2005) The Conjunction of Terrorist Opportunity (CTO): a theoretical framework for diagnosing and preventing acts of terrorism. *The Security Journal*, May.

Schweitzer, Y and Shay, S (2003) *The Globalisation of Terrorism*. London: Transaction Publishers.
Schmid, A and Jongman, A (1998) *Political Terrorism*. Amsterdam: North-Holland.
Surowiecki, J (2005) *The Wisdom of Crowds. Why The Many Are Smarter Than The Few*. London: Little, Brown.
US Department of State (2004) *Patterns of Global Terrorism – 2003*. Available at: http://www.state.gov/s/ct/
Veness, D (2002) The role of the police. In: *The Unlikely Counter Terrorists*. London: The Foreign Policy Centre.
Wald, G (1999) *Philosophy and Social Action*. Cited in Quotez: http://www.digiserve.co.uk/quotations
Whittaker, D J (2004) *Terrorists and Terrorism in the Contemporary World*. London: Routledge.

15

Understanding The Risk Management Universe – Consensus and Controversy

David Hillson

The chapters of this book have introduced us to the various dimensions of the risk management universe, with a variety of guides who are each expert in their own field of the discipline. After such a grand tour the reader may still be left wondering how to answer our opening question: 'What is risk management?', since we have been presented with a wide range of possible answers. And the true answer is not 'either/or' but 'both/and'. Each chapter has presented a concise summary of how risk management can be applied in a particular way, and where chapters offer different approaches it is not because one is right or another is wrong. The risk management universe is broad and diverse, with many elements and dimensions.

Despite the breadth of this topic, it is nevertheless possible to discern some common themes and messages, and this is the purpose of the final chapter of our guided tour. Given the wide range of different types of risk management described in this book, where are the underlying commonalities and which differences are most significant? After considering these, this chapter concludes with some thoughts on the future of the risk management universe and charts a possible way ahead for future explorers.

Universal laws?

Each preceding chapter describing the various types of risk management has mentioned some principles which apply to all, and which are underlying and constant throughout the risk management universe. These might be considered as 'laws of the risk management universe':

1. The first law of risk management is that *risk is related to uncertainty*. While there are good philosophical and theoretical reasons for treating risk and uncertainty as inherently different, and even mathematicians view them as distinct, in practice most risk specialists would agree that risk can be viewed as a variety of uncertainty. In every application area, from strategic risk to counter-terrorism, a risk is something which might or might not occur – in other words it is *uncertain*.

   This first characteristic may seem trivial, but it is vital to a proper understanding of risk, and to its effective management. Risks do not yet exist; indeed they may never exist at all. They are potential future events or sets of circumstances or conditions. As such, they are quite different from things which have happened in the past or which currently exist in the present. Past and present events can be analysed and measured, but future events can only be imagined or estimated. While some uncertainty may remain about what exactly happened in the past, there is usually no doubt that it actually did occur. Similarly present events and conditions are usually knowable and measurable. By contrast, a risk which may or may not exist in the future cannot be experienced directly unless or until it happens. This makes risks qualitatively different from issues, problems, concerns, constraints, etc. In every type of risk management described in the chapters of this book there is agreement that if risk exists at all, it exists in the future, which is inherently uncertain.
2. A second common theme which emerges from the various discussions of risk management is that *risk matters*. If they occur, risks will have *consequences* which make a difference in some way. It is not possible to have an inconsequential risk, by definition. While the various types of risk management focus on different sorts of consequence, all agree that a risk must affect something. One simple way to express this is that risks are inextricably linked to *objectives*. Wherever some field of human endeavour is attempting to achieve something, it is possible to identify uncertainties which might affect the chances of success. Whether the objectives are to

achieve good corporate governance, successful projects, business continuity or avoidance of fraud, risk management aims to identify those uncertainties which could influence achievement of the set objectives, and to enable the risks to be understood and managed effectively.

3. A third universal message repeated throughout the chapters is that *risk management is a process*. There are steps and stages to be followed, with varying degrees of rigour and definition, but all approaches to risk management provide a framework which is designed to maximize both efficiency and effectiveness. Although the details of the risk processes are different, each application area distinguishes two important parts: *analysis* and *action*. Before risk can be properly managed, it must first be identified, described, understood, assessed, etc. Analysis is a necessary prerequisite for what follows in the risk process. But analysis is not sufficient – it must be followed by action. A risk process which does not lead to implementation of actions to deal with identified risks is incomplete and useless. It is no accident that we speak about the 'risk management universe' and not the 'risk analysis universe', since the ultimate aim is to manage risk, not simply to analyse it.
4. Finally several chapter authors have emphasized the importance of the fact that *people perform risk management*. The *human aspects* of risk management are a vital contributor to its success and effectiveness. Most elements of the risk process are undertaken by people, though we may use machines to automate calculations, to record results, or to generate reports. People set risk thresholds, identify risks, assess the degree of uncertainty and extent of possible impact, propose appropriate responses and implement agreed actions. All of these require judgements, estimates and decisions to be made in the presence of uncertainty. And these judgements are subject to a range of influences, both explicit and hidden, which can significantly affect the outcome. Risk management at every level is exposed to sources of bias arising from overt and covert influences acting on individuals and groups who are trying to make risk-based decisions with imperfect or incomplete information.

Key differences

Despite the commonalities evident between the different types of risk management, including a focus on uncertainty and consequences, the need for a process which results in action, and the importance of people in the process, our guided tour has indicated a number of areas where risk management differs between the various areas where it is applied.

One of the main differences lies in the definition of risk itself. In some applications (for example, fraud, counter-terrorism, reputation risk or business continuity), risk is viewed as always and exclusively a bad thing, since it is defined as an uncertainty which, if it occurred, would have a harmful, negative, adverse or unwelcome effect. In other areas, such as project risk management, environmental risk, technical risk or strategic risk management, risks are defined as uncertainties with the potential of either positive of negative effects on achievement of objectives. In these application areas, the term 'risk' is used to encompass both threat and opportunity. This is a fundamental difference in the use of the key concept, and its significance cannot be understated. It is a cause of much misunderstanding between risk practitioners from different areas, since the most basic term is interpreted in two mutually exclusive ways. The resolution for this problem is for practitioners on both sides of the definitional divide to recognize and respect their differences, accepting that the common word 'risk' means different things in different contexts. It is also necessary for all risk practitioners to make clear the way in which they are defining and using the term 'risk', to avoid misunderstanding or miscommunication.

Apart from this most basic of differences, there are of course many places where the approach to risk management differs in detail between the various application areas. Each dimension of the risk management universe has developed its own concepts, language, processes and techniques, and each specific area represents a coherent approach to management of the types of risk which arise in that context. It is probably not useful to delineate every small variation between the application areas, since in many cases these are simply different ways of saying or doing the same thing. Users of risk management should merely be aware that in each area where risk management is applied there exists a particular and specific way of doing things which may differ in detail from other areas, but with a large degree of underlying consistency.

One area where confusion may arise between different approaches to risk management lies in the placement of uncertainty in the risk equation. Two basic positions can be adopted. In the first, uncertainty is a characteristic of the event or set of circumstances or condition which is recognized as 'the risk', and if this risk occurs then there is a consequence. Under this approach a risk might be defined as 'an uncertain event which, if it occurs, has a consequence'. The second approach attaches the uncertainty to the consequence, defining a risk as 'an event with an uncertain consequence'. Again this is more than mere semantics, since it determines the focus of the risk process. A simple example might illustrate the dilemma. If a construction contractor is required to dig a hole where the ground conditions are not known, what is the risk? Is the risk the possibility that something unexpected might be found when the hole is dug (i.e. an uncertain event), or is it the act of digging of the hole (an event with an uncertain consequence)? The answer to this question might lead to different risk responses being adopted, depending on whether the contractor thinks that the dig itself is the risk or that the risk lies in what may be found.

Fortunately the main differences between the various applications of risk management described in this book fall into the areas outlined above, namely definition of terms, or details of process. While these differences can cause problems and confusion, the solutions are simple, namely clarity of thinking and practice, unambiguous communication of intent and content, and mutual recognition of variations.

The expanding universe

Although the scope of this book is broad, it is not comprehensive. There are other areas where risk management is being applied to assist in the achievement of some area of human endeavour. Indeed if this book were to attempt to cover all the many and diverse forms of risk management it would be a very weighty tome. Instead we have concentrated on the main areas of interest to most businesses and risk practitioners.

But, like the physical universe, the risk management universe is expanding. This is true in two distinct ways, with enhanced depth of analysis and increased breadth of application.

First is the *micro* dimension, where new advances in risk analysis are providing improved insights into the nature of risk, and developing new approaches for the effective management of risk and its impacts. Risk practitioners are committed to their profession, and it is not static. The high rate of publication of research papers and case studies, and the release of new techniques and support tools, provide evidence of a dynamic and developing discipline. Risk management has not settled but is continuing to develop and break new ground.

Progress is also being made on the *macro* level, with discovery of new dimensions to the risk management universe. The use of a structured approach to understanding and managing significant uncertainty is proving valuable in hitherto unexpected areas. Several fields are adopting 'risk-based' approaches, including auditing, remuneration, social policy, communication, etc. It may only be a matter of time before these novel applications become full disciplines in their own right, adding new dimensions to the risk management universe.

Finally there is the question of 'dark matter'. Astronomers have realized that there is more to the physical universe than meets the eye or than can be detected using current instrumentation technology. They have been driven to postulate the existence of 'dark matter' to make their equations add up. This mysterious substance evades detection but its presence can be deduced from its effects. In the same way, the ever present 'unknown unknowns' pervade the risk management universe, with hidden risk making its effects known while remaining undetected. In the same way that astronomers and physicists are committed to exposing the nature of dark matter so that it can be understood, so risk practitioners should be relentless in their pursuit of hitherto undiscovered risk. Our understanding of the risk management universe will remain incomplete for as long as we passively accept the existence of unknown unknowns. And, since understanding is an essential prerequisite for effective action, risk management can never be fully effective unless and until this final barrier is broken.

One final thought in this regard is to remember that some astronomers believe that ours is not the only universe, and it may exist alongside a number of other parallel universes, some of which may be strange and exotic with many dimensions currently unknown to us (and possibly unimaginable by us). In the same way, it is clear that the risk management universe is not the only one in existence. There are many others which exist in parallel to ours, each with their own set of laws and dimensions, some of which may appear very strange to us in the risk management universe. We should keep an open mind about how these various universes might interact, and we must be alert to opportunities to learn from others outside our own field of experience. Indeed we would be wise to proactively seek 'close encounters' since it is clear that 'we are not alone'.

Towards a grand unified theory

Following Albert Einstein's failed attempts over several decades to develop one 'theory of everything' (or TOE), physicists have for many years sought to formulate a Grand Unified Theory (or GUT) to unify the various fundamental forces (weak, strong, electromagnetic and gravitational) and offer a more elegant understanding of the organization of the universe and the nature of matter, energy, space and time. While at the time of writing this remains elusive, due to the failure to confirm the existence of some crucial missing elements such as the Higgs particle, efforts are continuing. The drive towards a GUT is rooted in the conviction that everything in the universe is interconnected and interdependent, and that it must therefore be possible to describe this mathematically.

The possibility of a 'risk GUT' has also proved attractive to some, who seek an underlying paradigm or 'theory of everything' for risk. This has led to development of enterprise-wide risk management (sometimes called ERM), which aims to integrate the various elements of risk management into a cohesive whole. ERM takes the dimensions detailed in the various chapters of this book and provides a unifying and unitary framework within which they can each operate, specializing in addressing the different types of risk, but communicating with and supporting each other, recognizing that they are both interconnected and interdependent.

One way of thinking about ERM is to construct a 'hierarchy of objectives', for example, seeing a business as a set of overarching objectives defined in the vision or mission statement. This is then implemented through various lower-level structures such as departments and functions, each with their own set of objectives, where the sum of the lower-level objectives fully describes the top set. Further decomposition is possible, for example, implementing operational objectives via a hierarchy of portfolios, programmes, projects and tasks, each with objectives at an increasing level of detail. Since risk is defined as uncertainty which can affect achievement of objectives, it is also possible to construct a hierarchical risk management framework to match the set of objectives. Risk management can then be applied in a cohesive and integrated manner from top to bottom across the hierarchy of objectives. This approach might serve as a Grand Unifying Theory for application of risk management within an organization, drawing together all the various applications of risk management into a single framework.

The idea of a 'risk GUT' has also found favour among the standards-setting bodies. Chapter 1 discussed the existence of a wide range of professional standards and guidelines covering different types of risk management (see Table 1.2). Although there is some consensus and convergence over the content of these standards, there is currently no single 'theory of everything' which can be applied across all dimensions of the risk management universe. It is not yet clear whether one 'universal risk management standard' might be developed to which all other standards will be subservient, or whether the best that can be achieved is a family of risk standards each covering one or more specialist areas but with a consistent and coherent underlying philosophy.

The future of the universe

Experts who study the physical universe hold a variety of views about where it is heading. While there is no doubt that the universe is currently expanding, there is no consensus about what might happen next. One camp holds that the universe will continue expanding indefinitely, while another believes that expansion will eventually reach a maximum and will be followed by a collapse, possibly reversing all the way to a 'Big Crunch'. A third view adopts a cyclic position, seeing repeating iterations of expansion and collapse. One thing on which all cosmologists seem to agree is that the universe we inhabit is not in a 'steady state'.

Each of these different positions finds echoes among observers of the risk management universe.

Some believe that the scope of risk management will continue to expand and include more and more elements of personal, business and social life, until 'Everything is just risk management'. Their vision is of a risk-based world where all decisions are taken in the light of the identification and assessment of relevant uncertainty. Like their cosmologist counterparts, some even detect an accelerating rate of growth as more and more space becomes occupied by risk management. This expansionist view is exemplified by some project risk management practitioners whose slogan is 'Manage the risk = manage the project'. This implies that normal planned activity needs no special attention, and all that is required is management of variations from the plan. By looking ahead to identify potential variations, both positive and negative, and focusing management attention on addressing just these aspects, proponents of this position claim that success is ensured. Managers should allow non-risky elements to continue without intervention, but concentrate on proactive management of risk.

While expansionism serves to emphasize the importance of risk management in the overall scheme of things, it is an extreme position whose adoption denies the reality of much normal work. For example, in the project management arena there are many required tasks which are not risk-based, including performing the actual technical work to produce the project deliverables. Much of project management may be about managing risk, but project work is more than project management. Similar comments apply equally to other fields of endeavour, where the risk element is not the whole picture, and concentrating wholly on managing risk to the exclusion of other aspects would be detrimental and counter-productive.

Nevertheless, it is probably true that the scope and influence of risk management will continue to expand, at least in the short term, as more areas of application are found for risk-based approaches. The question is whether such expansion is limitless, or whether some critical point might be reached when further growth is unsustainable, to be followed by a collapse and eventual 'Big Crunch'. It is possible that risk management might just be the latest management fad, although admittedly it is already rather more long-lasting than most. The recent emphasis on risk management started in the 1970s, and though it shows little sign of reducing, it is conceivable that future society and business might place less emphasis on risk than their forebears. If risk management goes the way of other fads, it could disappear from the scene very quickly, becoming just a memory or a footnote in the annals of management history.

There is another way in which risk management might disappear, rather than fading away into oblivion. If risk management becomes all-pervasive to the point where it is absorbed into the nature of business at all levels, it could become invisible as a result. The statement of Roman philosopher Seneca the Younger '*Nusquam est qui ubique est*' ('He who is everywhere is nowhere') could equally be applied to risk management. If everyone naturally and habitually 'thinks risk' and manages it as a normal part of daily life, then it might no longer be necessary to have a separate discipline called 'risk management', since this would be accepted and practised by all. Risk management could vanish as a result of its own success, leaving risk specialists and practitioners as outdated purveyors of a universally recognized self-evident truth.

A third option for the future of risk management is possible, combining expansionism and catastrophism. Maybe the size of the risk management universe might vary cyclically, increasing for a time then contracting. A review of the broader story of risk management across the span of human history reveals periods when it was more prominent than others. Social commentators suggest that advances in technology, law and religion can be seen as human responses to uncertainty, seeking to make sense of the ineffable, and attempting to impose control wherever possible. If this is true then the major changes in civilizations might be interpreted as cycles of risk management, though not within the same process-driven framework we see in modern business. And maybe the expansion we are witnessing today is merely part of the latest cycle.

Only time will tell whether the risk management universe is expanding indefinitely until it encompasses everything, or whether a turning-point might be reached to be followed by collapse to a 'Big Crunch' where risk management disappears, or whether some cycle of growth and decline might occur. What is certain is that, like our physical universe, risk management is not in steady state. The reason that risk management is such a fascinating topic is precisely because it is constantly changing. The guided tour of the risk management universe offered in this book presents a view from today's perspective, but this is almost guaranteed to change with time as new approaches and application areas emerge, new dimensions of risk management are discovered, and new insights into the meaning of risk are revealed. Explorers of this intriguing universe can be sure of an exciting journey as the future of risk management unfolds before them in novel and unexpected ways, challenging them 'to boldly go where no man has gone before' in their continuing exploration of risk management.

Index